JUDGE  5

YOSHIKI TONOGAI

Translation and Lettering: Alexis Eckerman

JUDGE Vol. 5 © 2012 Yoshiki Tonogai / SQUARE ENIX. First published in Japan in 2012 by SQUARE ENIX CO., LTD. English translation rights arranged with SQUARE ENIX CO., LTD. and Hachette Book Group through Tuttle-Mori Agency, Inc.

Translation © 2014 by SQUARE ENIX CO., LTD.

Yen Press
Hachette Book Group
1290 Avenue of the Americas
New York, NY 10104

www.HachetteBookGroup.com
www.YenPress.com

Yen Press is an imprint of Hachette Book Group, Inc. The Yen Press name and logo are trademarks of Hachette Book Group, Inc.

First Yen Press Edition: October 2014

ISBN: 978-0-316-24035-2

10 9 8 7 6 5 4 3 2 1

BVG

Printed in the United States of America

CAN'T WAIT FOR THE NEXT VOLUME?
YOU DON'T HAVE TO!

Follow the latest adventures of Max and the flock each month DIGITALLY!

New chapters go live every month at your favorite ebook retailer, and the Yen Press App.

www.YenPress.com

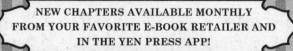

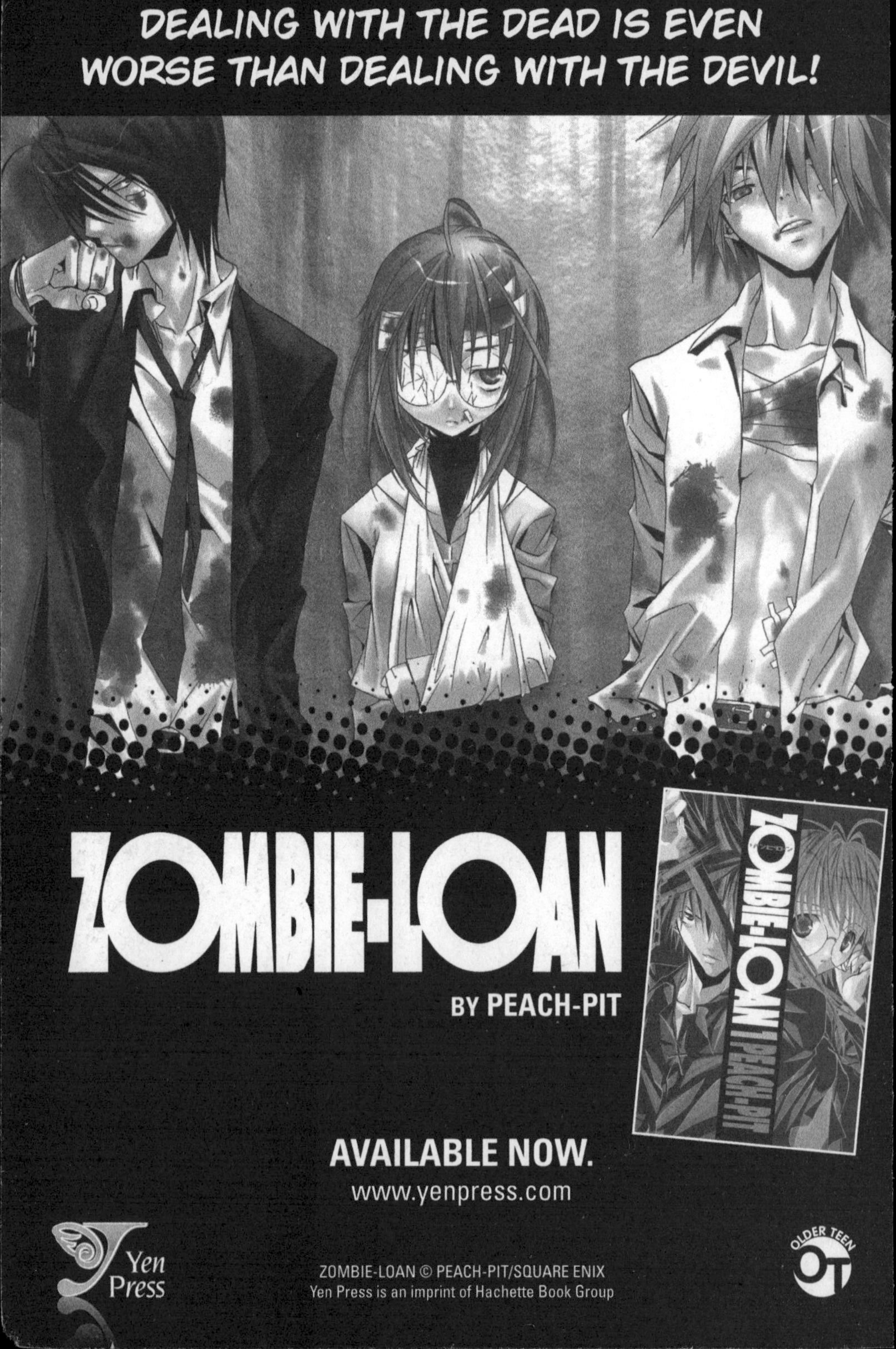
DEALING WITH THE DEAD IS EVEN WORSE THAN DEALING WITH THE DEVIL!
ZOMBIE-LOAN
BY PEACH-PIT
ZOMBIE-LOAN 1 PEACH-PIT
AVAILABLE NOW.
www.yenpress.com
Yen Press
OLDER TEEN OT
ZOMBIE-LOAN © PEACH-PIT/SQUARE ENIX
Yen Press is an imprint of Hachette Book Group

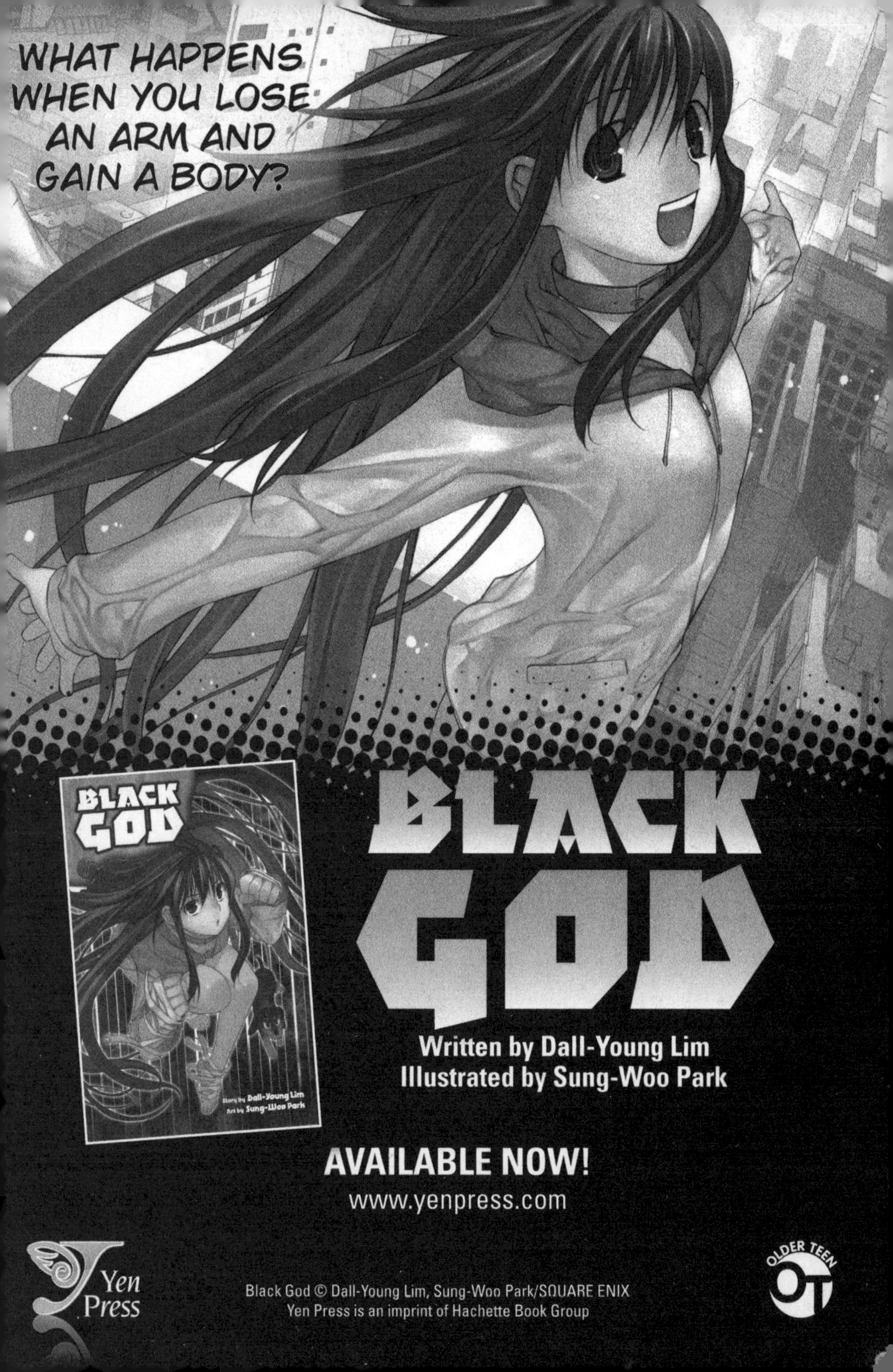
WHAT HAPPENS WHEN YOU LOSE AN ARM AND GAIN A BODY?
BLACK GOD
Story by Dall-Young Lim
Art by Sung-Woo Park
BLACK GOD
Written by Dall-Young Lim
Illustrated by Sung-Woo Park
AVAILABLE NOW!
www.yenpress.com
Yen Press
OLDER TEEN
OT
Black God © Dall-Young Lim, Sung-Woo Park/SQUARE ENIX
Yen Press is an imprint of Hachette Book Group

WELCOME TO IKEBUKURO, WHERE TOKYO'S WILDEST CHARACTERS GATHER!!

AS THEIR PATHS CROSS, THIS ECCENTRIC CAST WEAVES A TWISTED, CRACKED LOVE STORY...

AVAILABLE NOW!!

THE POWER
TO RULE THE
HIDDEN WORLD
OF SHINOBI...

THE POWER
COVETED BY
EVERY NINJA
CLAN...

...LIES WITHIN
THE MOST
APATHETIC,
DISINTERESTED
VESSEL
IMAGINABLE.

Nabari No Ou
Yuhki Kamatani

COMPLETE SERIES 1-14
NOW AVAILABLE

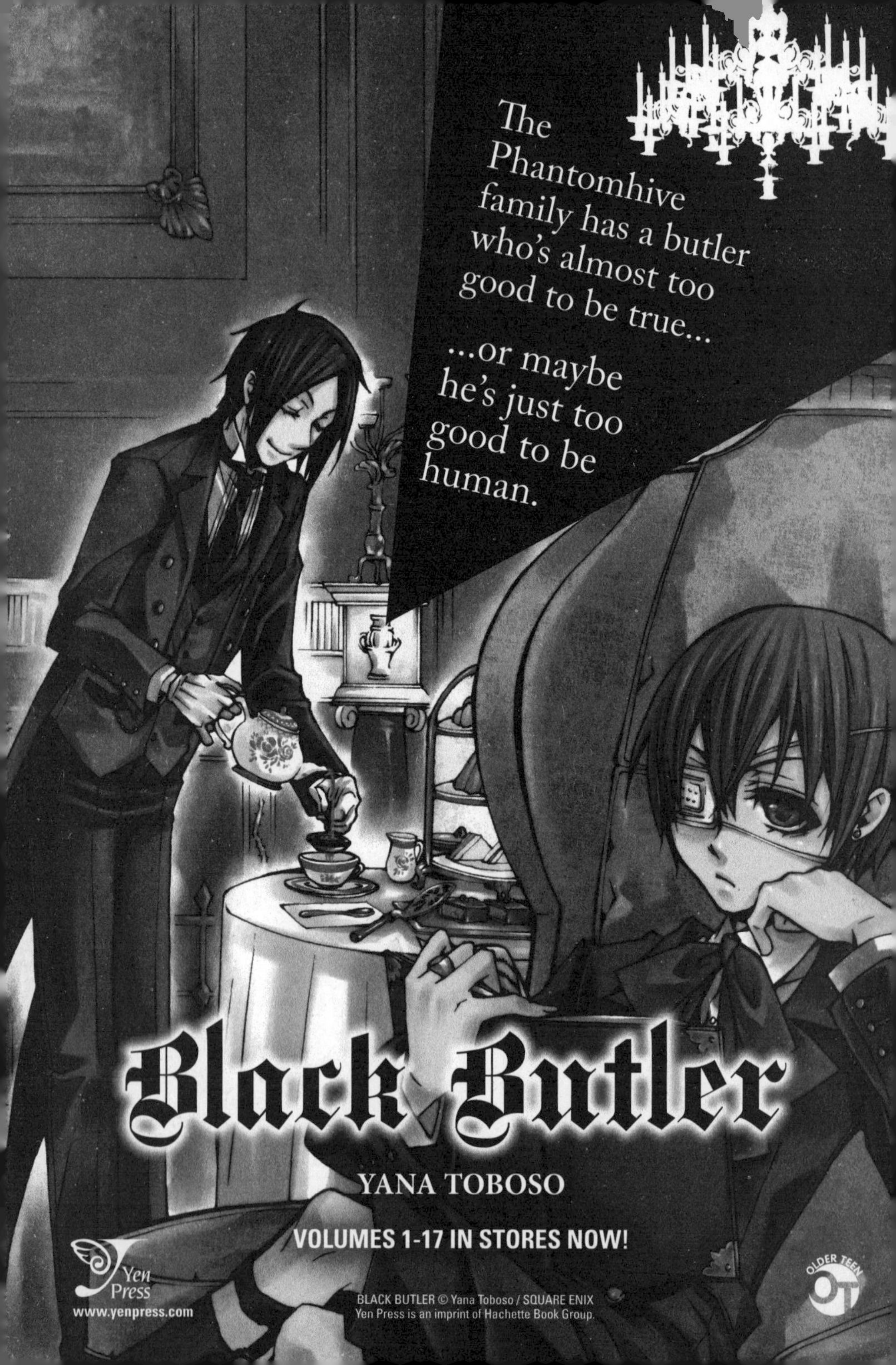
The Phantomhive family has a butler who's almost too good to be true...
...or maybe he's just too good to be human.
Black Butler
YANA TOBOSO
VOLUMES 1-17 IN STORES NOW!
Yen Press
www.yenpress.com
BLACK BUTLER © Yana Toboso / SQUARE ENIX
Yen Press is an imprint of Hachette Book Group.
OLDER TEEN
OT

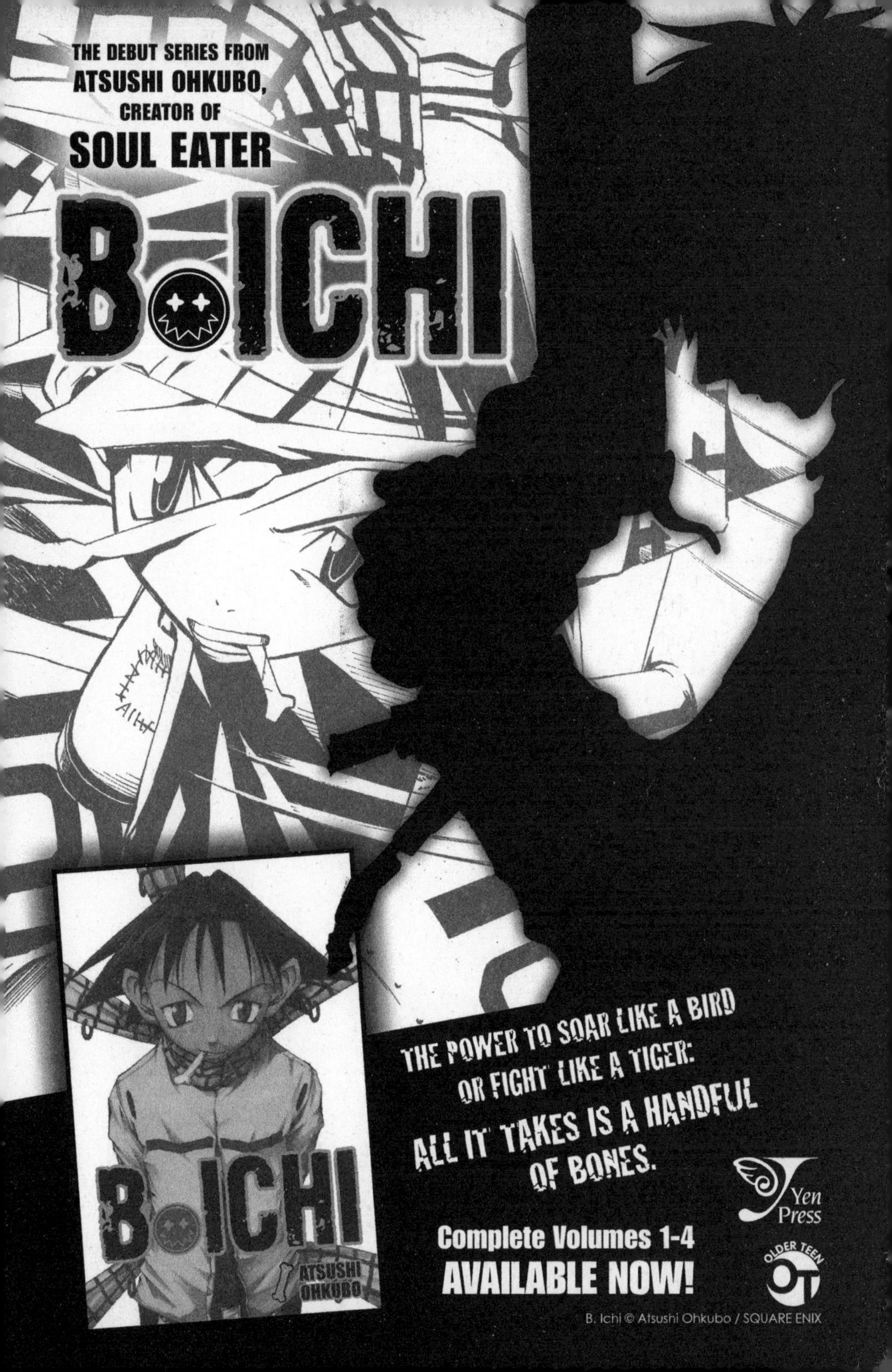
THE DEBUT SERIES FROM
ATSUSHI OHKUBO,
CREATOR OF
SOUL EATER
B. ICHI
THE POWER TO SOAR LIKE A BIRD
OR FIGHT LIKE A TIGER:
ALL IT TAKES IS A HANDFUL
OF BONES.
B. ICHI
ATSUSHI OHKUBO
Yen Press
Complete Volumes 1-4
AVAILABLE NOW!
OLDER TEEN
OT
B. Ichi © Atsushi Ohkubo / SQUARE ENIX

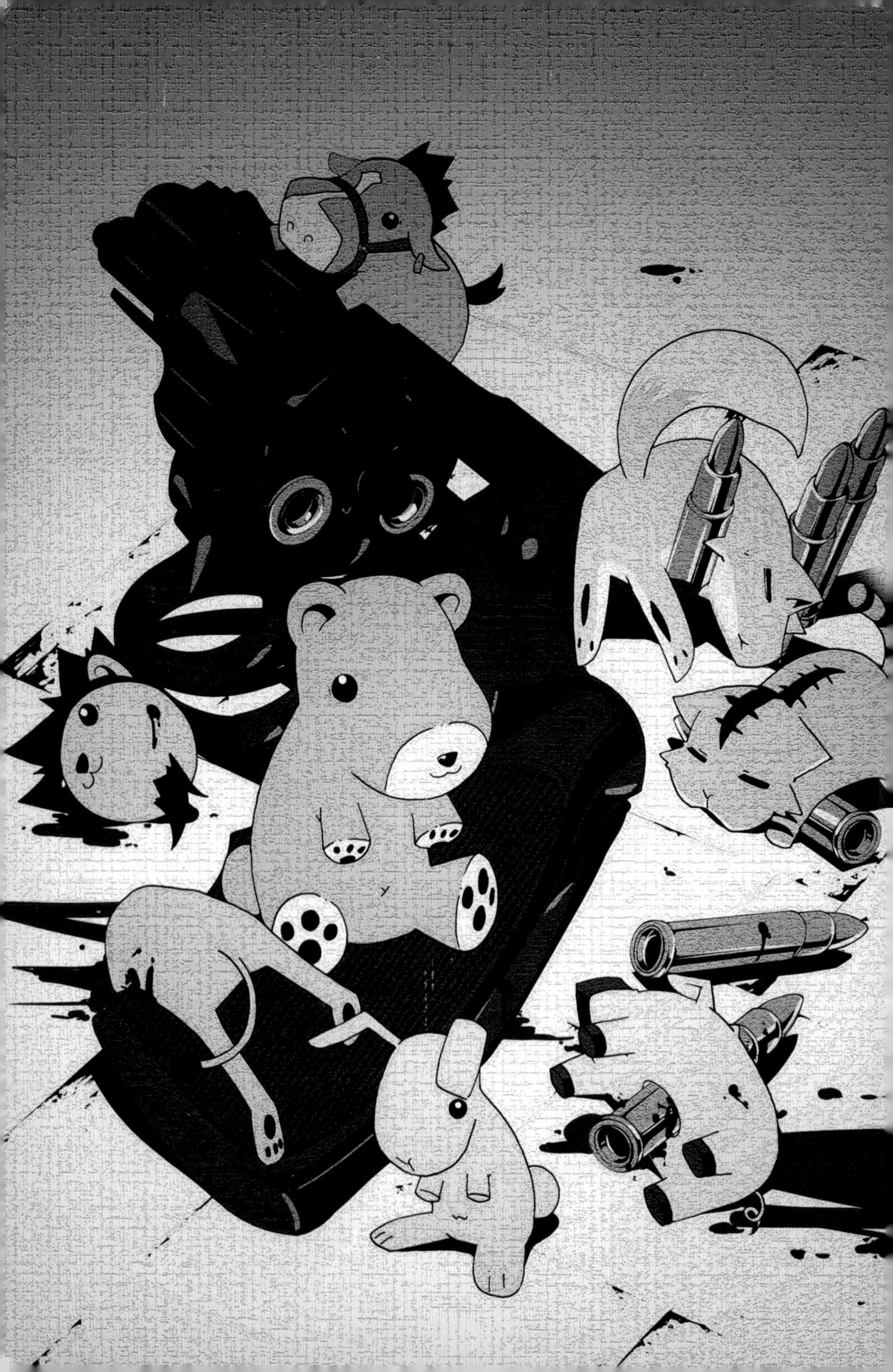

JUDGE

YOSHIKI TONOGAI

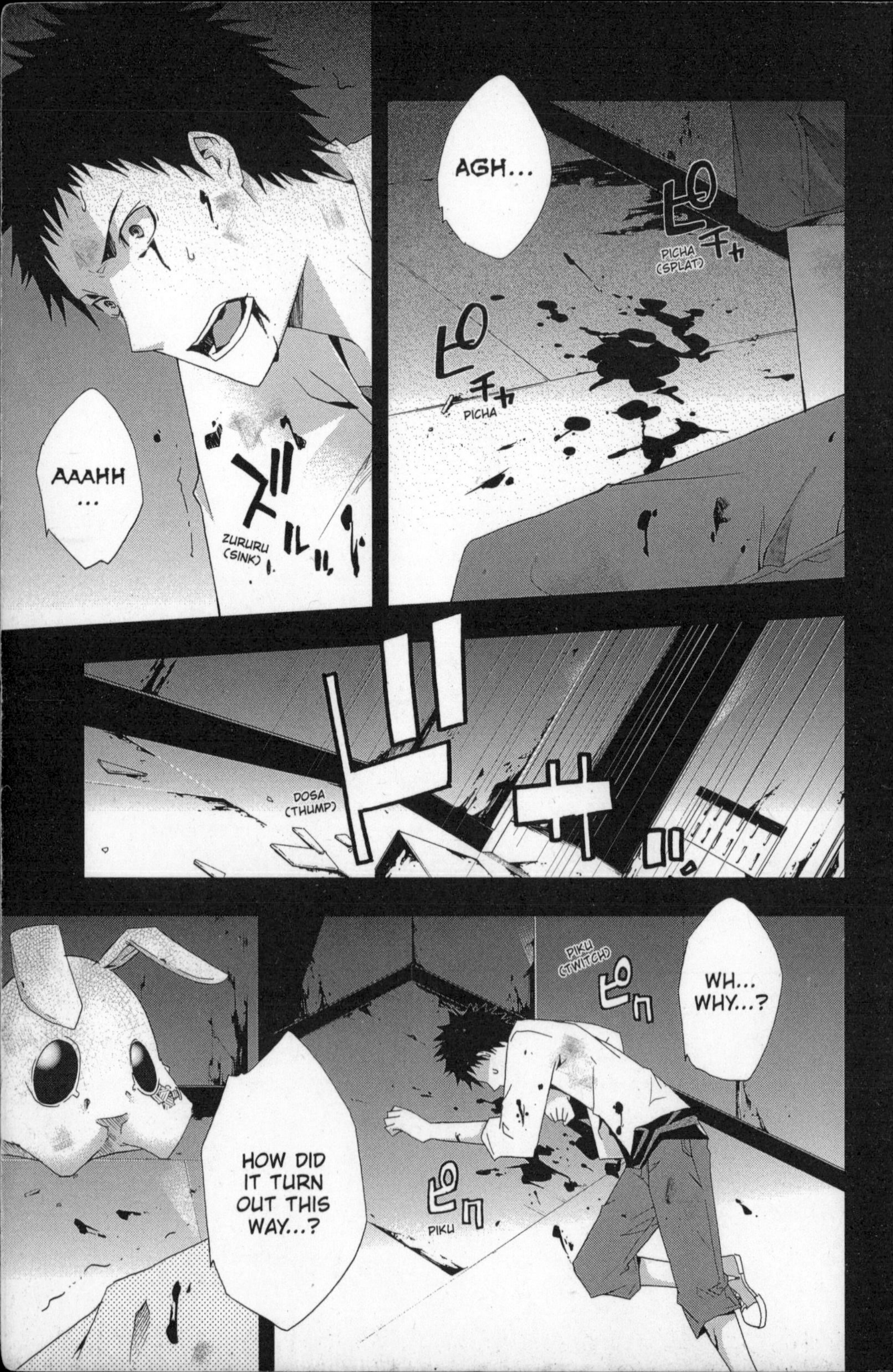
AGH...
ピチャ
PICHA (SPLAT)
ピチャ
PICHA
AAAHH...
ズルル
ZURURU (SINK)
ドサッ
DOSA (THUMP)
WH... WHY...?
PIKU (TWITCH)
ピク
ピク
PIKU
HOW DID IT TURN OUT THIS WAY...?

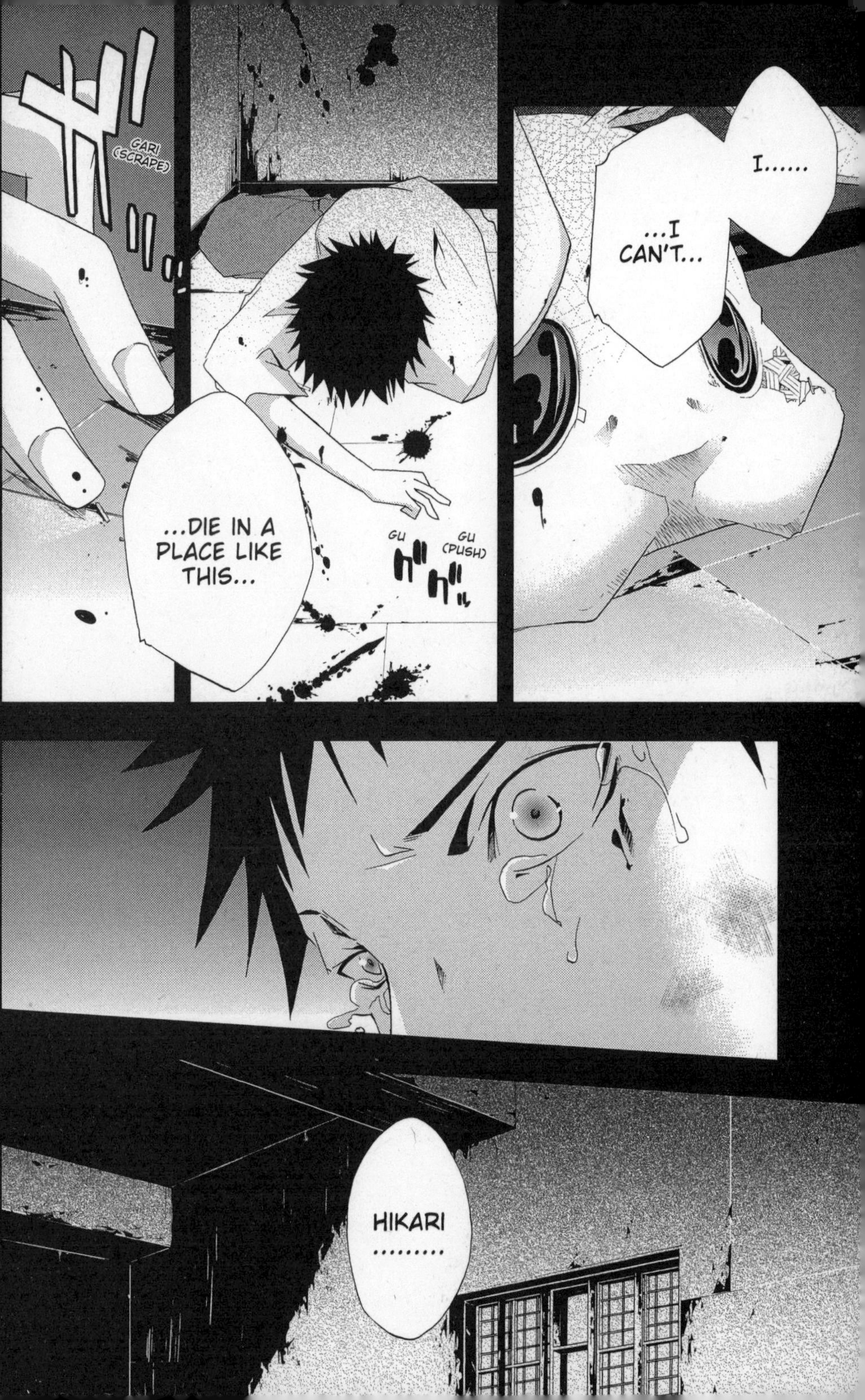

I......
...I CAN'T...
...DIE IN A PLACE LIKE THIS...
GU GU (PUSH)
GARI (SCRAPE)
HIKARI ....

CHAPTER 21 THREE SUSPECTS

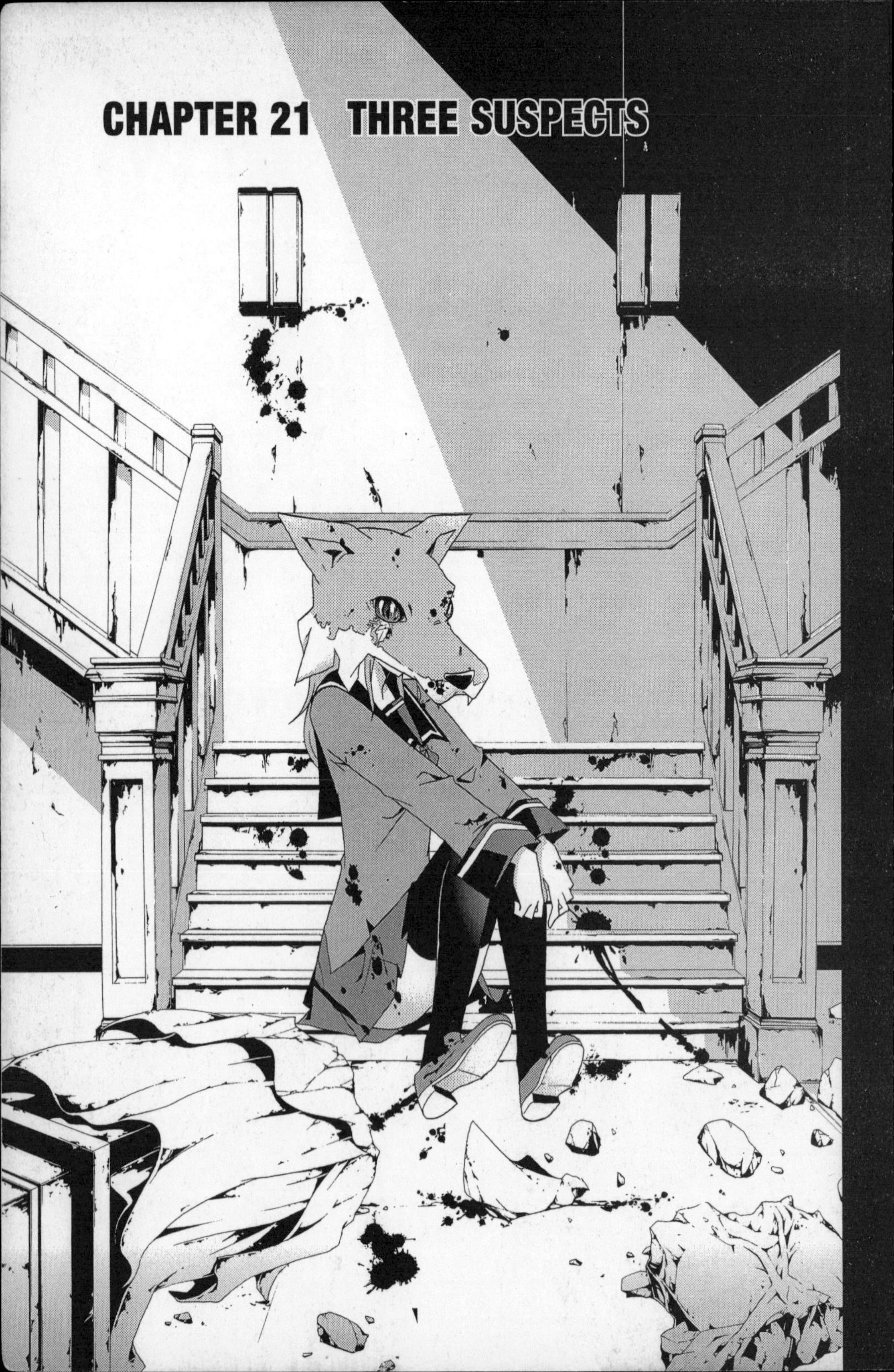

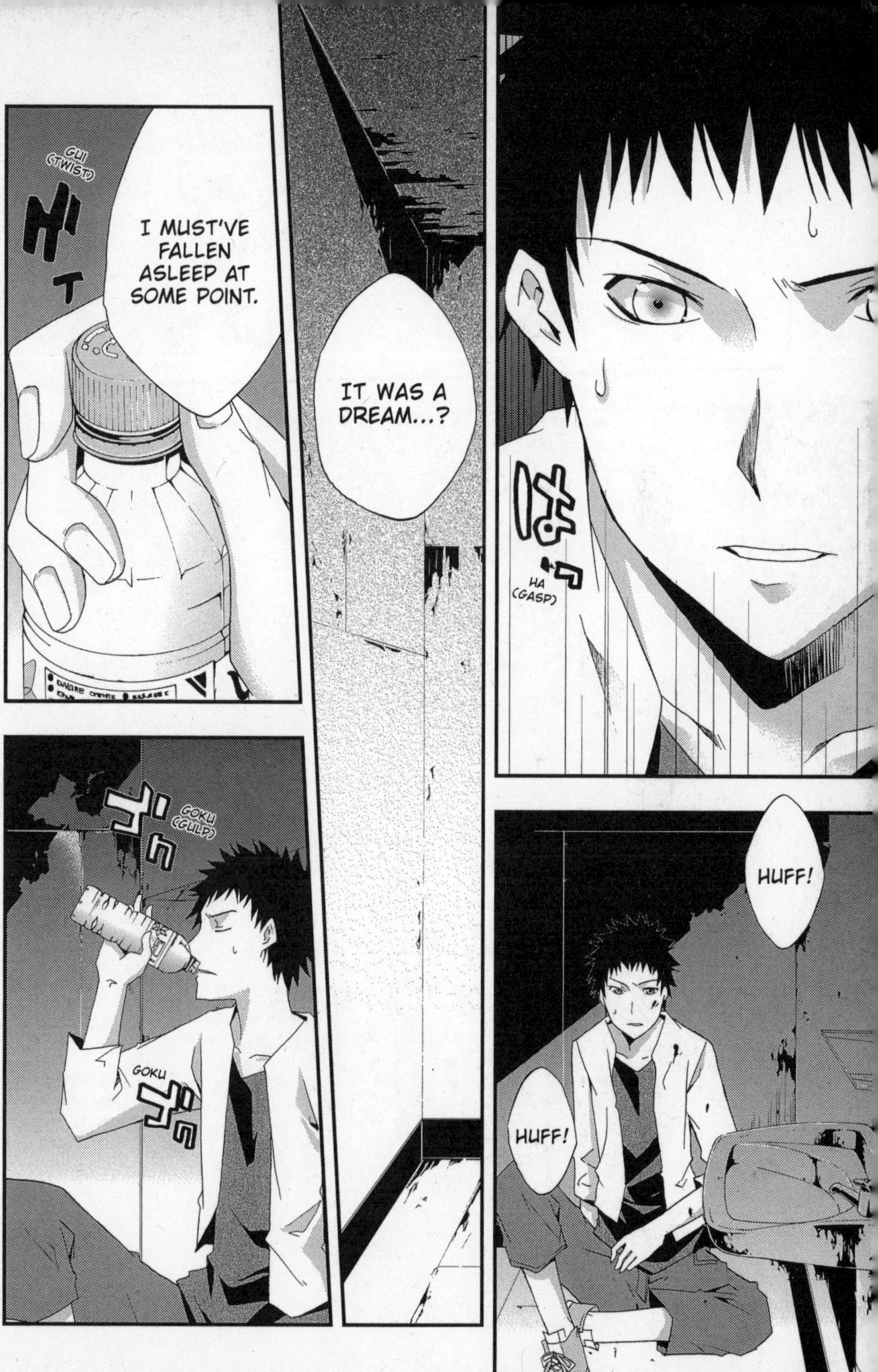

HA (GASP)
HUFF!
HUFF!
IT WAS A DREAM...?
I MUST'VE FALLEN ASLEEP AT SOME POINT.
GUI (TWIST)
GOKU (GULP)
GOKU

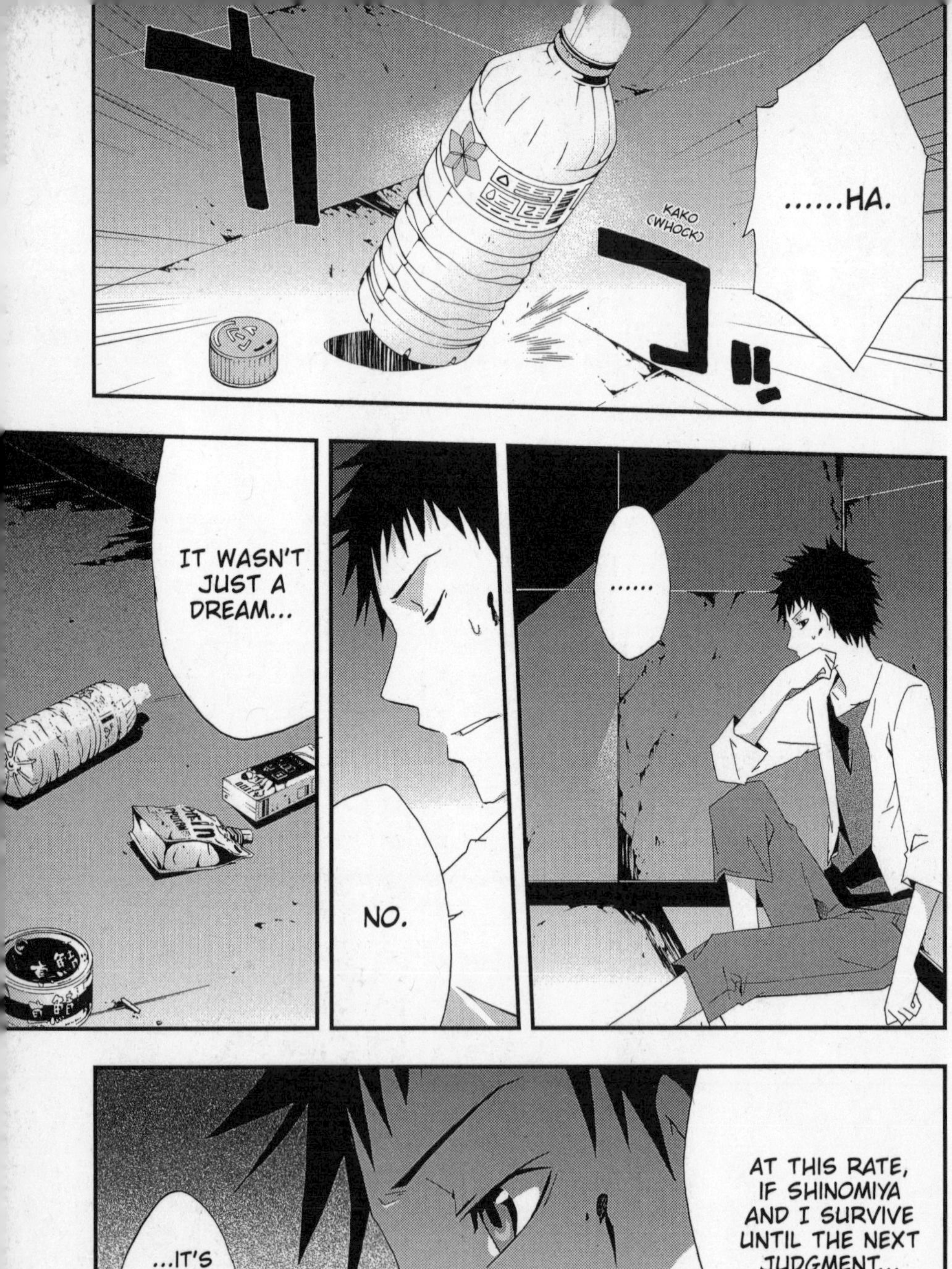

......HA.
KAKO (WHOCK)
......
NO.
IT WASN'T JUST A DREAM...
AT THIS RATE, IF SHINOMIYA AND I SURVIVE UNTIL THE NEXT JUDGMENT...
...IT'S ONLY A MATTER OF TIME ...

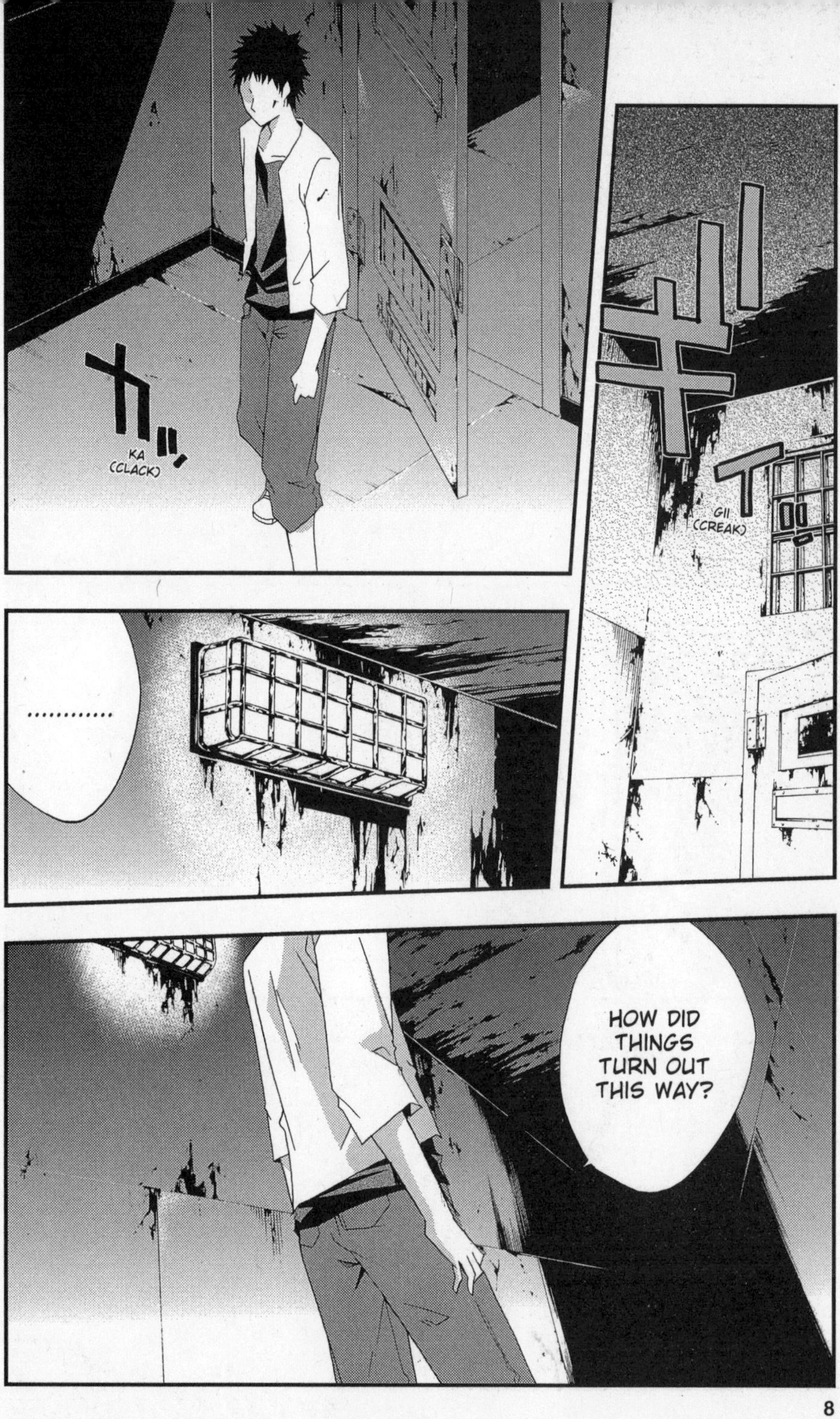
GII
(CREAK)
KA
(CLACK)
....
HOW DID THINGS TURN OUT THIS WAY?

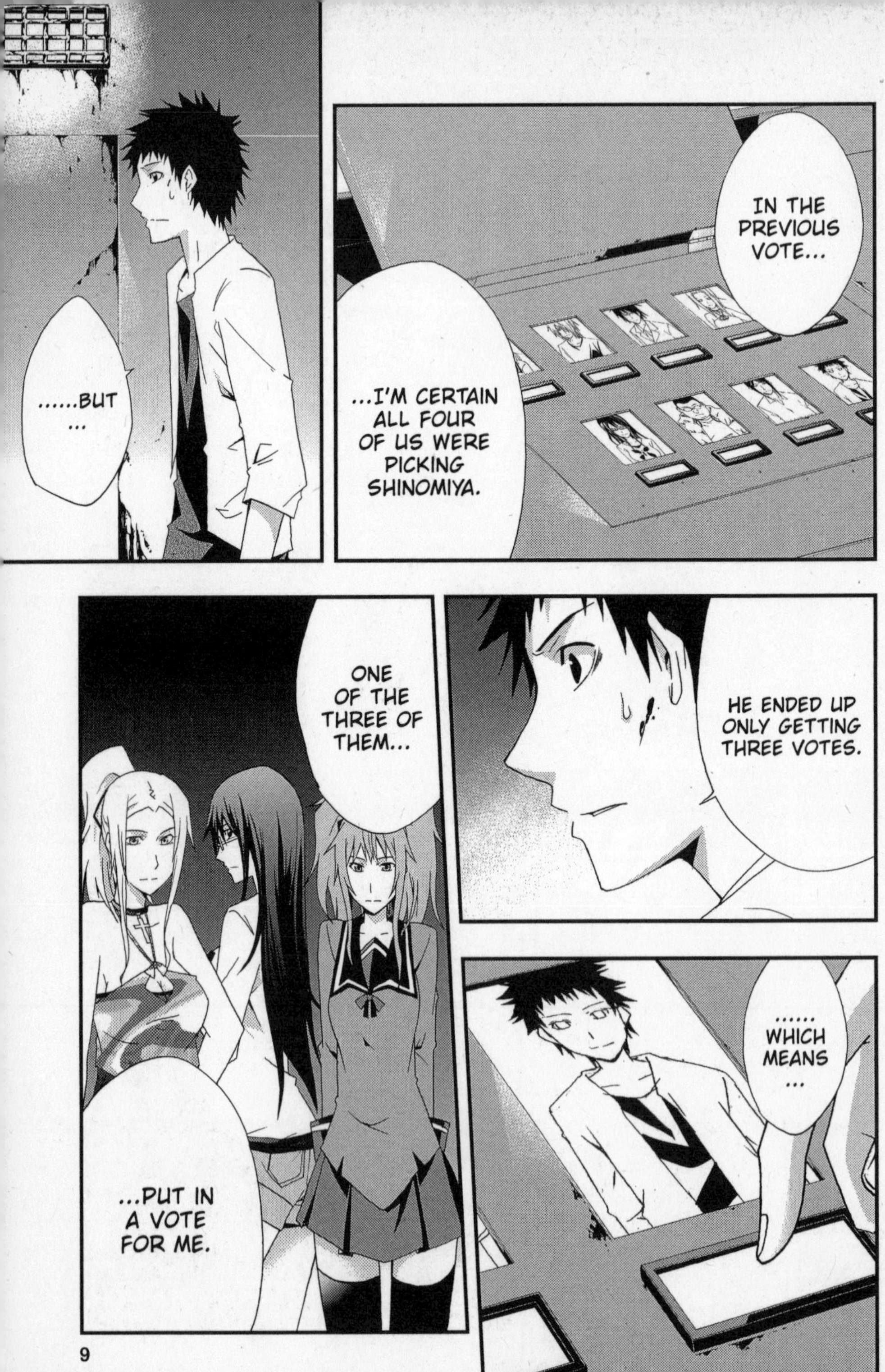
IN THE PREVIOUS VOTE...
...I'M CERTAIN ALL FOUR OF US WERE PICKING SHINOMIYA.
......BUT ...
HE ENDED UP ONLY GETTING THREE VOTES.
...... WHICH MEANS ...
ONE OF THE THREE OF THEM...
...PUT IN A VOTE FOR ME.

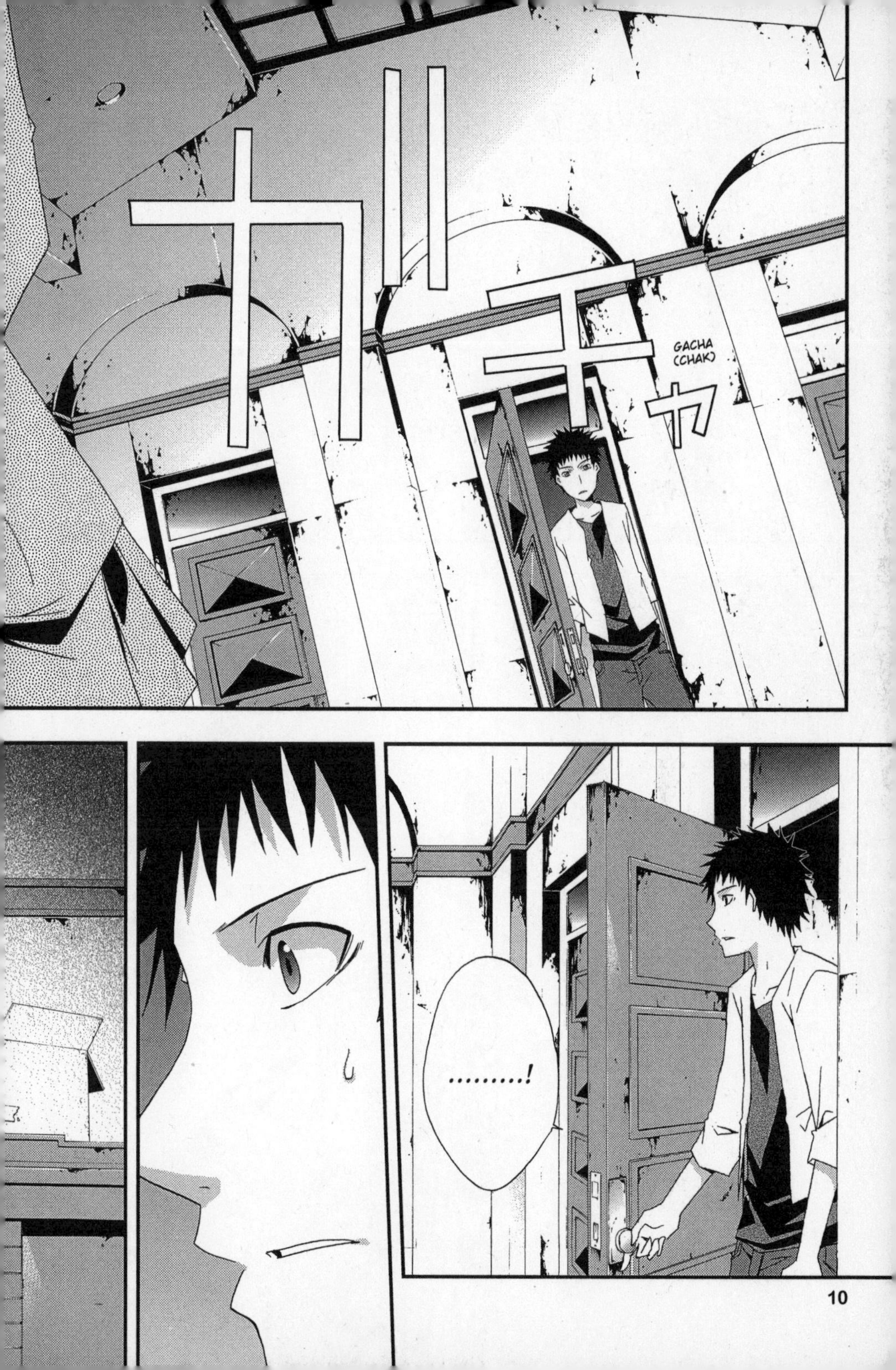
GACHA (CHAK)
.........!

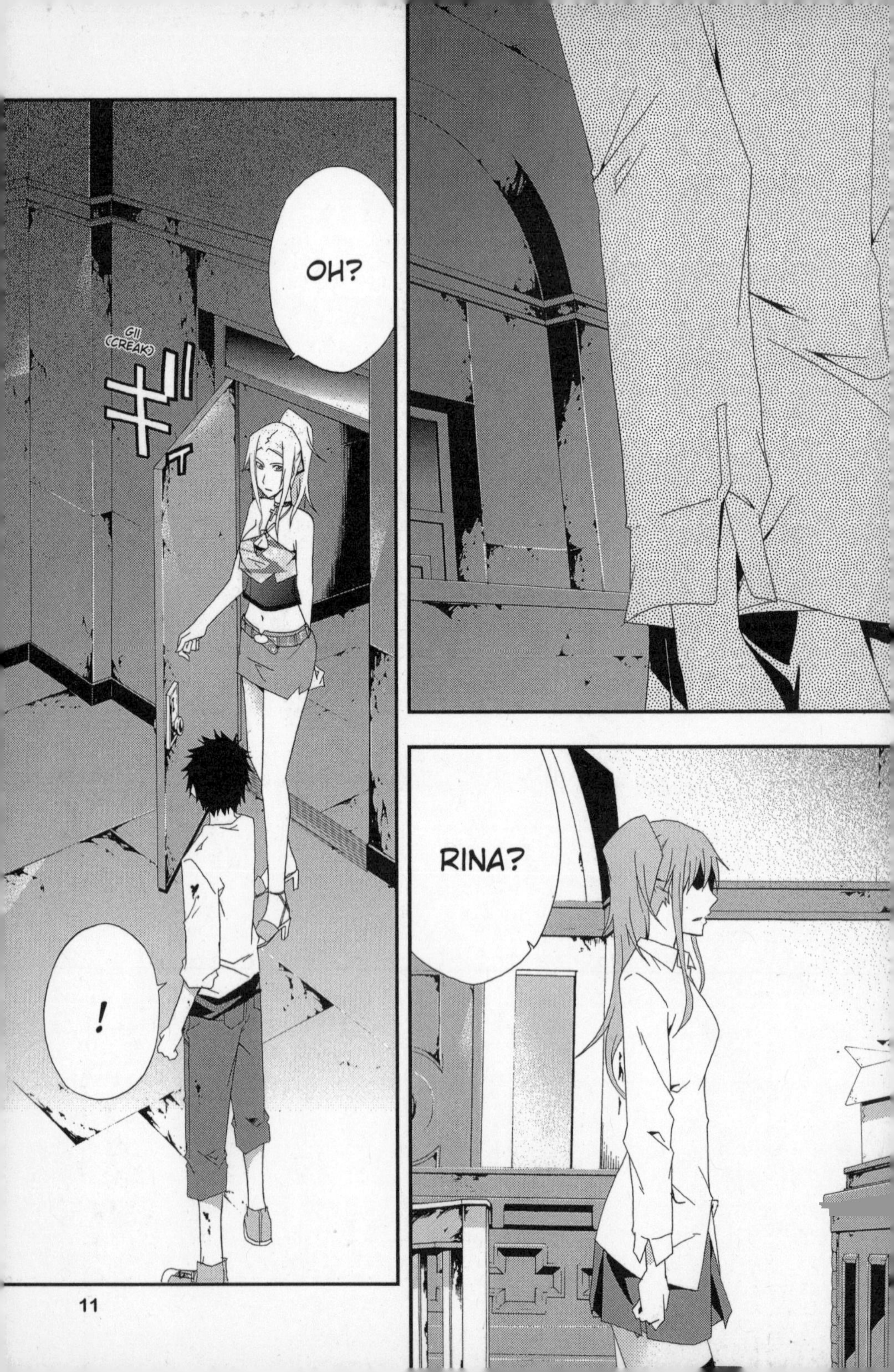
RINA?
OH?
GII (CREAK)
!

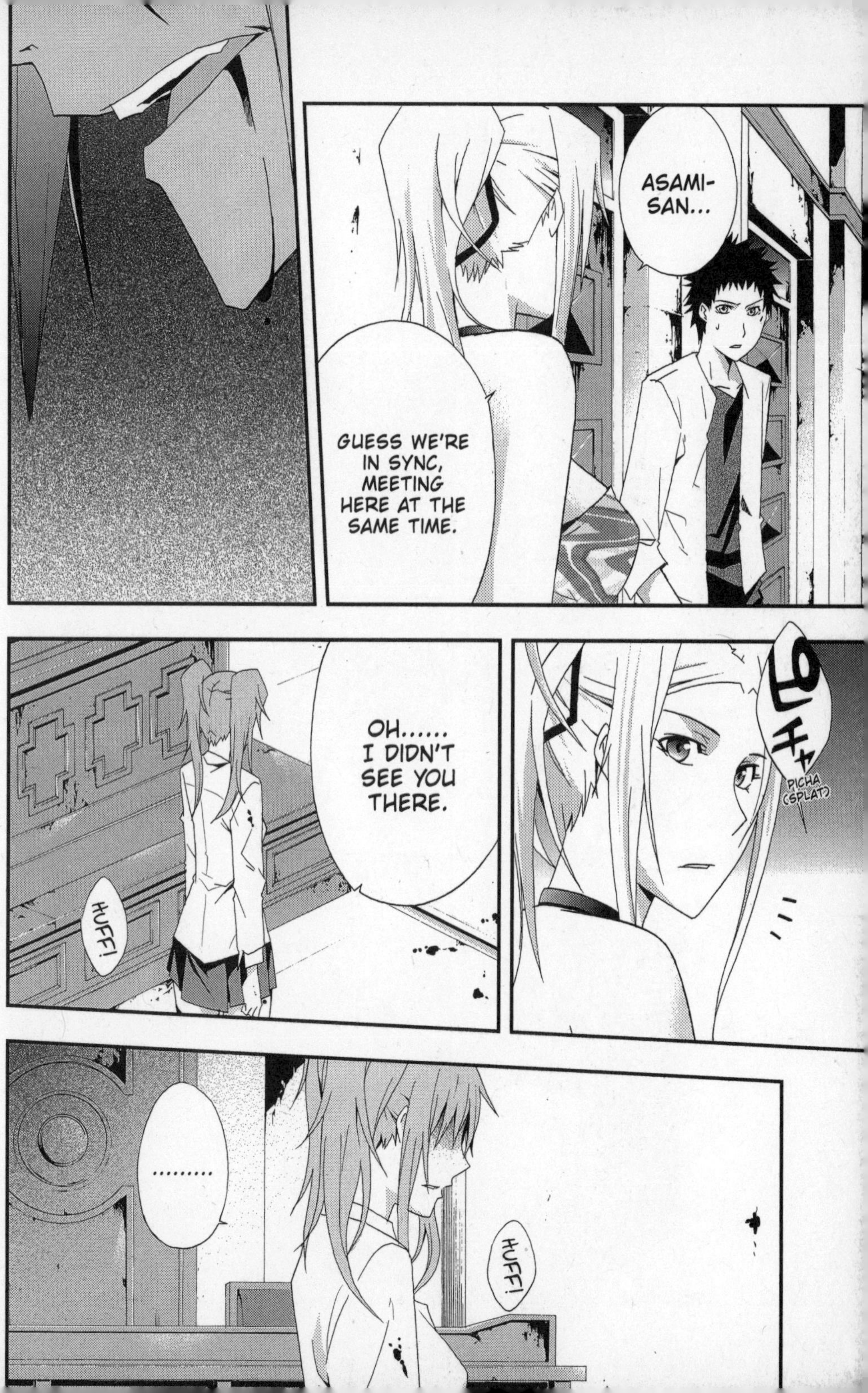
ASAMI-SAN...
GUESS WE'RE IN SYNC, MEETING HERE AT THE SAME TIME.
ピチャ
PICHA (SPLAT)
OH...... I DIDN'T SEE YOU THERE.
HUFF!
....
HUFF!

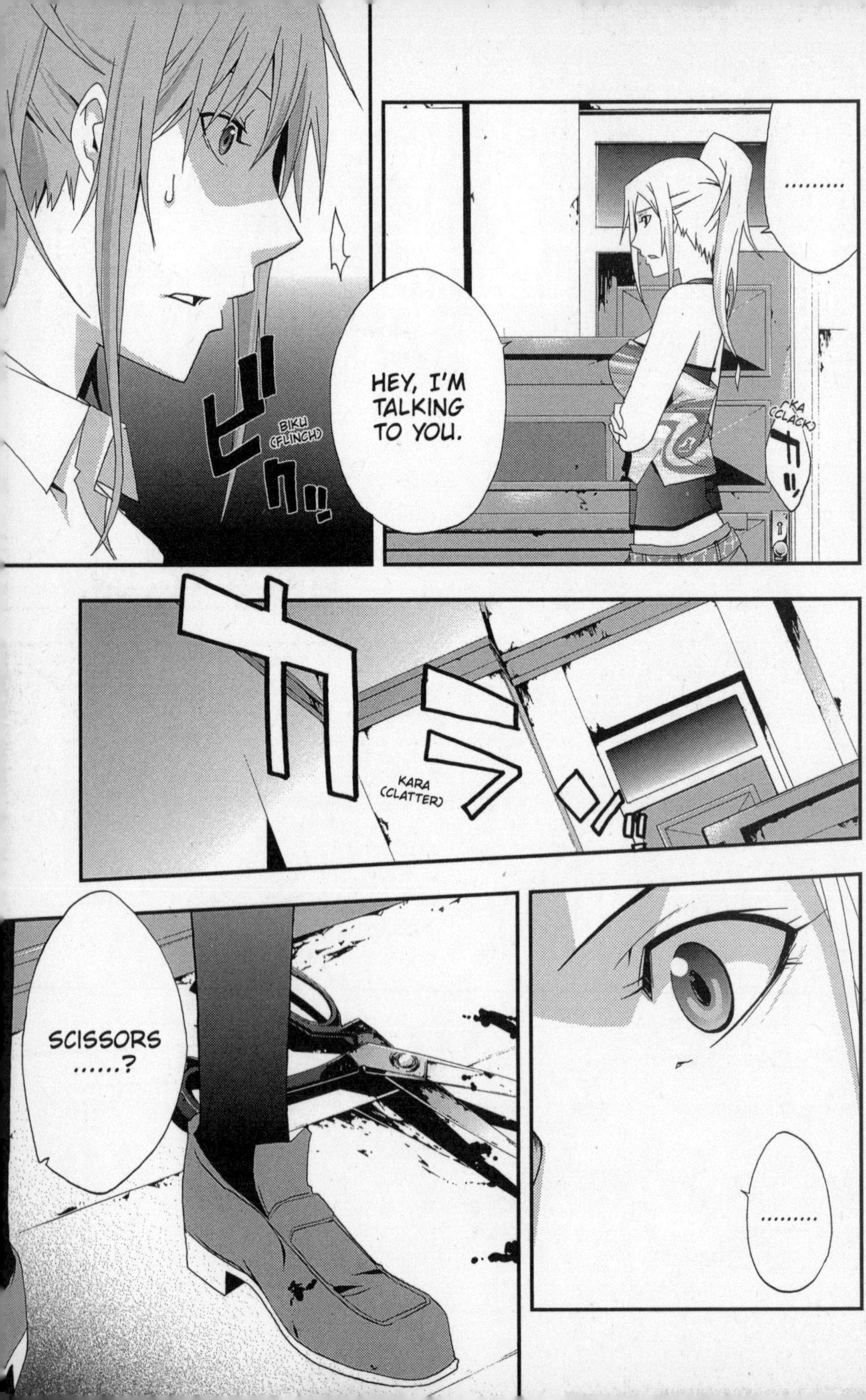
....
HEY, I'M TALKING TO YOU.
KA (CLACK)
BIKU (FLINCH)
KARA (CLATTER)
....
SCISSORS ......?

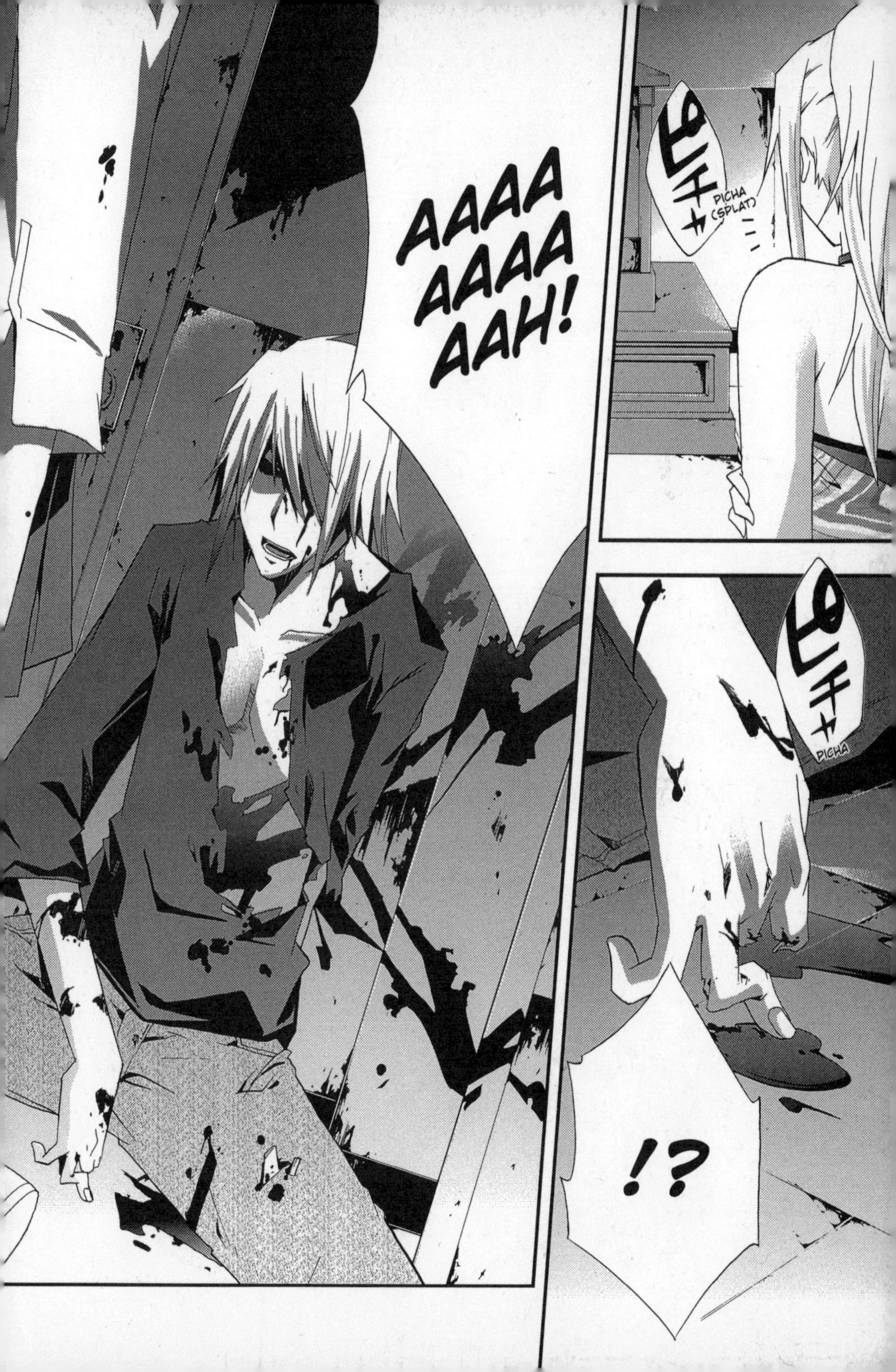
ピチャ
PICHA (SPLAT)
ピチャ
PICHA
!?
AAAA AAAA AAH!

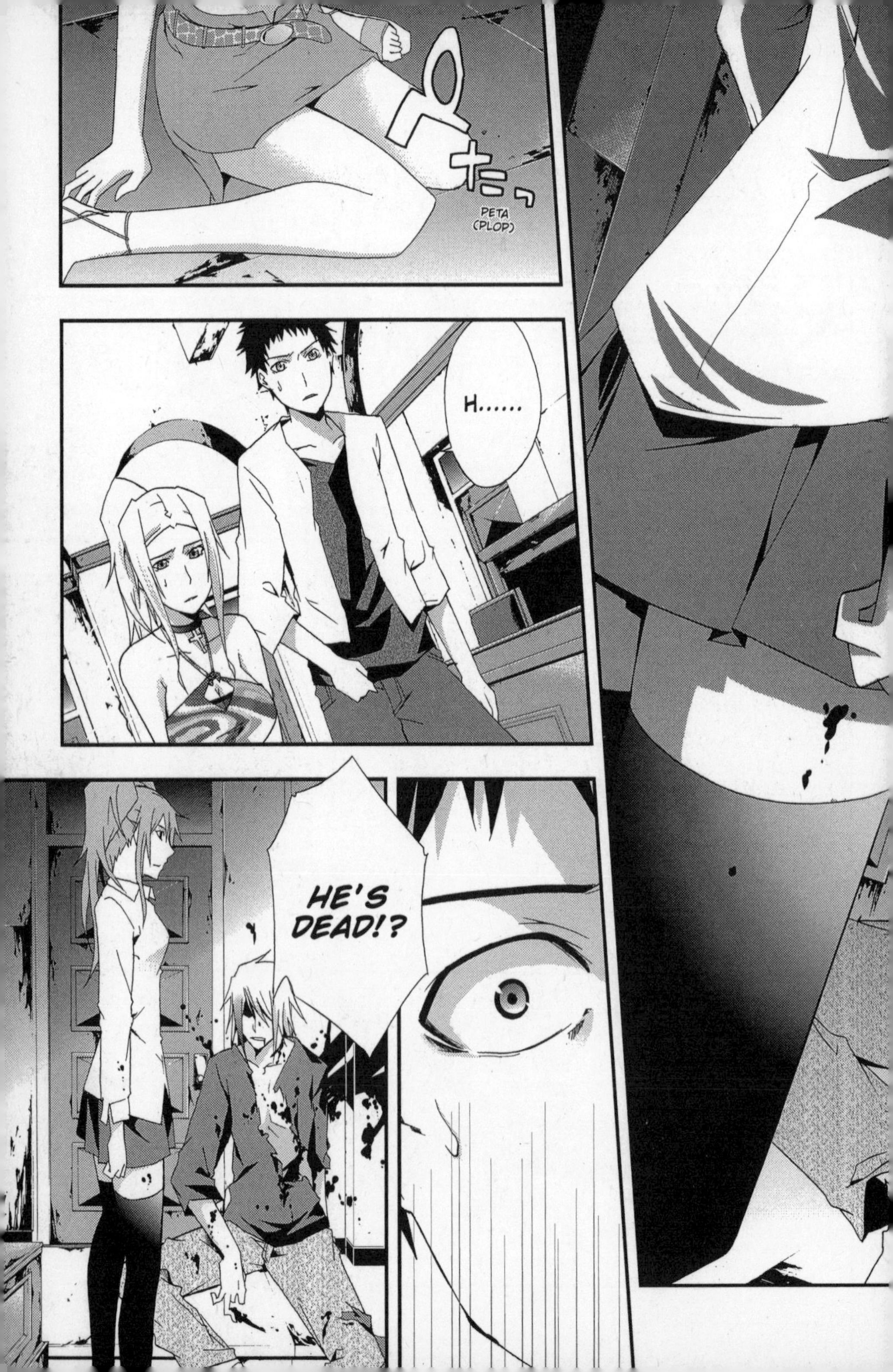
ペタッ
PETA (PLOP)
H......
HE'S DEAD!?

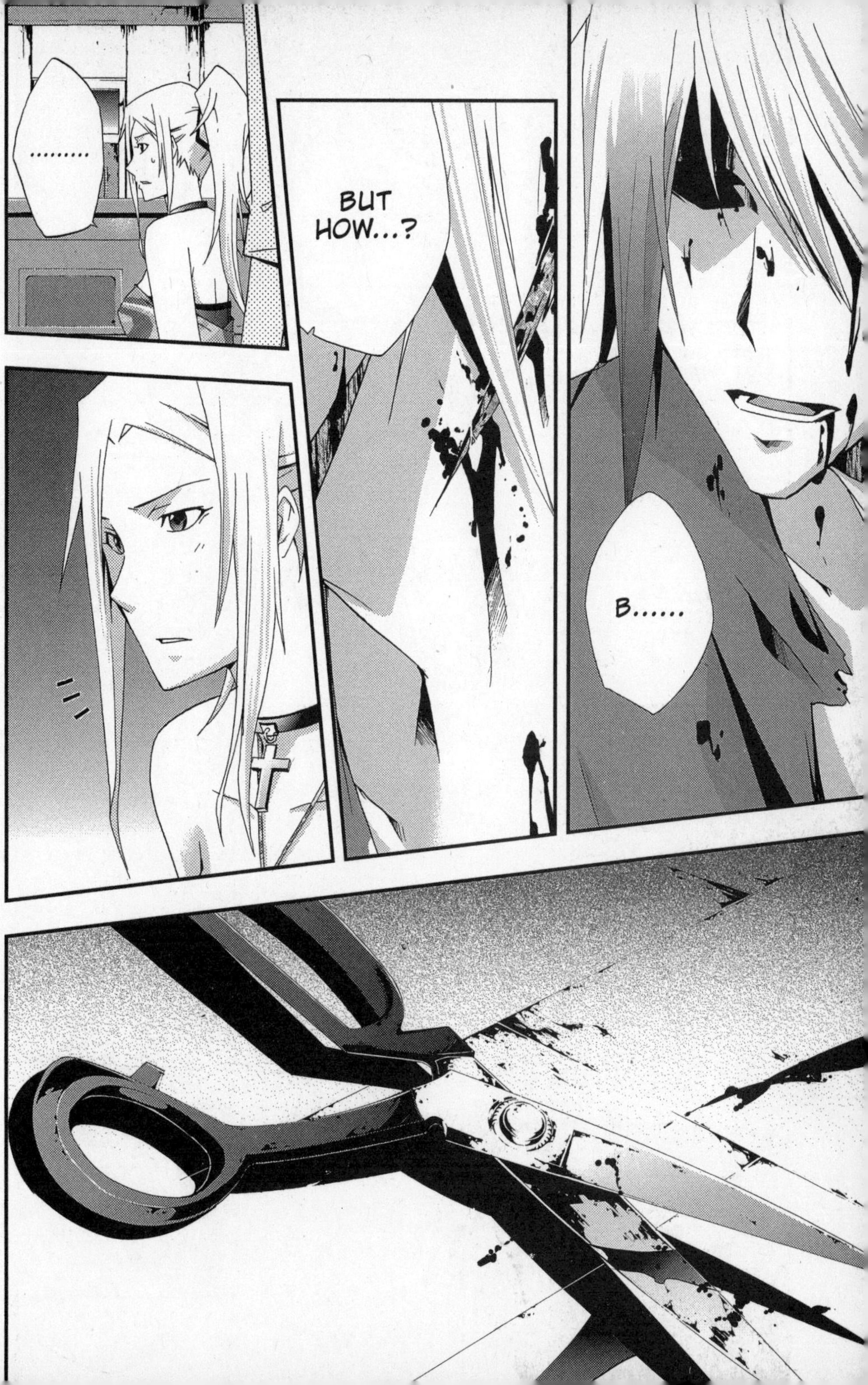
B......
BUT HOW...?
....

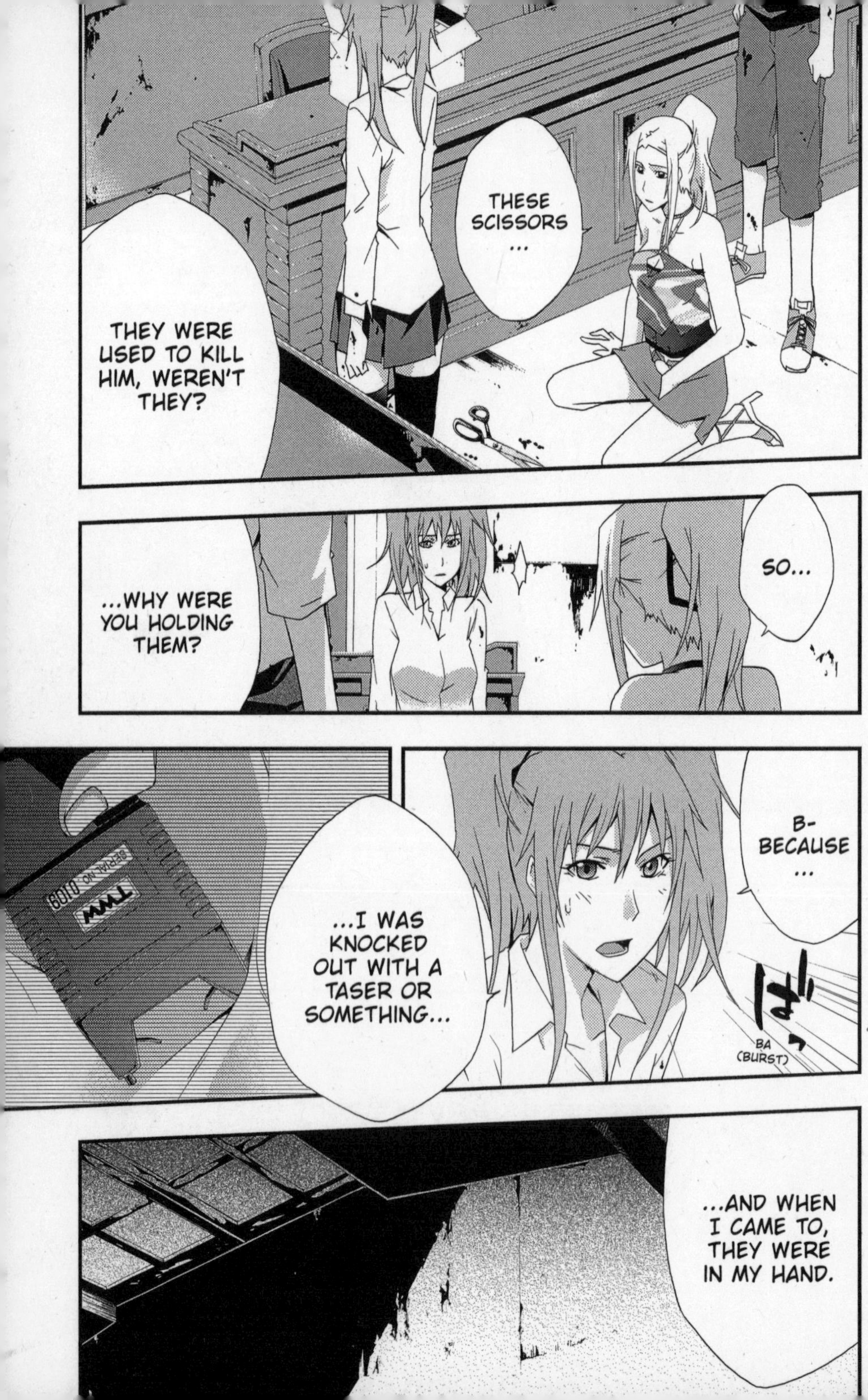
THESE SCISSORS ...
THEY WERE USED TO KILL HIM, WEREN'T THEY?
SO...
...WHY WERE YOU HOLDING THEM?
B-BECAUSE ...
...I WAS KNOCKED OUT WITH A TASER OR SOMETHING...
BA (BURST)
TWW
SERIAL NO. 0109
...AND WHEN I CAME TO, THEY WERE IN MY HAND.

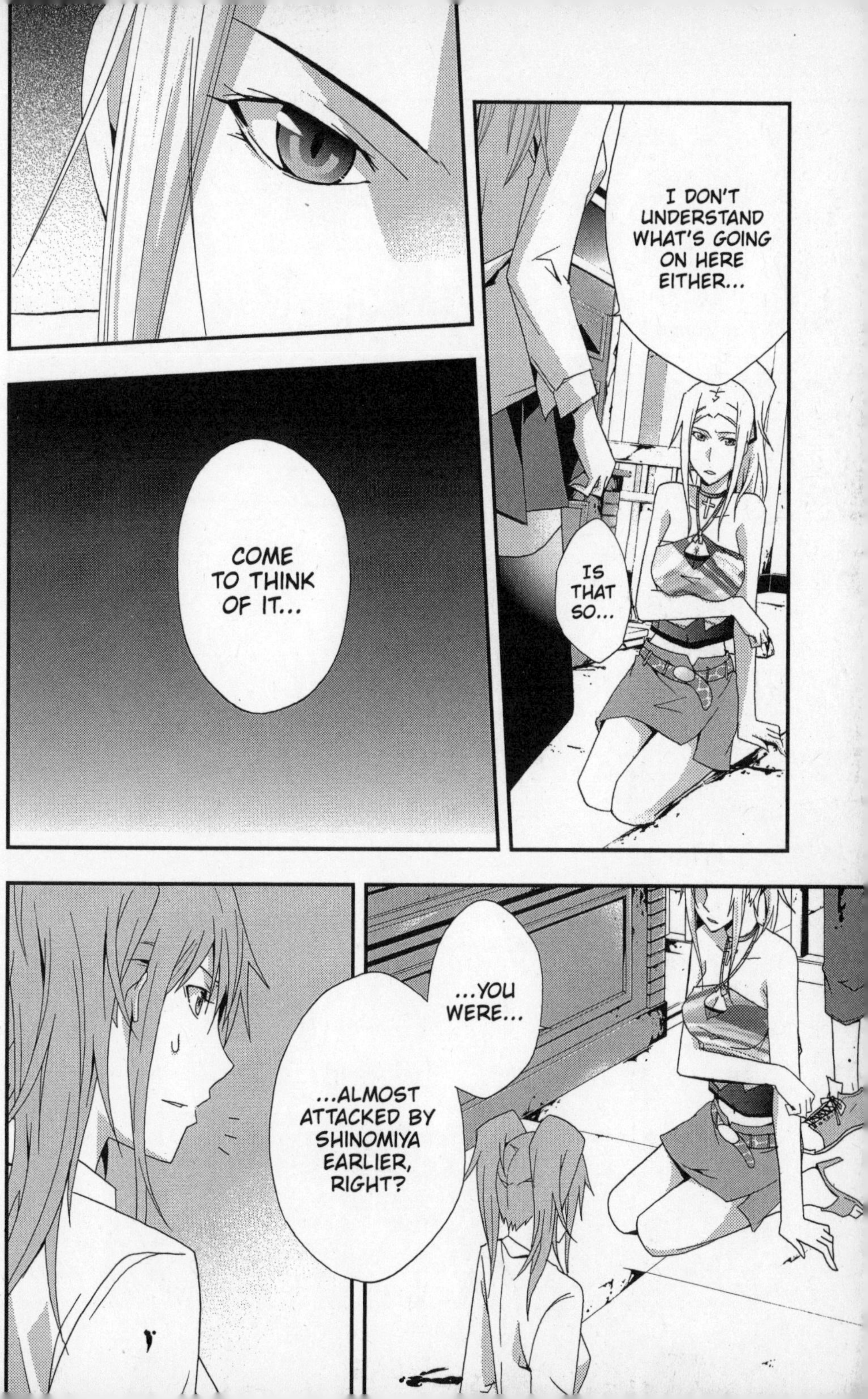
I DON'T UNDERSTAND WHAT'S GOING ON HERE EITHER...
IS THAT SO...
COME TO THINK OF IT...
...YOU WERE...
...ALMOST ATTACKED BY SHINOMIYA EARLIER, RIGHT?

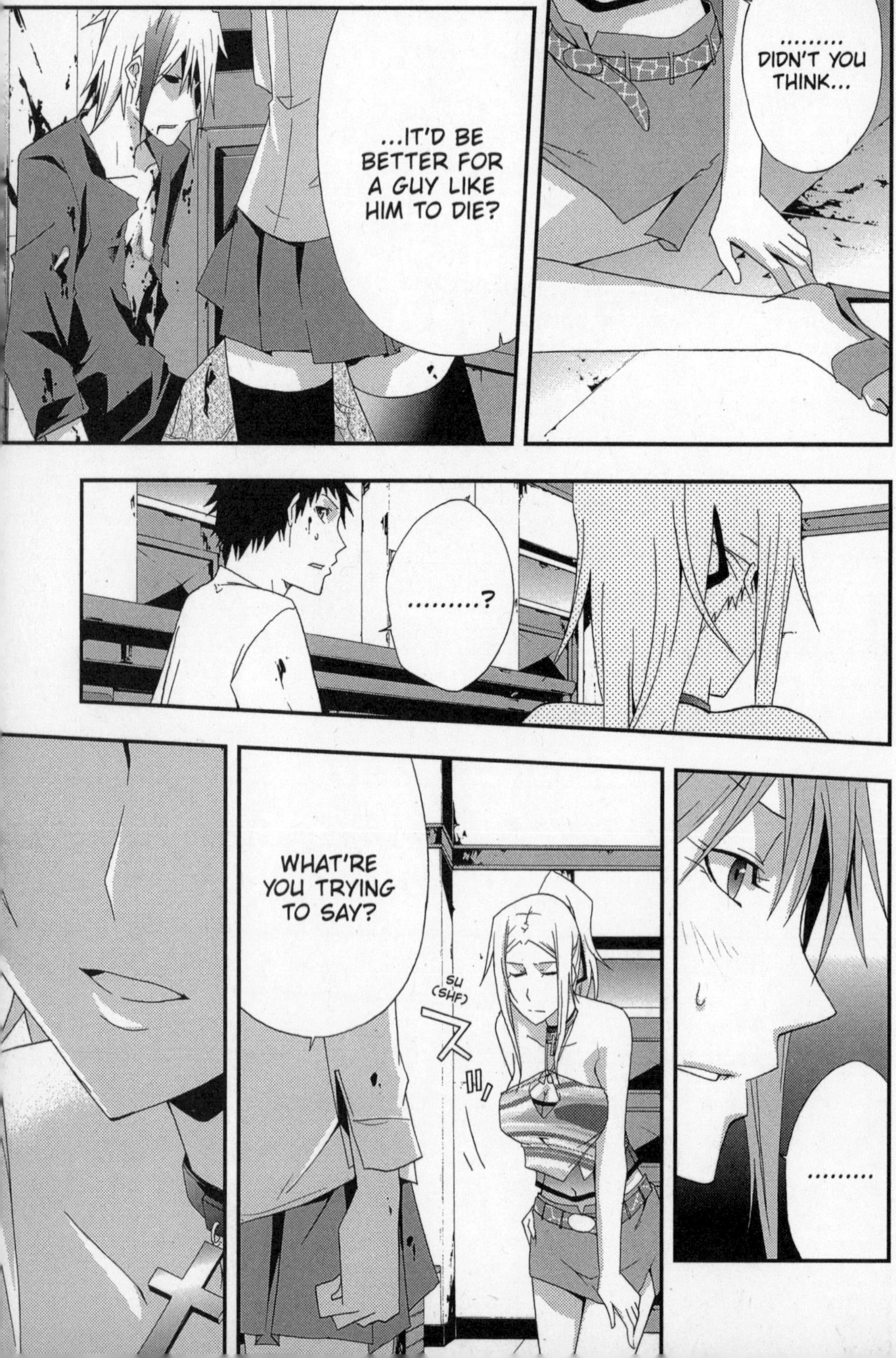
....
DIDN'T YOU THINK...
...IT'D BE BETTER FOR A GUY LIKE HIM TO DIE?
.........?
....
WHAT'RE YOU TRYING TO SAY?
SU (SHF)

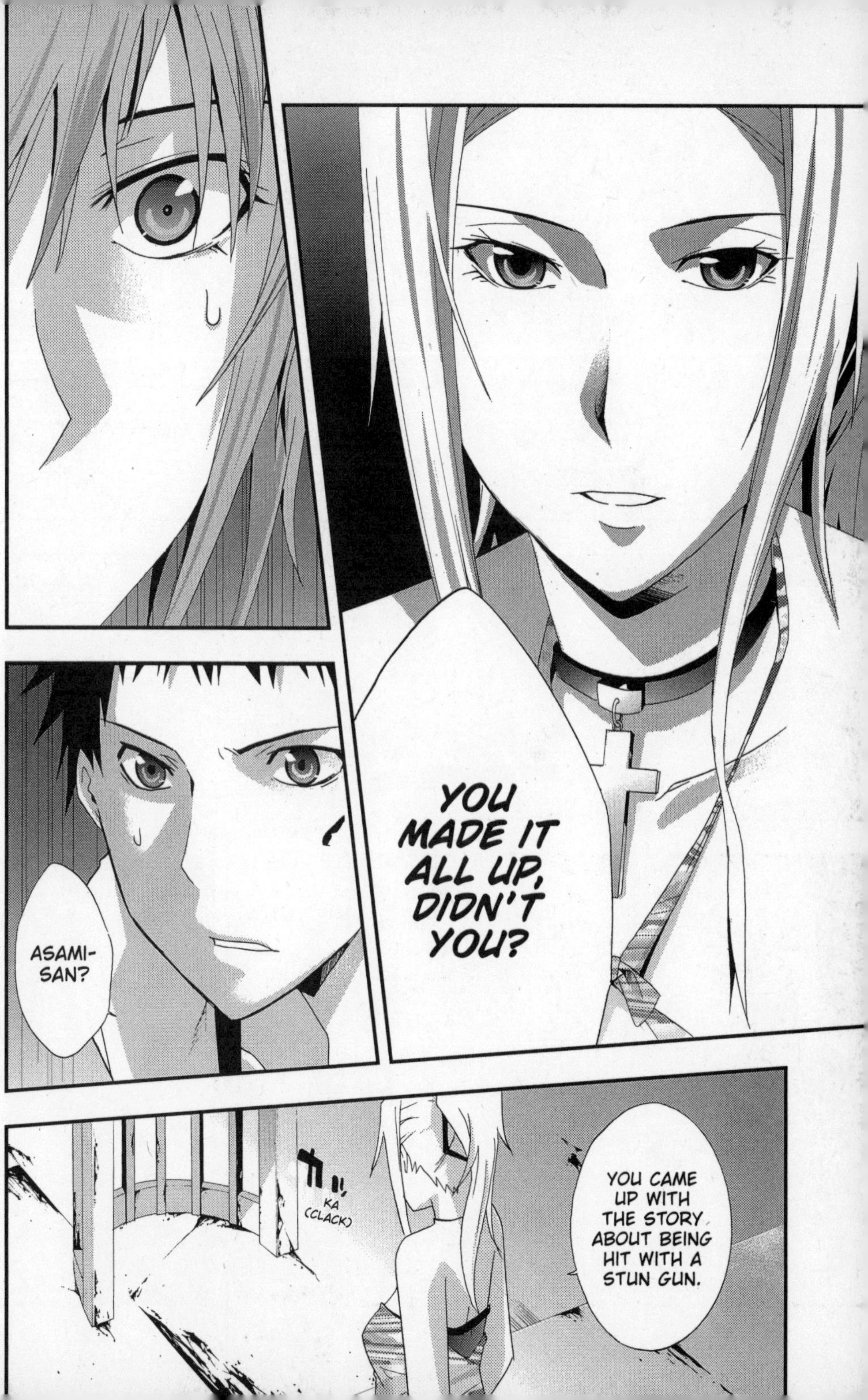
YOU MADE IT ALL UP, DIDN'T YOU?
ASAMI-SAN?
YOU CAME UP WITH THE STORY ABOUT BEING HIT WITH A STUN GUN.
KA (CLACK)

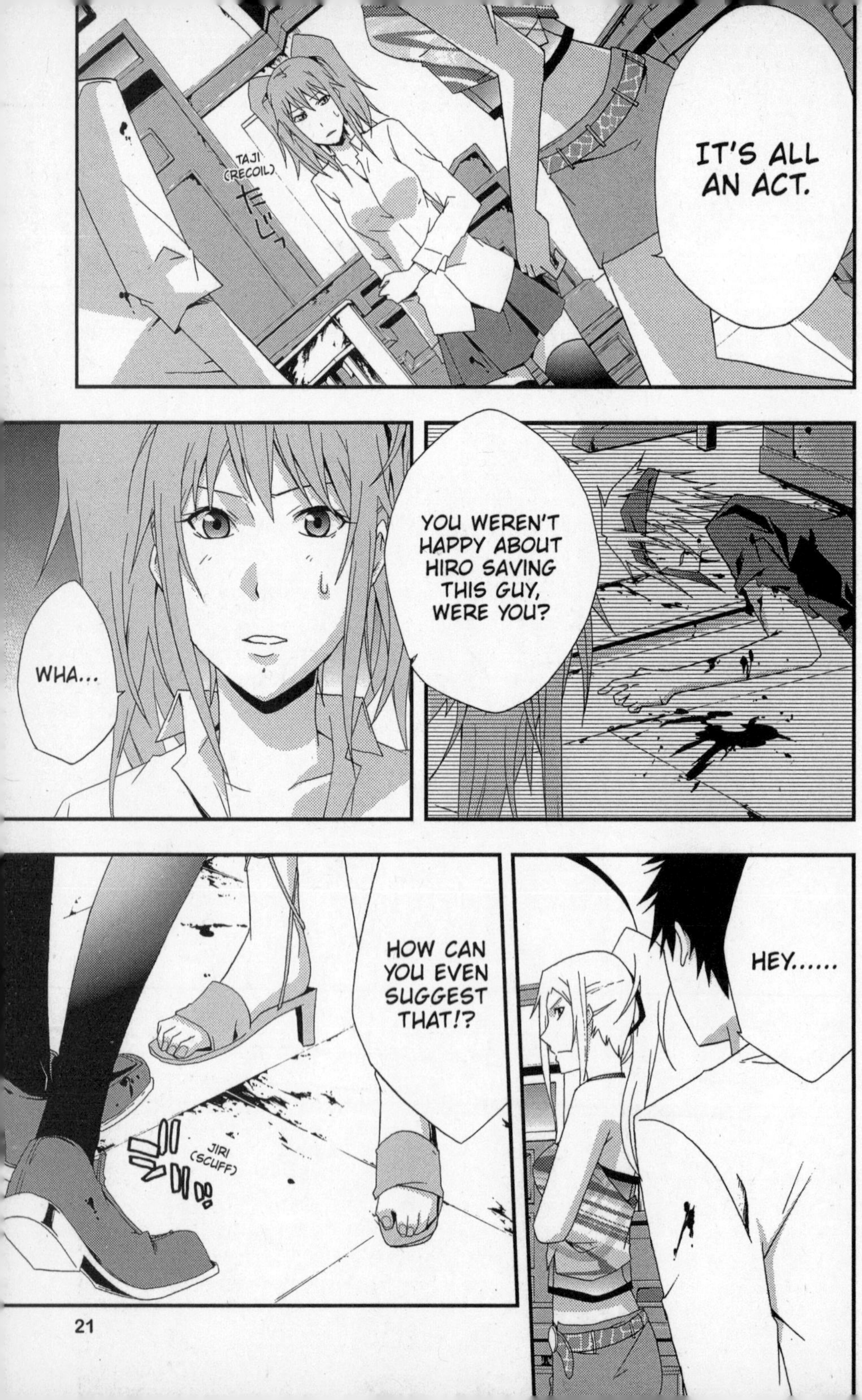
IT'S ALL AN ACT.
TAJI (RECOIL)
たじっ
YOU WEREN'T HAPPY ABOUT HIRO SAVING THIS GUY, WERE YOU?
WHA...
HEY......
HOW CAN YOU EVEN SUGGEST THAT!?
JIRI (SCUFF)

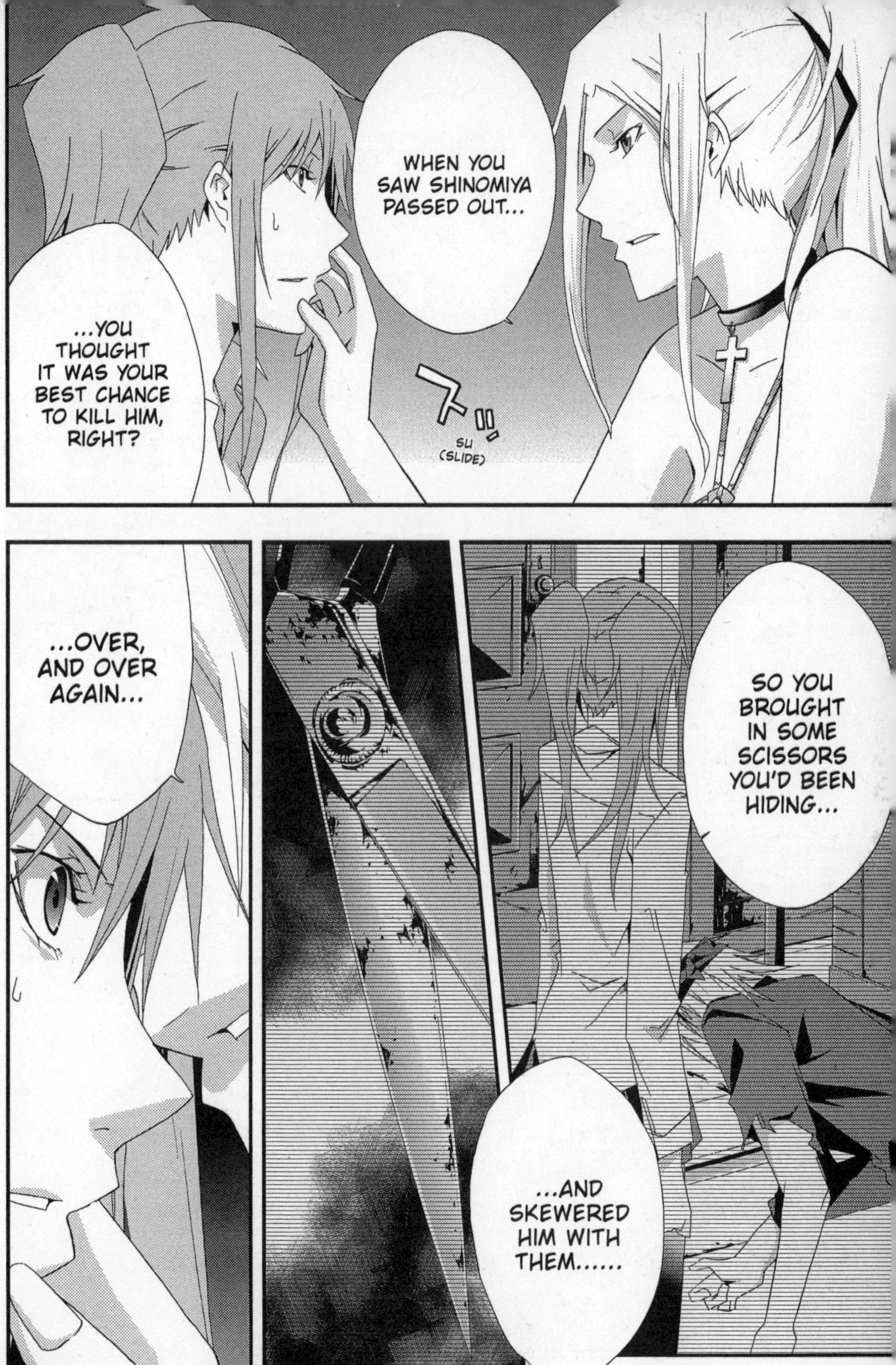
WHEN YOU SAW SHINOMIYA PASSED OUT...
SU (SLIDE)
...YOU THOUGHT IT WAS YOUR BEST CHANCE TO KILL HIM, RIGHT?
SO YOU BROUGHT IN SOME SCISSORS YOU'D BEEN HIDING...
...AND SKEWERED HIM WITH THEM......
...OVER, AND OVER AGAIN...

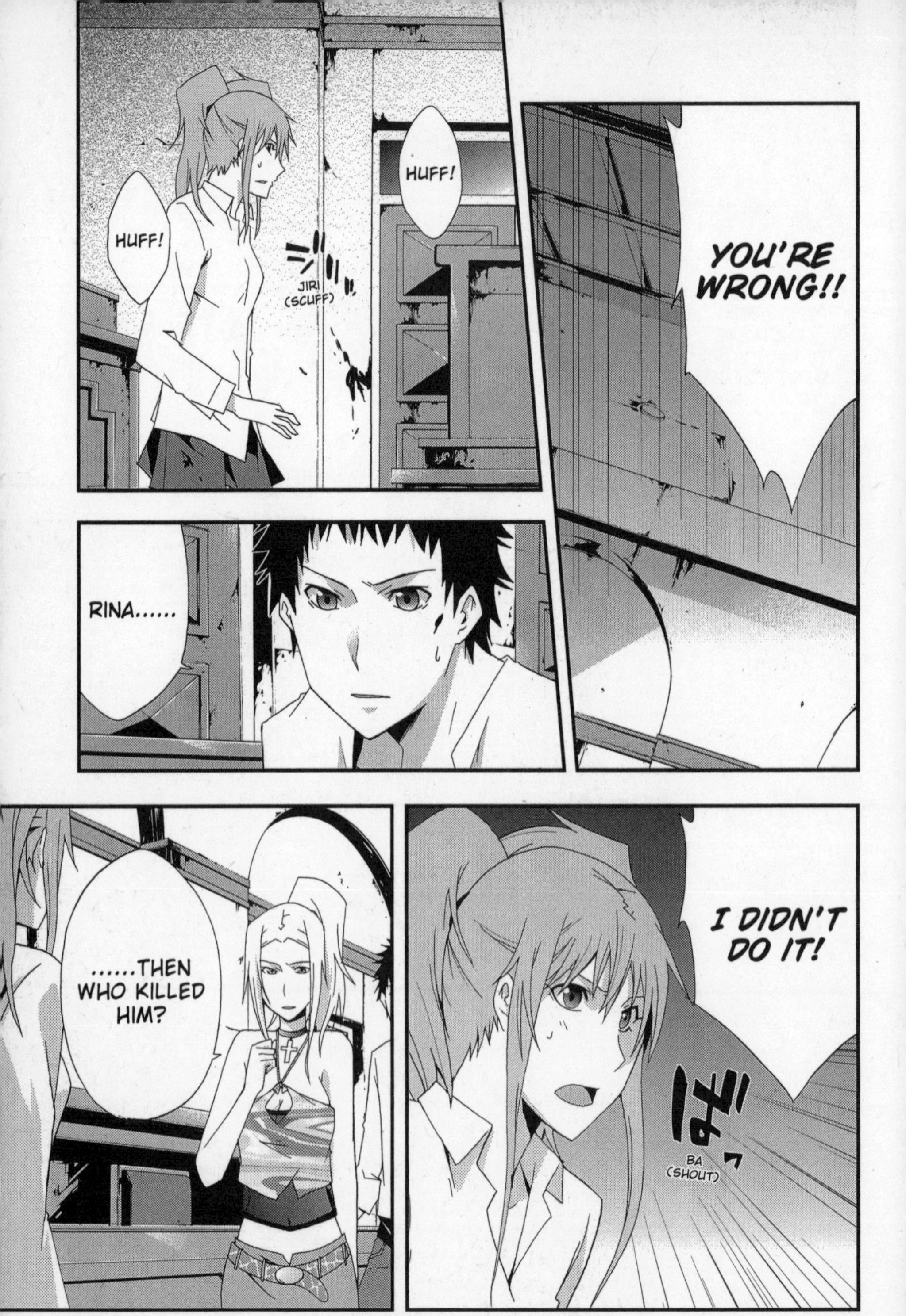
YOU'RE WRONG!!
HUFF!
JIRI (SCUFF)
HUFF!
RINA......
I DIDN'T DO IT!
ば
BA (SHOUT)
......THEN WHO KILLED HIM?

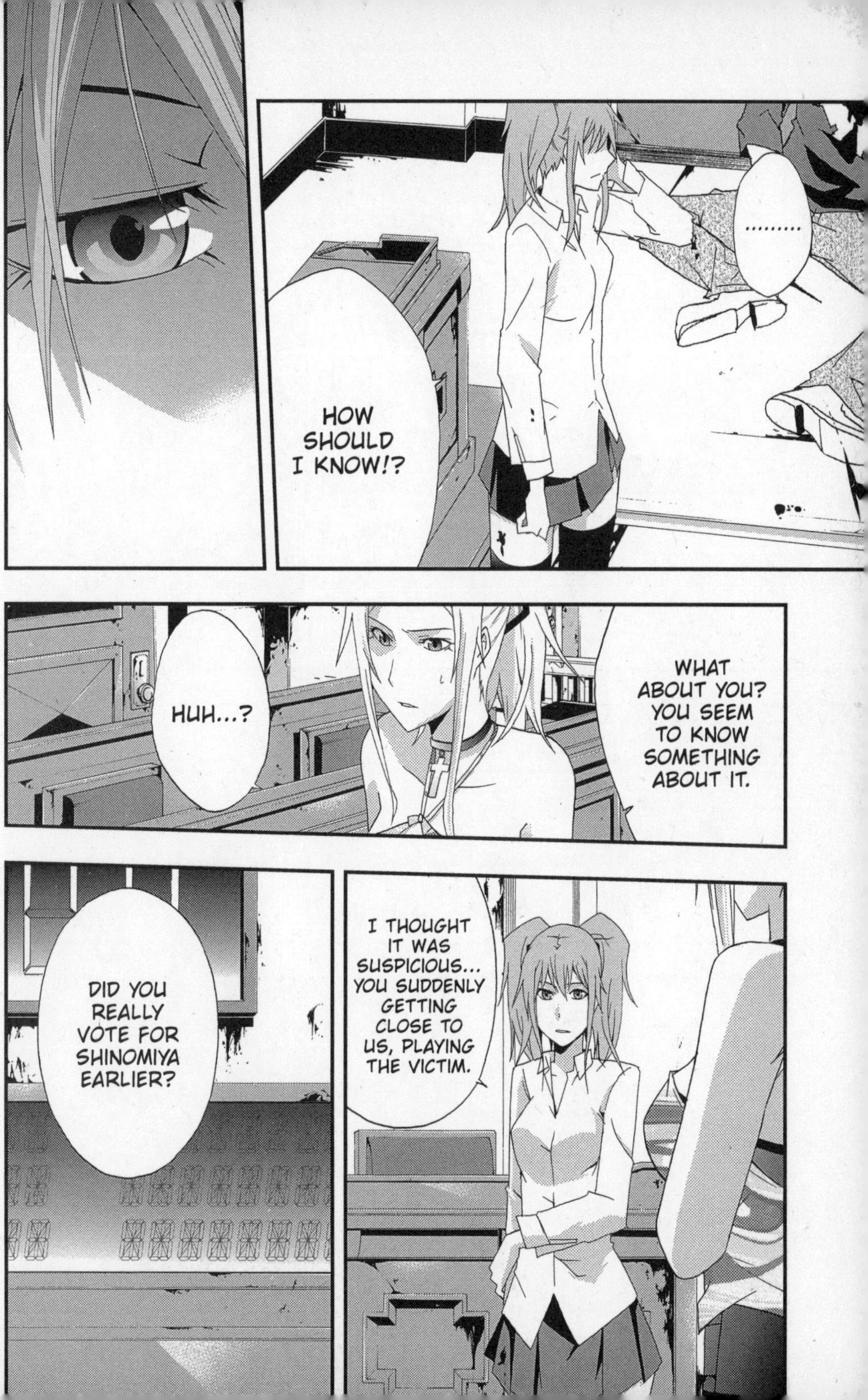
....
HOW SHOULD I KNOW!?
WHAT ABOUT YOU? YOU SEEM TO KNOW SOMETHING ABOUT IT.
HUH...?
I THOUGHT IT WAS SUSPICIOUS... YOU SUDDENLY GETTING CLOSE TO US, PLAYING THE VICTIM.
DID YOU REALLY VOTE FOR SHINOMIYA EARLIER?

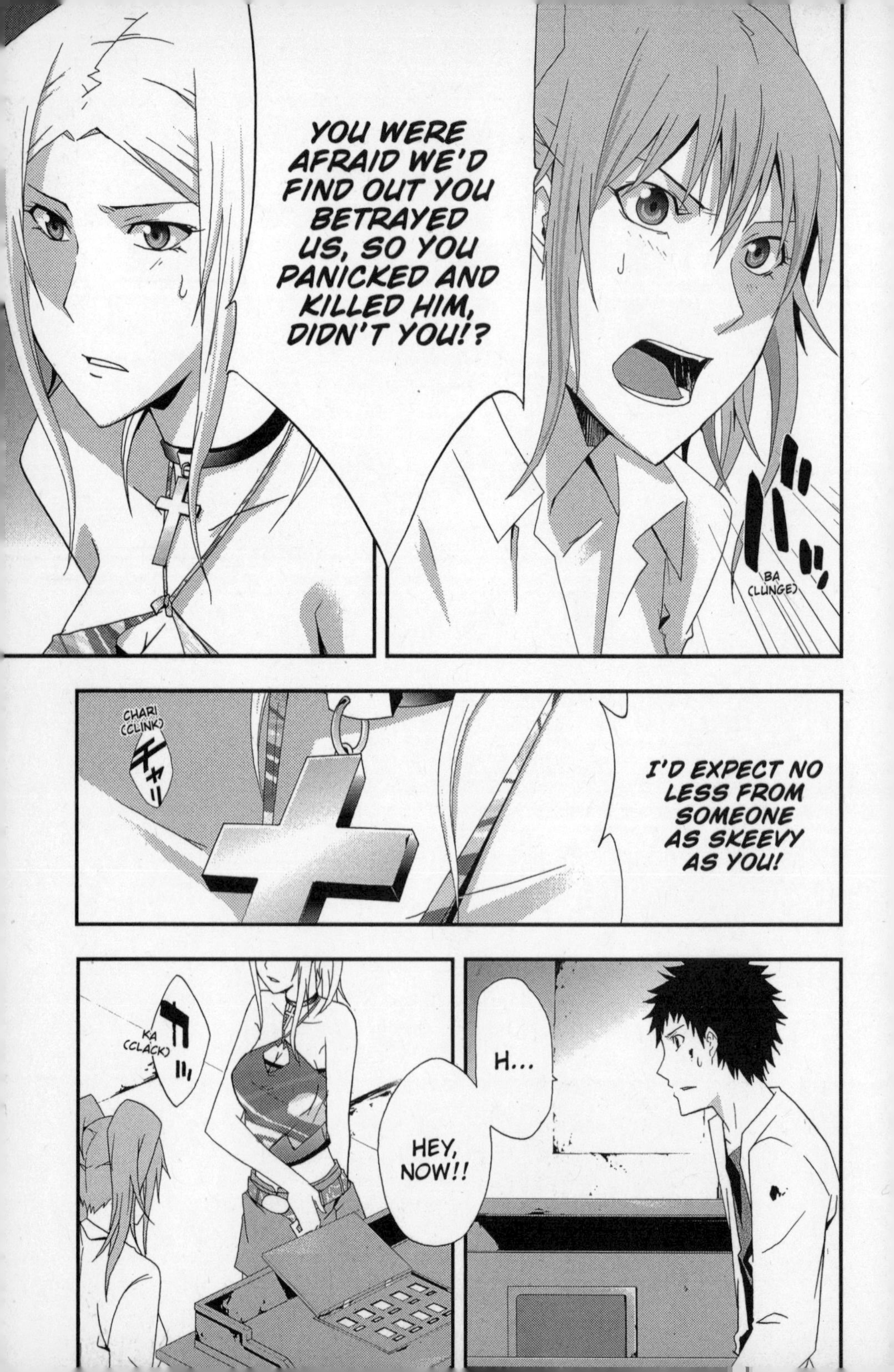

YOU WERE AFRAID WE'D FIND OUT YOU BETRAYED US, SO YOU PANICKED AND KILLED HIM, DIDN'T YOU!?
BA (LUNGE)
I'D EXPECT NO LESS FROM SOMEONE AS SKEEVY AS YOU!
CHARI (CLINK)
H...
HEY, NOW!!
KA (CLACK)

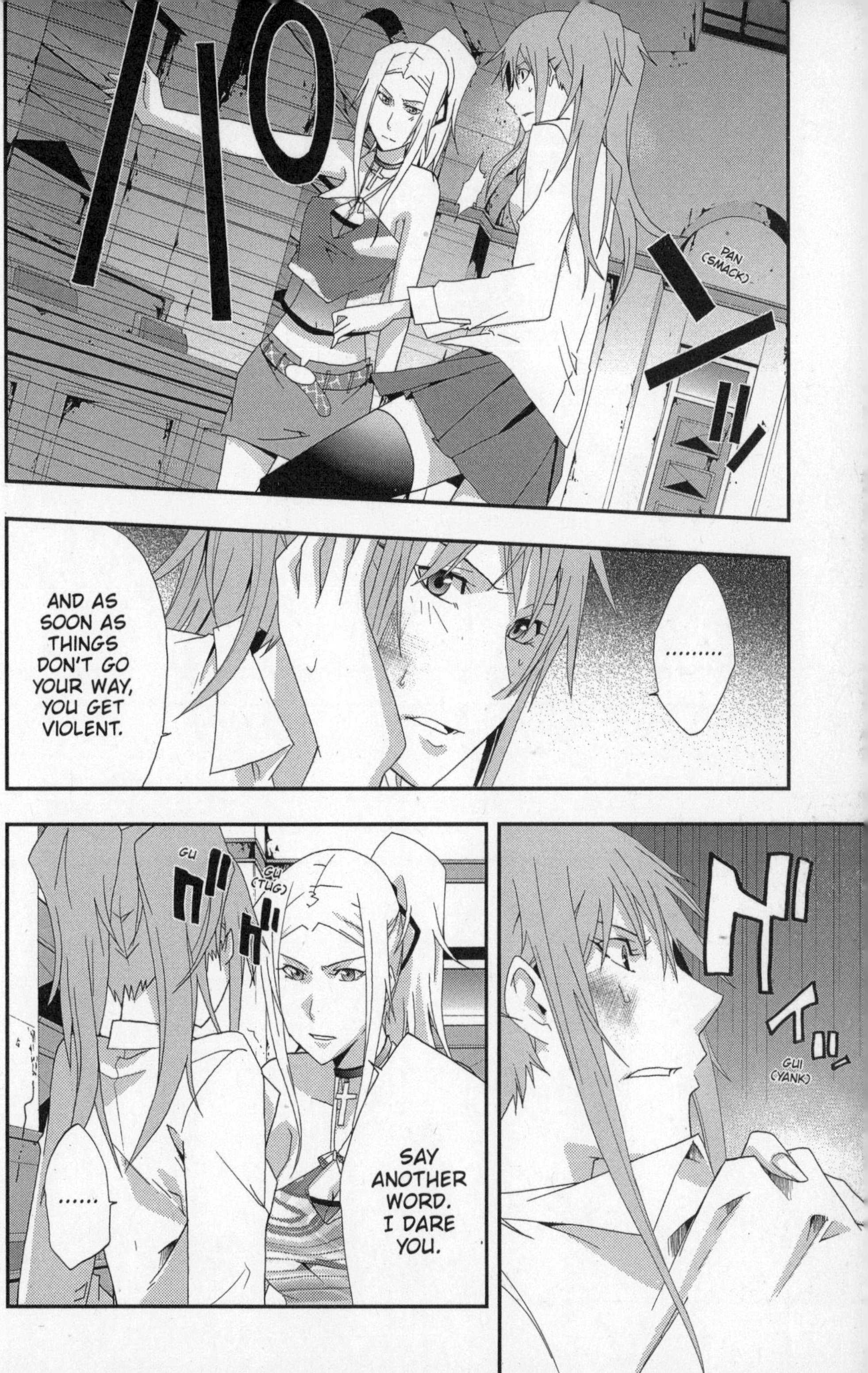
PAN
(SMACK)
....
AND AS SOON AS THINGS DON'T GO YOUR WAY, YOU GET VIOLENT.
GUI
(YANK)
GU
GU
(TUG)
SAY ANOTHER WORD. I DARE YOU.
......

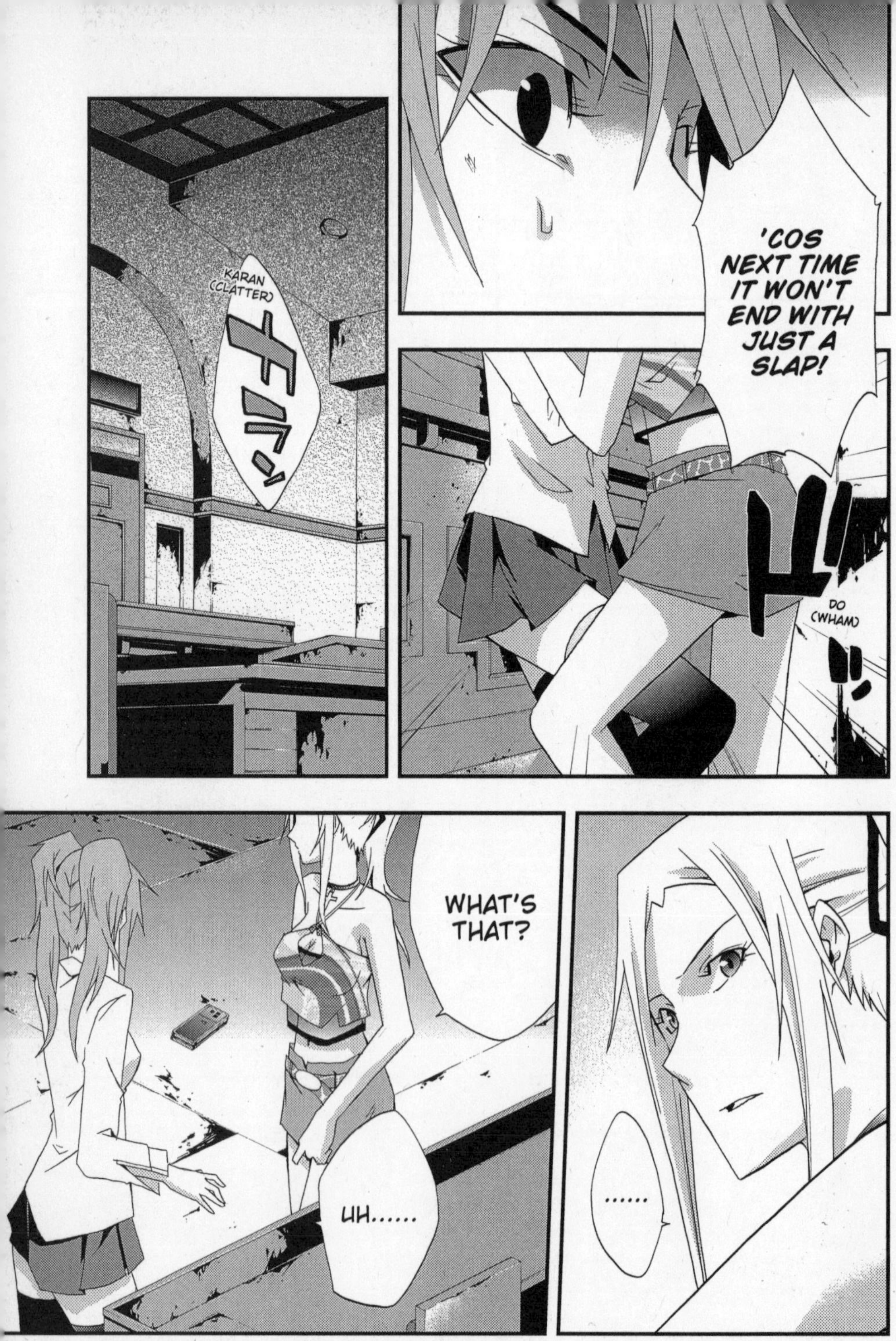
'COS NEXT TIME IT WON'T END WITH JUST A SLAP!
DO (WHAM)
KARAN (CLATTER)
......
WHAT'S THAT?
UH......

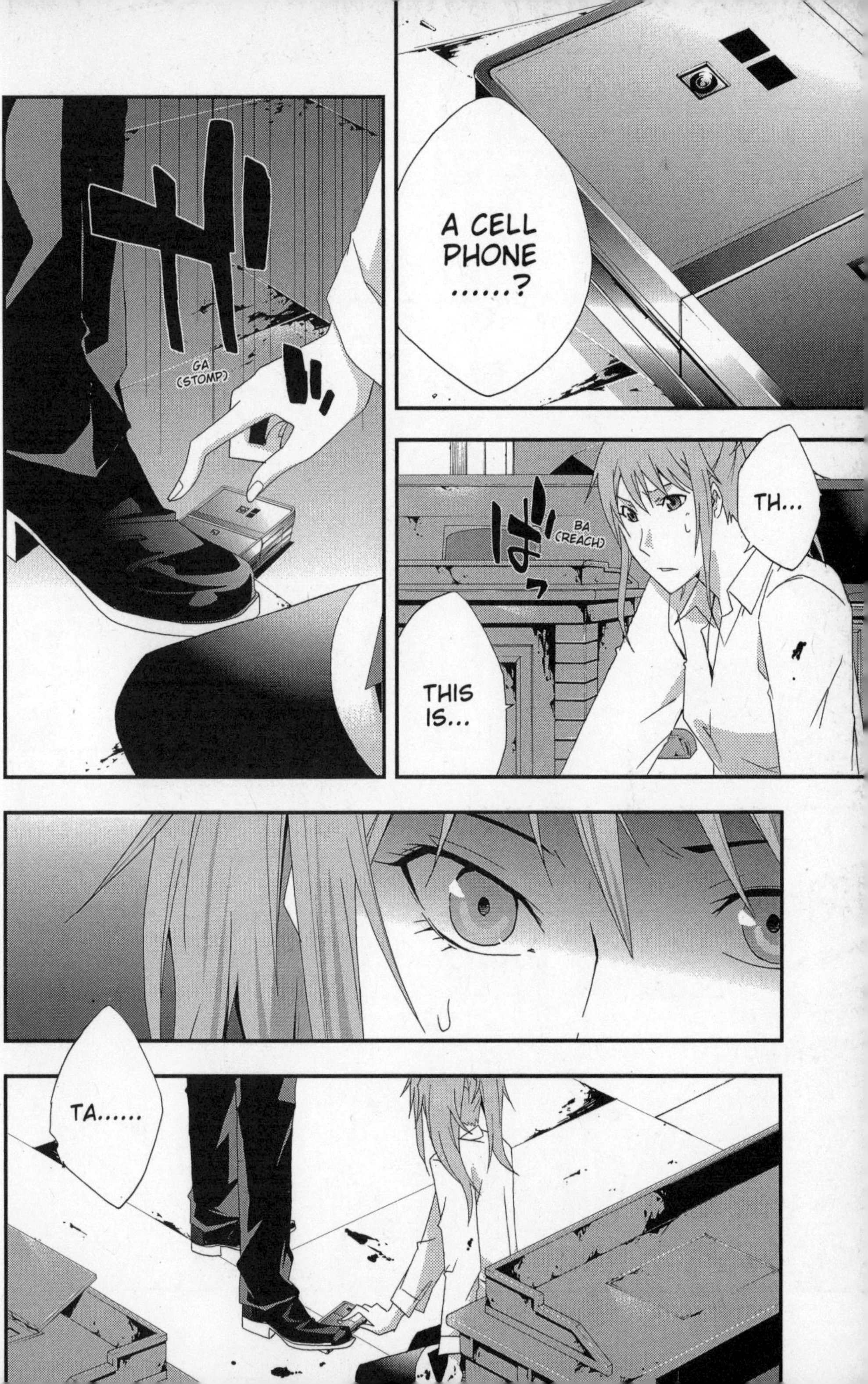

A CELL PHONE ......?
TH...
BA (REACH)
THIS IS...
GA (STOMP)
TA......

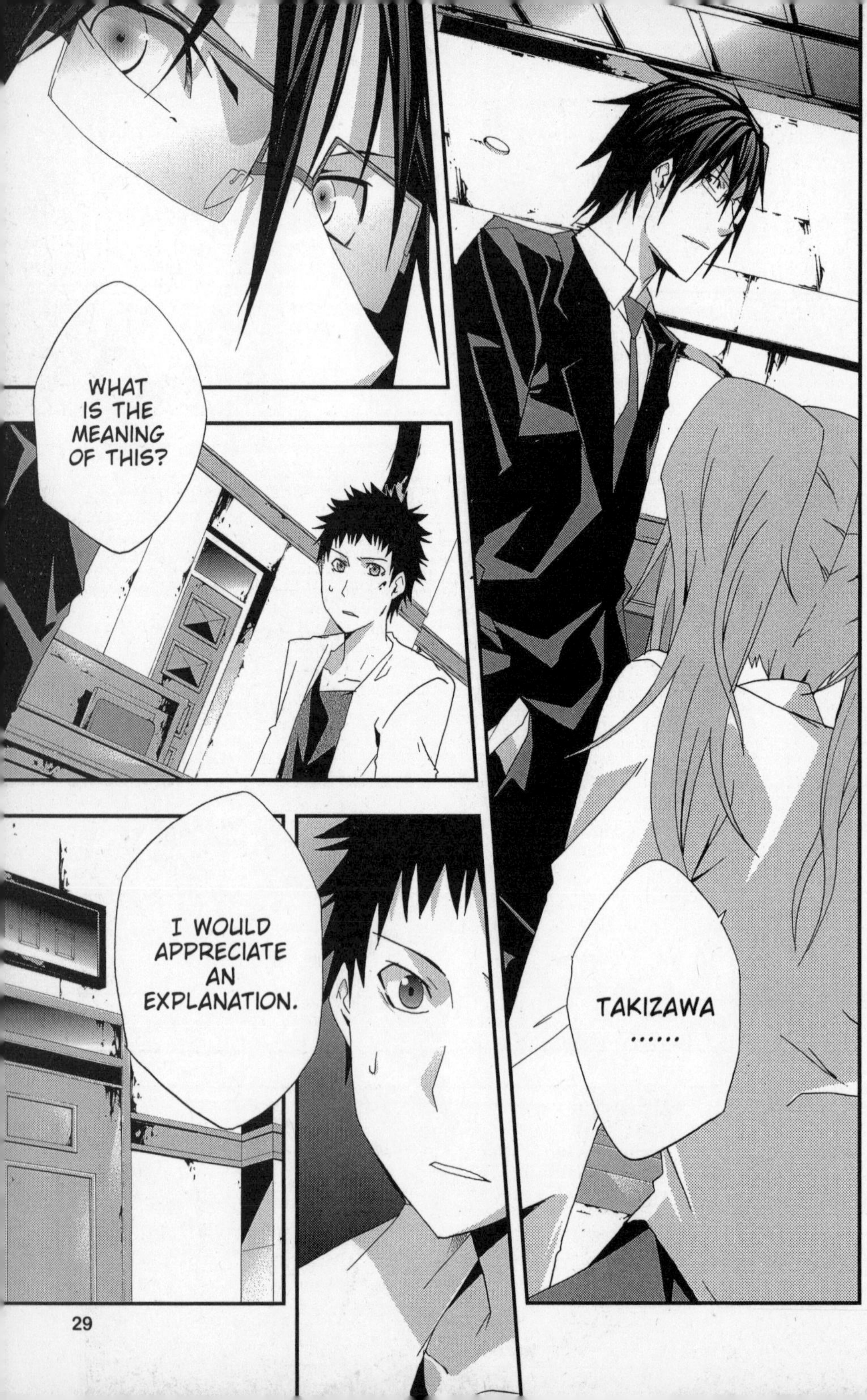
TAKIZAWA ......
WHAT IS THE MEANING OF THIS?
I WOULD APPRECIATE AN EXPLANATION.

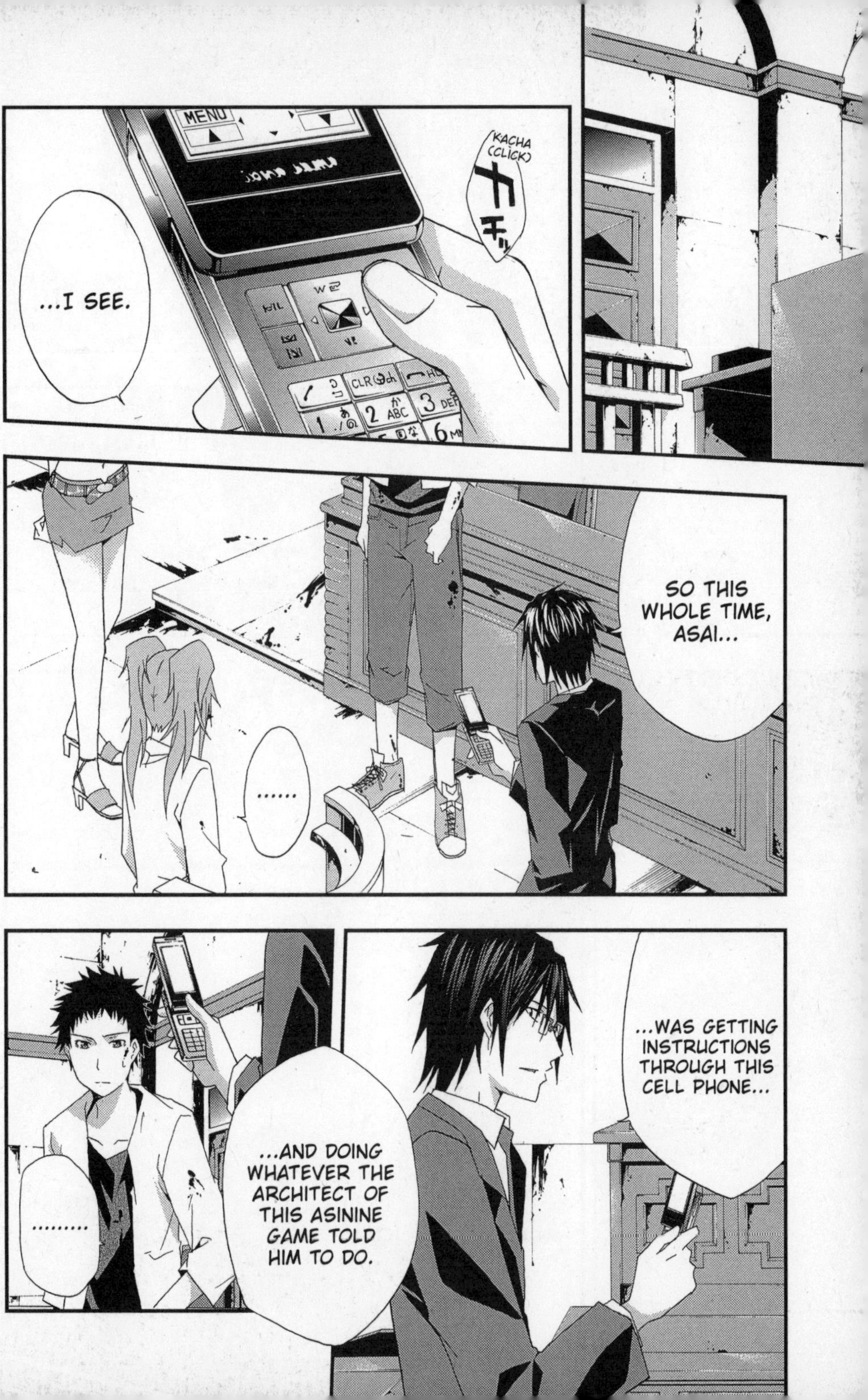
MENU
KACHA (CLICK)
カチッ
...I SEE.
SO THIS WHOLE TIME, ASAI...
......
...WAS GETTING INSTRUCTIONS THROUGH THIS CELL PHONE...
...AND DOING WHATEVER THE ARCHITECT OF THIS ASININE GAME TOLD HIM TO DO.
....

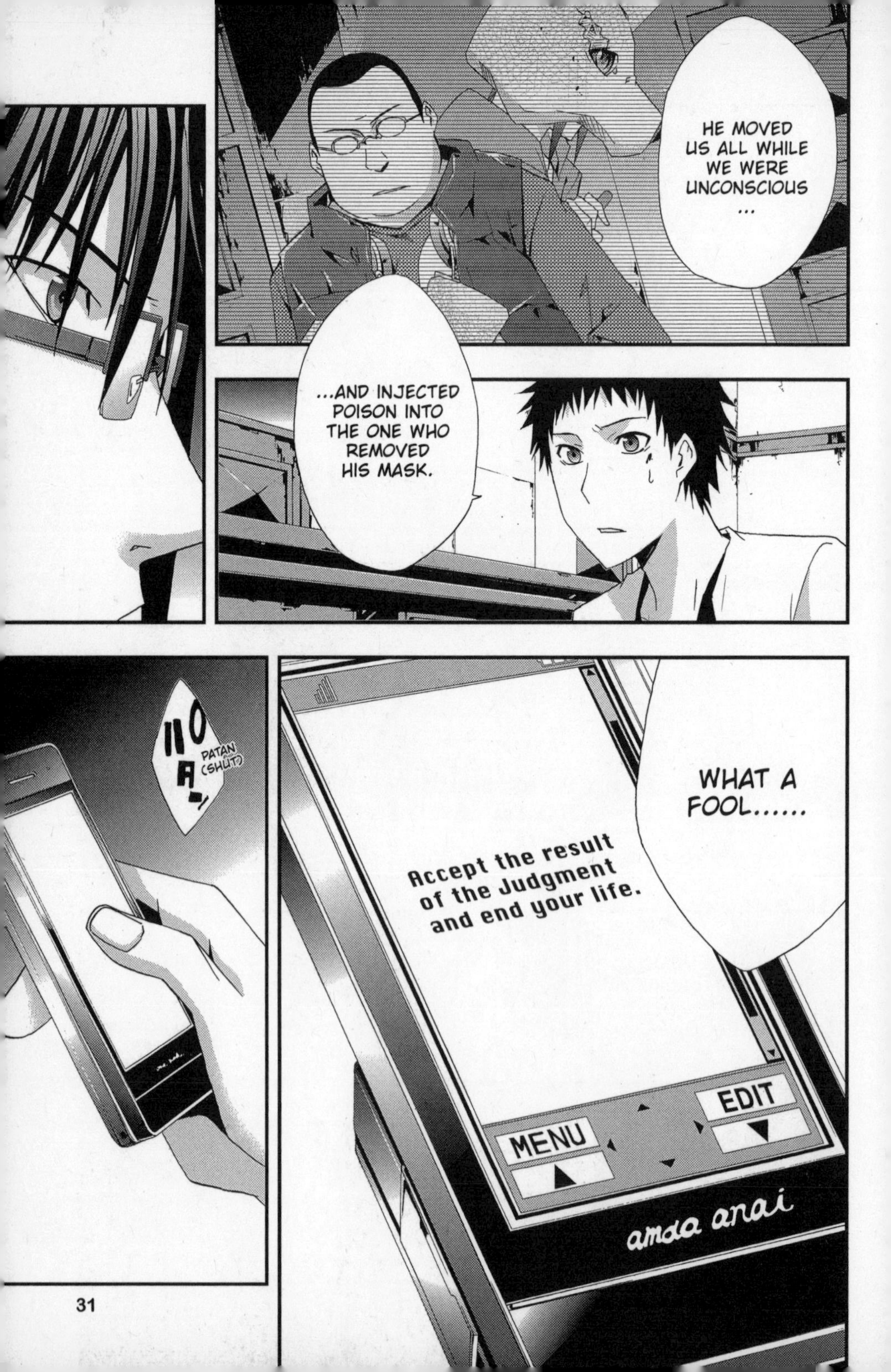
HE MOVED US ALL WHILE WE WERE UNCONSCIOUS ...
...AND INJECTED POISON INTO THE ONE WHO REMOVED HIS MASK.
WHAT A FOOL......
Accept the result of the Judgment and end your life.
MENU
EDIT
amda anai
PATAN (SHUT)

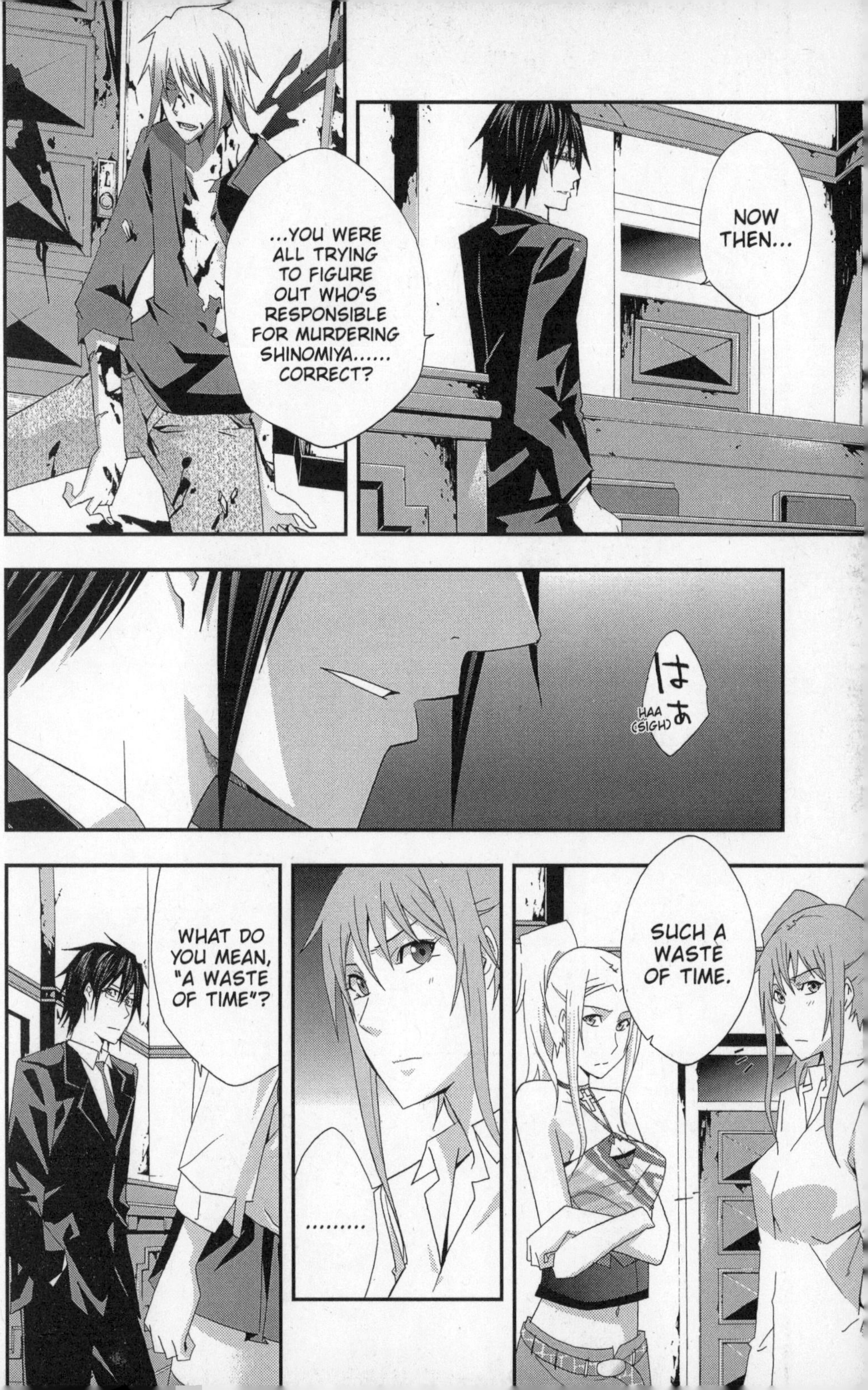
NOW THEN...
...YOU WERE ALL TRYING TO FIGURE OUT WHO'S RESPONSIBLE FOR MURDERING SHINOMIYA...... CORRECT?
はあ
HAA (SIGH)
SUCH A WASTE OF TIME.
....
WHAT DO YOU MEAN, "A WASTE OF TIME"?

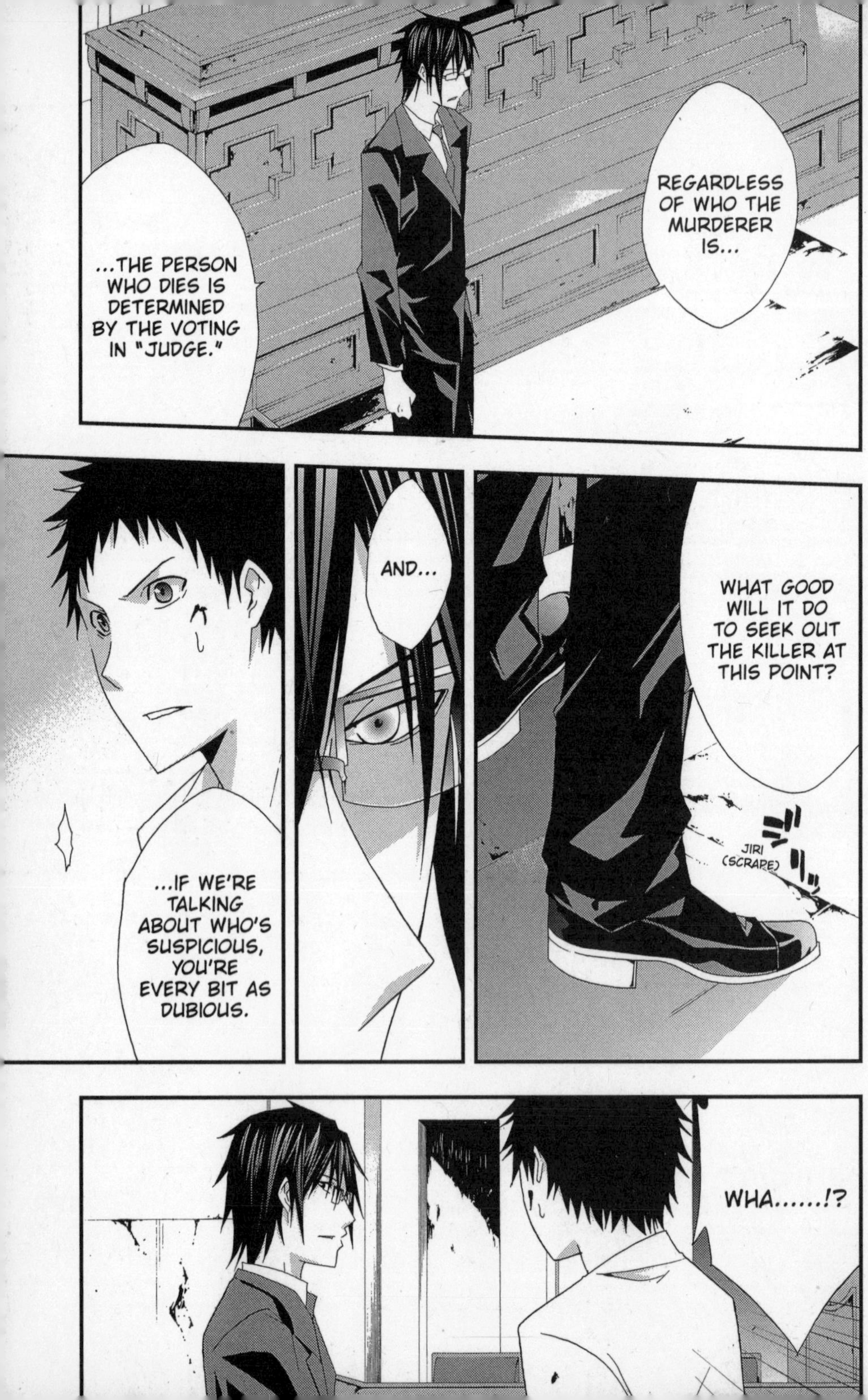
REGARDLESS OF WHO THE MURDERER IS...
...THE PERSON WHO DIES IS DETERMINED BY THE VOTING IN "JUDGE."
WHAT GOOD WILL IT DO TO SEEK OUT THE KILLER AT THIS POINT?
JIRI (SCRAPE)
AND...
...IF WE'RE TALKING ABOUT WHO'S SUSPICIOUS, YOU'RE EVERY BIT AS DUBIOUS.
WHA......!?

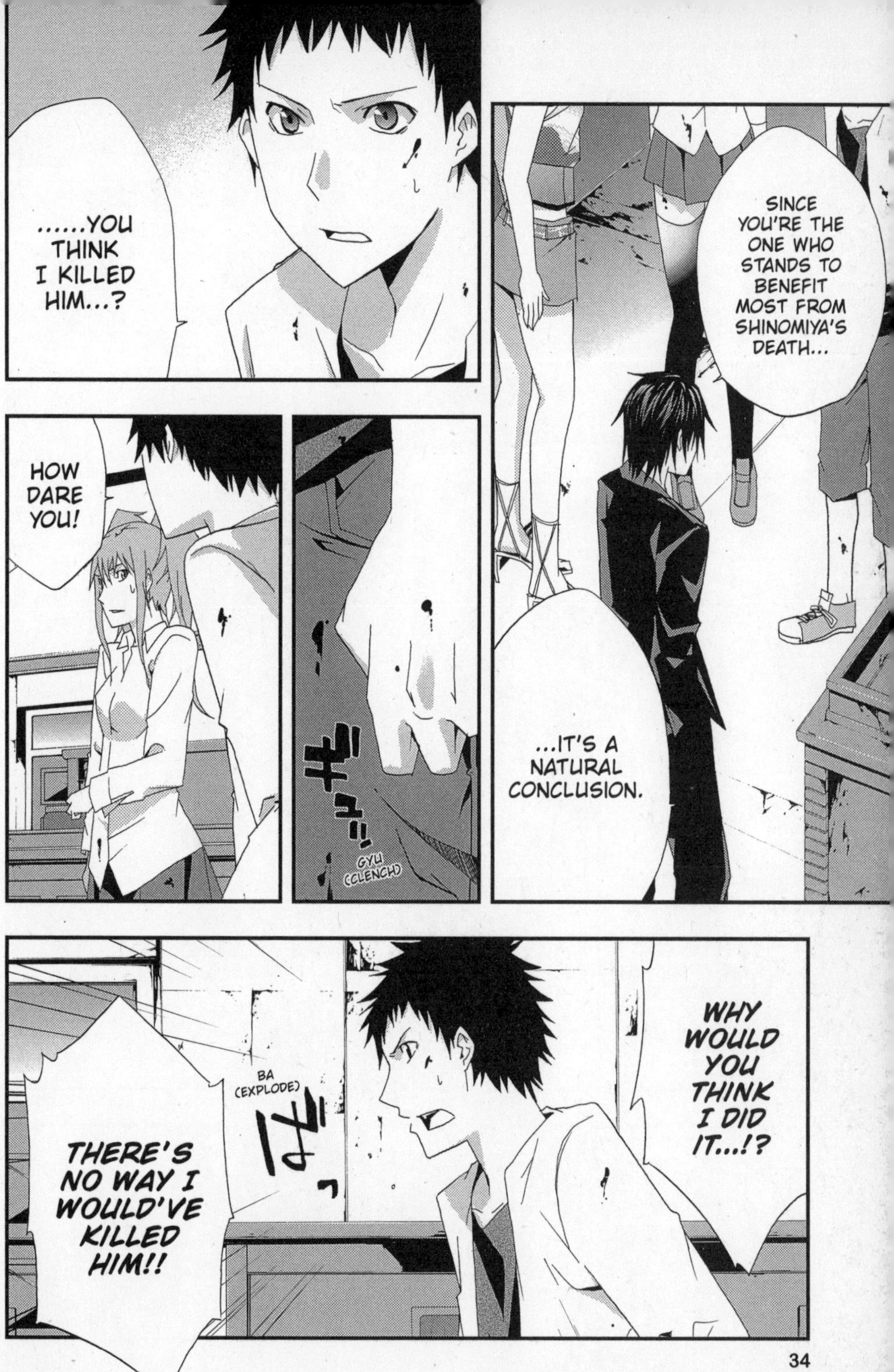
SINCE YOU'RE THE ONE WHO STANDS TO BENEFIT MOST FROM SHINOMIYA'S DEATH...
...IT'S A NATURAL CONCLUSION.
......YOU THINK I KILLED HIM...?
GYU (CLENCH)
HOW DARE YOU!
WHY WOULD YOU THINK I DID IT...!?
BA (EXPLODE)
THERE'S NO WAY I WOULD'VE KILLED HIM!!

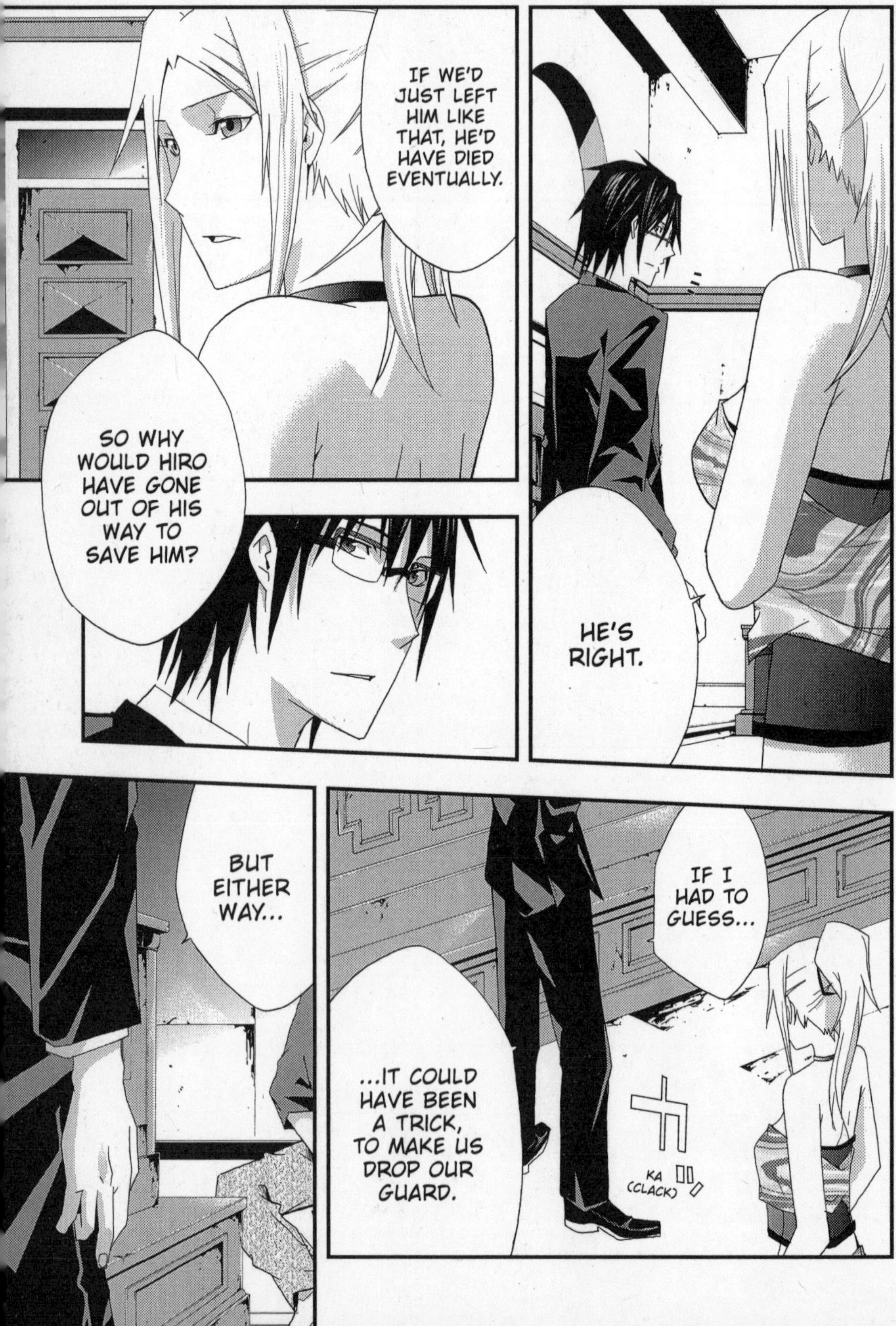
HE'S RIGHT.
IF WE'D JUST LEFT HIM LIKE THAT, HE'D HAVE DIED EVENTUALLY.
SO WHY WOULD HIRO HAVE GONE OUT OF HIS WAY TO SAVE HIM?
IF I HAD TO GUESS...
...IT COULD HAVE BEEN A TRICK, TO MAKE US DROP OUR GUARD.
KA (CLACK)
BUT EITHER WAY...

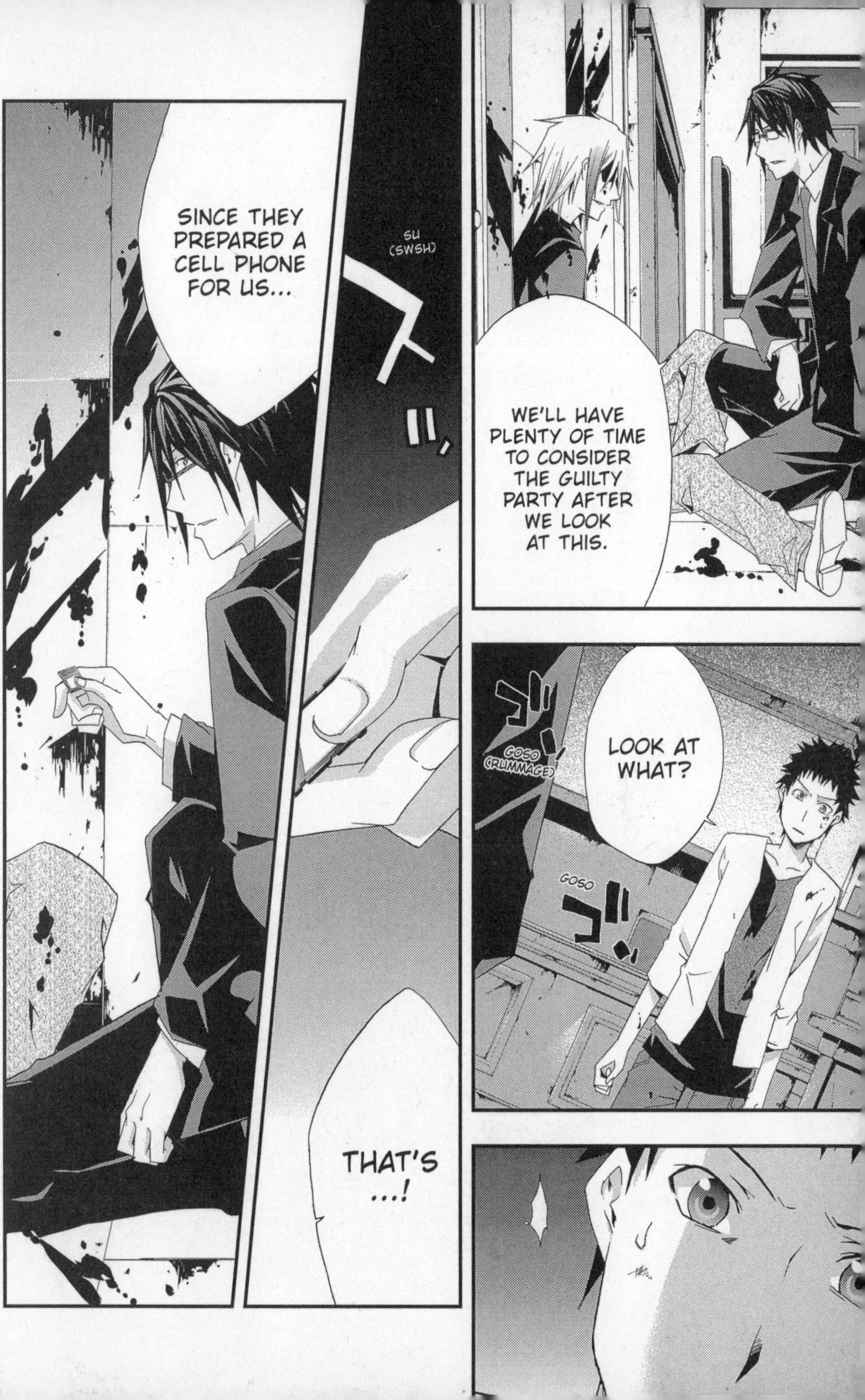
WE'LL HAVE PLENTY OF TIME TO CONSIDER THE GUILTY PARTY AFTER WE LOOK AT THIS.
GOSO (RUMMAGE)
LOOK AT WHAT?
GOSO
SU (SWSH)
THAT'S ...!
SINCE THEY PREPARED A CELL PHONE FOR US...

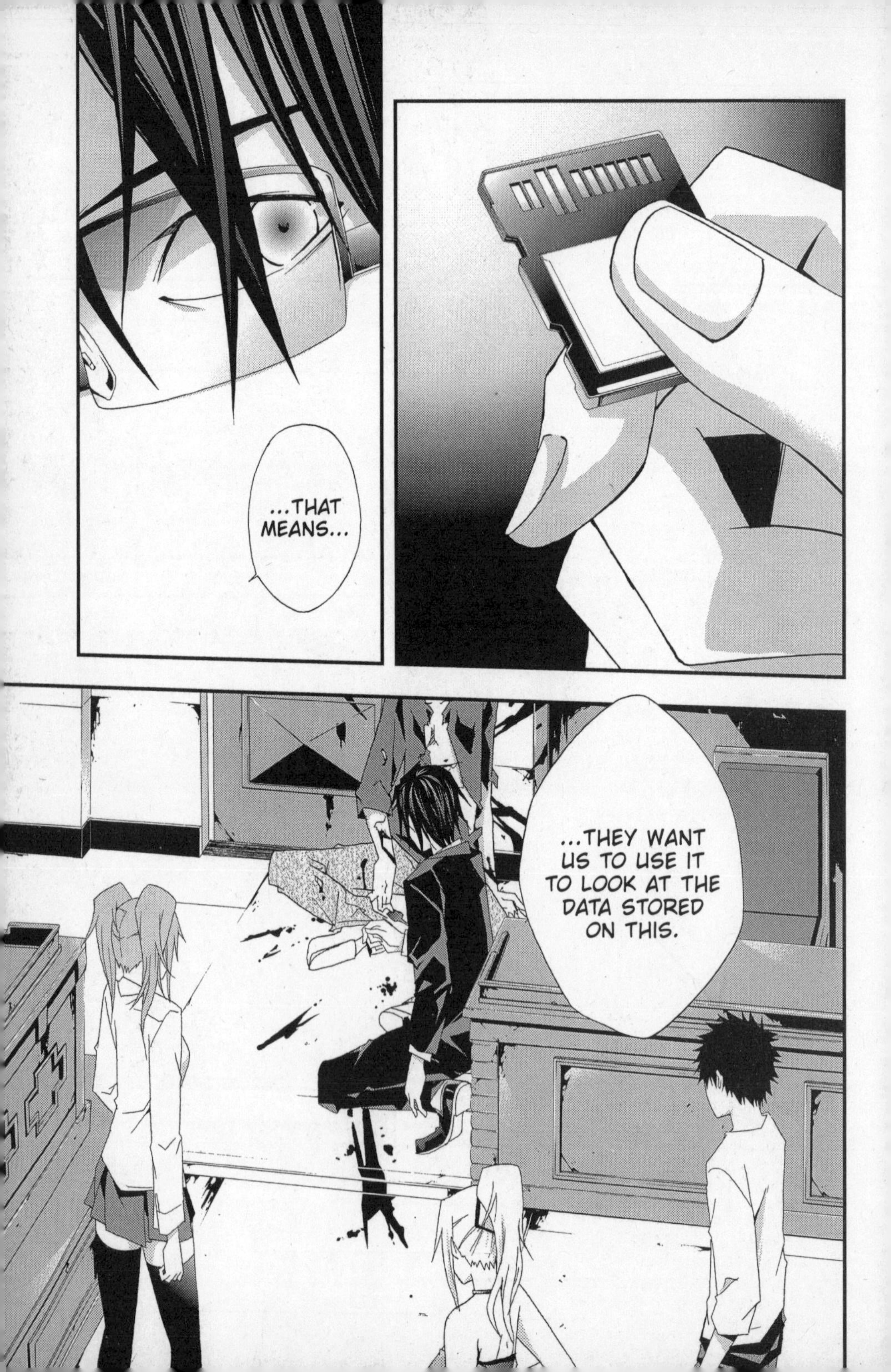
...THAT MEANS...
...THEY WANT US TO USE IT TO LOOK AT THE DATA STORED ON THIS.

JUDGE

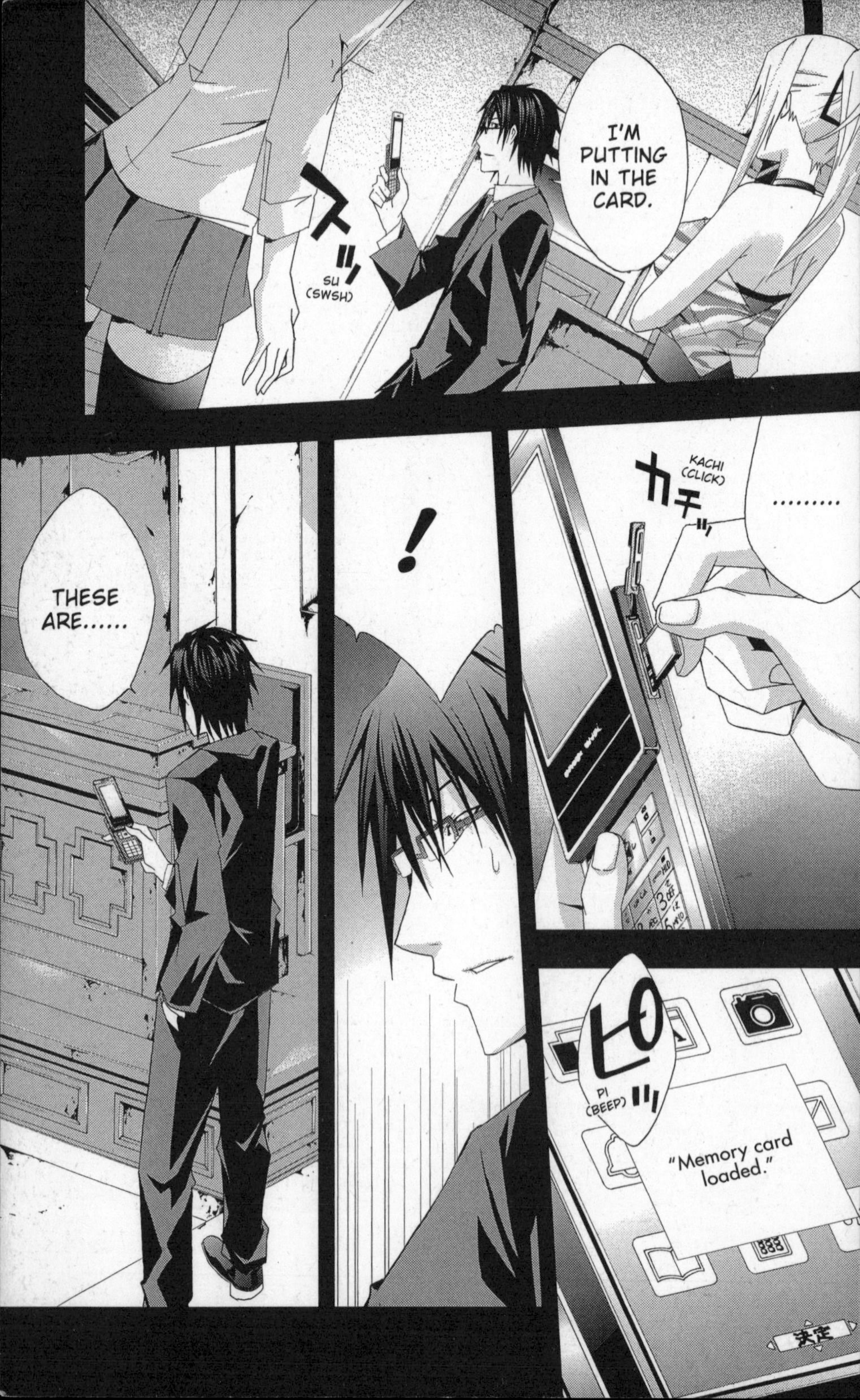
I'M PUTTING IN THE CARD.
スッ
SU (SWSH)
....
カチッ
KACHI (CLICK)
ピッ
PI (BEEP)
"Memory card loaded."
決定
!
THESE ARE......

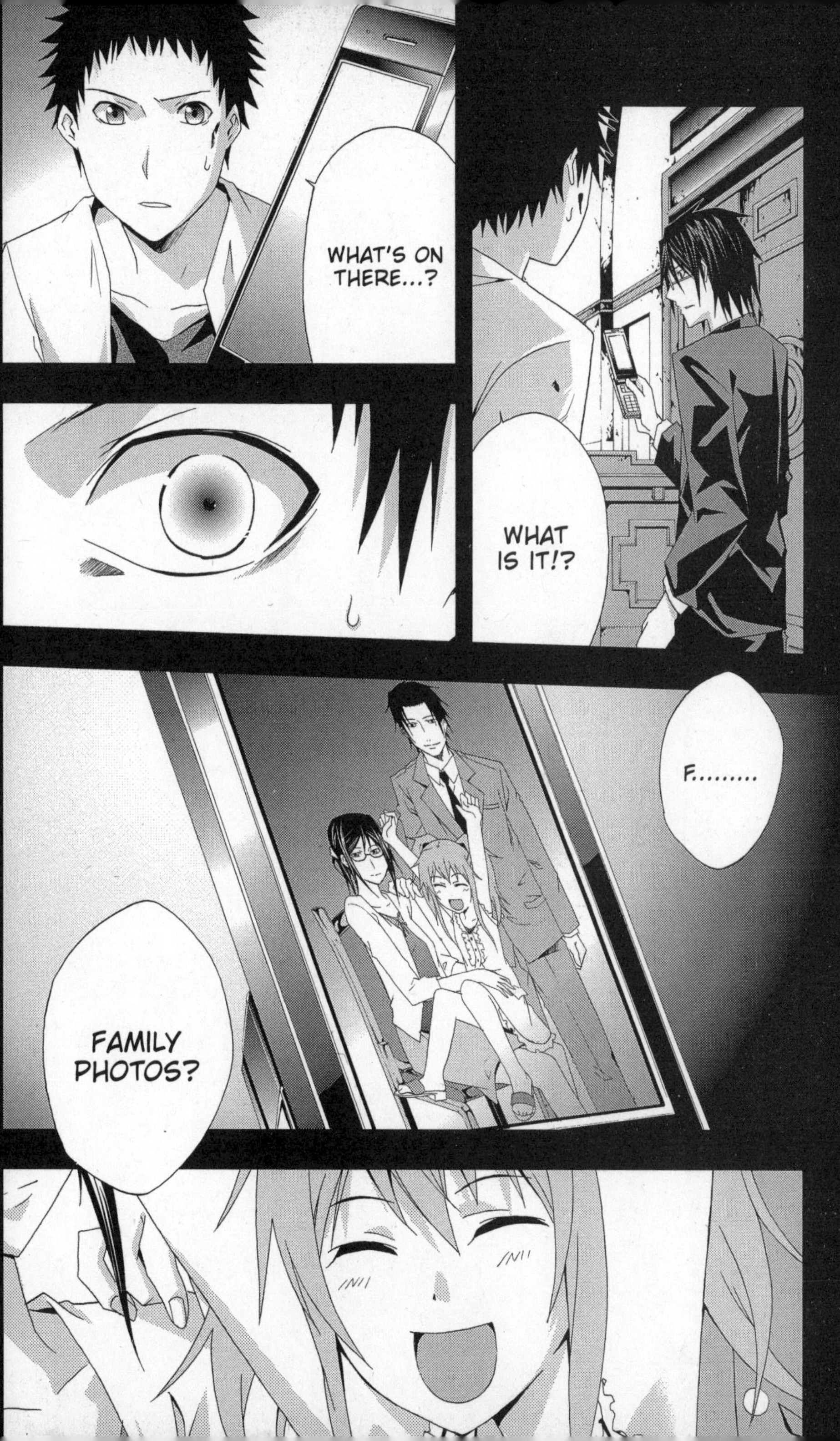
WHAT IS IT!?
WHAT'S ON THERE...?
F.........
FAMILY PHOTOS?

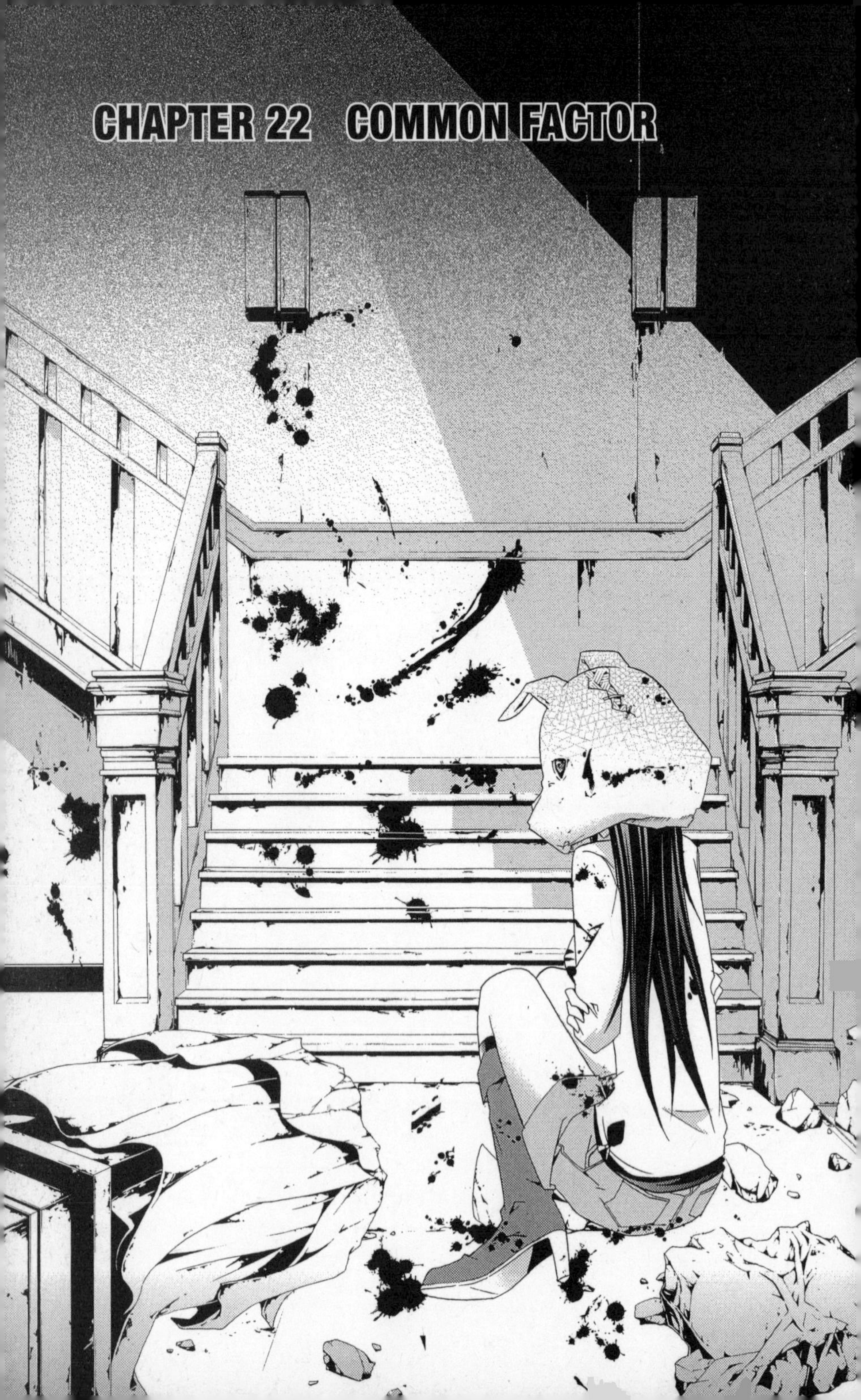
CHAPTER 22 COMMON FACTOR

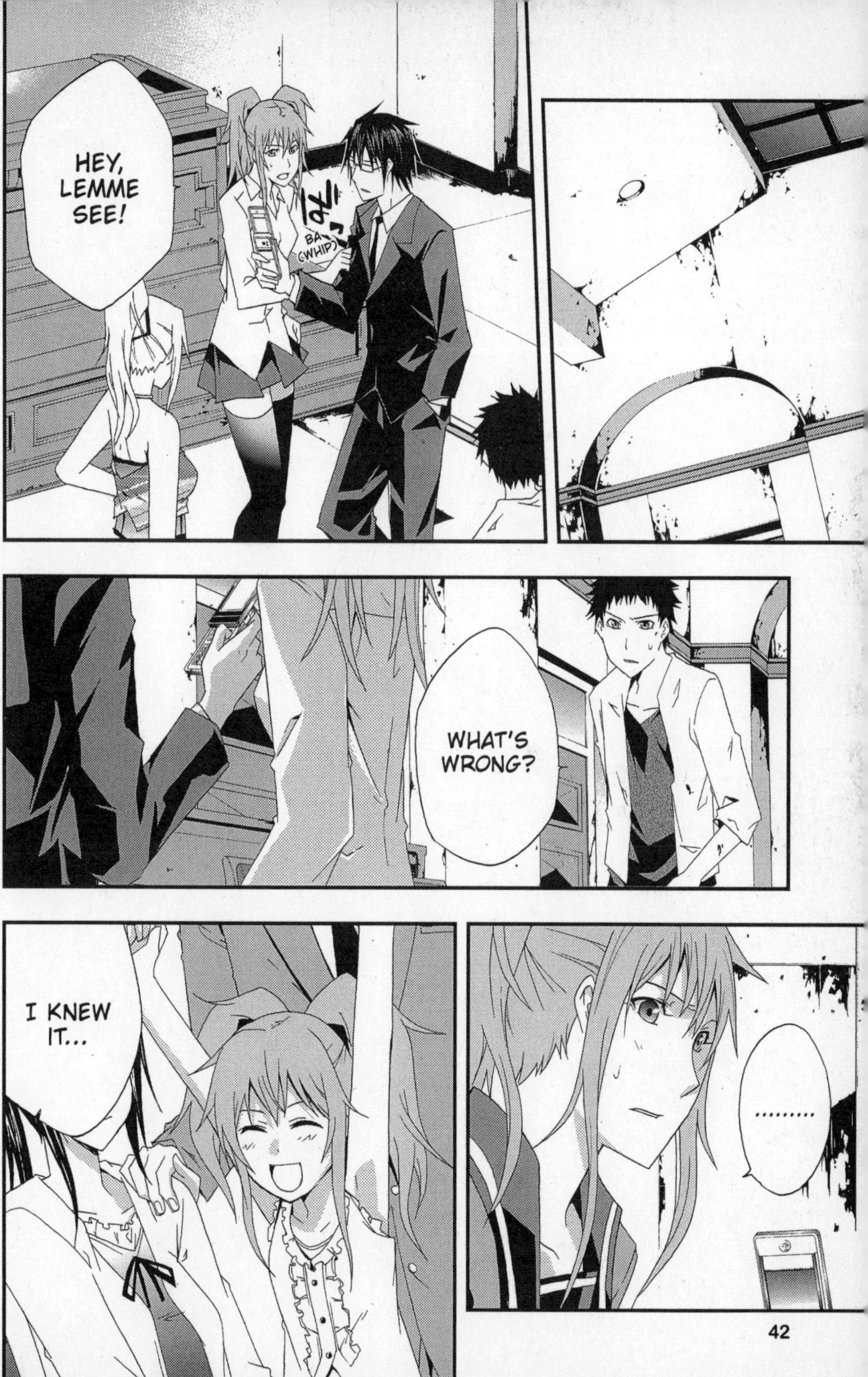
HEY, LEMME SEE!
ばっ
BA (WHIP)
WHAT'S WRONG?
....
I KNEW IT...

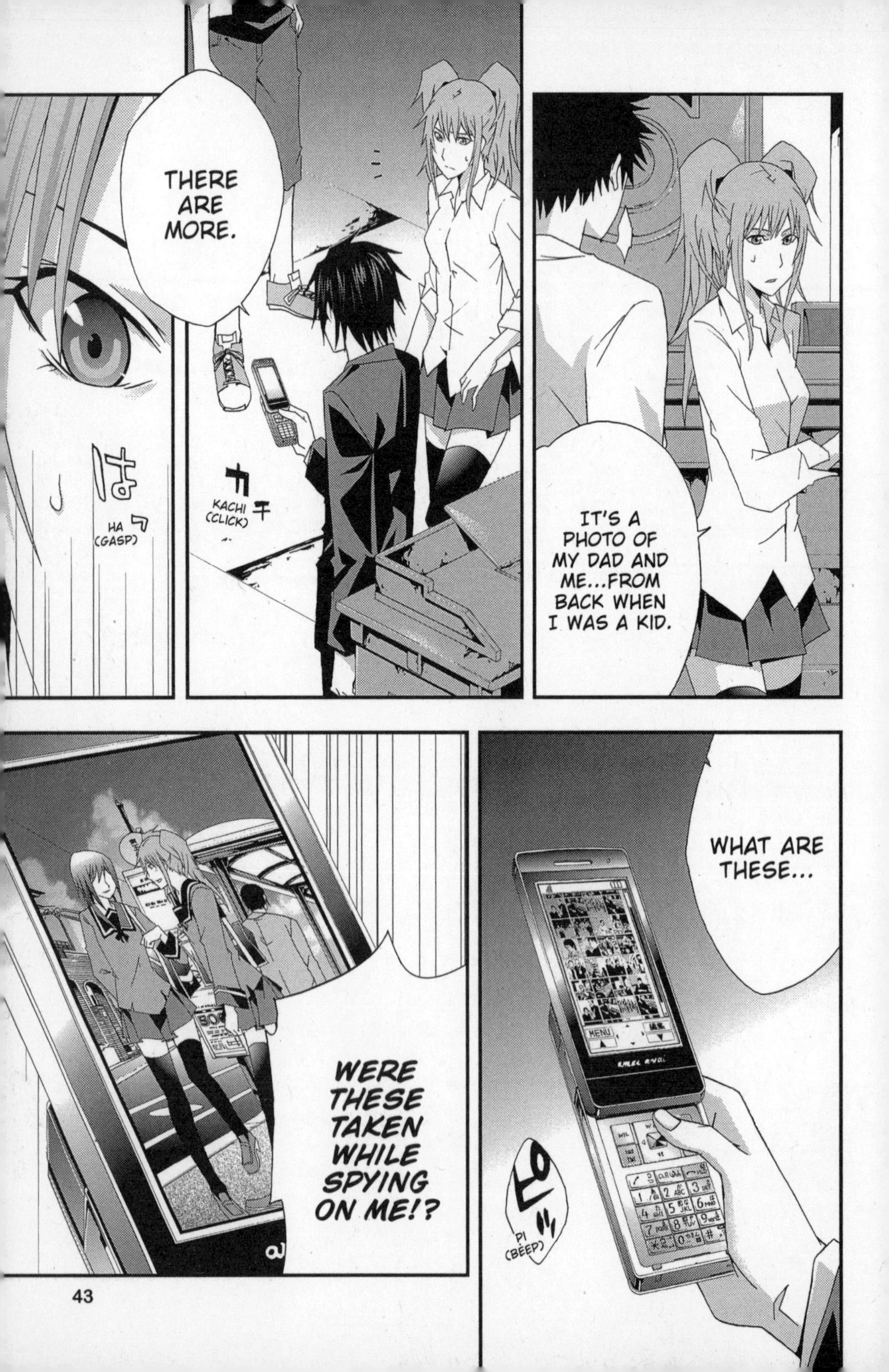
IT'S A PHOTO OF MY DAD AND ME...FROM BACK WHEN I WAS A KID.
THERE ARE MORE.
カチ
KACHI (CLICK)
はっ
HA (GASP)
WHAT ARE THESE...
ピッ
PI (BEEP)
WERE THESE TAKEN WHILE SPYING ON ME!?

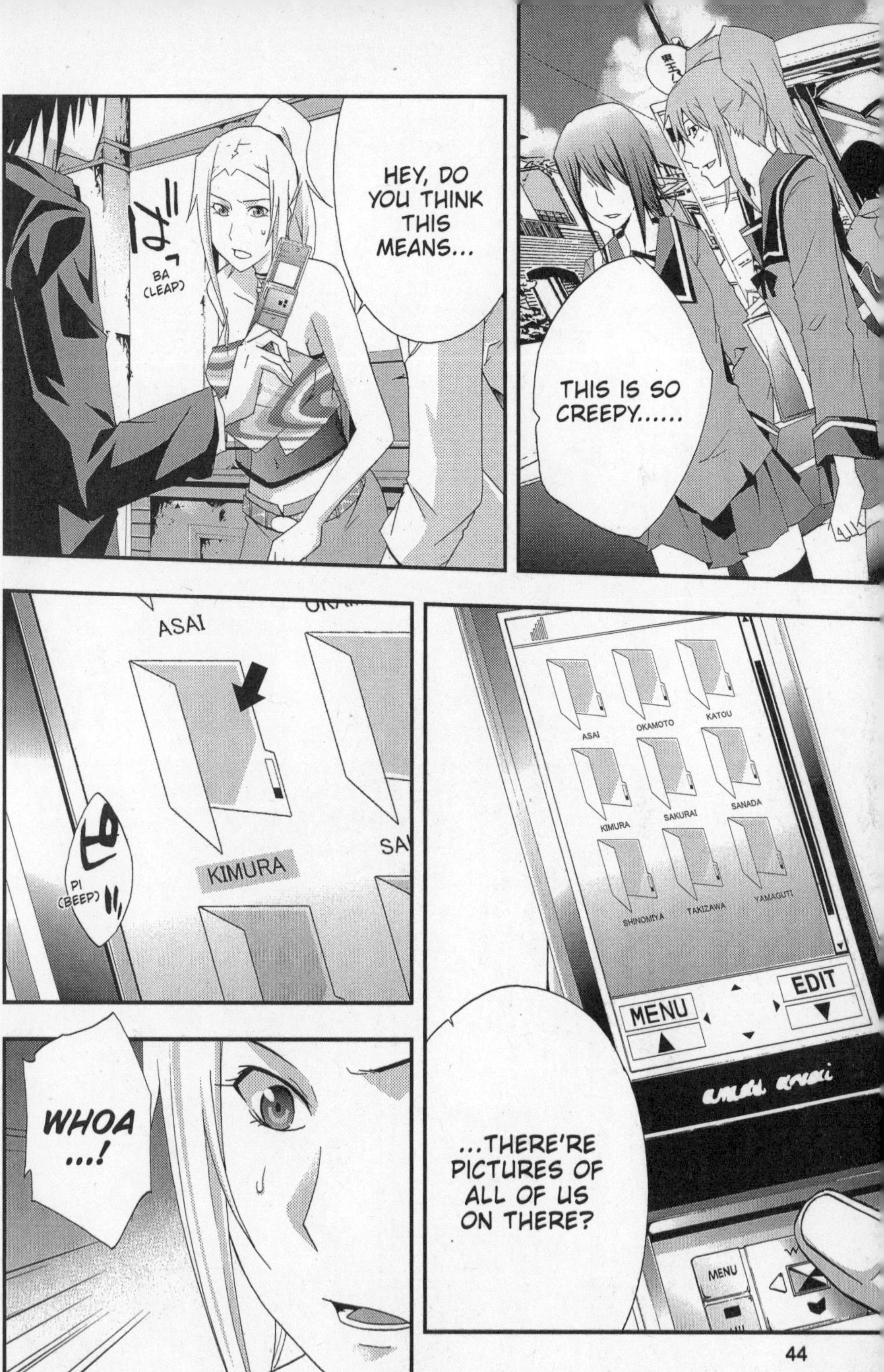
THIS IS SO CREEPY......
HEY, DO YOU THINK THIS MEANS...
BA (LEAP)
EDIT
MENU
ASAI
OKAMOTO
KATOU
KIMURA
SAKURAI
SANADA
SHINOMIYA
TAKIZAWA
YAMAGUTI
MENU
...THERE'RE PICTURES OF ALL OF US ON THERE?
ASAI
KIMURA
PI (BEEP)
WHOA ...!

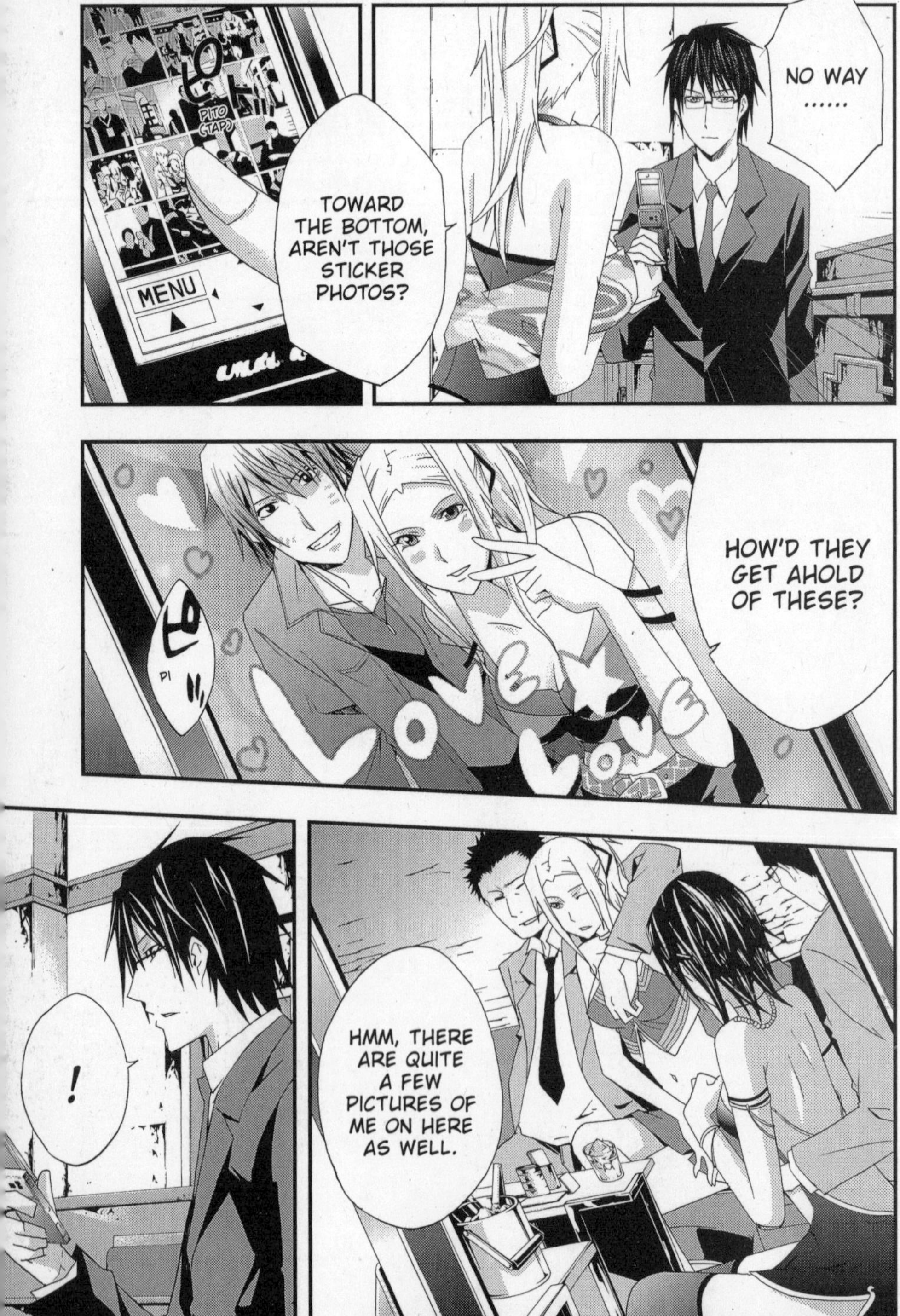
NO WAY ......
TOWARD THE BOTTOM, AREN'T THOSE STICKER PHOTOS?
PITO (TAP)
MENU
HOW'D THEY GET AHOLD OF THESE?
PI
HMM, THERE ARE QUITE A FEW PICTURES OF ME ON HERE AS WELL.
!

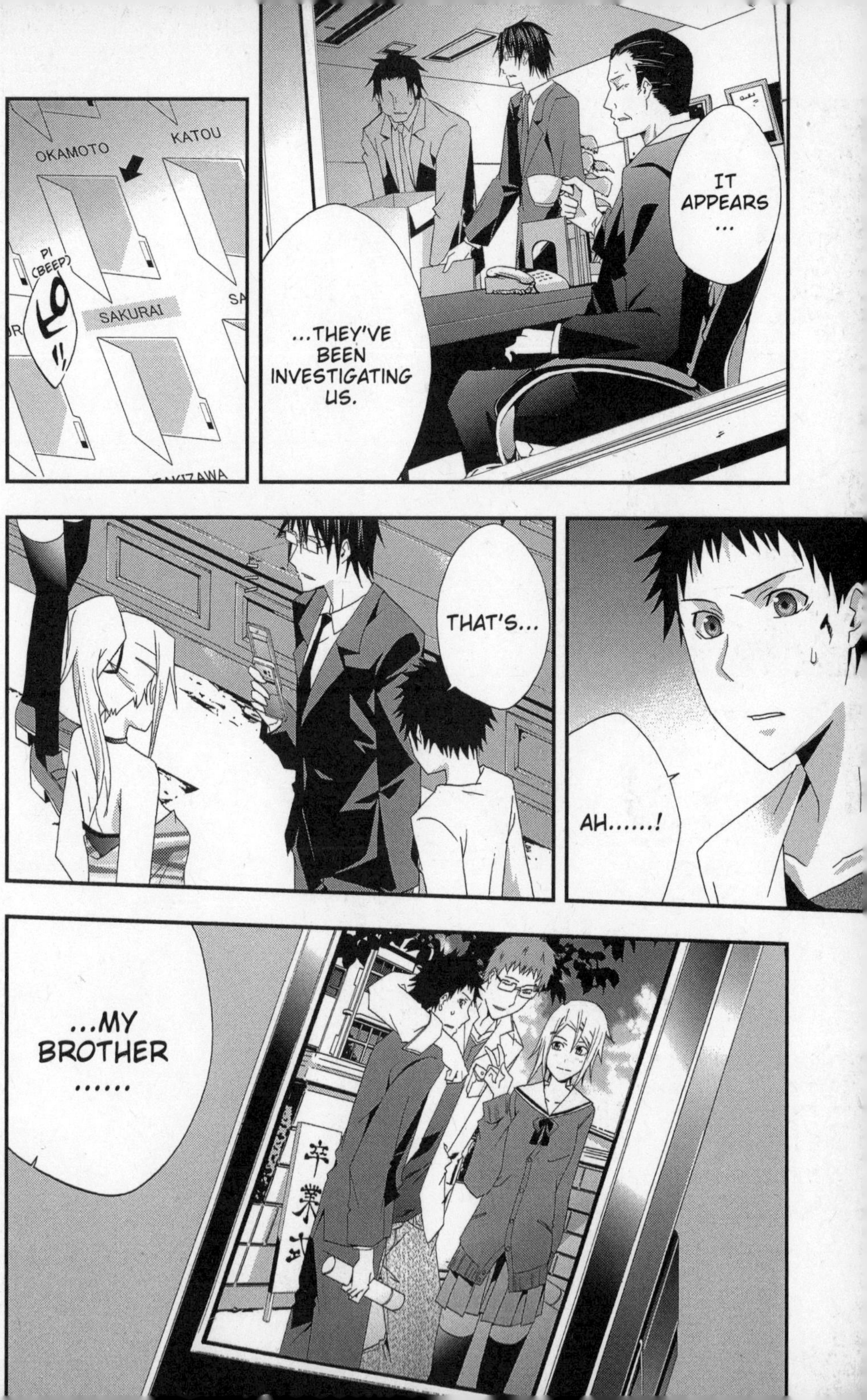
IT APPEARS ...
...THEY'VE BEEN INVESTIGATING US.
KATOU
OKAMOTO
PI (BEEP)
SAKURAI
AH......!
THAT'S...
...MY BROTHER ......
卒業式

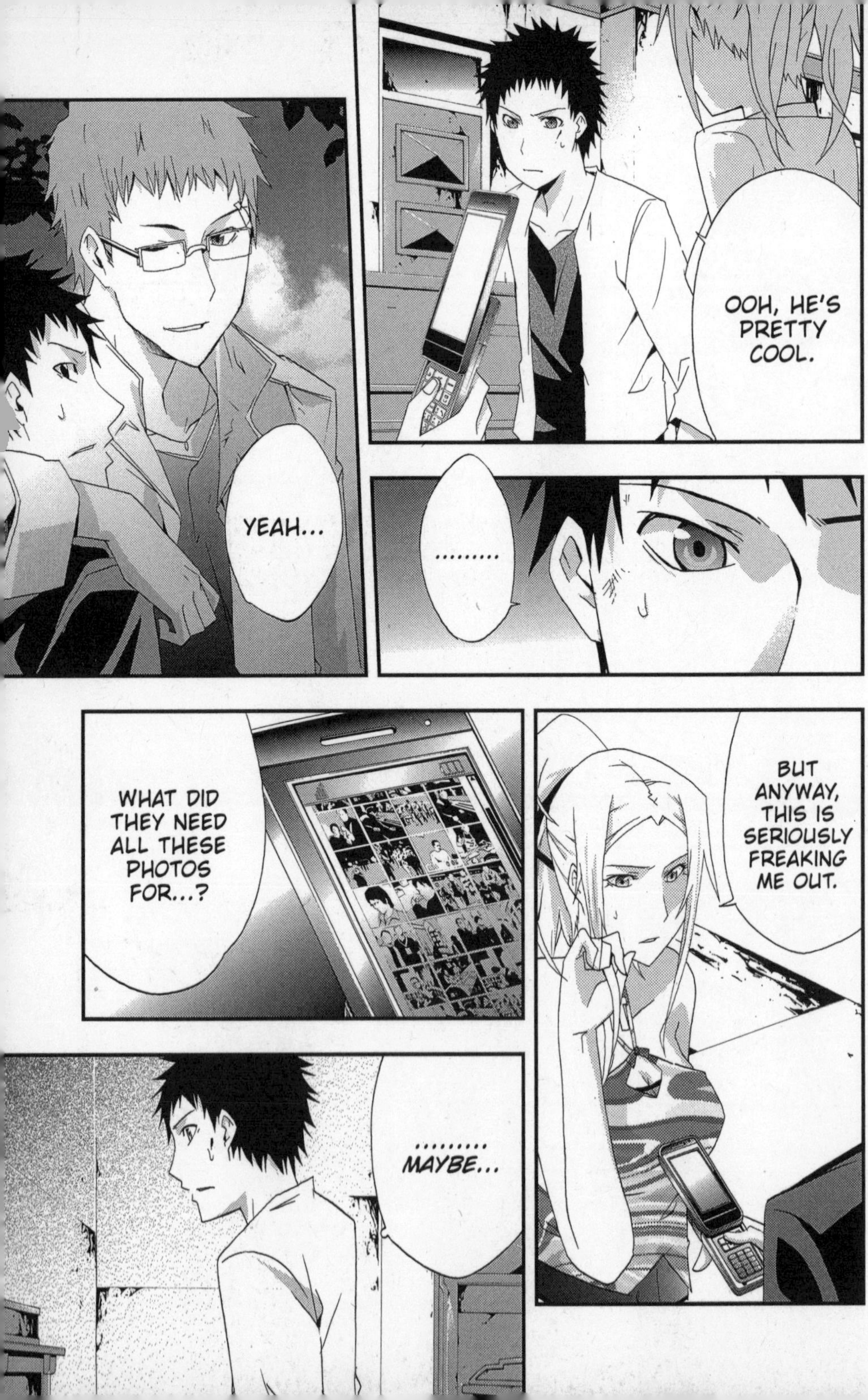
OOH, HE'S PRETTY COOL.
....
YEAH...
BUT ANYWAY, THIS IS SERIOUSLY FREAKING ME OUT.
WHAT DID THEY NEED ALL THESE PHOTOS FOR...?
.... MAYBE...

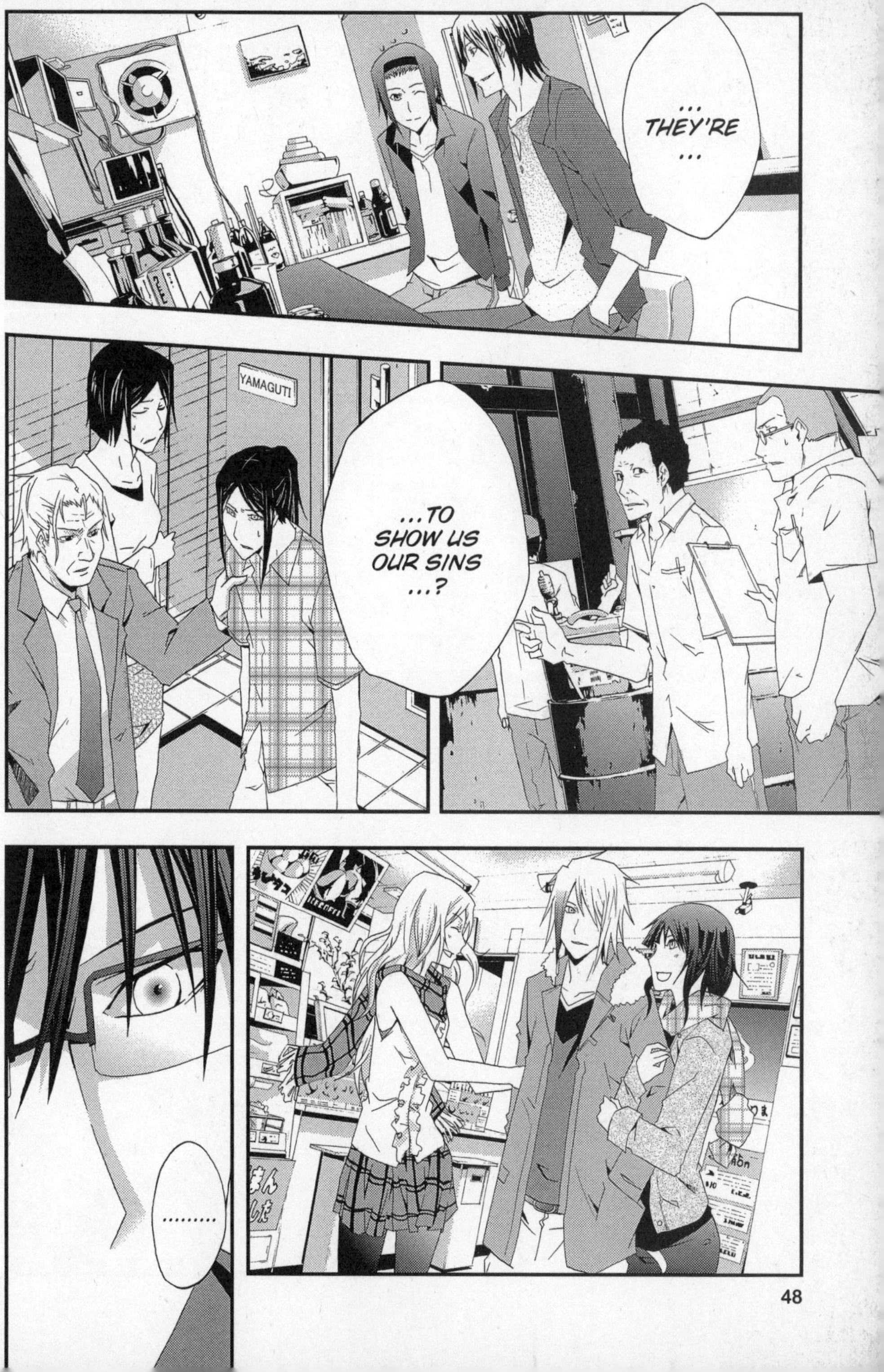
... THEY'RE ...
...TO SHOW US OUR SINS ...?
....

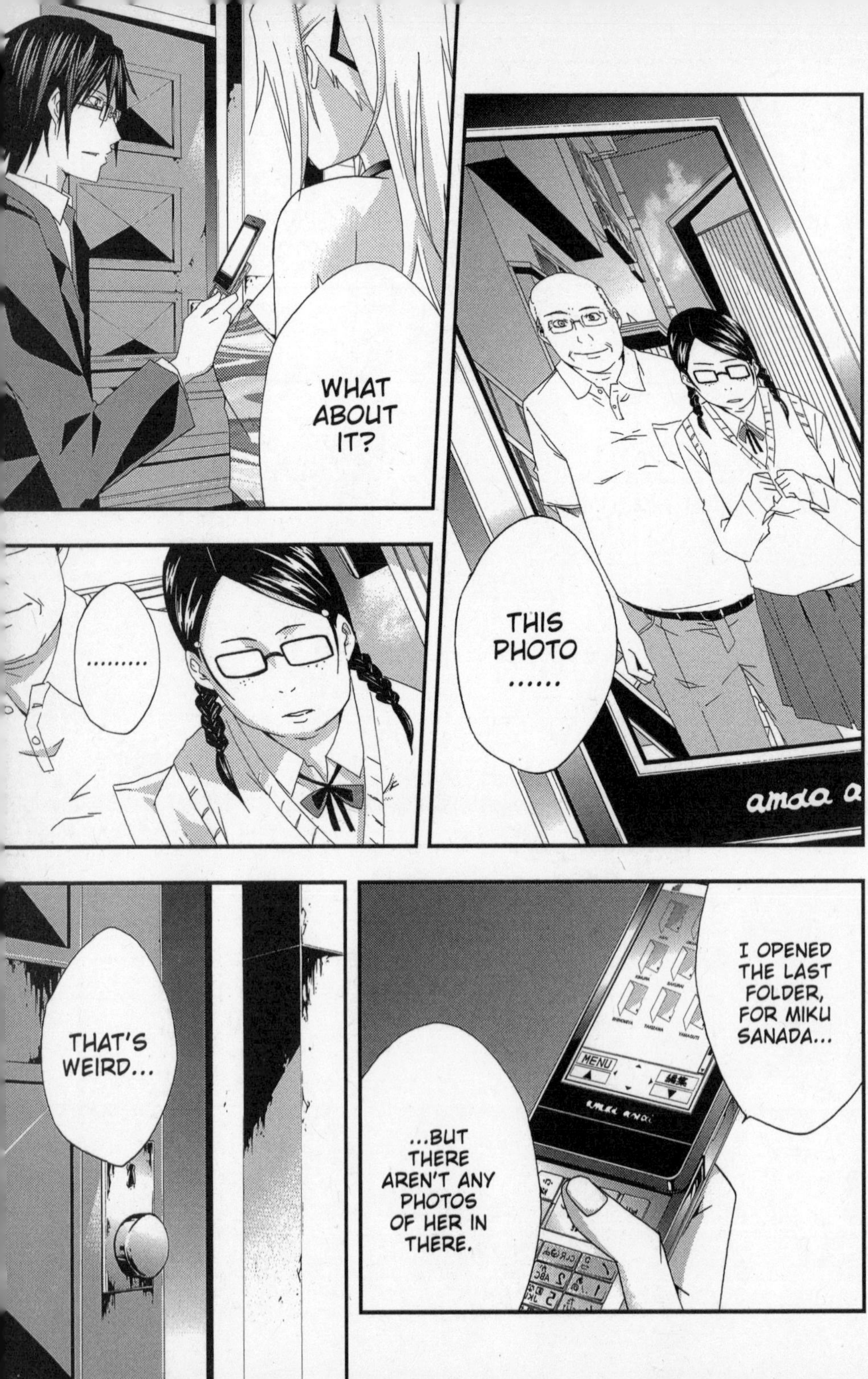
WHAT ABOUT IT?
THIS PHOTO ......
....
I OPENED THE LAST FOLDER, FOR MIKU SANADA...
...BUT THERE AREN'T ANY PHOTOS OF HER IN THERE.
THAT'S WEIRD...

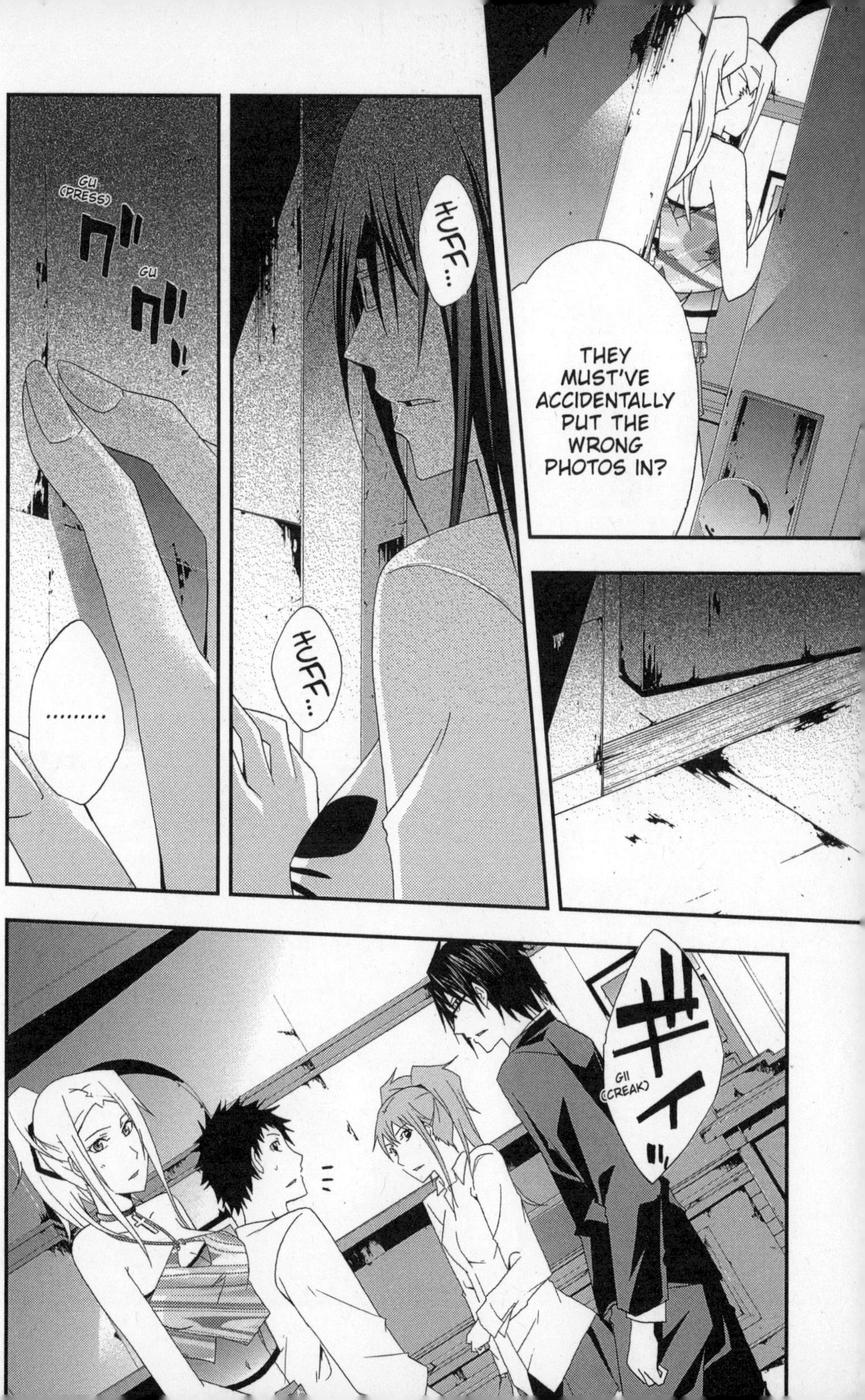
THEY MUST'VE ACCIDENTALLY PUT THE WRONG PHOTOS IN?
HUFF...
HUFF...
GU (PRESS)
GU
....
GII (CREAK)

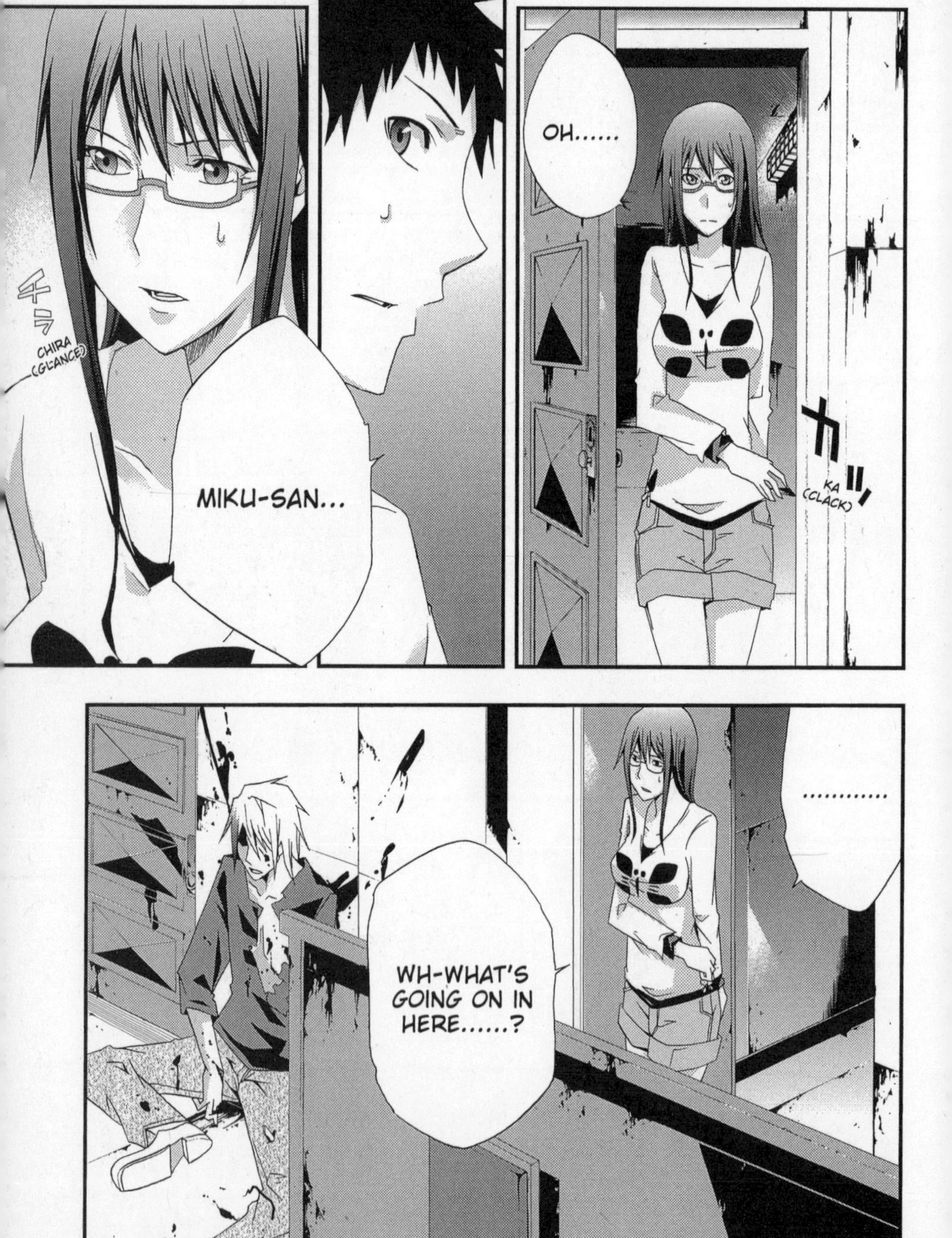
OH......
カッ
KA (CLACK)
MIKU-SAN...
チラ
CHIRA (GLANCE)
....
WH-WHAT'S GOING ON IN HERE......?

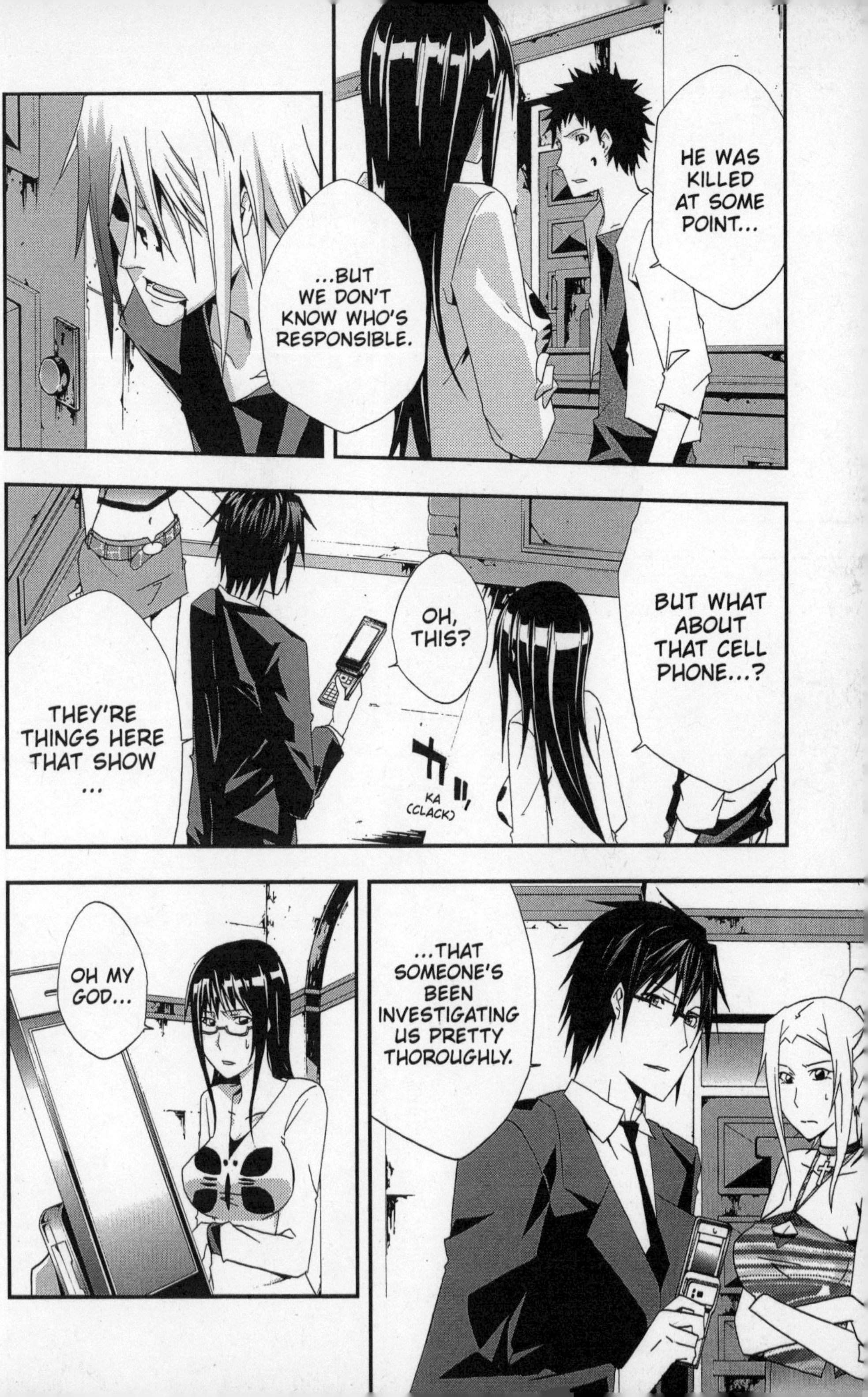
HE WAS KILLED AT SOME POINT...
...BUT WE DON'T KNOW WHO'S RESPONSIBLE.
BUT WHAT ABOUT THAT CELL PHONE...?
OH, THIS?
KA (CLACK)
THEY'RE THINGS HERE THAT SHOW ...
...THAT SOMEONE'S BEEN INVESTIGATING US PRETTY THOROUGHLY.
OH MY GOD...

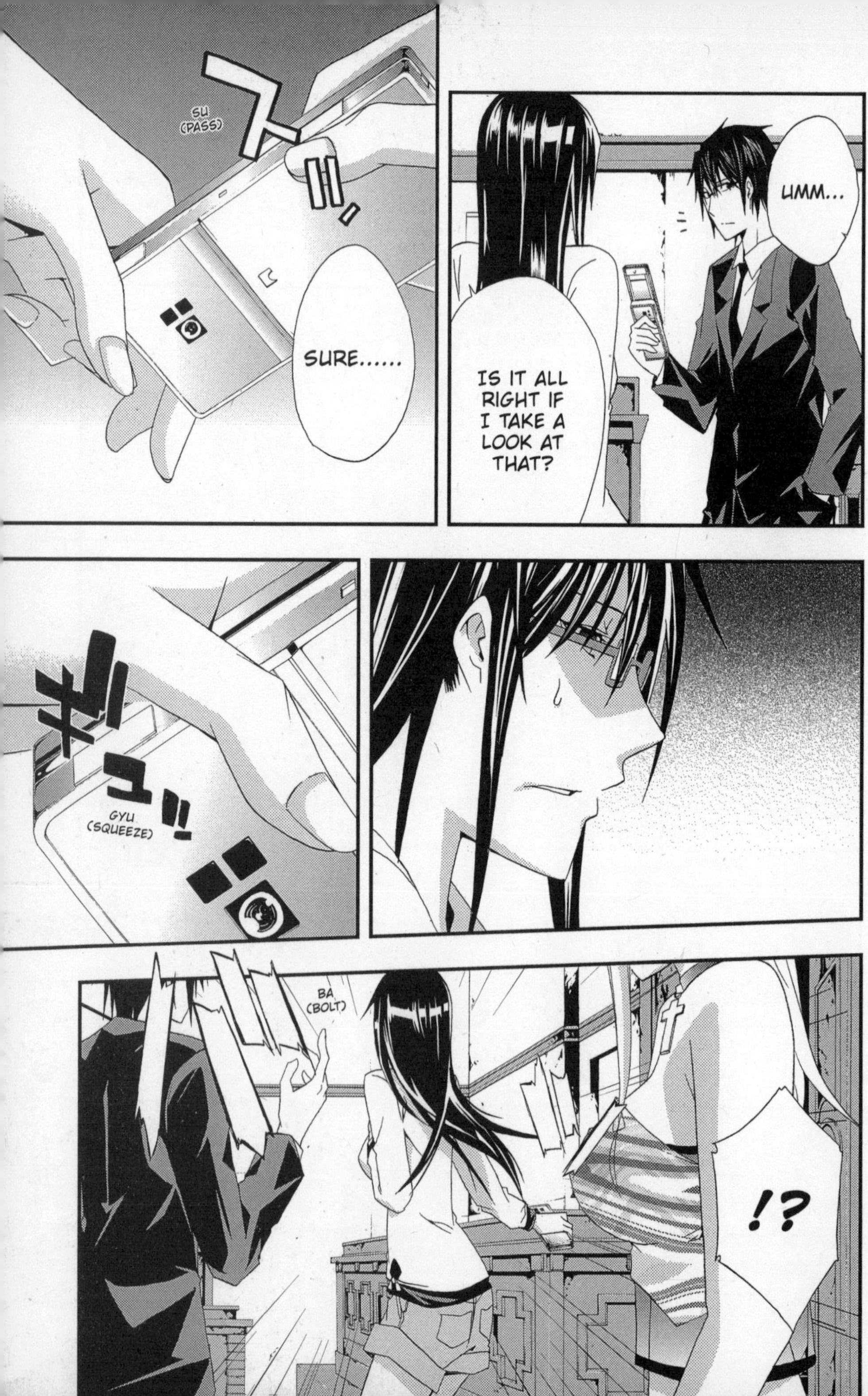
UMM...
IS IT ALL RIGHT IF I TAKE A LOOK AT THAT?
SU (PASS)
SURE......
GYU (SQUEEZE)
BA (BOLT)
!?

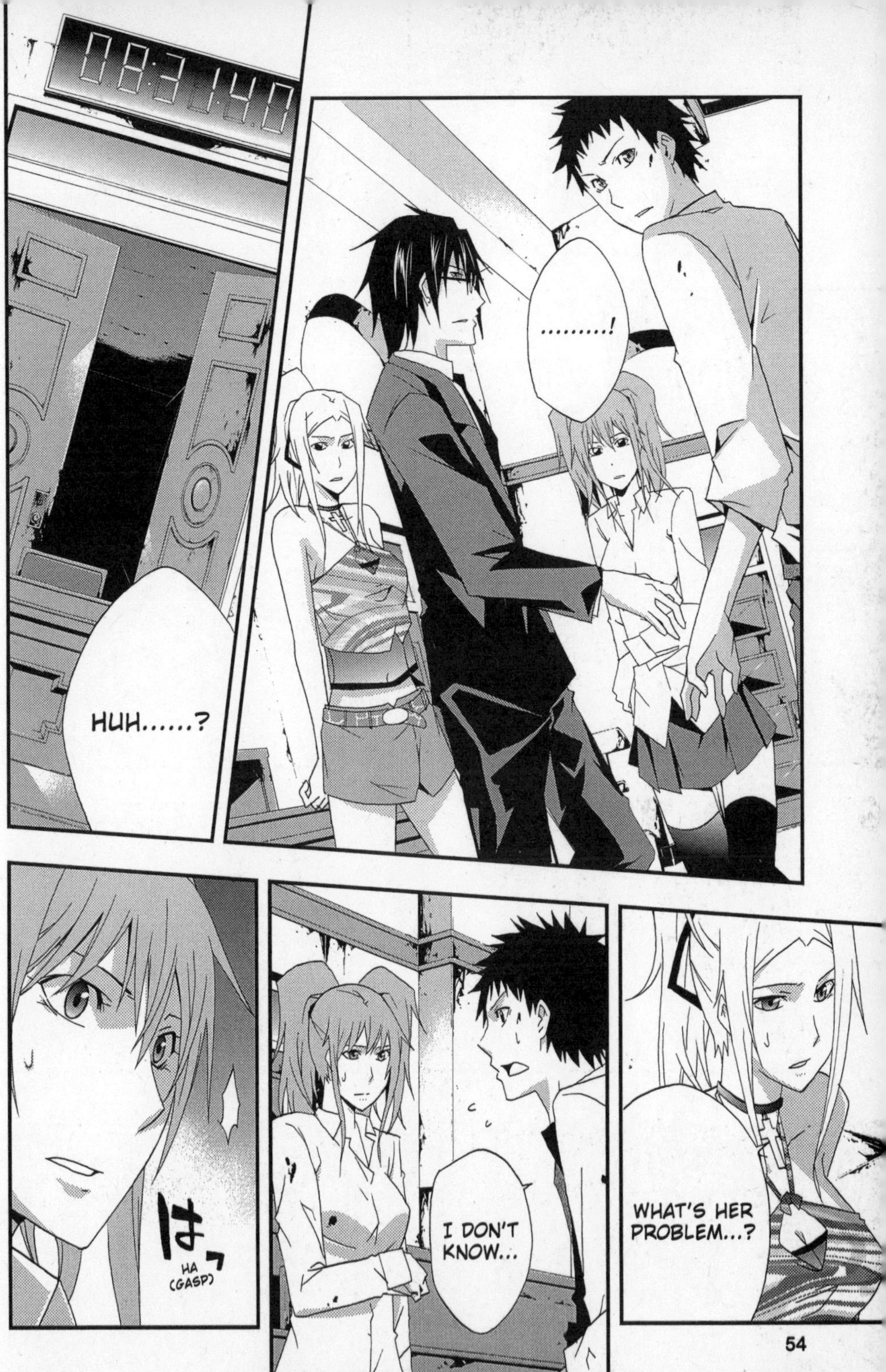

08:31:40
.........!
HUH......?
WHAT'S HER PROBLEM...?
I DON'T KNOW...
は
HA (GASP)

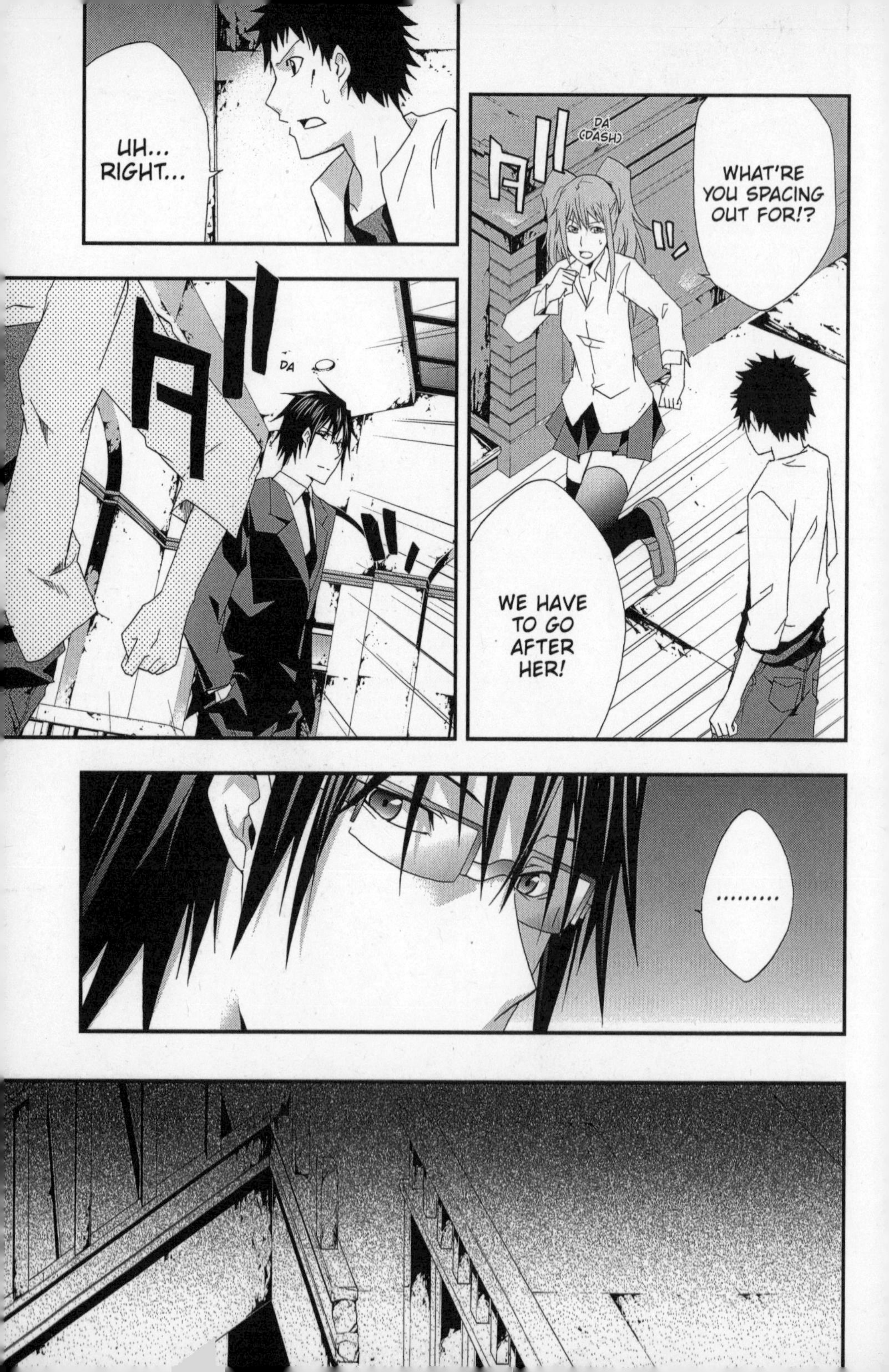
DA
(DASH)
WHAT'RE YOU SPACING OUT FOR!?
WE HAVE TO GO AFTER HER!
UH... RIGHT...
DA
....

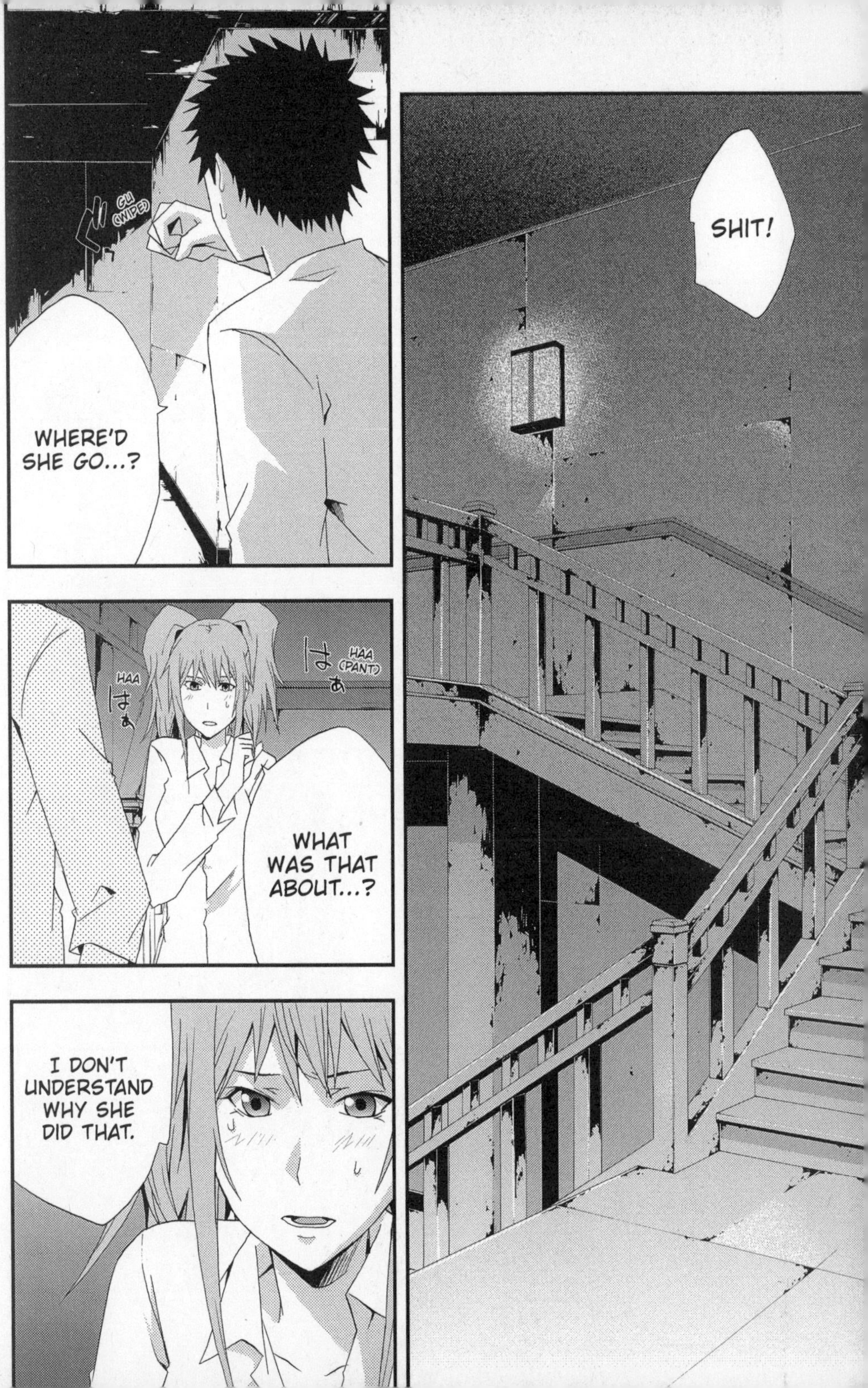
SHIT!
GU (WIPE)
WHERE'D SHE GO...?
HAA
HAA (PANT)
WHAT WAS THAT ABOUT...?
I DON'T UNDERSTAND WHY SHE DID THAT.

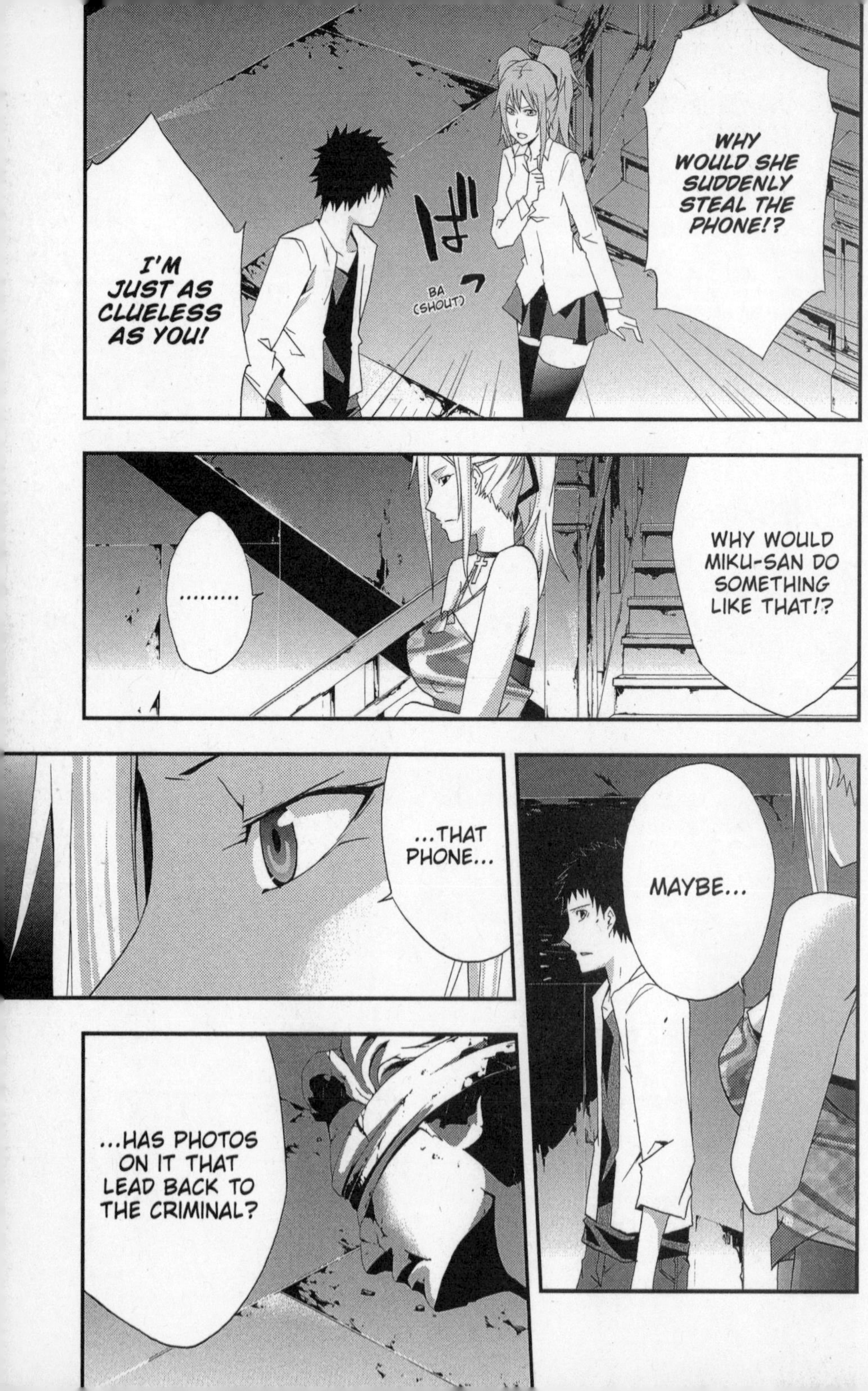
WHY WOULD SHE SUDDENLY STEAL THE PHONE!?
ばっ
BA (SHOUT)
I'M JUST AS CLUELESS AS YOU!
WHY WOULD MIKU-SAN DO SOMETHING LIKE THAT!?
....
MAYBE...
...THAT PHONE...
...HAS PHOTOS ON IT THAT LEAD BACK TO THE CRIMINAL?

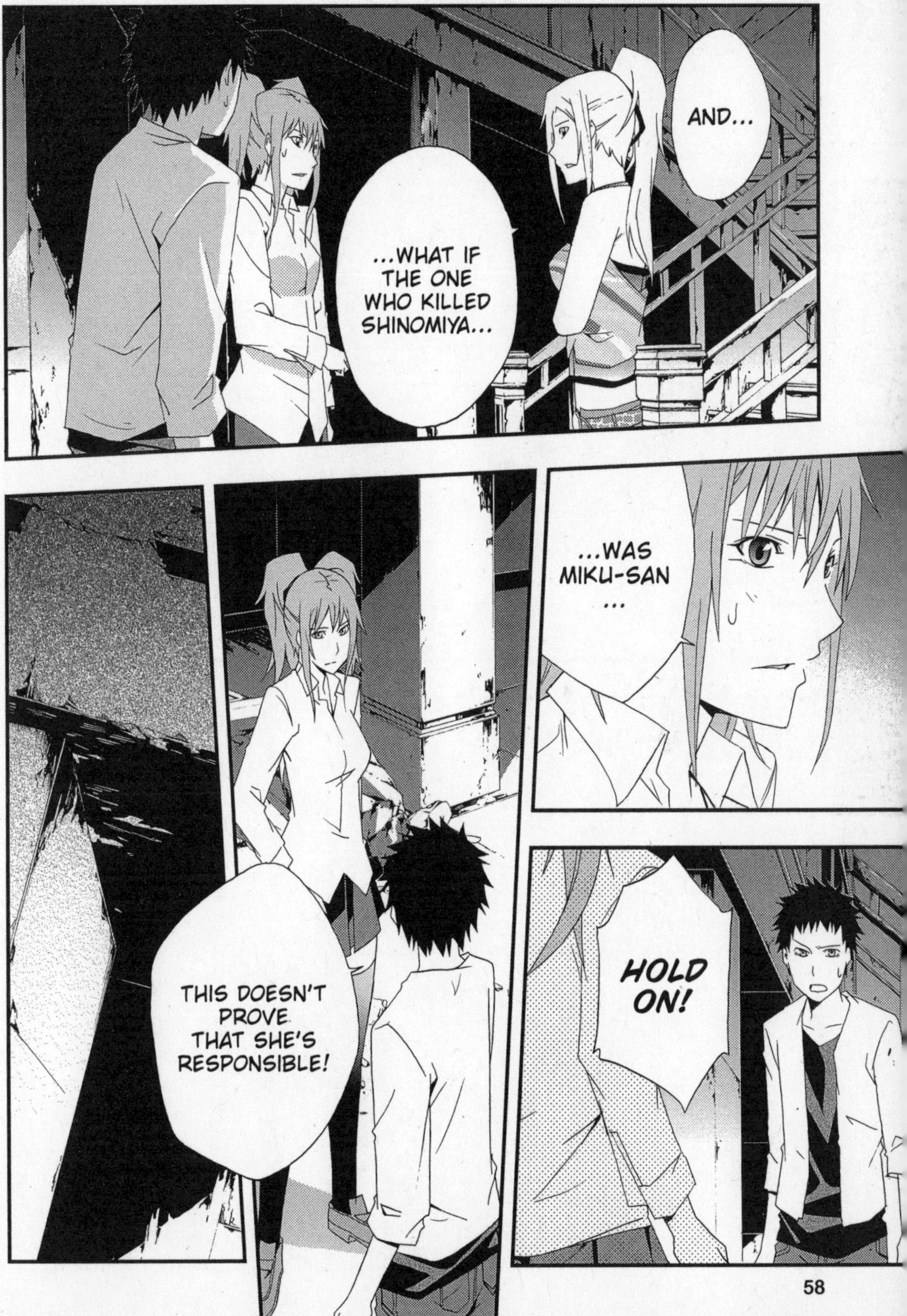
AND...
...WHAT IF THE ONE WHO KILLED SHINOMIYA...
...WAS MIKU-SAN ...
HOLD ON!
THIS DOESN'T PROVE THAT SHE'S RESPONSIBLE!

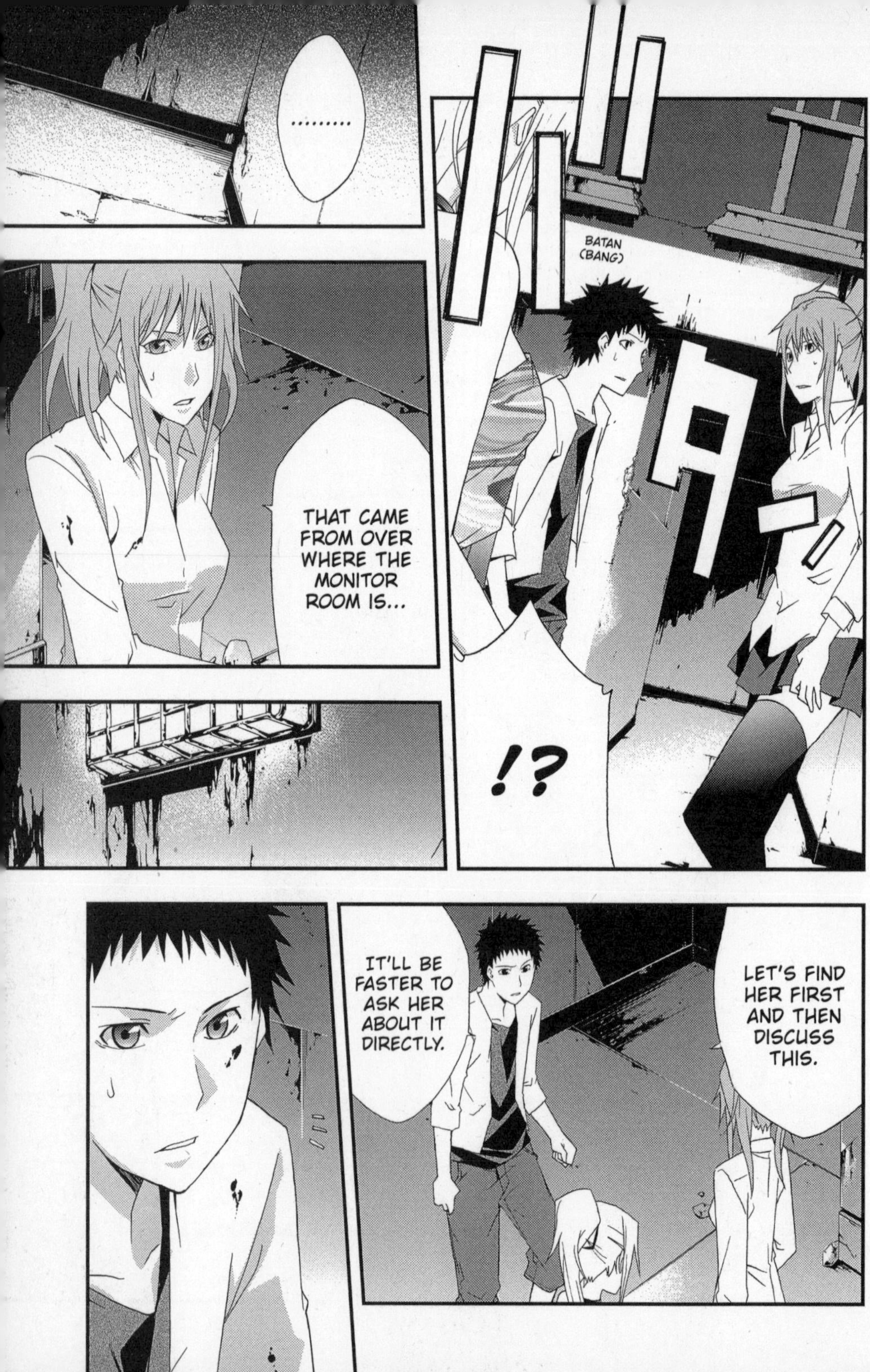
BATAN (BANG)
!?
....
THAT CAME FROM OVER WHERE THE MONITOR ROOM IS...
LET'S FIND HER FIRST AND THEN DISCUSS THIS.
IT'LL BE FASTER TO ASK HER ABOUT IT DIRECTLY.

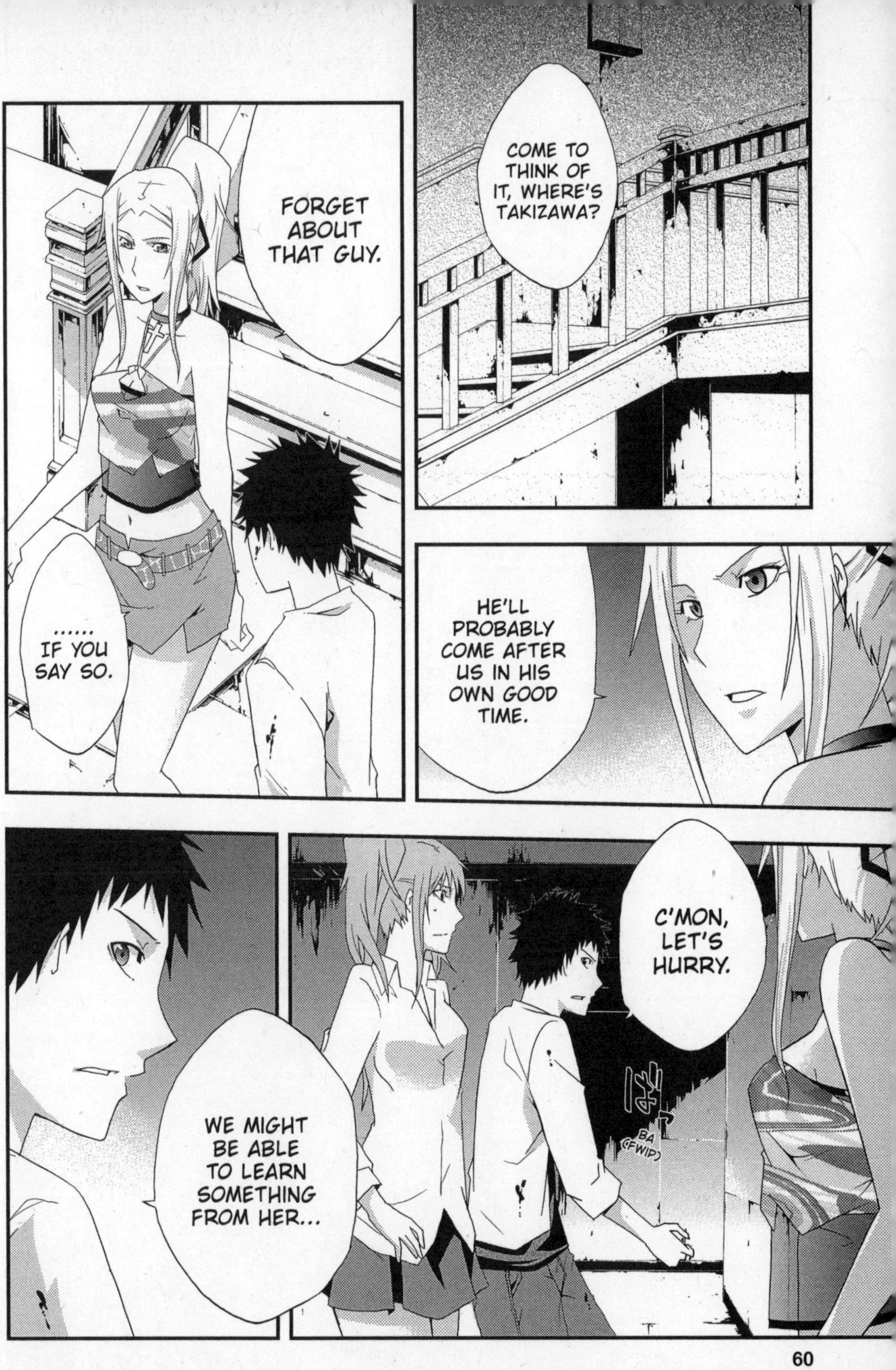
COME TO THINK OF IT, WHERE'S TAKIZAWA?
HE'LL PROBABLY COME AFTER US IN HIS OWN GOOD TIME.
FORGET ABOUT THAT GUY.
...... IF YOU SAY SO.
C'MON, LET'S HURRY.
BA (FWIP)
WE MIGHT BE ABLE TO LEARN SOMETHING FROM HER...

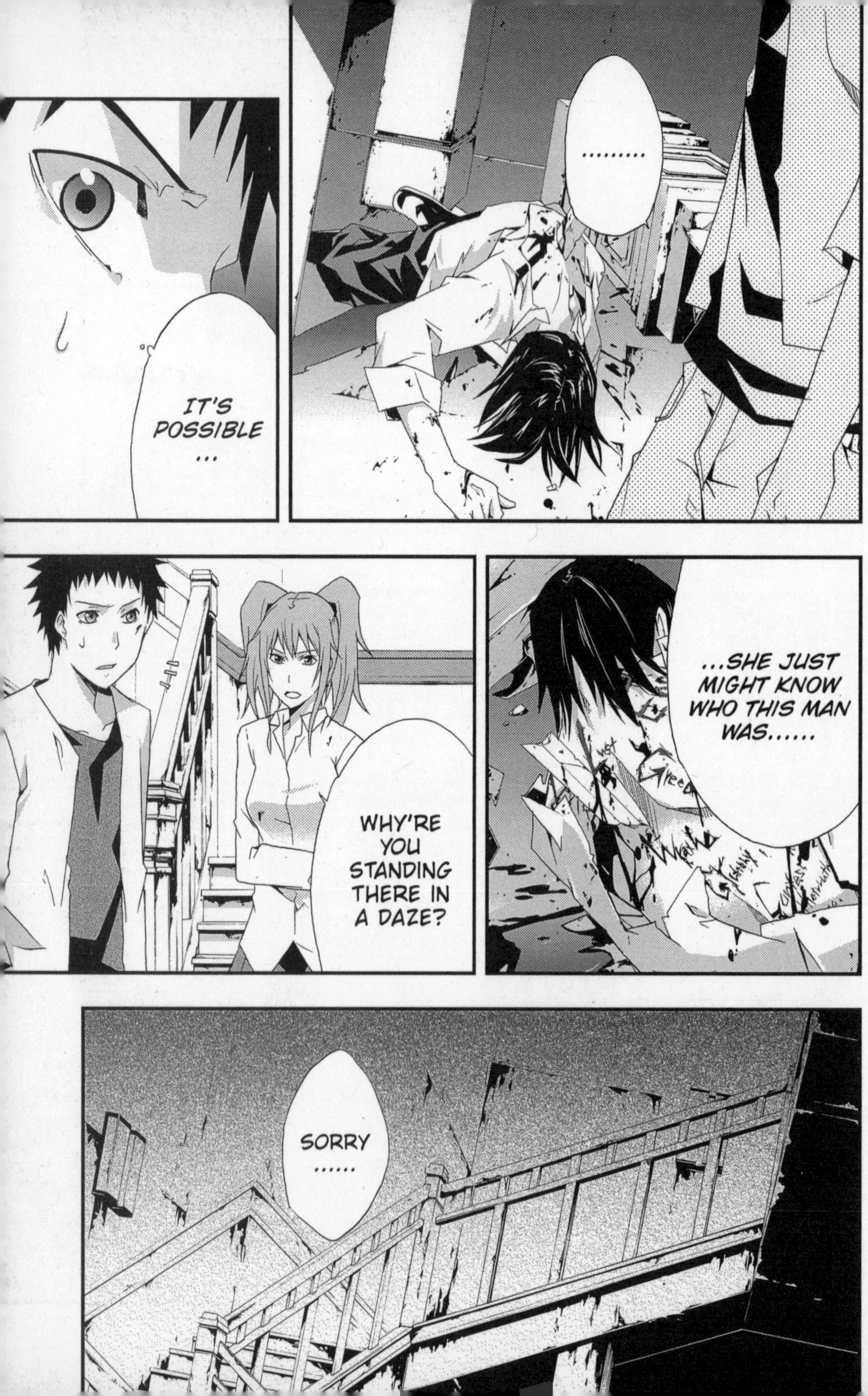
....
IT'S POSSIBLE ...
...SHE JUST MIGHT KNOW WHO THIS MAN WAS......
WHY'RE YOU STANDING THERE IN A DAZE?
SORRY ......

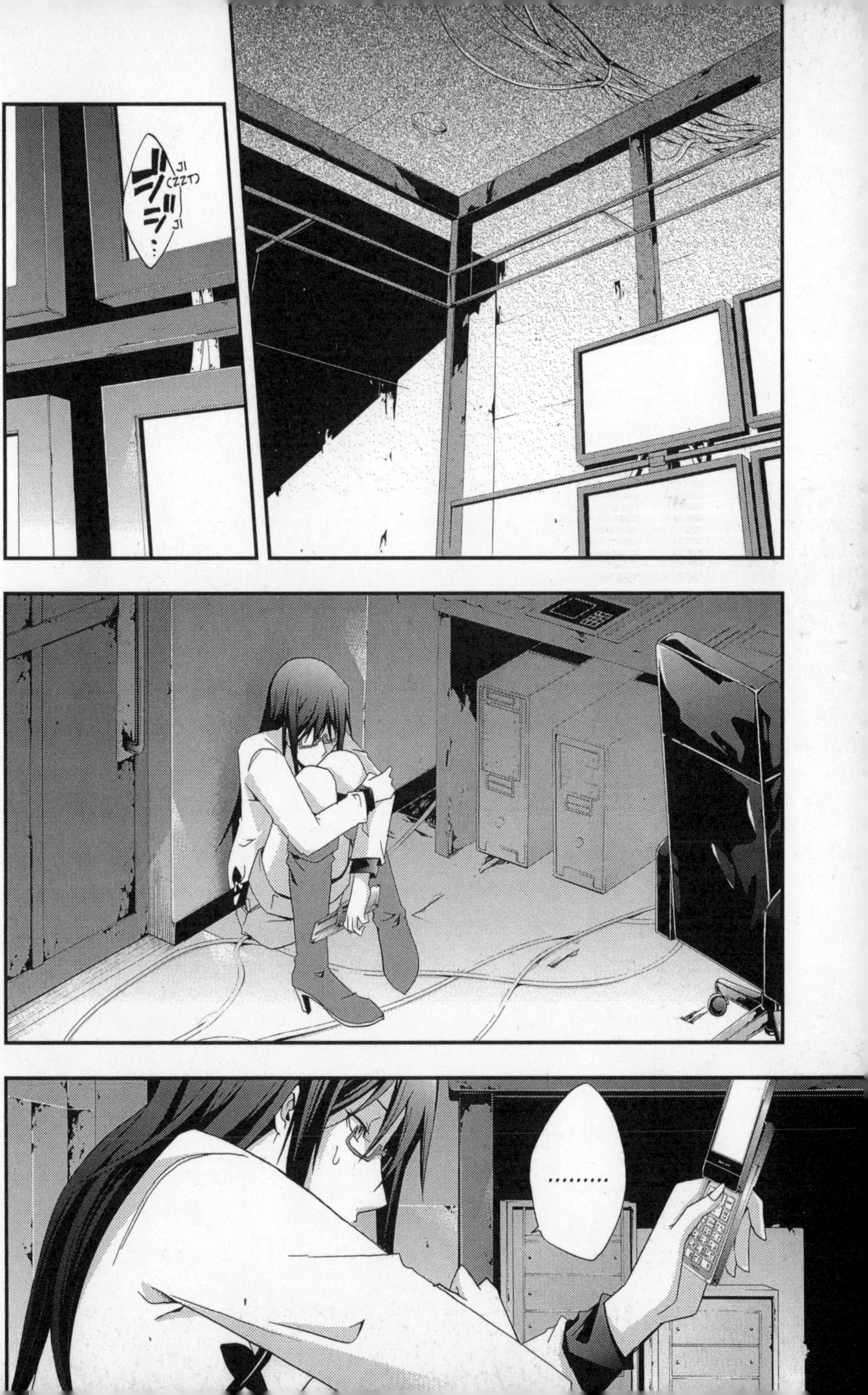
ジ…ジジ…
JI (ZZT) JI
………

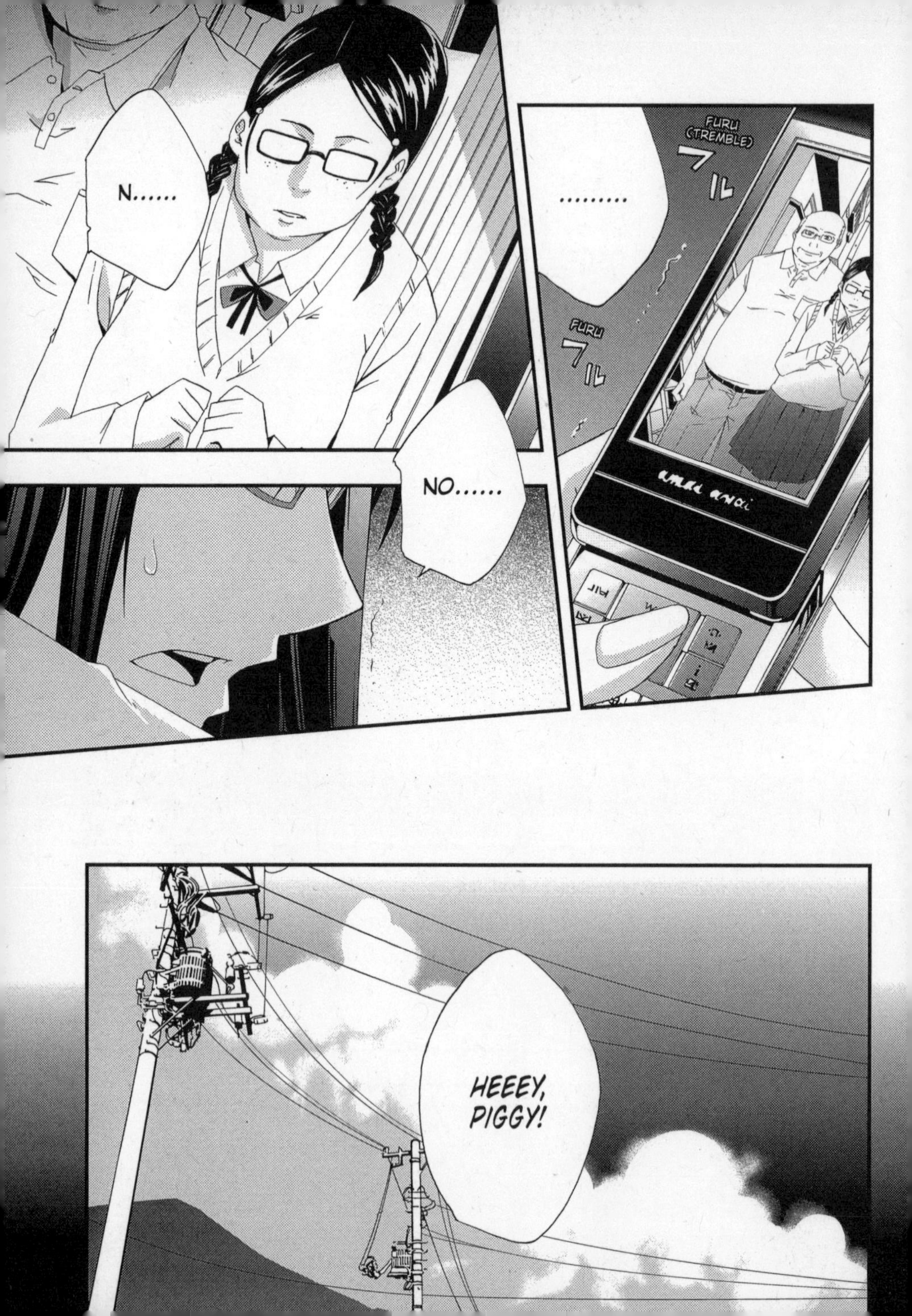
FURU (TREMBLE)
....
FURU
N......
NO......
HEEEY, PIGGY!

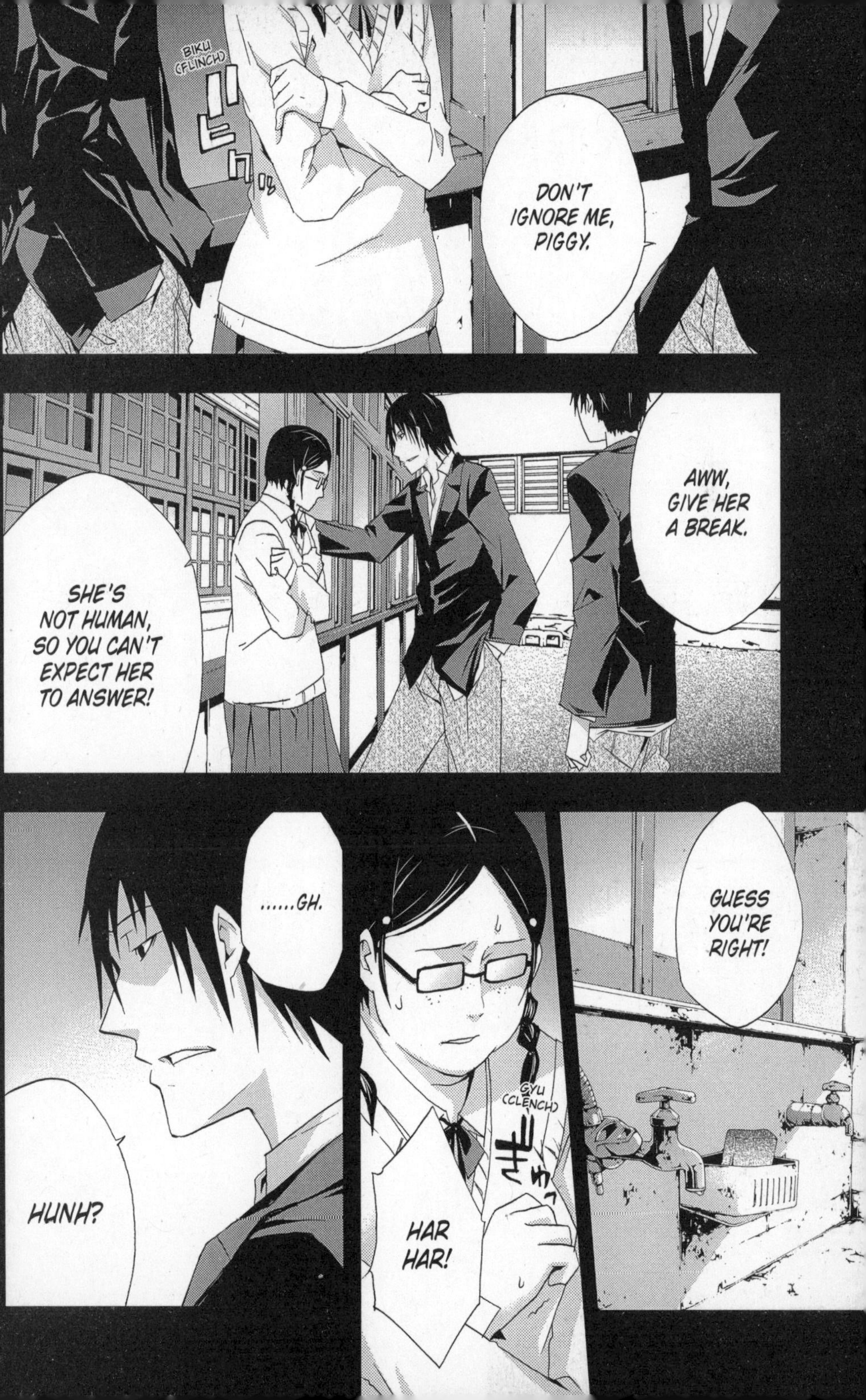
DON'T IGNORE ME, PIGGY.
BIKU (FLINCH)
AWW, GIVE HER A BREAK.
SHE'S NOT HUMAN, SO YOU CAN'T EXPECT HER TO ANSWER!
GUESS YOU'RE RIGHT!
GYU (CLENCH)
HAR HAR!
......GH.
HUNH?

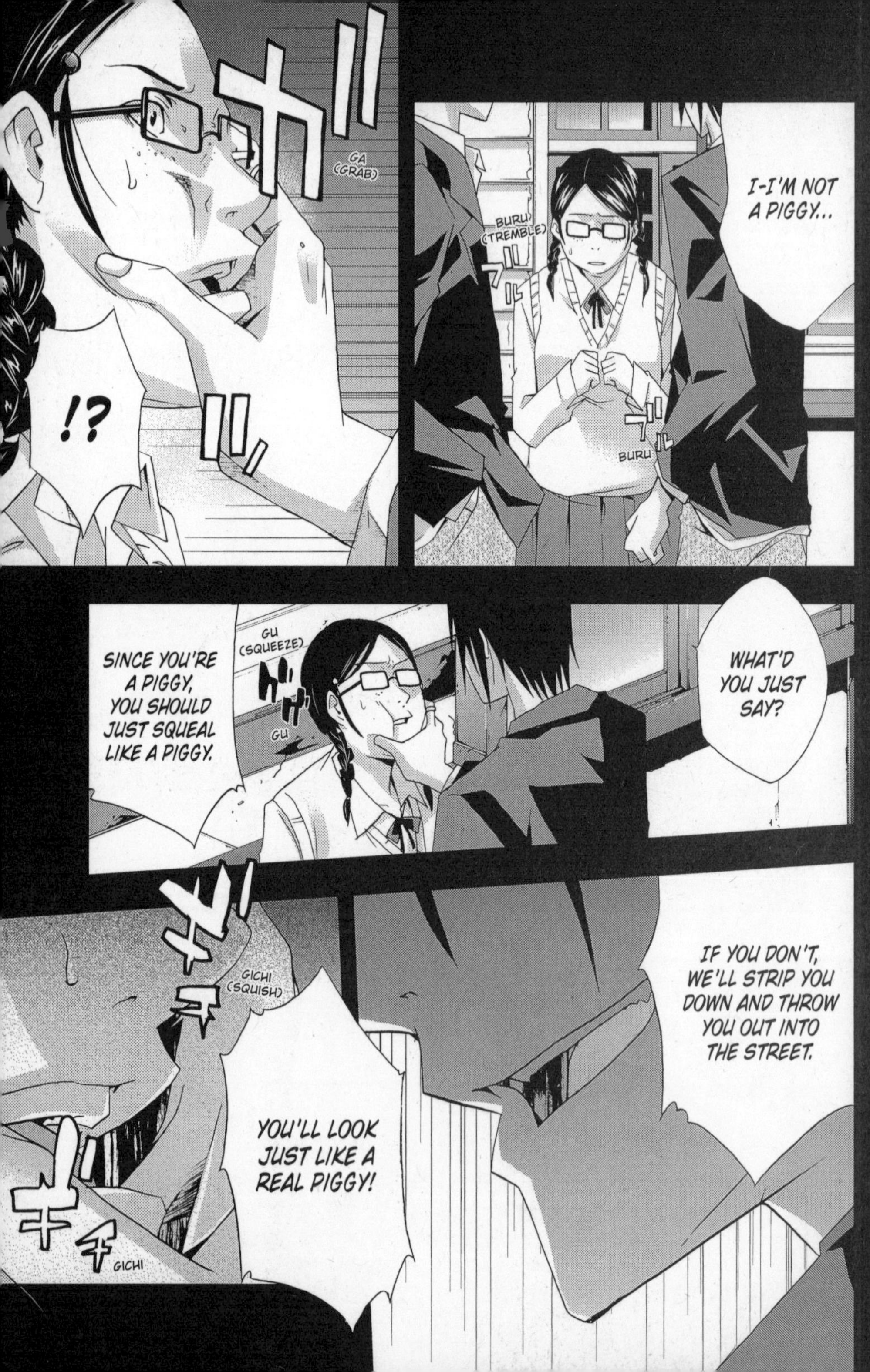
I-I'M NOT A PIGGY...
BURU (TREMBLE)
BURU
GA (GRAB)
!?
WHAT'D YOU JUST SAY?
GU (SQUEEZE)
GU
SINCE YOU'RE A PIGGY, YOU SHOULD JUST SQUEAL LIKE A PIGGY.
IF YOU DON'T, WE'LL STRIP YOU DOWN AND THROW YOU OUT INTO THE STREET.
GICHI (SQUISH)
YOU'LL LOOK JUST LIKE A REAL PIGGY!
GICHI

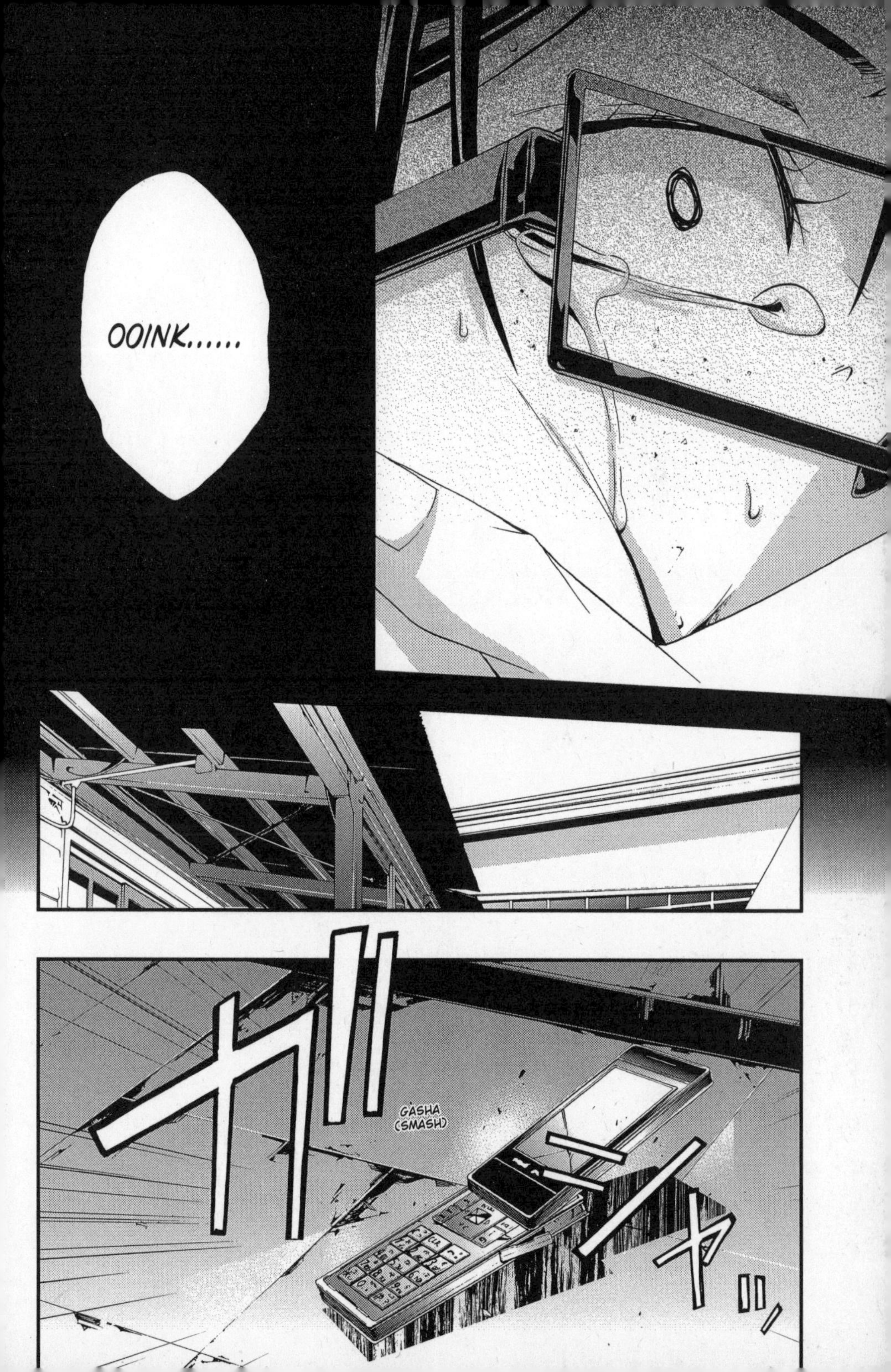
OOINK......
GASHA
(SMASH)

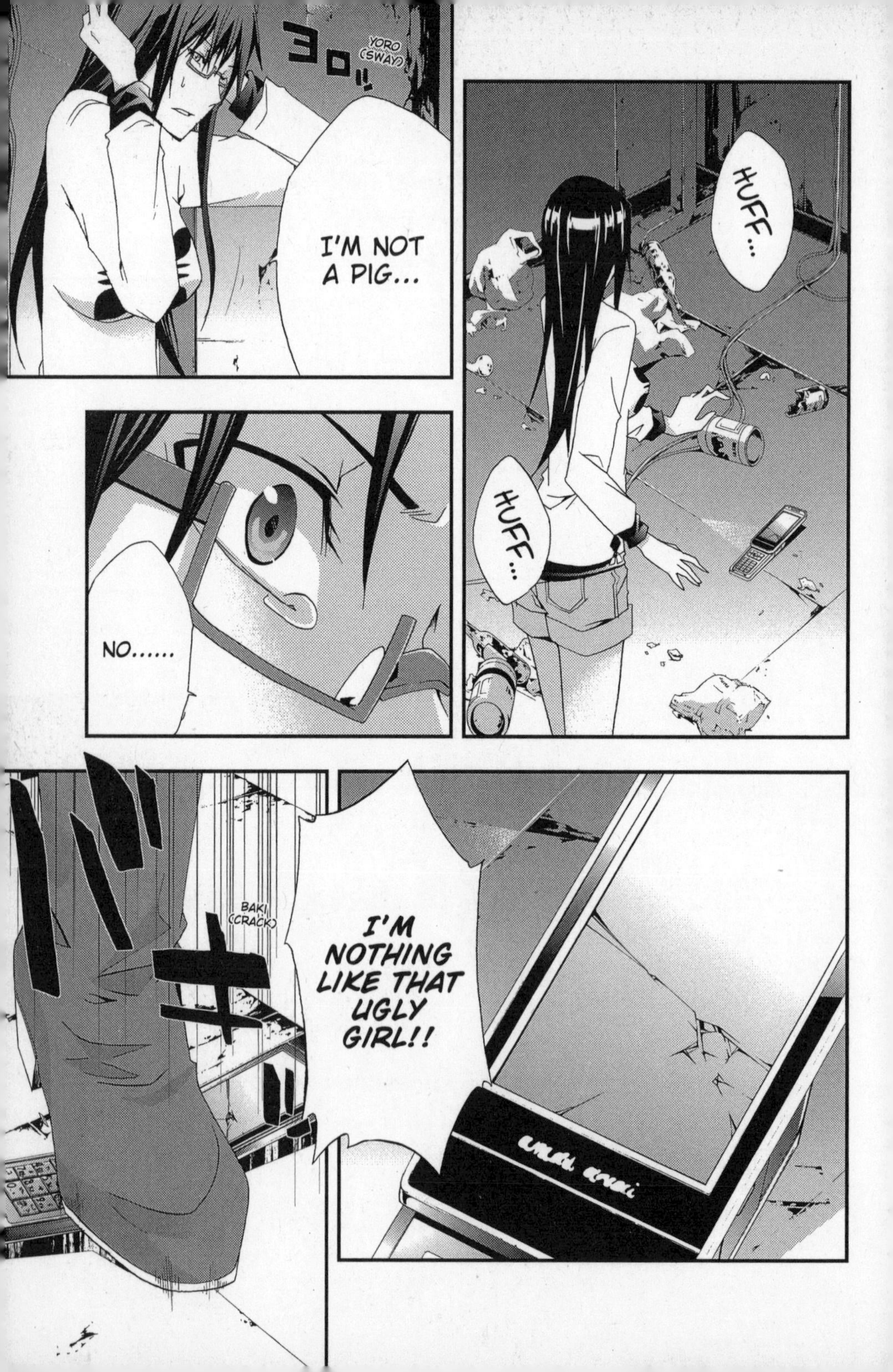

HUFF...
HUFF...
YORO (SWAY)
I'M NOT A PIG...
NO......
I'M NOTHING LIKE THAT UGLY GIRL!!
BAKI (CRACK)

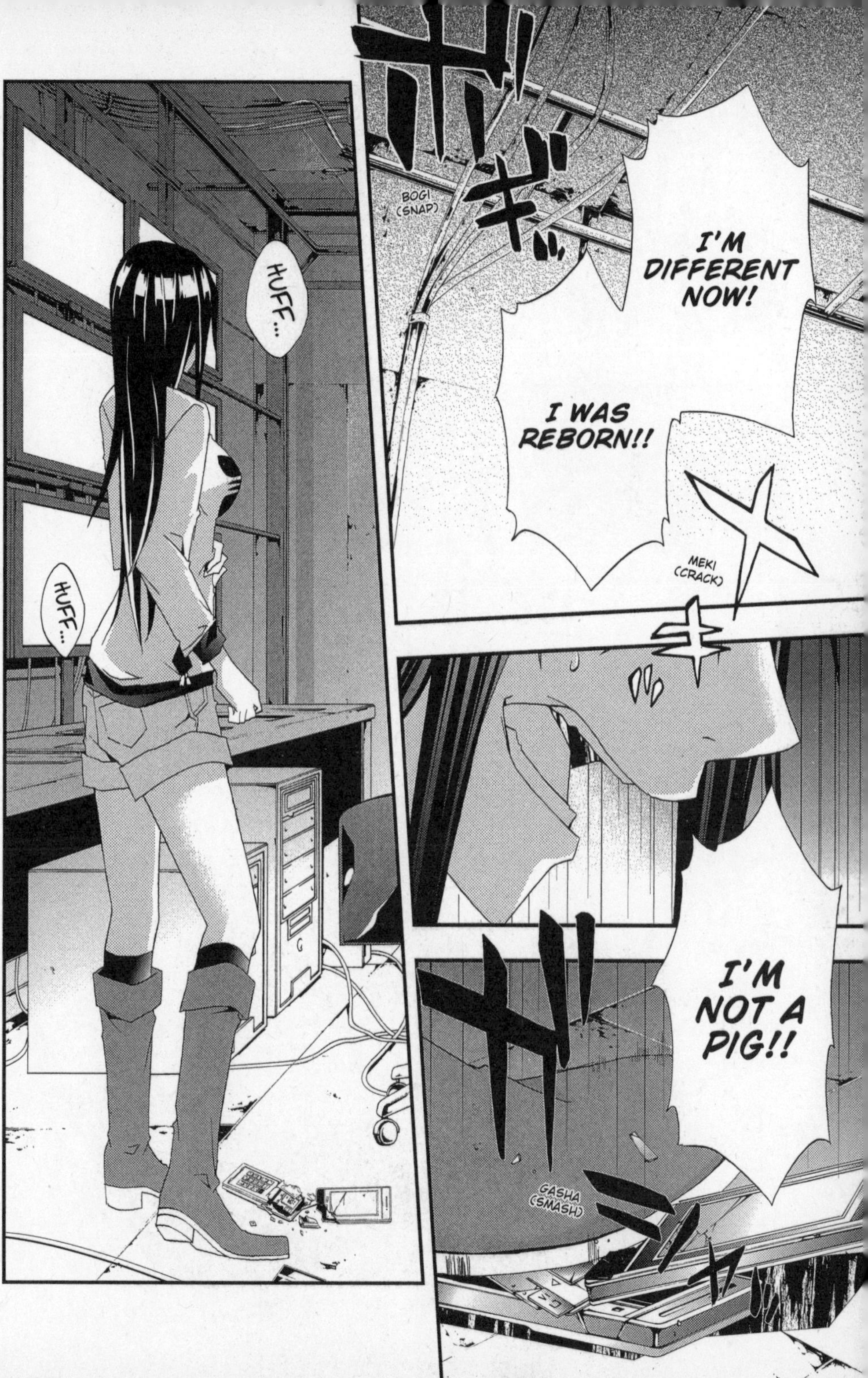
I'M DIFFERENT NOW!
BOGI (SNAP)
I WAS REBORN!!
MEKI (CRACK)
I'M NOT A PIG!!
GASHA (SMASH)
HUFF...
HUFF...

MIKU-SAN
...

GACHA
(CHK)

BIKU
(FLINCH)

WHAT
HAVE
YOU
DONE!!?

BA
(LUNGE)

AH......

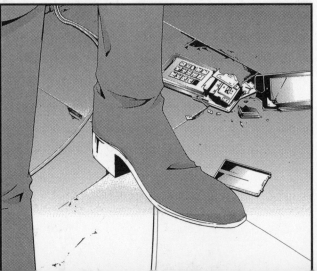

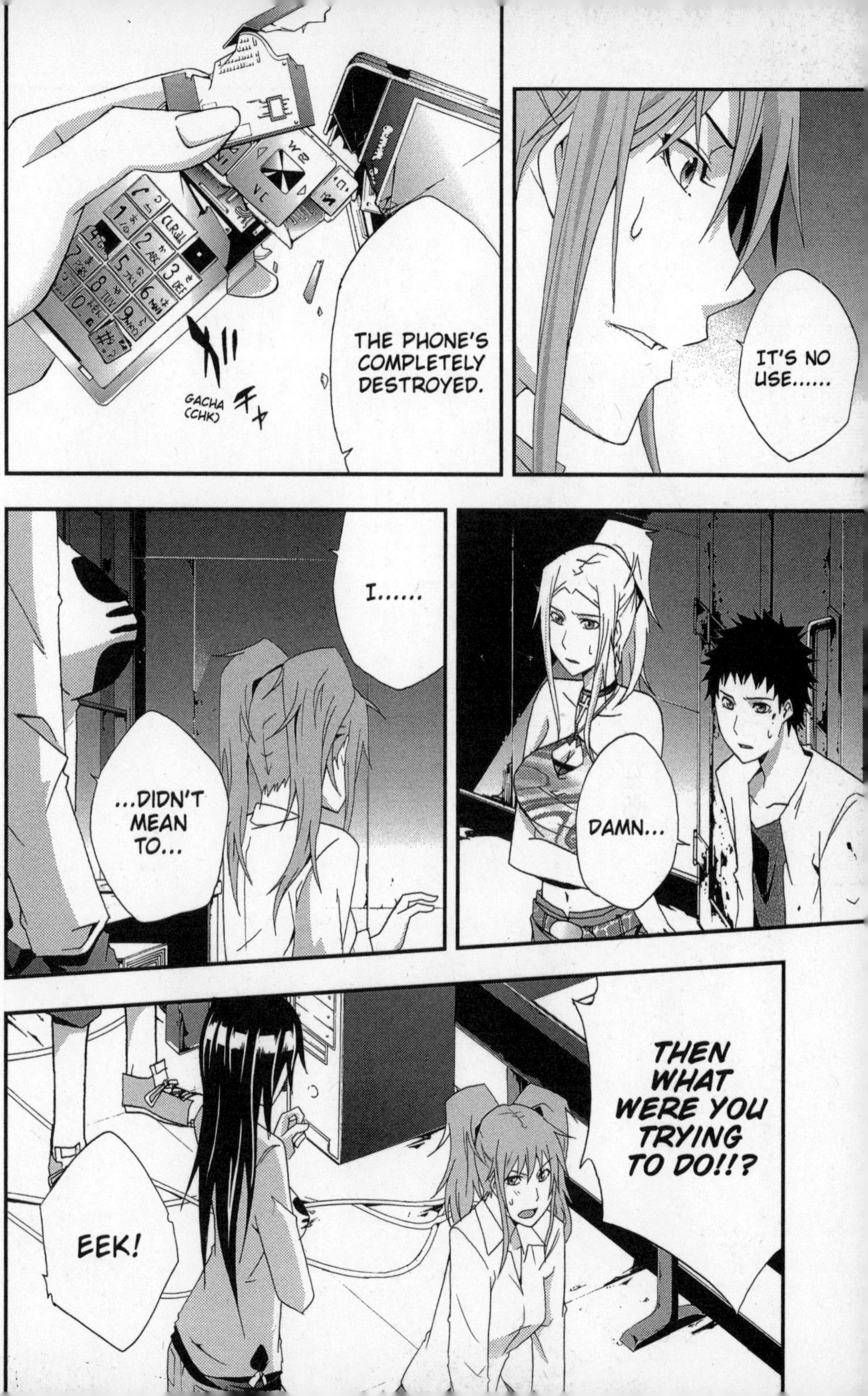
IT'S NO USE......
THE PHONE'S COMPLETELY DESTROYED.
GACHA (CHK)
DAMN...
I......
...DIDN'T MEAN TO...
THEN WHAT WERE YOU TRYING TO DO!!?
EEK!

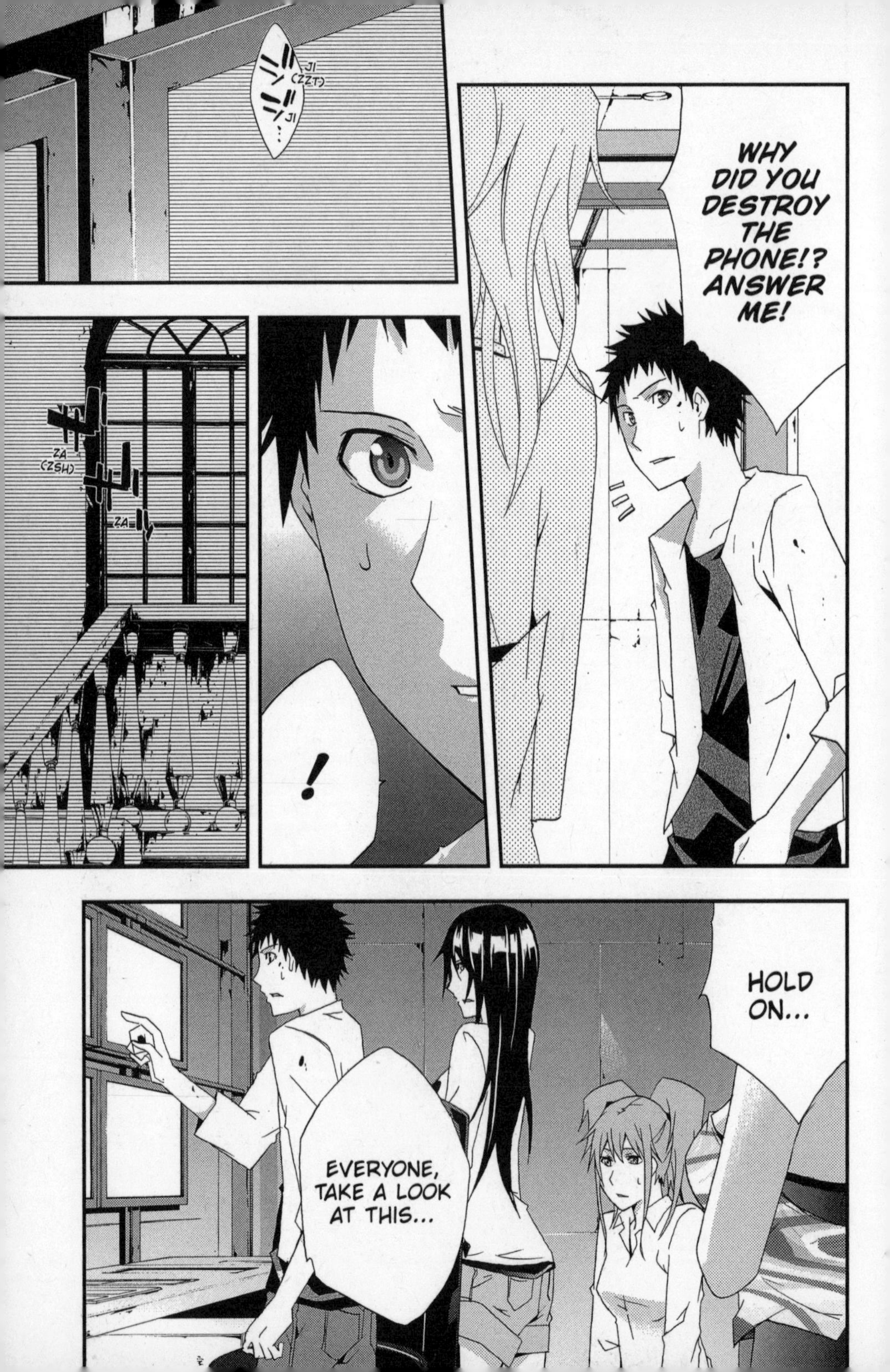
WHY DID YOU DESTROY THE PHONE!? ANSWER ME!
JI (ZZZT) JI
!
ZA (ZSH) ZA
HOLD ON...
EVERYONE, TAKE A LOOK AT THIS...

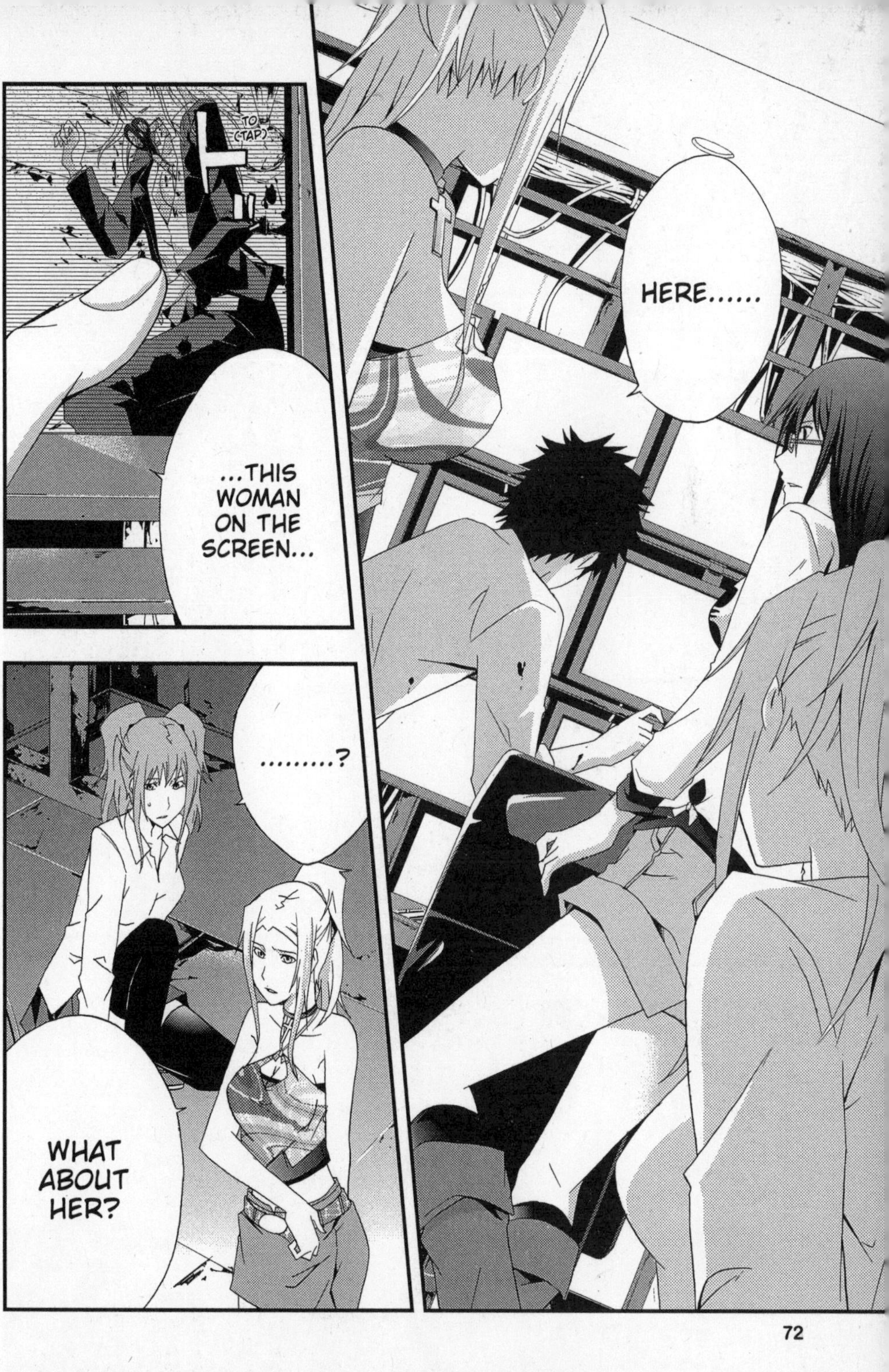
HERE......
TO (TAP)
...THIS WOMAN ON THE SCREEN...
.........?
WHAT ABOUT HER?

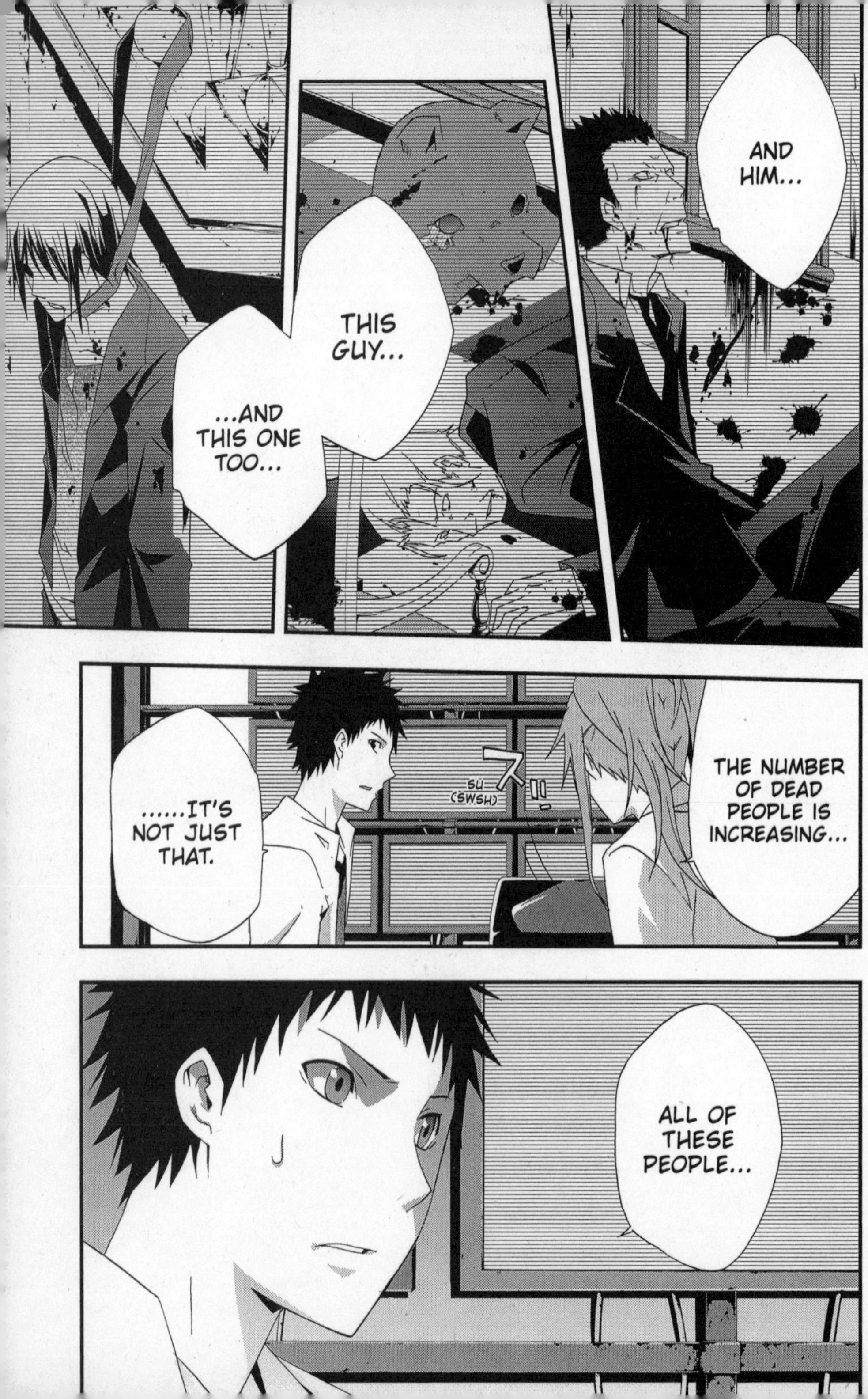
AND HIM...
THIS GUY...
...AND THIS ONE TOO...
THE NUMBER OF DEAD PEOPLE IS INCREASING...
SU (SWSH)
......IT'S NOT JUST THAT.
ALL OF THESE PEOPLE...

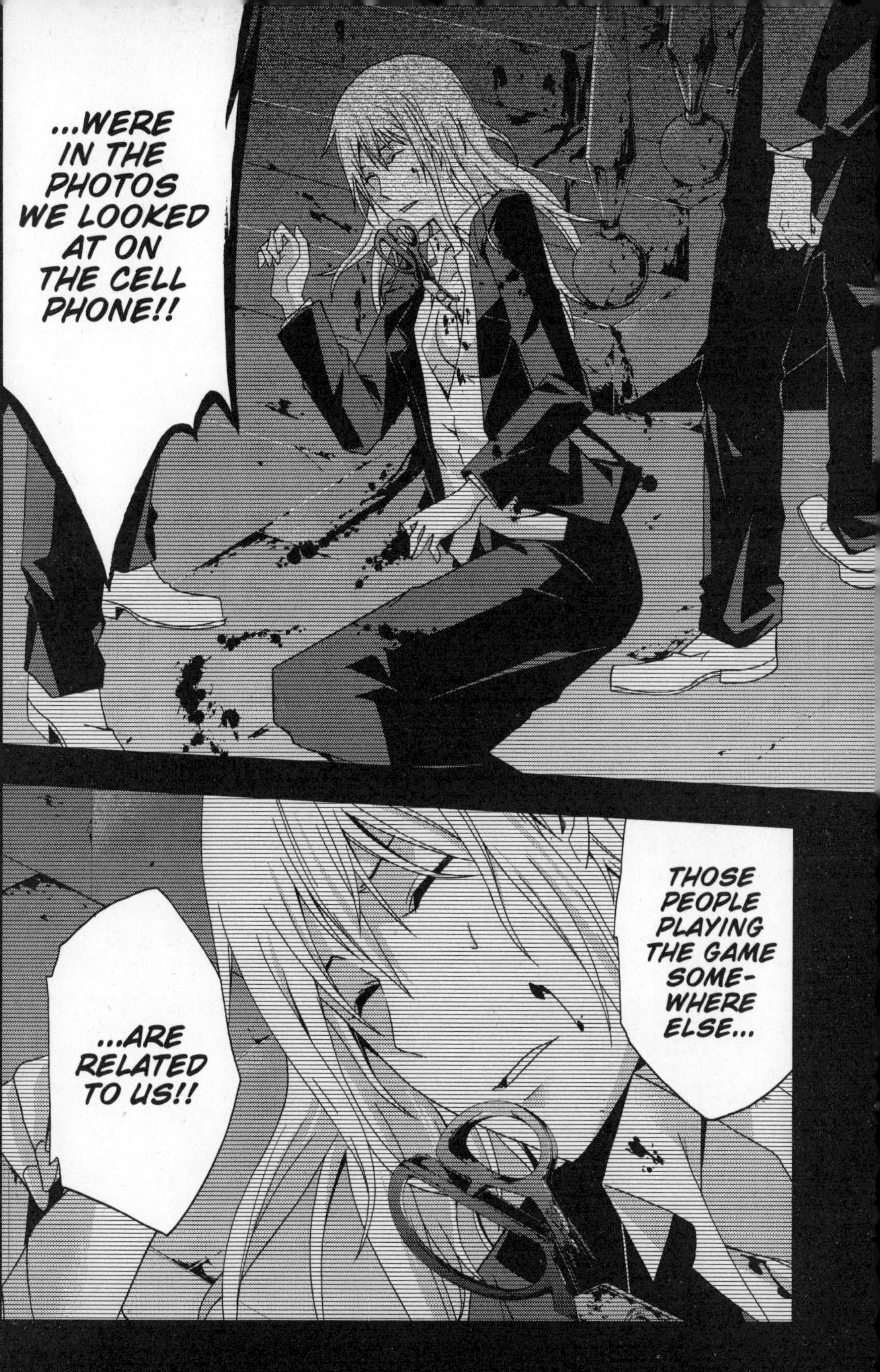
...WERE IN THE PHOTOS WE LOOKED AT ON THE CELL PHONE!!
THOSE PEOPLE PLAYING THE GAME SOME-WHERE ELSE...
...ARE RELATED TO US!!

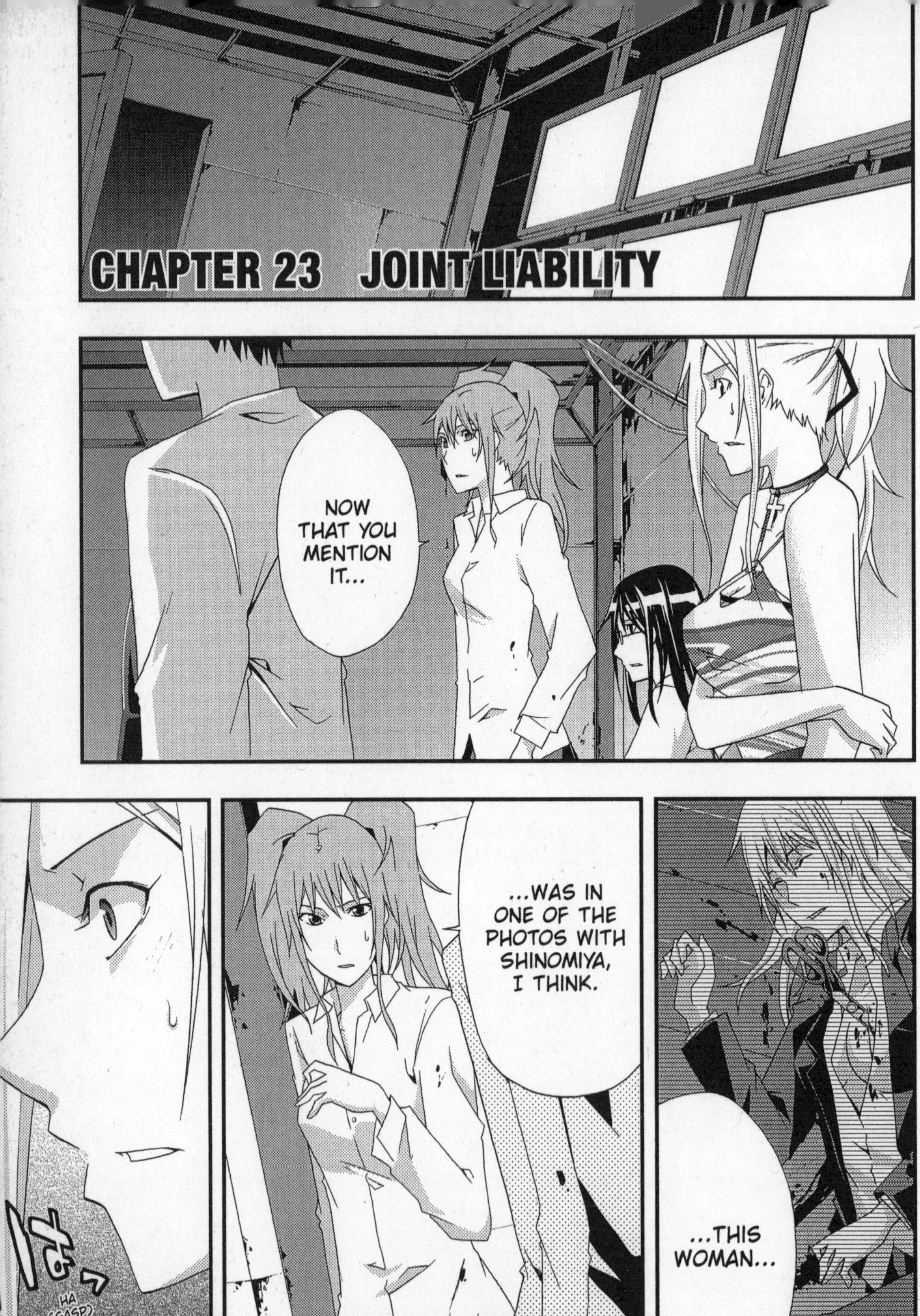
CHAPTER 23 JOINT LIABILITY
NOW THAT YOU MENTION IT...
...THIS WOMAN...
...WAS IN ONE OF THE PHOTOS WITH SHINOMIYA, I THINK.
HA (GASP)

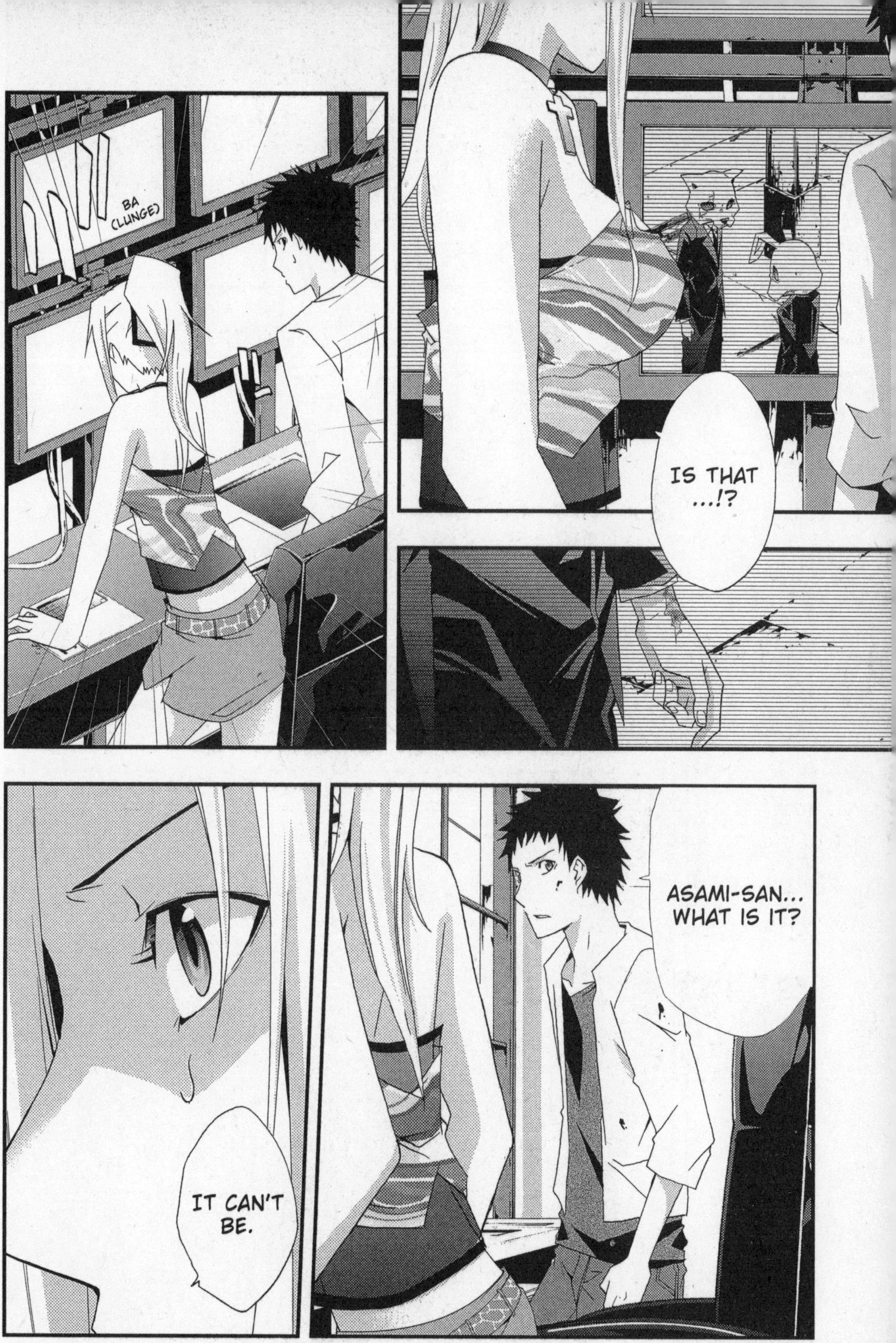
IS THAT ...!?
BA (LUNGE)
ASAMI-SAN... WHAT IS IT?
IT CAN'T BE.

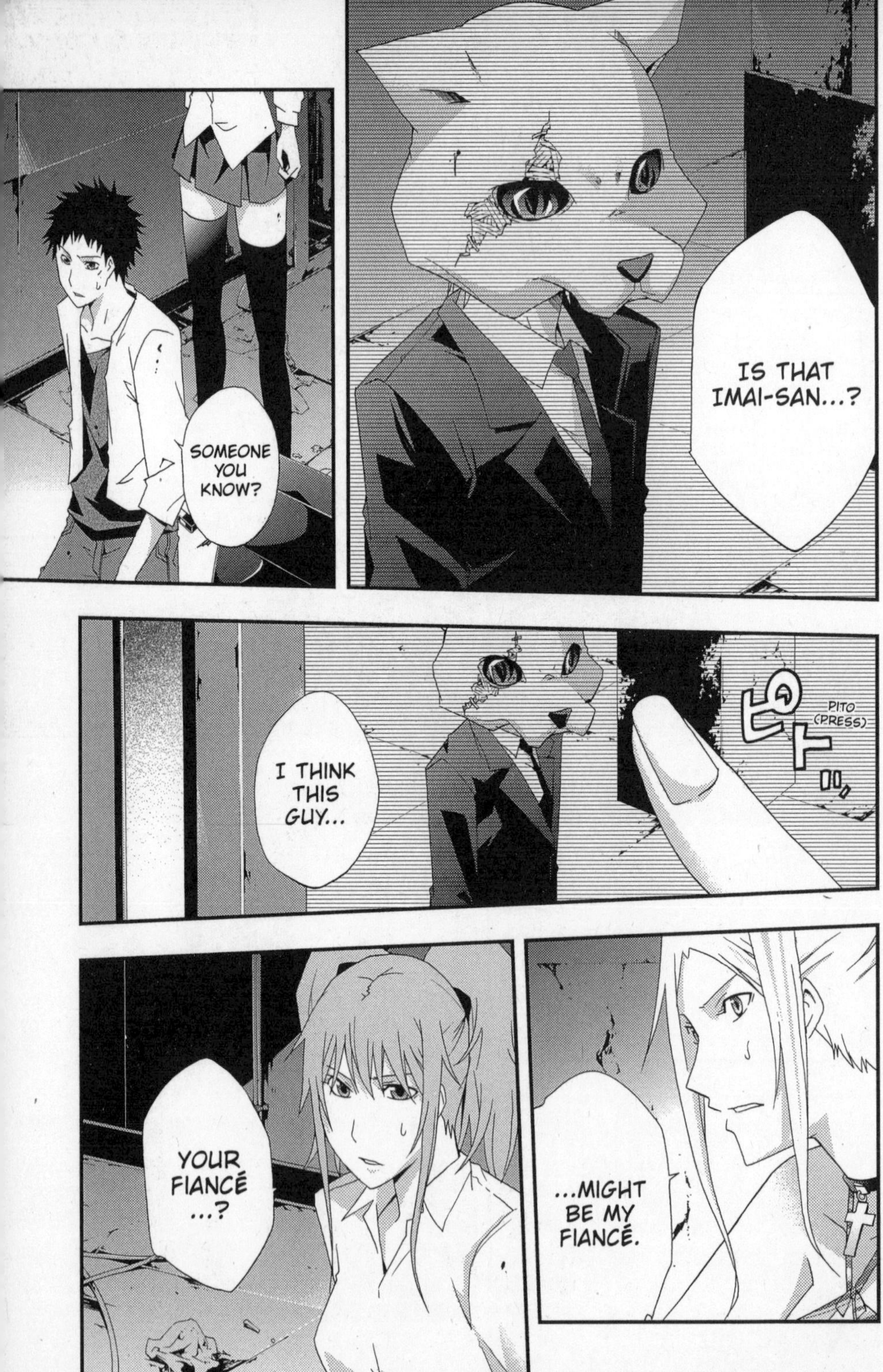
IS THAT IMAI-SAN...?
SOMEONE YOU KNOW?
ピトッ
PITO (PRESS)
I THINK THIS GUY...
...MIGHT BE MY FIANCÉ.
YOUR FIANCÉ ...?

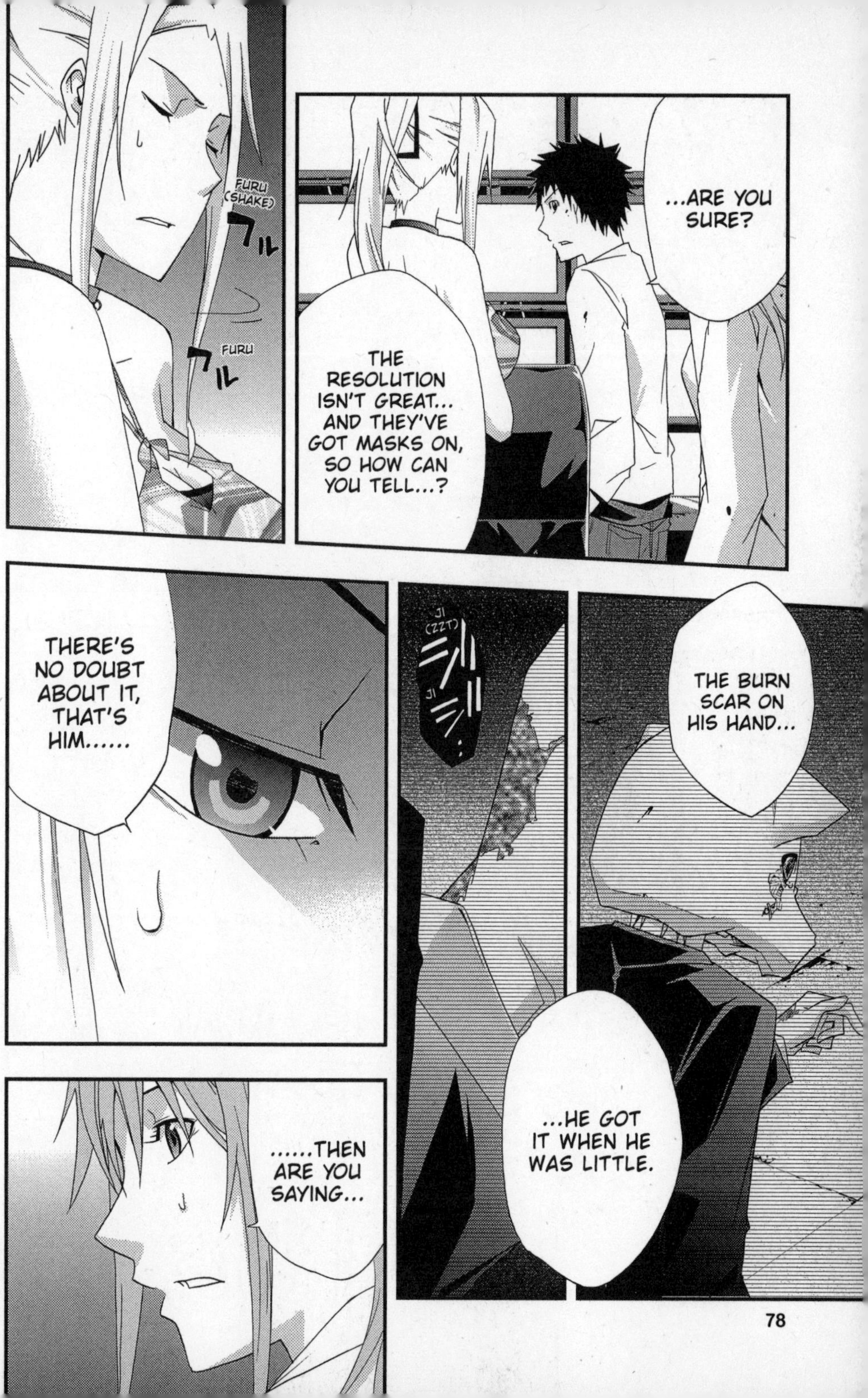
...ARE YOU SURE?
THE RESOLUTION ISN'T GREAT... AND THEY'VE GOT MASKS ON, SO HOW CAN YOU TELL...?
FURU (SHAKE)
FURU
THE BURN SCAR ON HIS HAND...
...HE GOT IT WHEN HE WAS LITTLE.
JI (ZZT)
JI
THERE'S NO DOUBT ABOUT IT, THAT'S HIM......
......THEN ARE YOU SAYING...

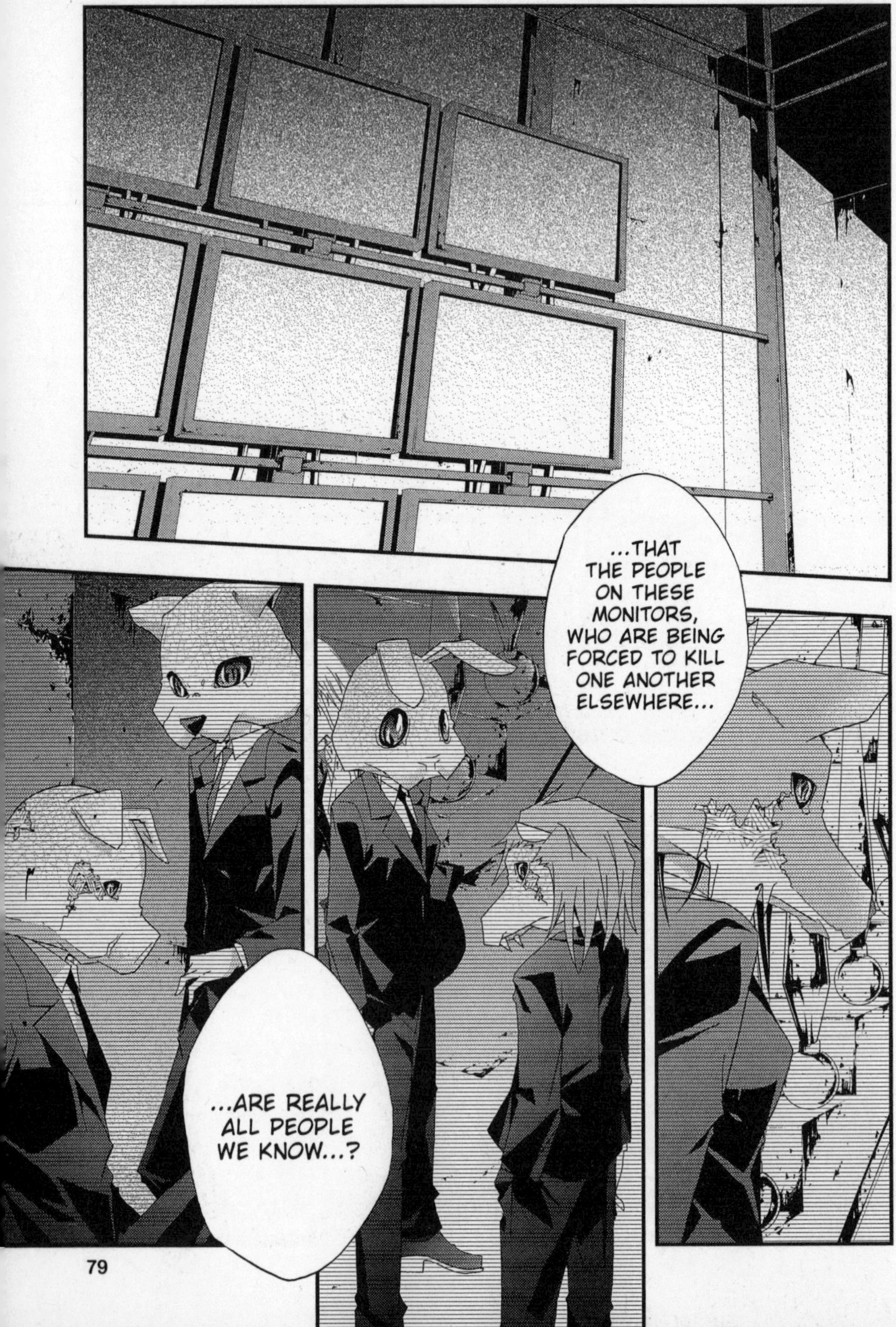
...THAT THE PEOPLE ON THESE MONITORS, WHO ARE BEING FORCED TO KILL ONE ANOTHER ELSEWHERE...
...ARE REALLY ALL PEOPLE WE KNOW...?

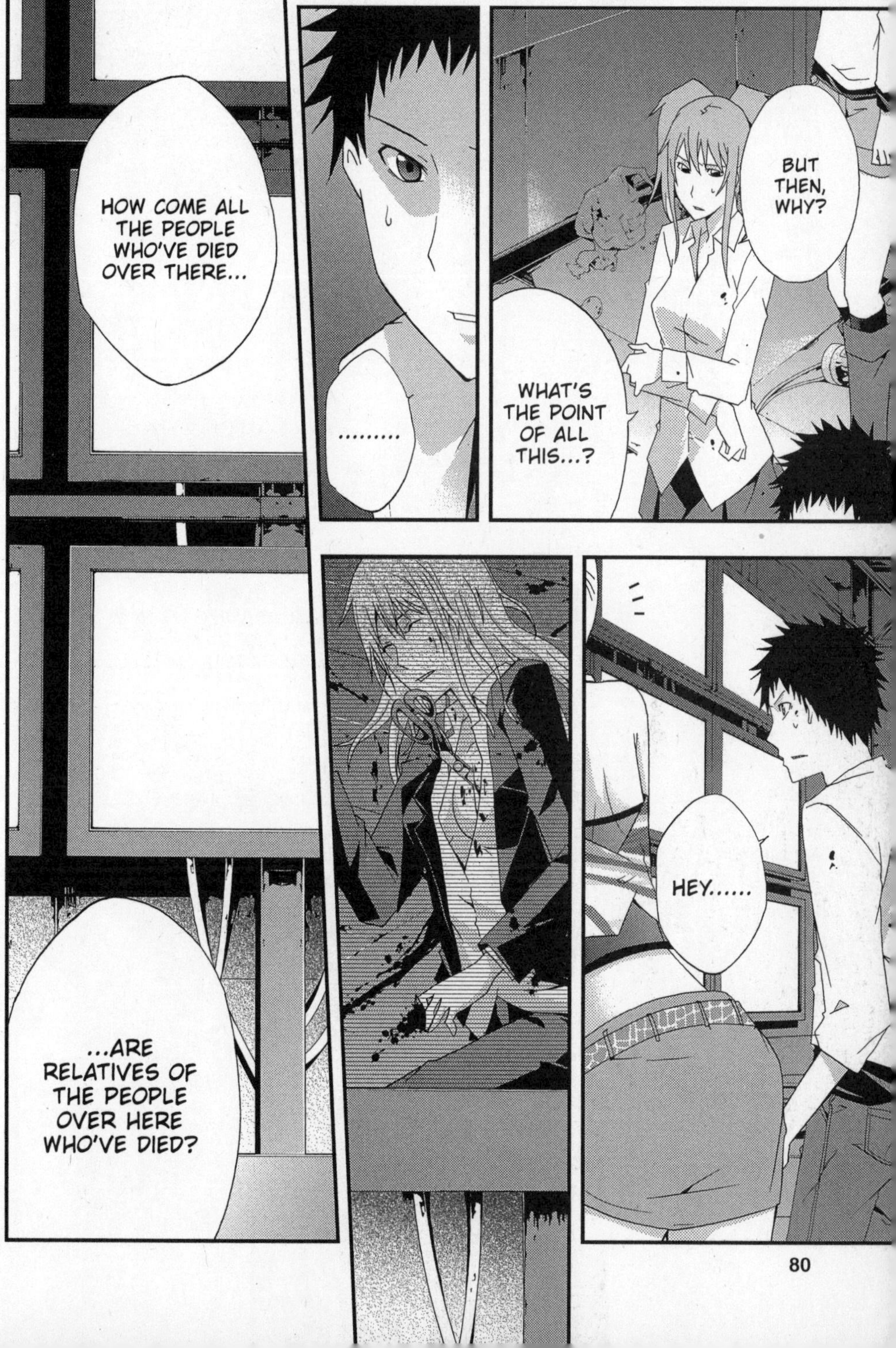
BUT THEN, WHY?
WHAT'S THE POINT OF ALL THIS...?
....
HEY......
HOW COME ALL THE PEOPLE WHO'VE DIED OVER THERE...
...ARE RELATIVES OF THE PEOPLE OVER HERE WHO'VE DIED?

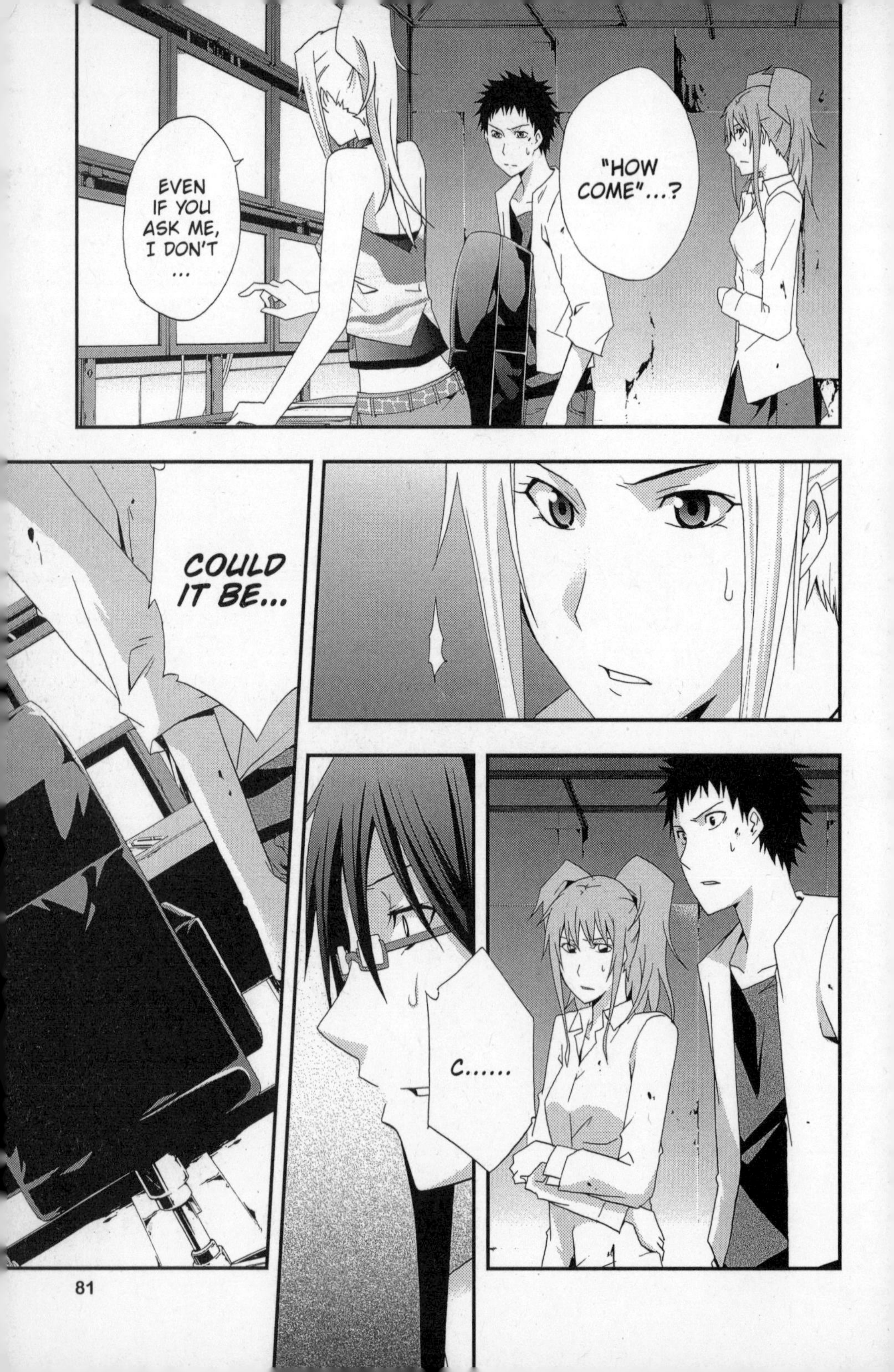
"HOW COME"...?
EVEN IF YOU ASK ME, I DON'T ...
C......
COULD IT BE...

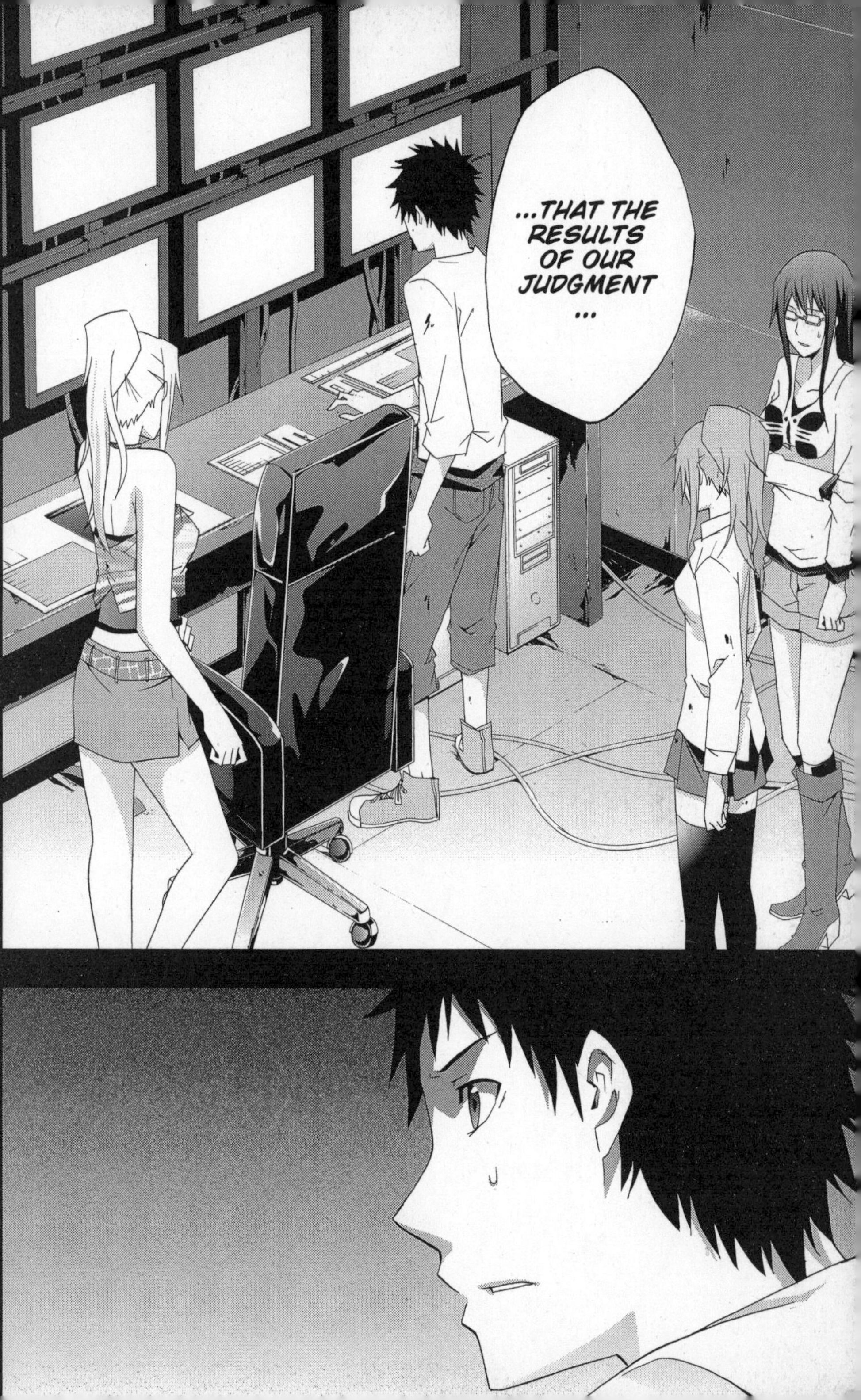
...THAT THE RESULTS OF OUR JUDGMENT ...

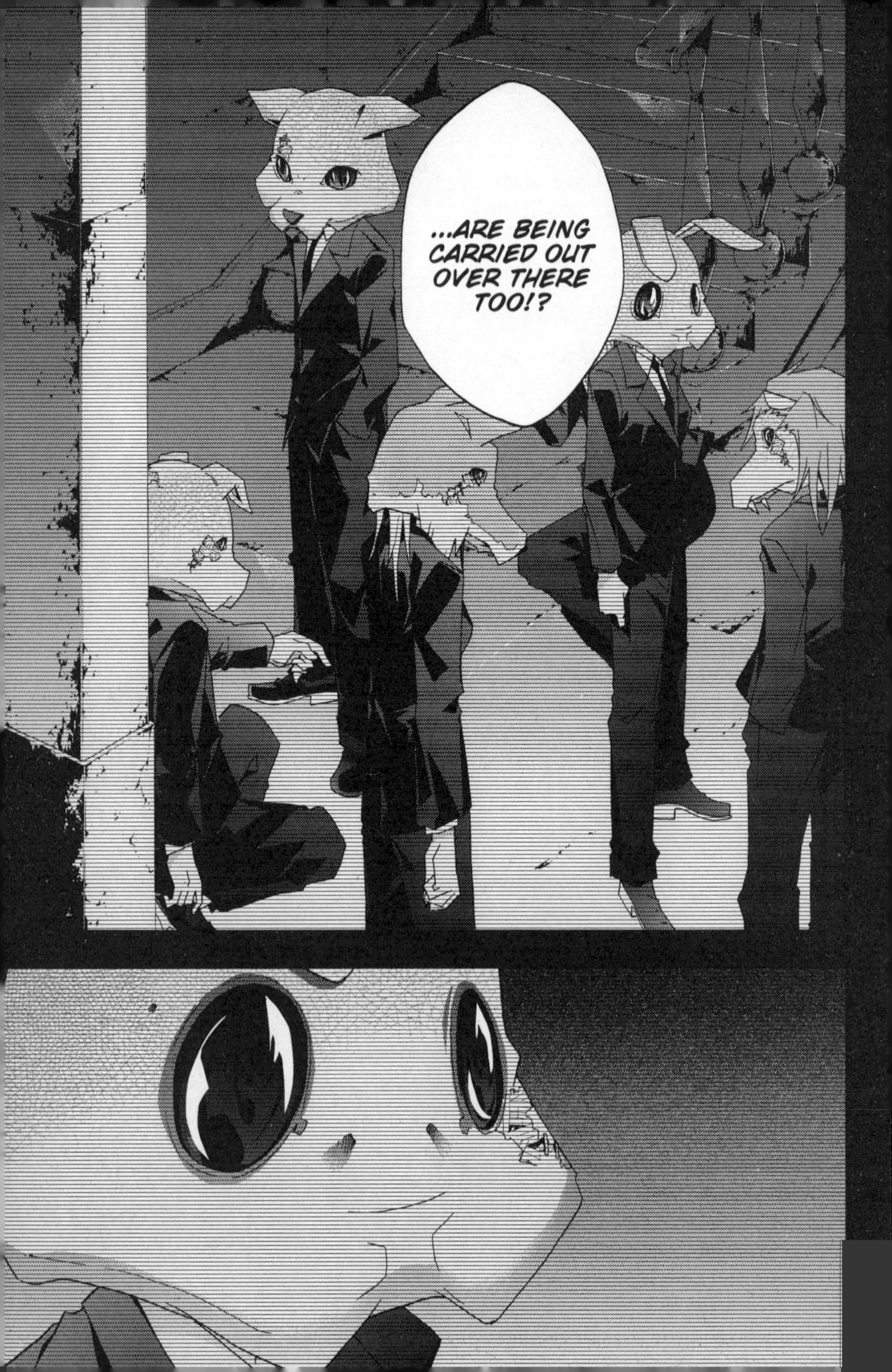
...ARE BEING CARRIED OUT OVER THERE TOO!?

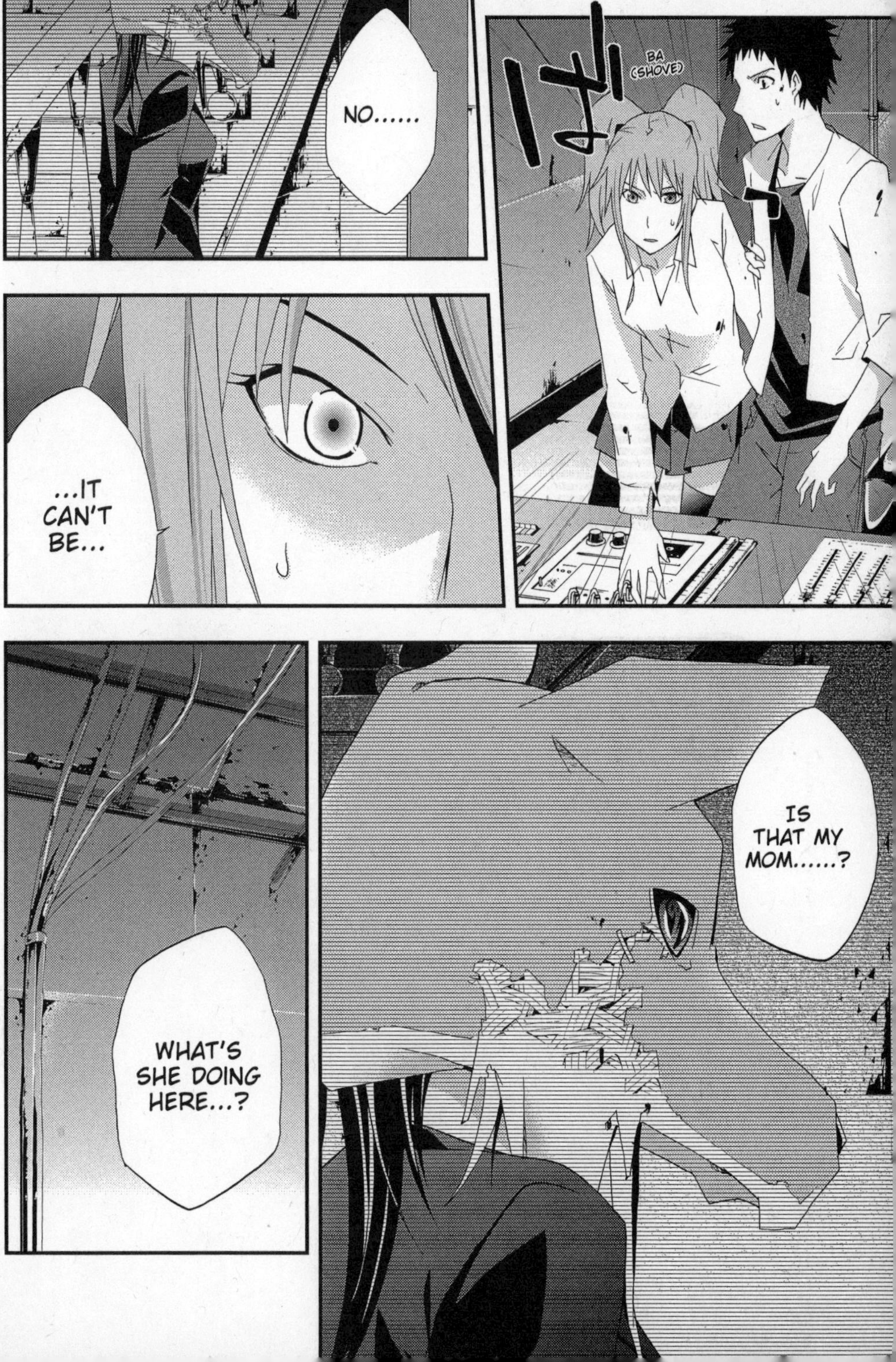
ば
BA (SHOVE)
NO......
...IT CAN'T BE...
IS THAT MY MOM......?
WHAT'S SHE DOING HERE...?

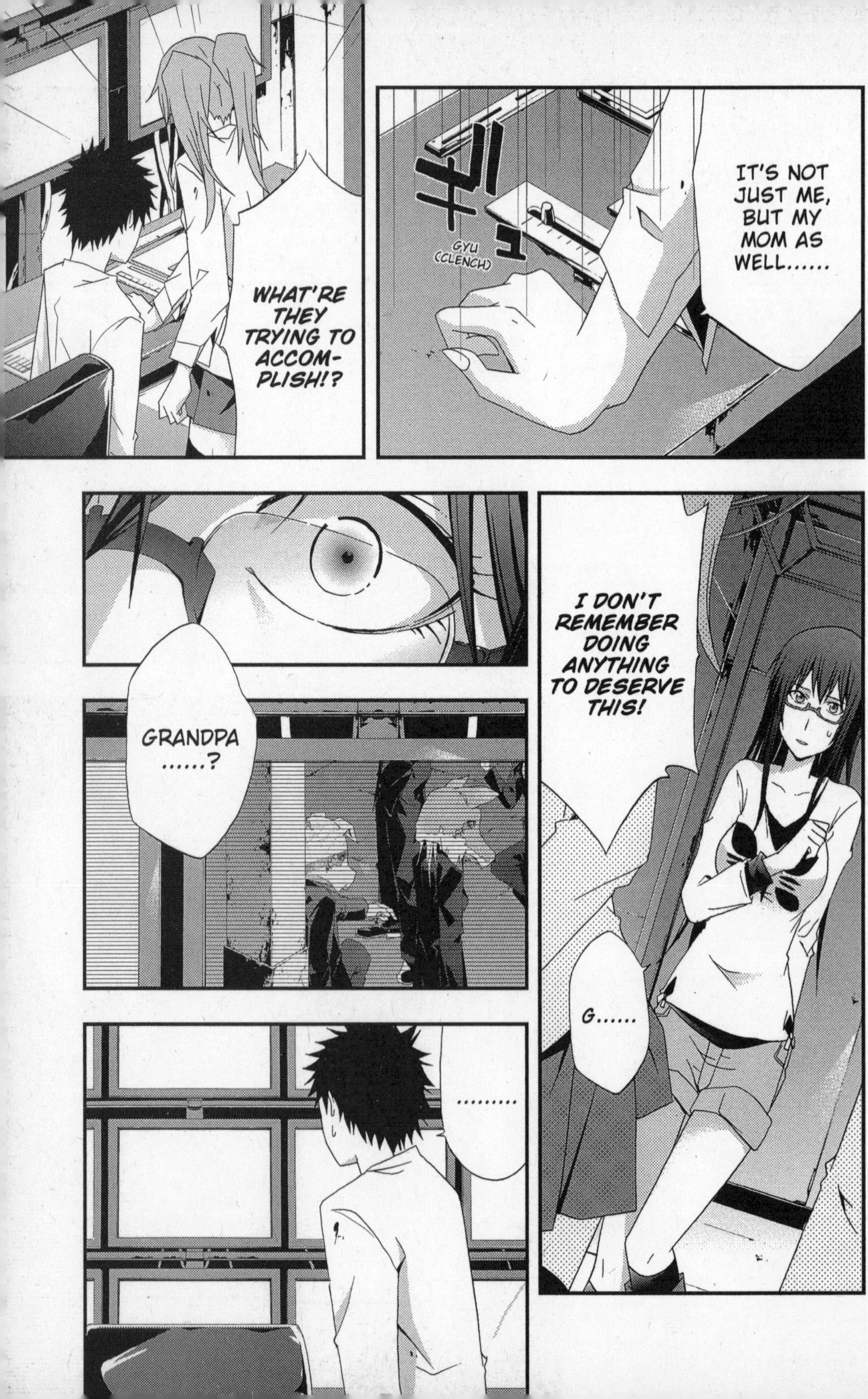
GYU (CLENCH)
IT'S NOT JUST ME, BUT MY MOM AS WELL......
WHAT'RE THEY TRYING TO ACCOM-PLISH!?
I DON'T REMEMBER DOING ANYTHING TO DESERVE THIS!
G......
GRANDPA ......?
....

MY BROTHER'S PASSED, SO I DON'T HAVE ANY FAMILY LEFT...

WHICH MEANS THE PERSON OVER THERE MUST BE...

GYU (SQUEAK)

...HIKARI...

KA (CLACK)

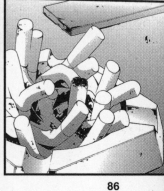

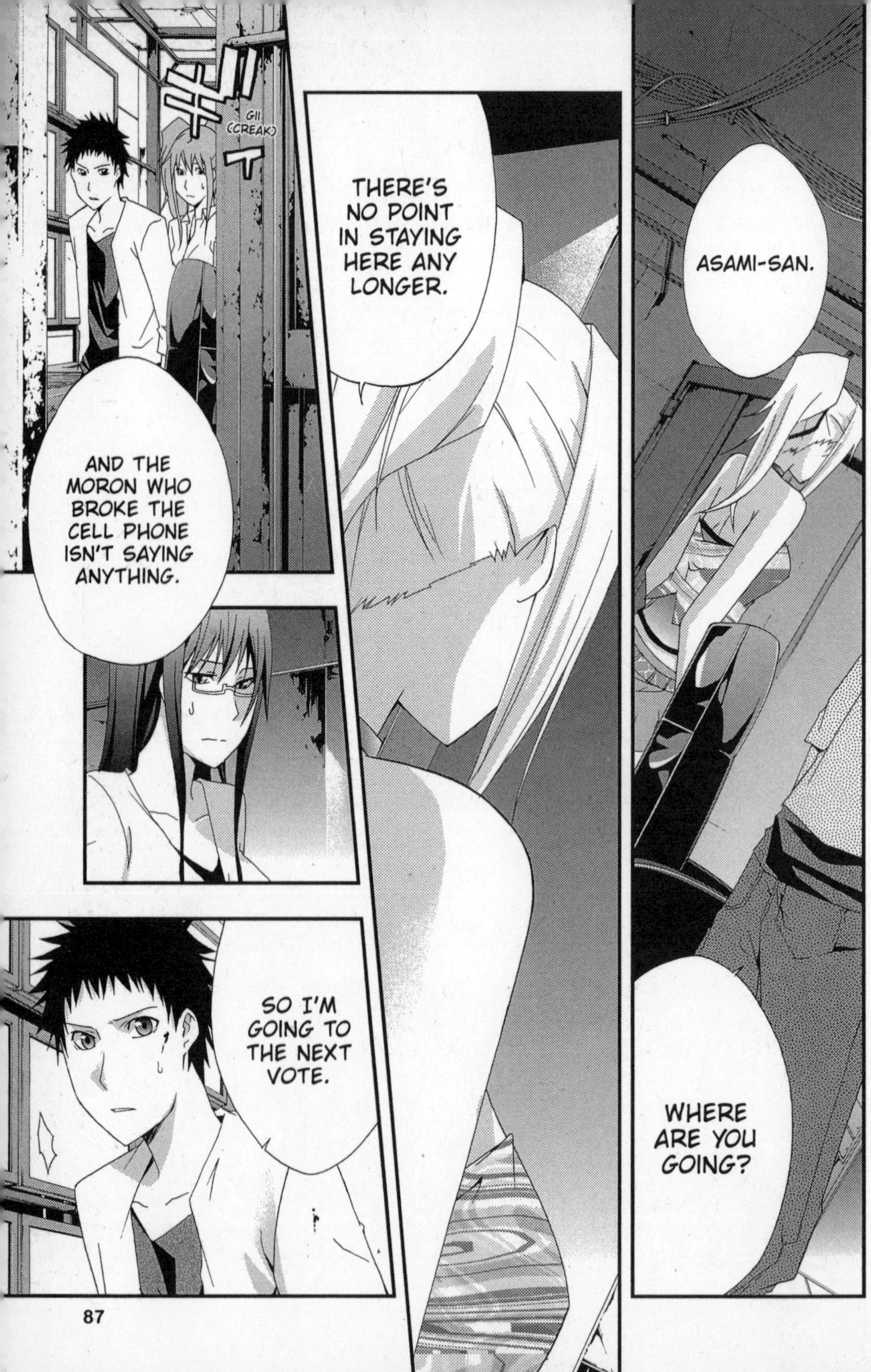
ASAMI-SAN.
WHERE ARE YOU GOING?
THERE'S NO POINT IN STAYING HERE ANY LONGER.
GII (CREAK)
AND THE MORON WHO BROKE THE CELL PHONE ISN'T SAYING ANYTHING.
SO I'M GOING TO THE NEXT VOTE.

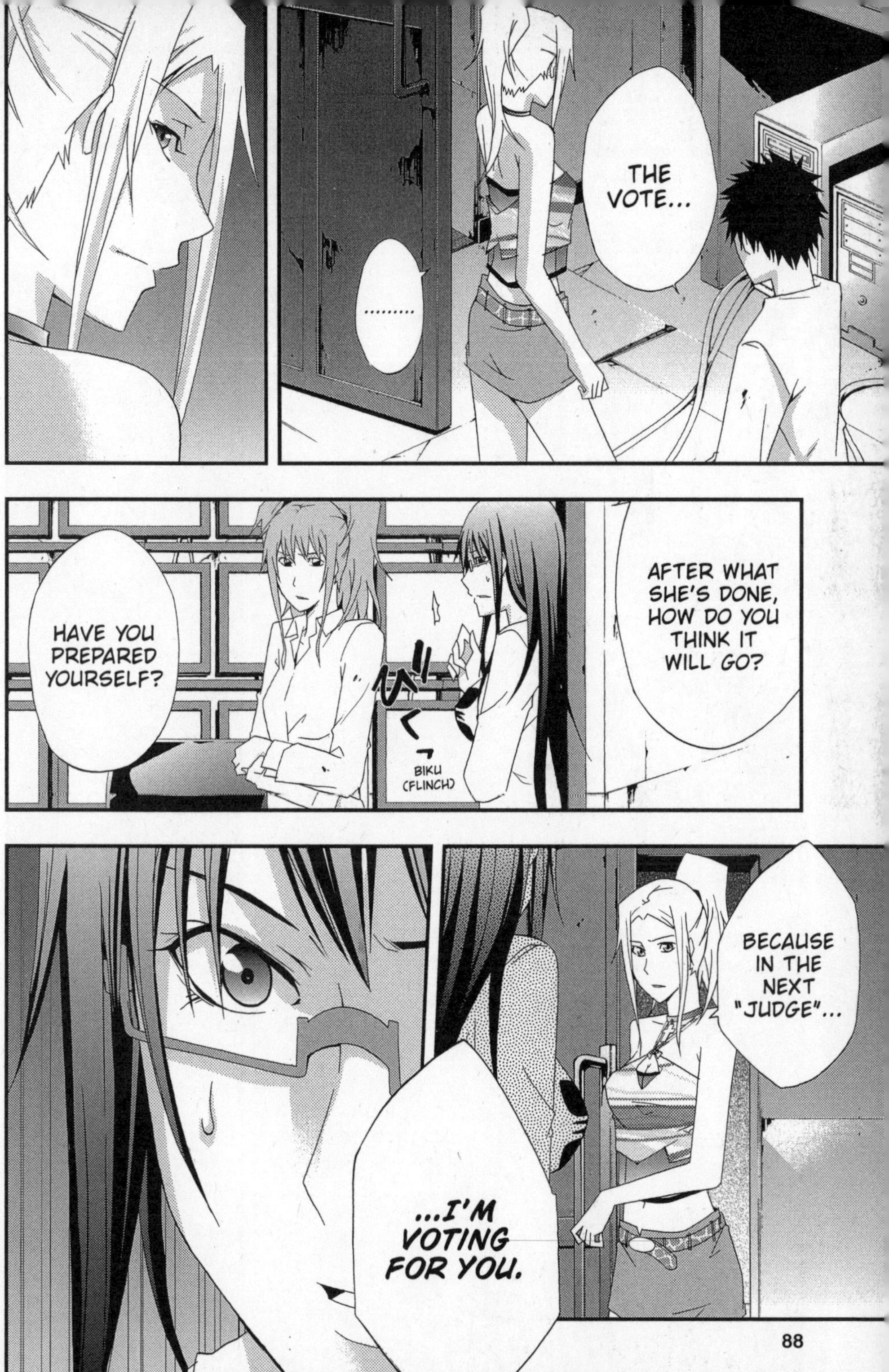
THE VOTE...
....
AFTER WHAT SHE'S DONE, HOW DO YOU THINK IT WILL GO?
びくっ
BIKU (FLINCH)
HAVE YOU PREPARED YOURSELF?
BECAUSE IN THE NEXT "JUDGE"...
...I'M VOTING FOR YOU.

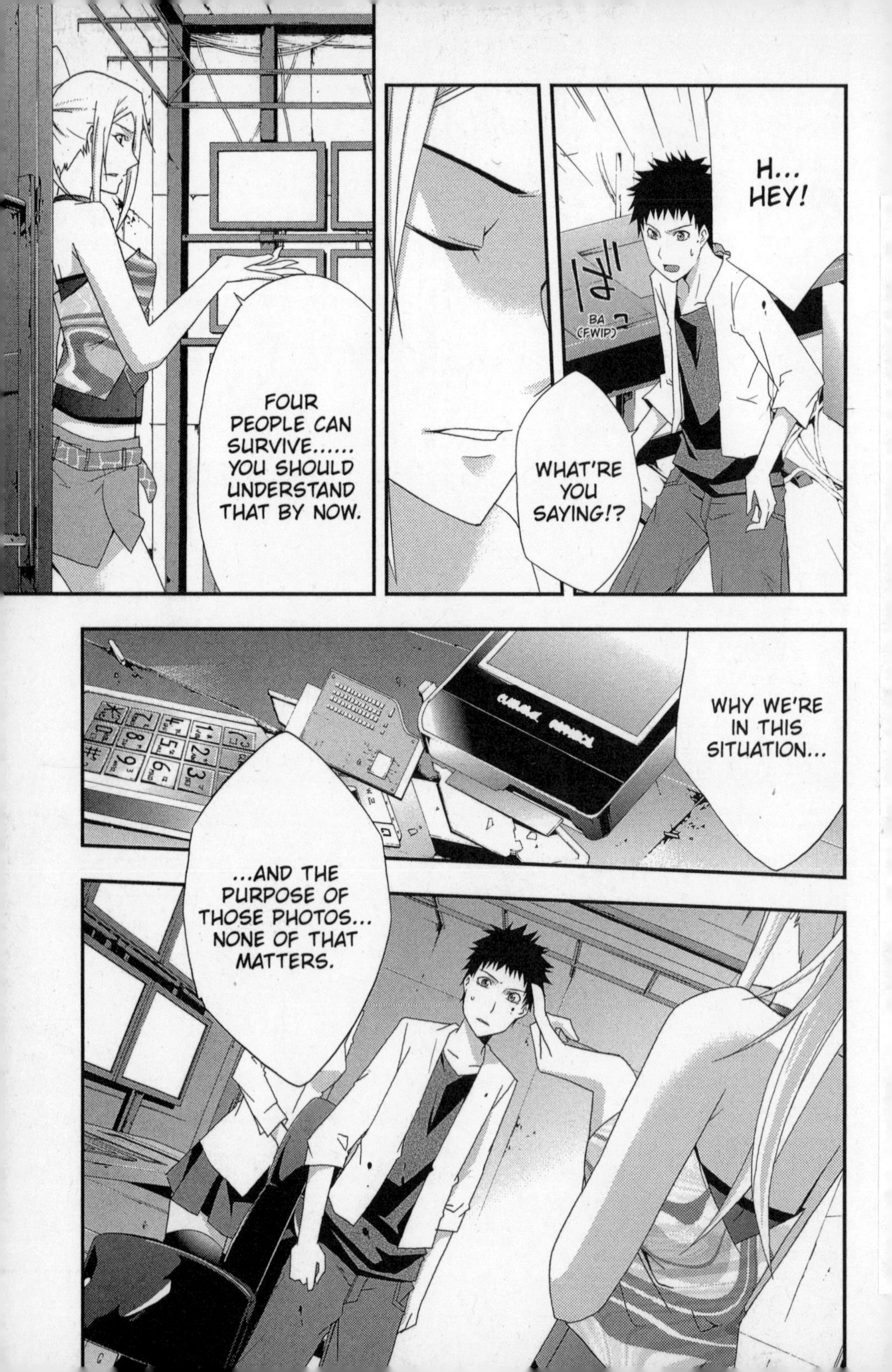
H...
HEY!
BA (FWIP)
WHAT'RE YOU SAYING!?
FOUR PEOPLE CAN SURVIVE...... YOU SHOULD UNDERSTAND THAT BY NOW.
WHY WE'RE IN THIS SITUATION...
...AND THE PURPOSE OF THOSE PHOTOS... NONE OF THAT MATTERS.

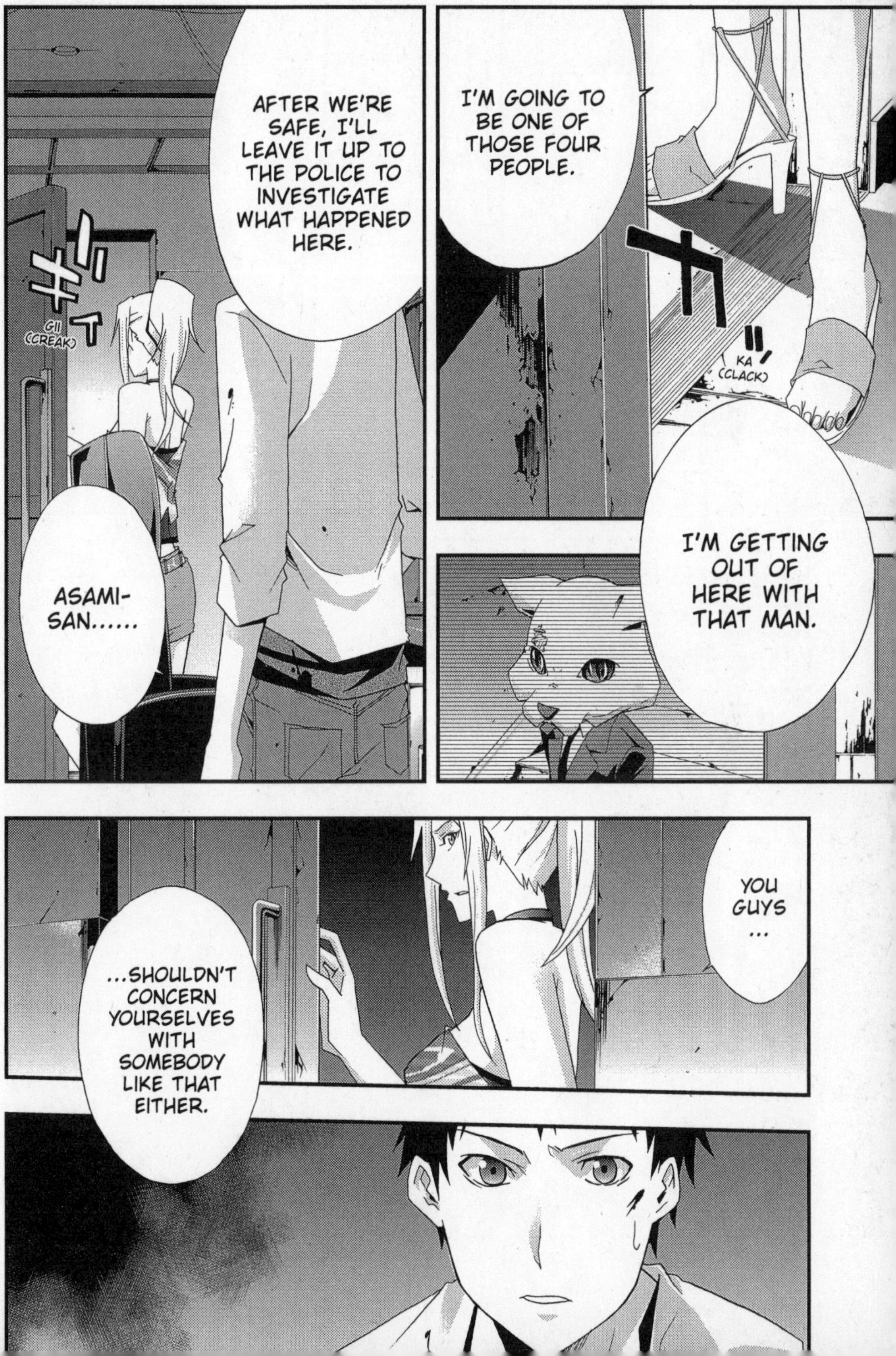
I'M GOING TO BE ONE OF THOSE FOUR PEOPLE.
KA (CLACK)
I'M GETTING OUT OF HERE WITH THAT MAN.
AFTER WE'RE SAFE, I'LL LEAVE IT UP TO THE POLICE TO INVESTIGATE WHAT HAPPENED HERE.
GII (CREAK)
ASAMI-SAN......
YOU GUYS ...
...SHOULDN'T CONCERN YOURSELVES WITH SOMEBODY LIKE THAT EITHER.

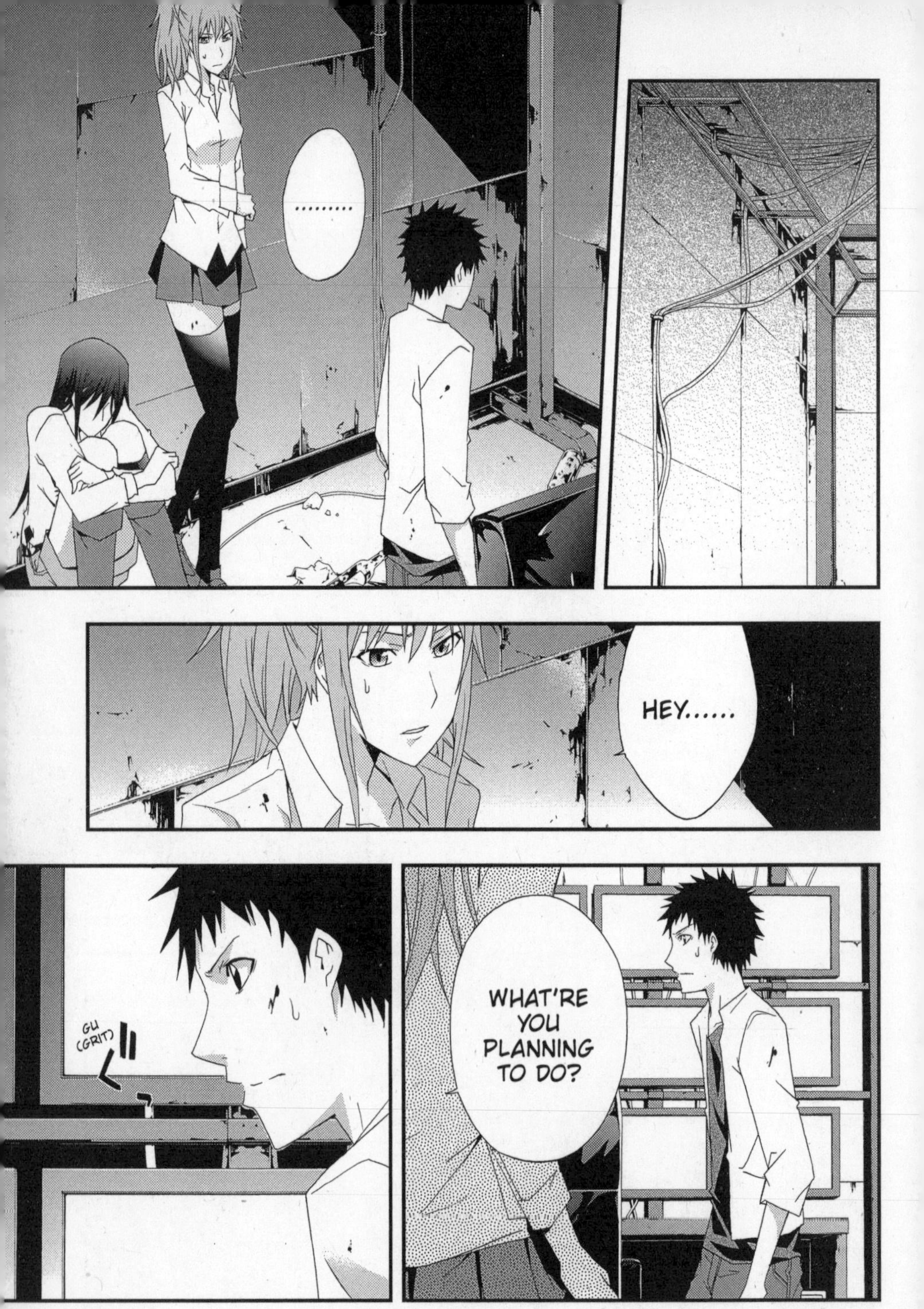
....
HEY......
WHAT'RE YOU PLANNING TO DO?
GU (GRIT)

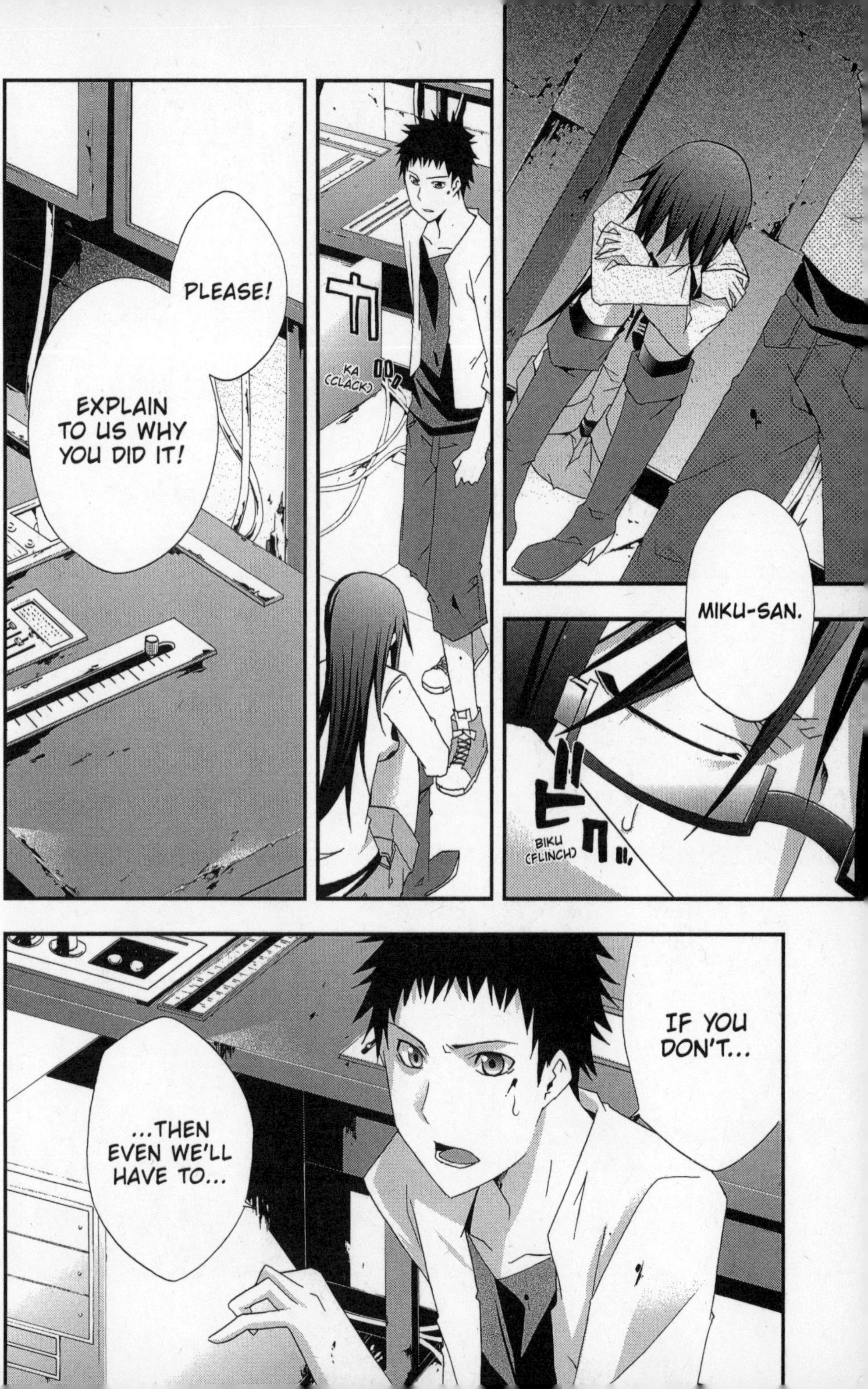
MIKU-SAN.
BIKU (FLINCH)
KA (CLACK)
PLEASE!
EXPLAIN TO US WHY YOU DID IT!
IF YOU DON'T...
...THEN EVEN WE'LL HAVE TO...

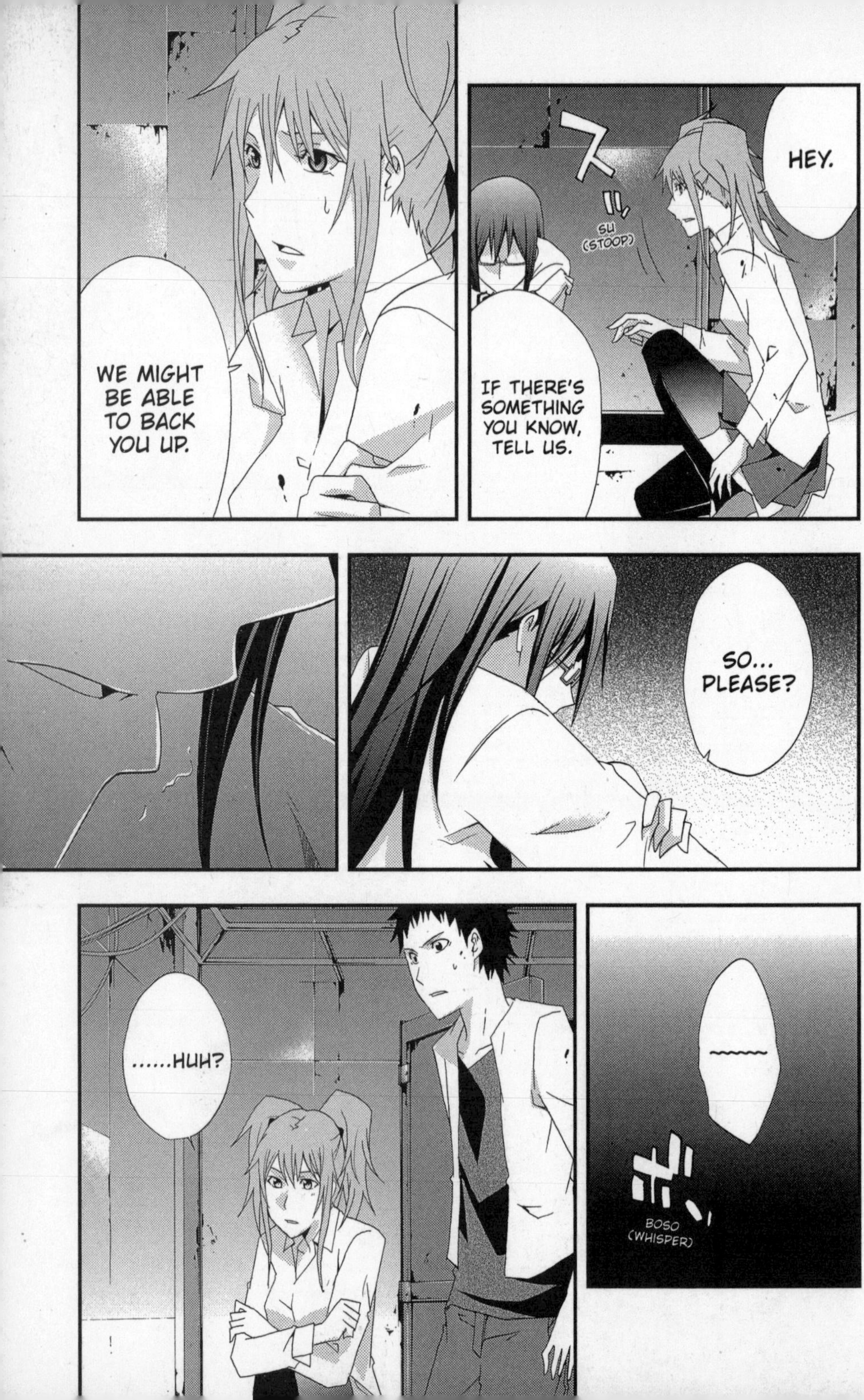
HEY.
スル
SU (STOOP)
IF THERE'S SOMETHING YOU KNOW, TELL US.
WE MIGHT BE ABLE TO BACK YOU UP.
SO... PLEASE?
~~~~~
ボソ
BOSO (WHISPER)
......HUH?
~~~~~

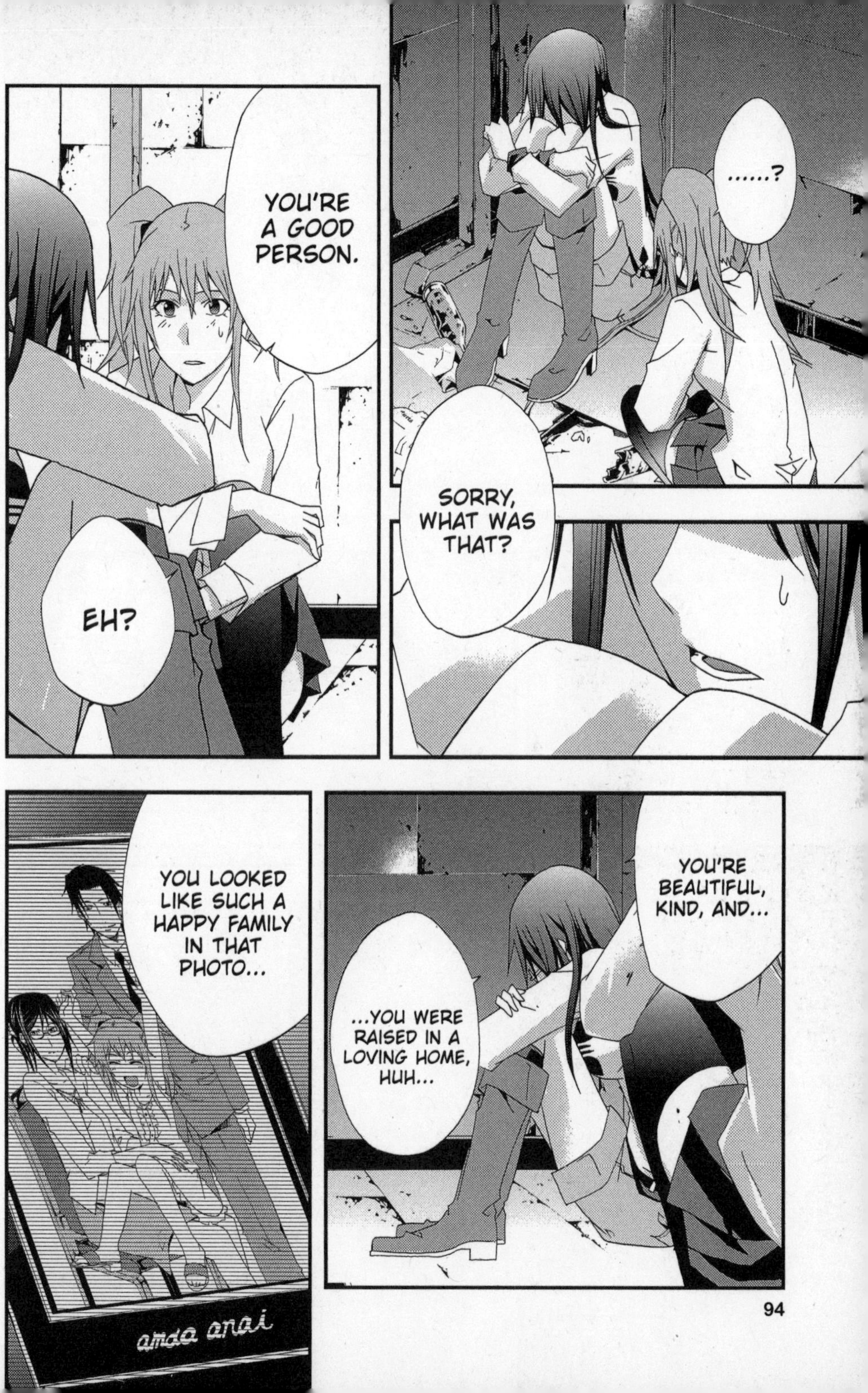
......?
SORRY, WHAT WAS THAT?
YOU'RE A GOOD PERSON.
EH?
YOU'RE BEAUTIFUL, KIND, AND...
...YOU WERE RAISED IN A LOVING HOME, HUH...
YOU LOOKED LIKE SUCH A HAPPY FAMILY IN THAT PHOTO...
amda anai

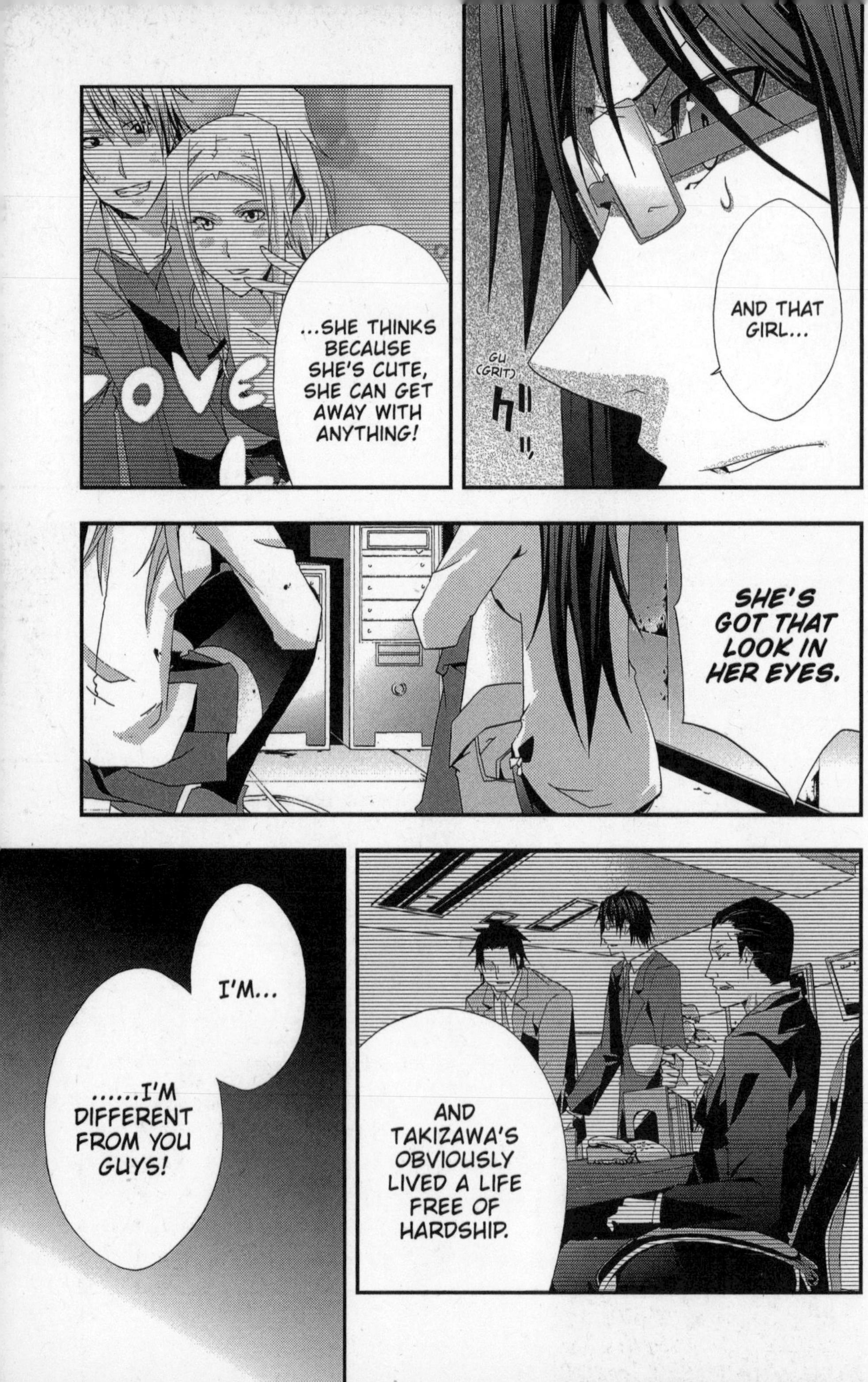
AND THAT GIRL...
GU (GRIT)
...SHE THINKS BECAUSE SHE'S CUTE, SHE CAN GET AWAY WITH ANYTHING!
SHE'S GOT THAT LOOK IN HER EYES.
AND TAKIZAWA'S OBVIOUSLY LIVED A LIFE FREE OF HARDSHIP.
I'M...
......I'M DIFFERENT FROM YOU GUYS!

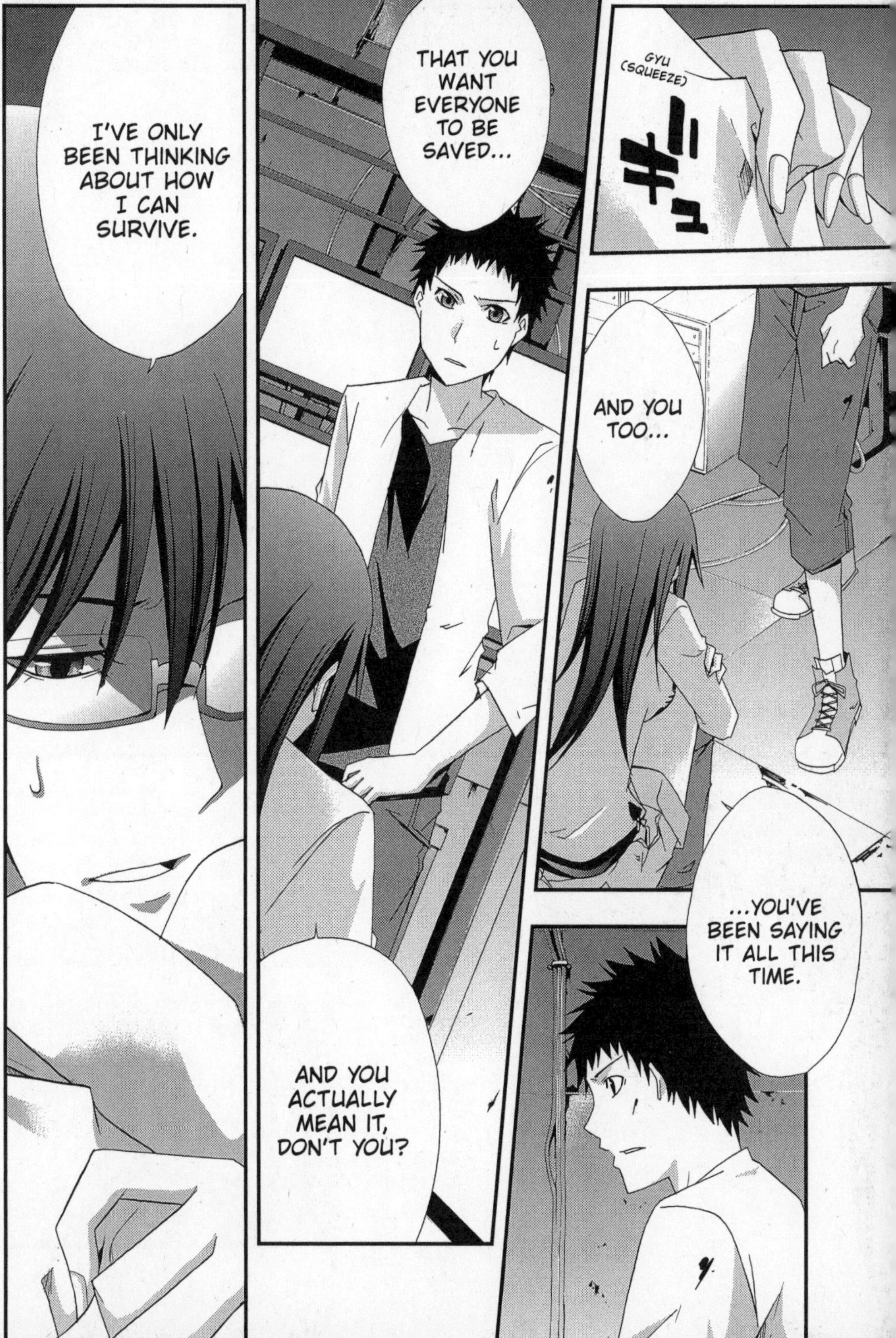
GYU (SQUEEZE)
ギュ
AND YOU TOO...
...YOU'VE BEEN SAYING IT ALL THIS TIME.
THAT YOU WANT EVERYONE TO BE SAVED...
AND YOU ACTUALLY MEAN IT, DON'T YOU?
I'VE ONLY BEEN THINKING ABOUT HOW I CAN SURVIVE.

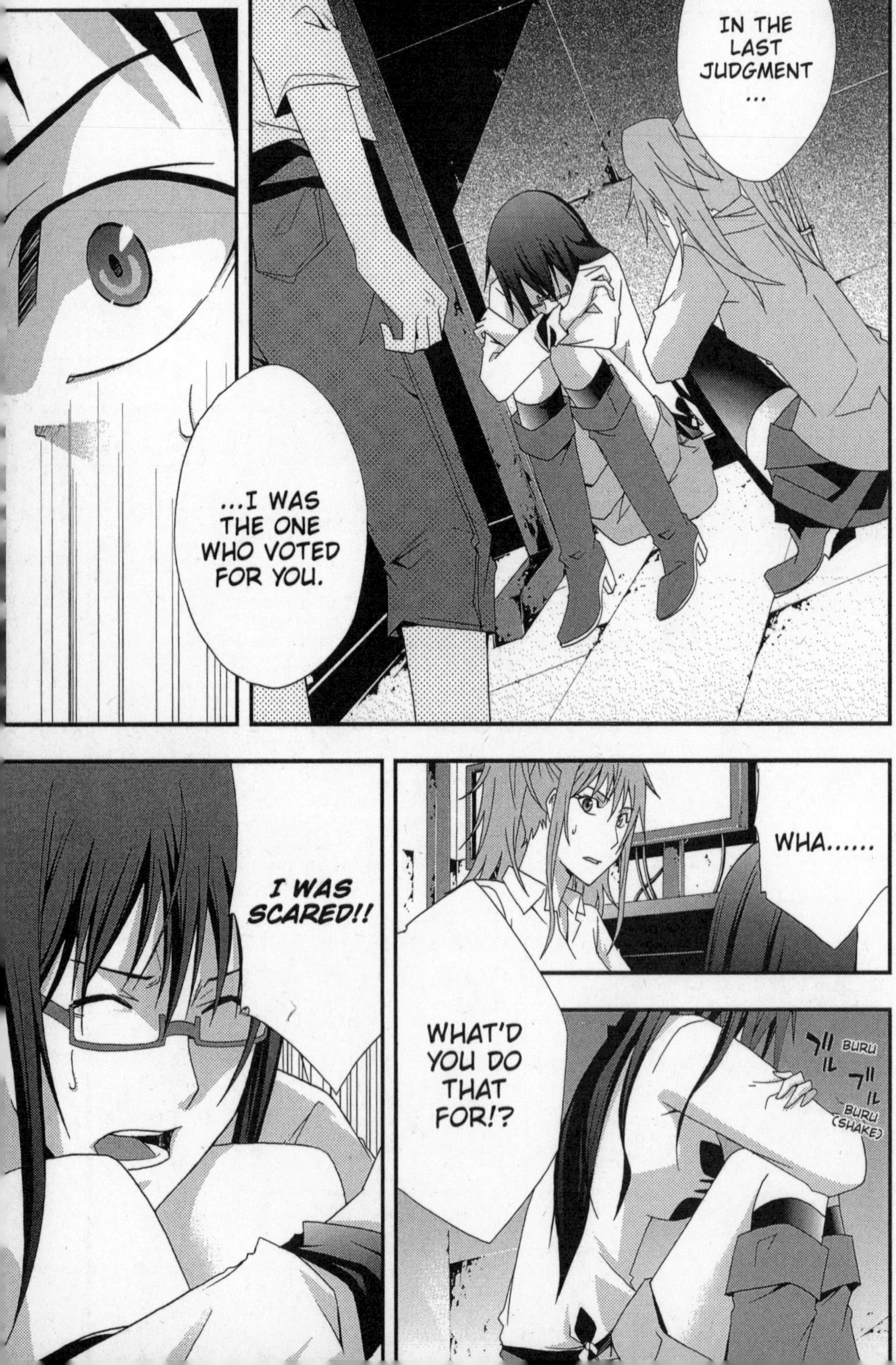
IN THE LAST JUDGMENT ...
...I WAS THE ONE WHO VOTED FOR YOU.
WHA......
WHAT'D YOU DO THAT FOR!?
BURU BURU (SHAKE)
I WAS SCARED!!

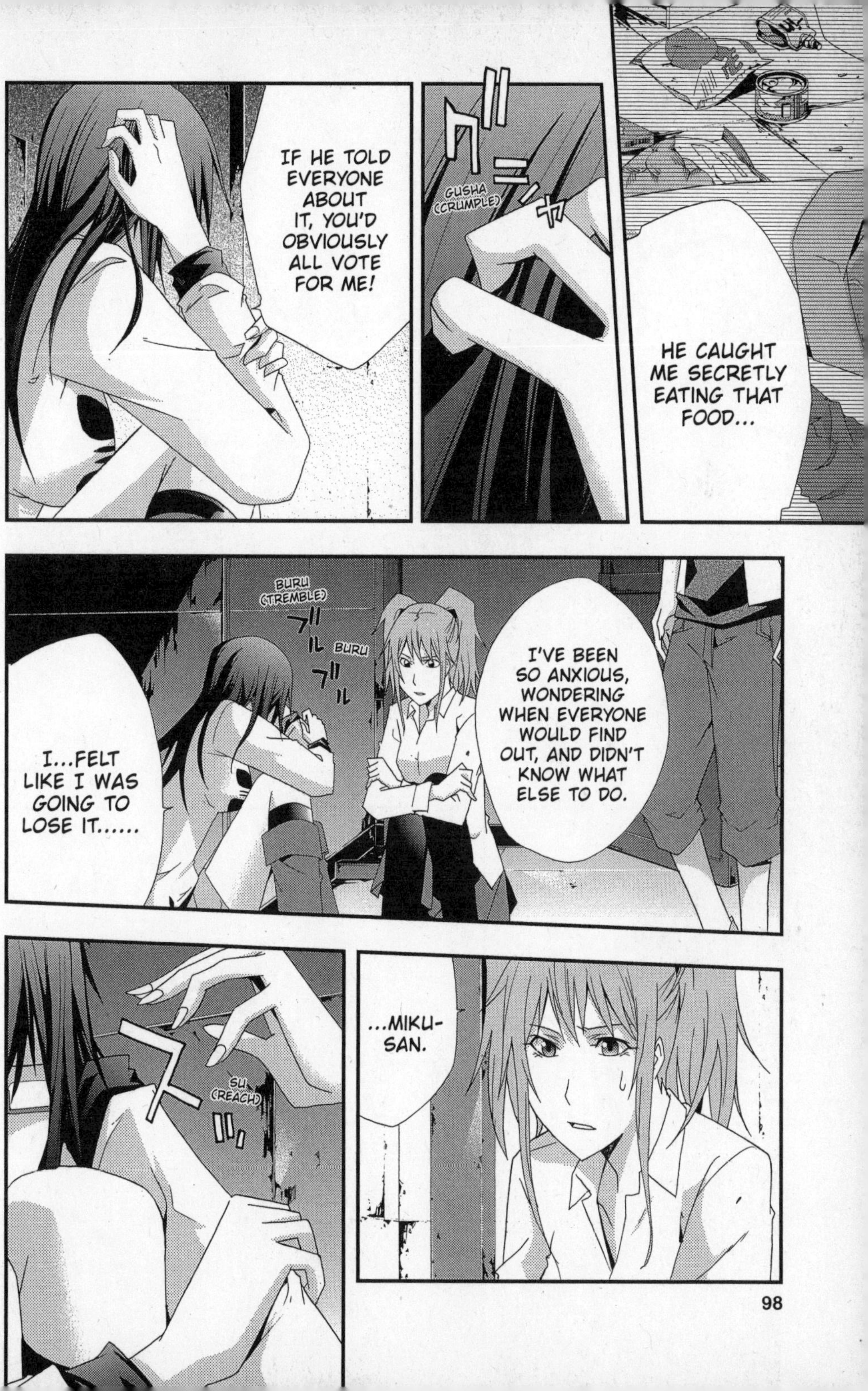
HE CAUGHT ME SECRETLY EATING THAT FOOD...
GUSHA (CRUMPLE)
IF HE TOLD EVERYONE ABOUT IT, YOU'D OBVIOUSLY ALL VOTE FOR ME!
I'VE BEEN SO ANXIOUS, WONDERING WHEN EVERYONE WOULD FIND OUT, AND DIDN'T KNOW WHAT ELSE TO DO.
BURU (TREMBLE)
BURU
I...FELT LIKE I WAS GOING TO LOSE IT......
...MIKU-SAN.
SU (REACH)

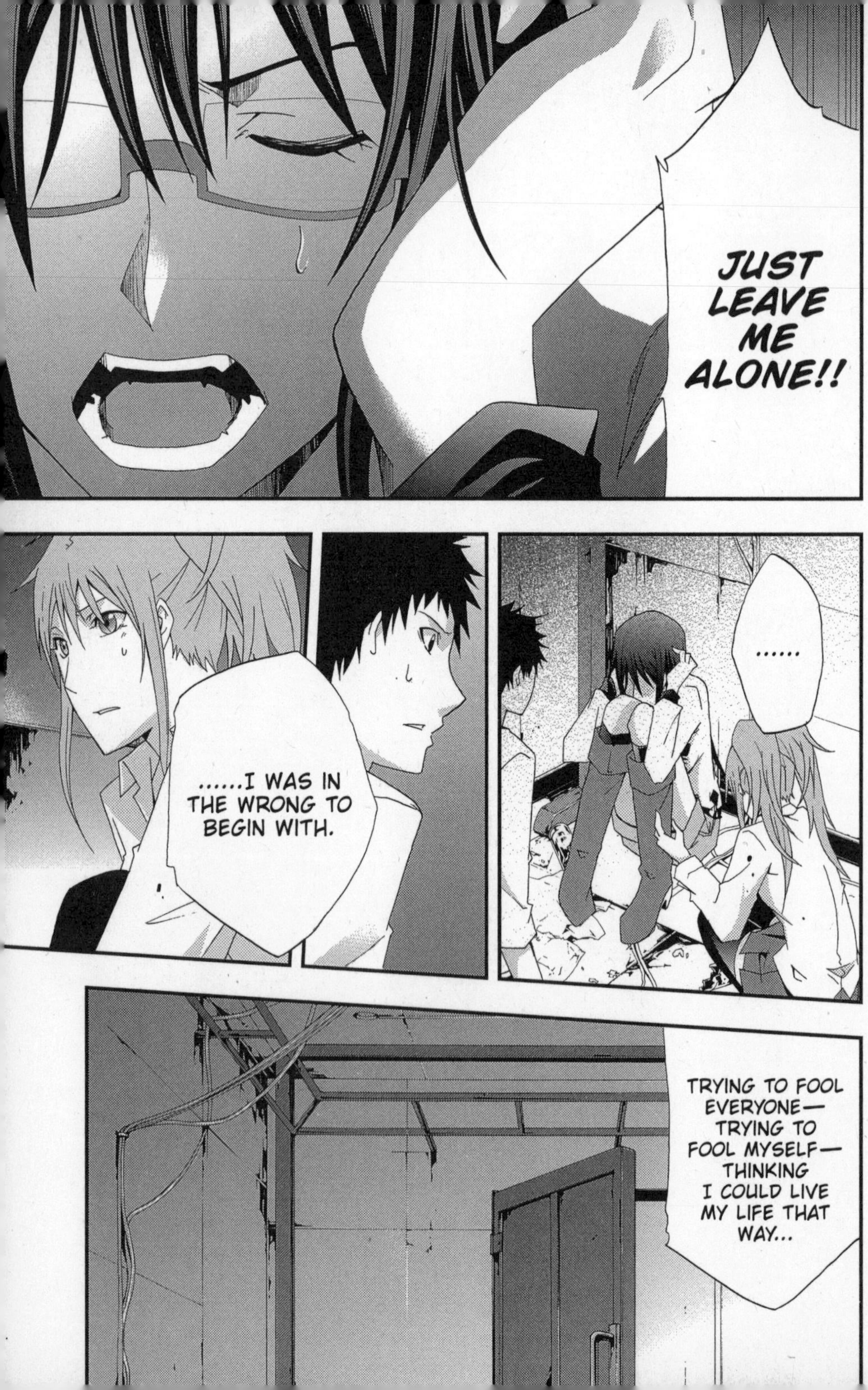
JUST LEAVE ME ALONE!!
......
......I WAS IN THE WRONG TO BEGIN WITH.
TRYING TO FOOL EVERYONE—TRYING TO FOOL MYSELF—THINKING I COULD LIVE MY LIFE THAT WAY...

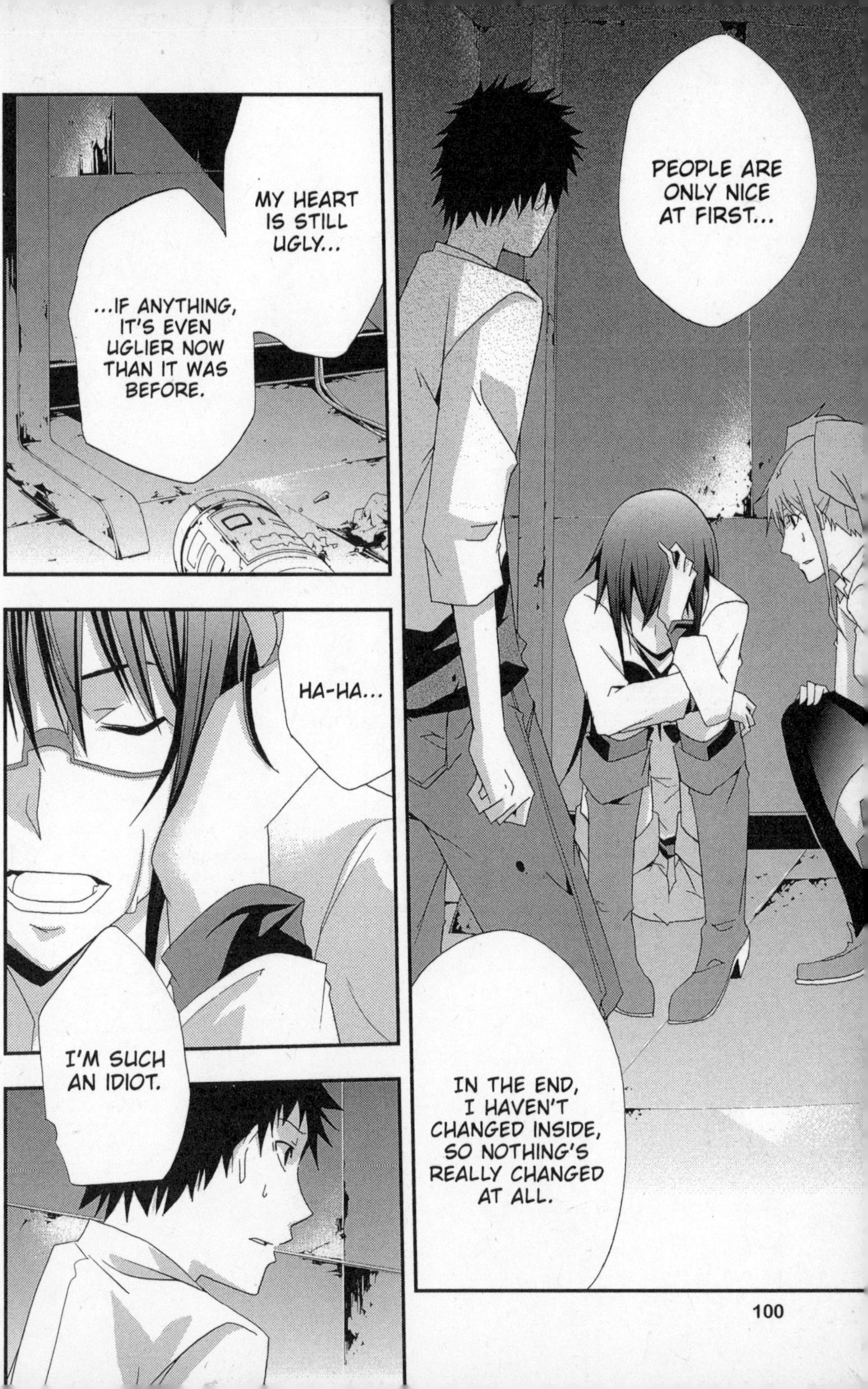
PEOPLE ARE ONLY NICE AT FIRST...
IN THE END, I HAVEN'T CHANGED INSIDE, SO NOTHING'S REALLY CHANGED AT ALL.
MY HEART IS STILL UGLY...
...IF ANYTHING, IT'S EVEN UGLIER NOW THAN IT WAS BEFORE.
HA-HA...
I'M SUCH AN IDIOT.

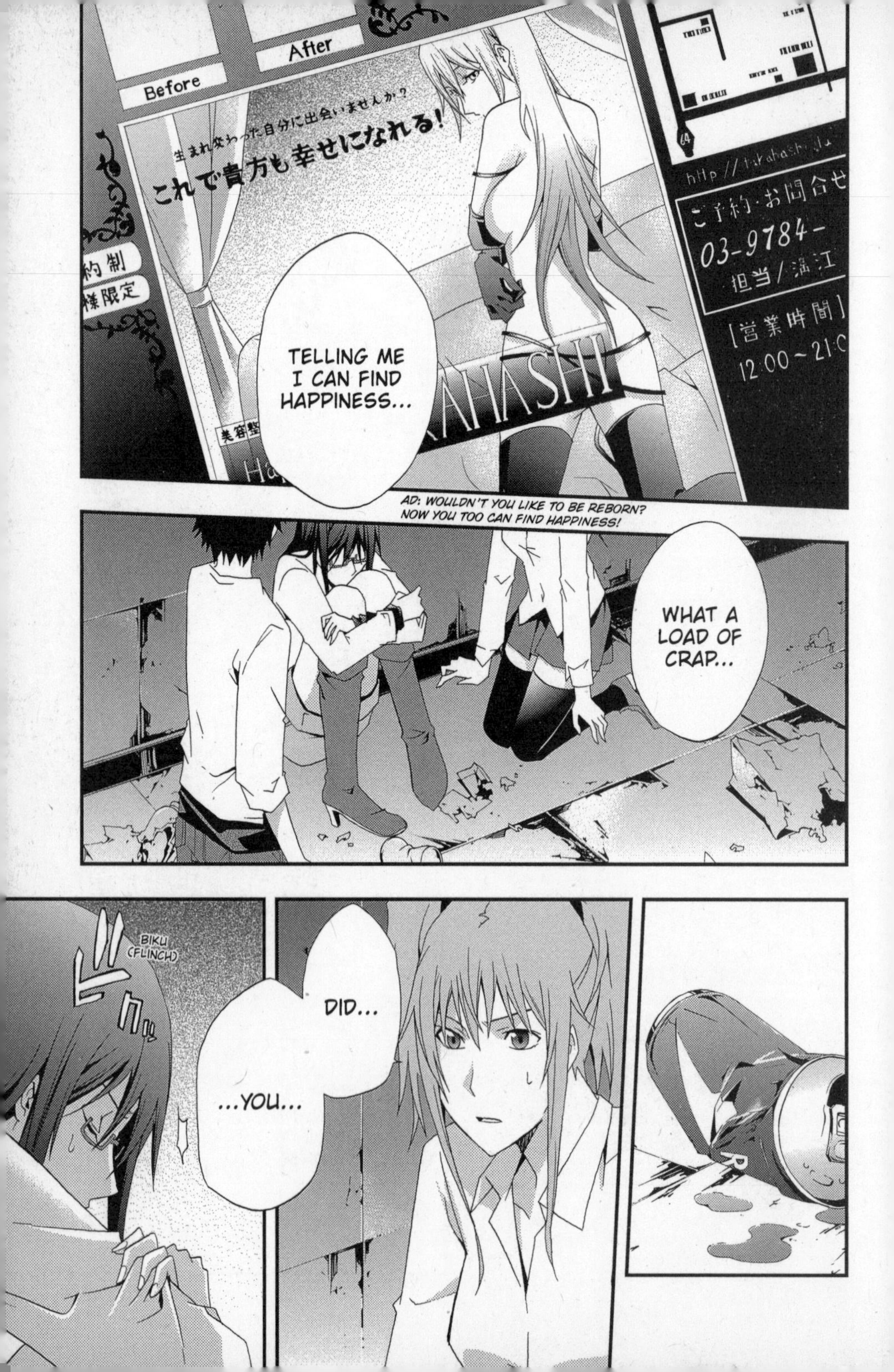
Before
After
生まれ変わった自分に出会いませんか？
これで貴方も幸せになれる！
ご予約・お問合せ
03-9784-
TELLING ME I CAN FIND HAPPINESS...
AD: WOULDN'T YOU LIKE TO BE REBORN? NOW YOU TOO CAN FIND HAPPINESS!
WHAT A LOAD OF CRAP...
DID...
...YOU...
BIKU (FLINCH)

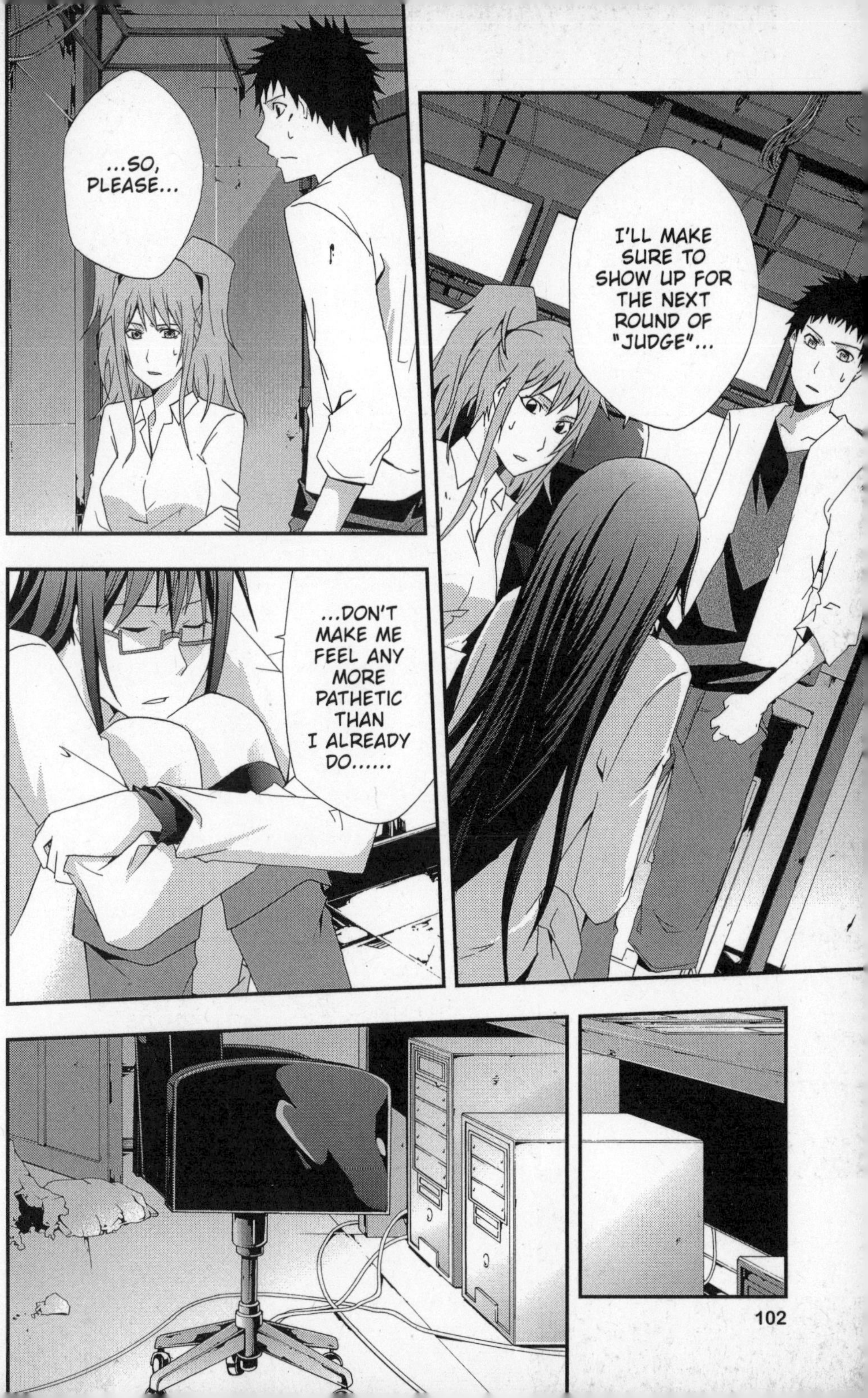
I'LL MAKE SURE TO SHOW UP FOR THE NEXT ROUND OF "JUDGE"...
...SO, PLEASE...
...DON'T MAKE ME FEEL ANY MORE PATHETIC THAN I ALREADY DO......

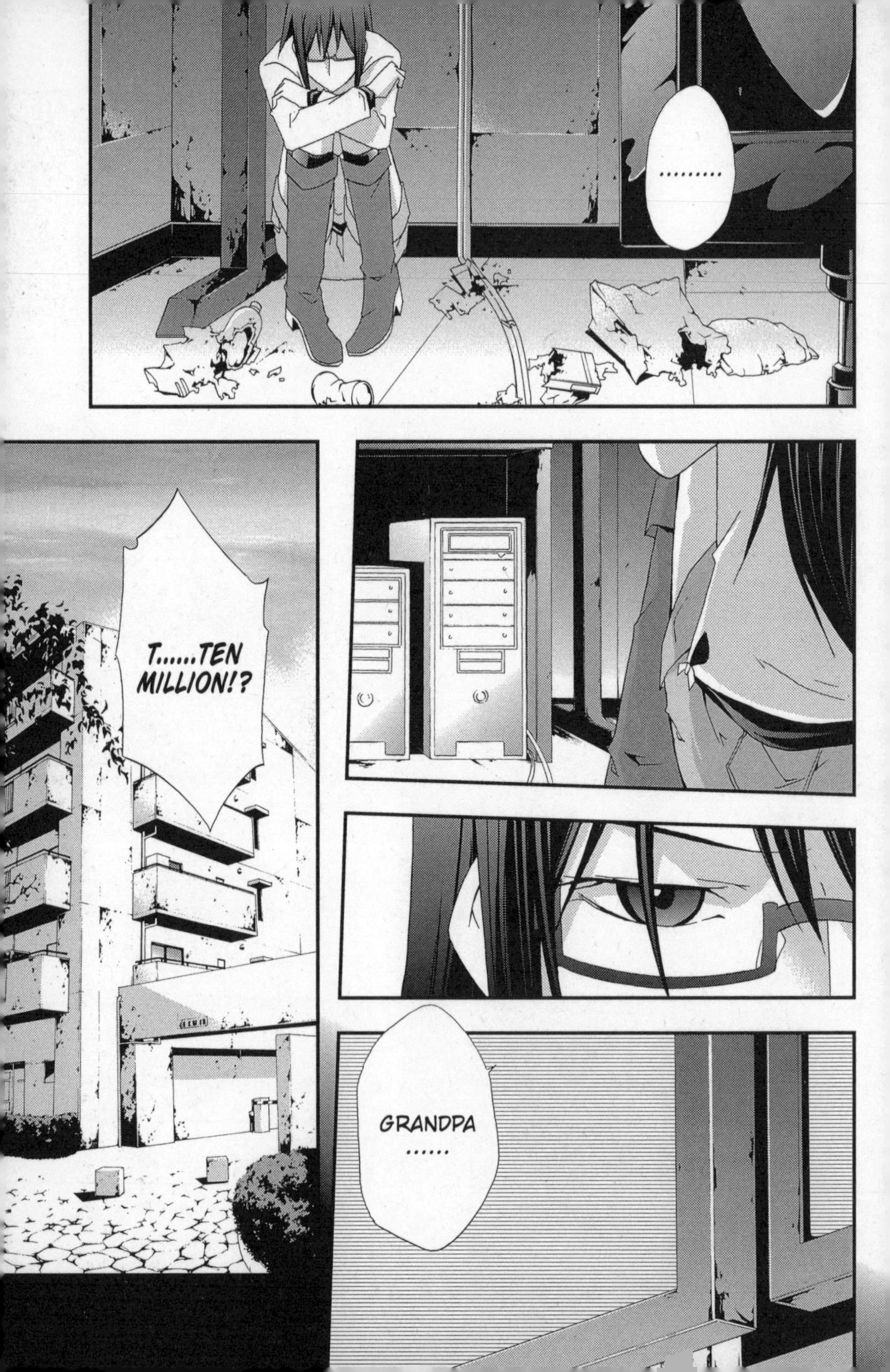
....
GRANDPA ......
T......TEN MILLION!?

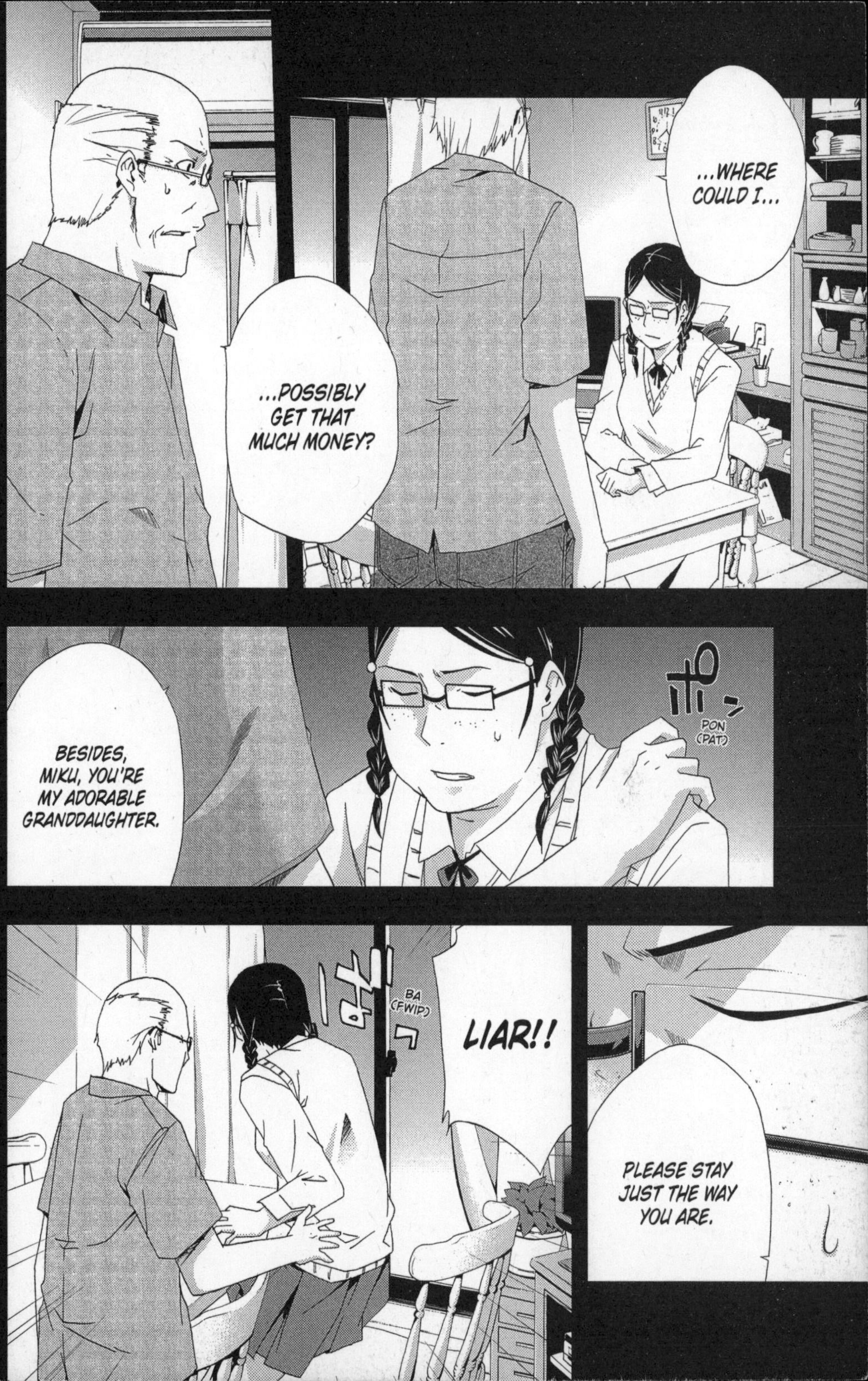
...WHERE COULD I...
...POSSIBLY GET THAT MUCH MONEY?
ポッ
PON (PAT)
BESIDES, MIKU, YOU'RE MY ADORABLE GRANDDAUGHTER.
PLEASE STAY JUST THE WAY YOU ARE.
LIAR!!
ぱっ
BA (FWIP)

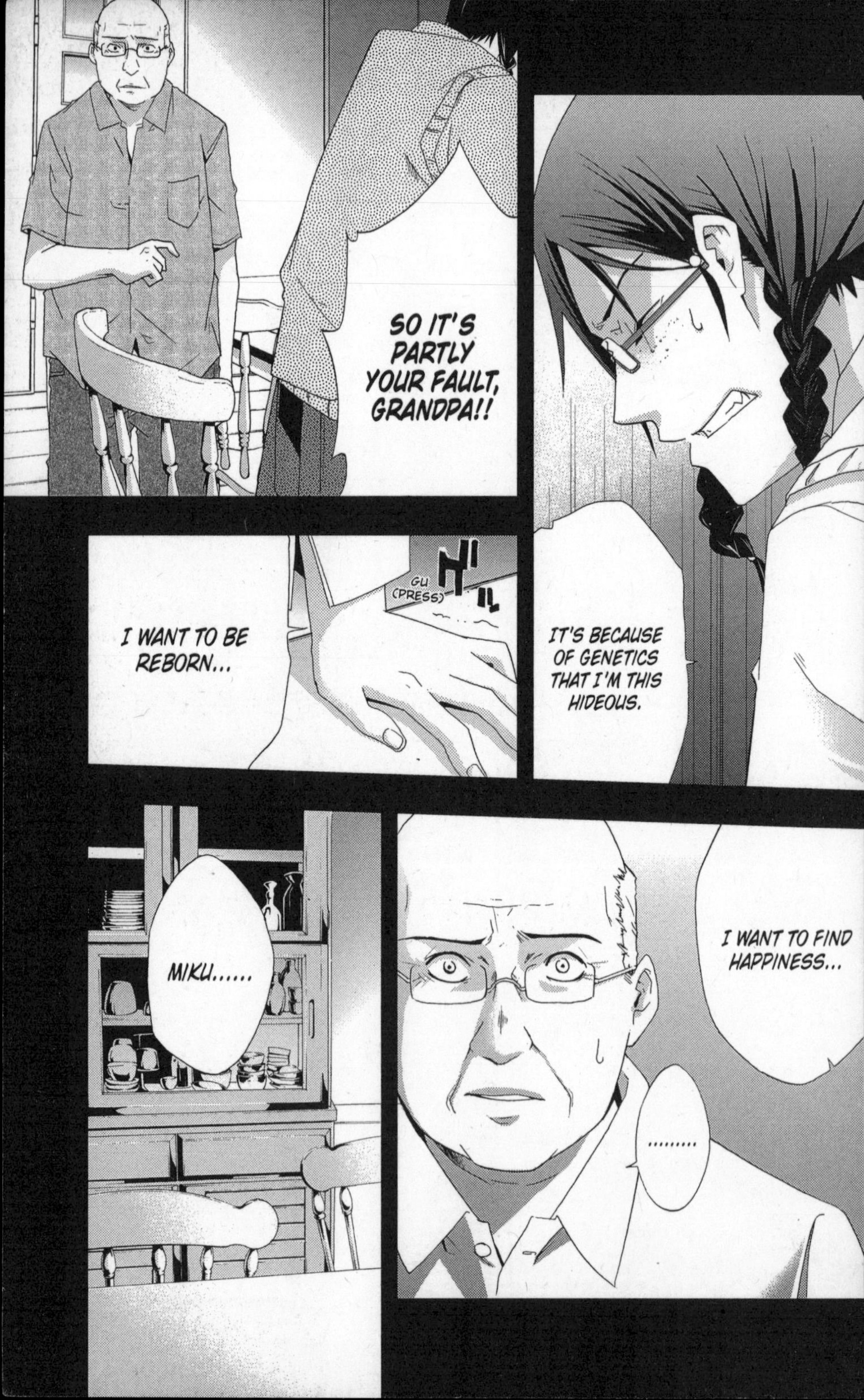
IT'S BECAUSE OF GENETICS THAT I'M THIS HIDEOUS.
SO IT'S PARTLY YOUR FAULT, GRANDPA!!
GU (PRESS)
I WANT TO BE REBORN...
I WANT TO FIND HAPPINESS...
....
MIKU......

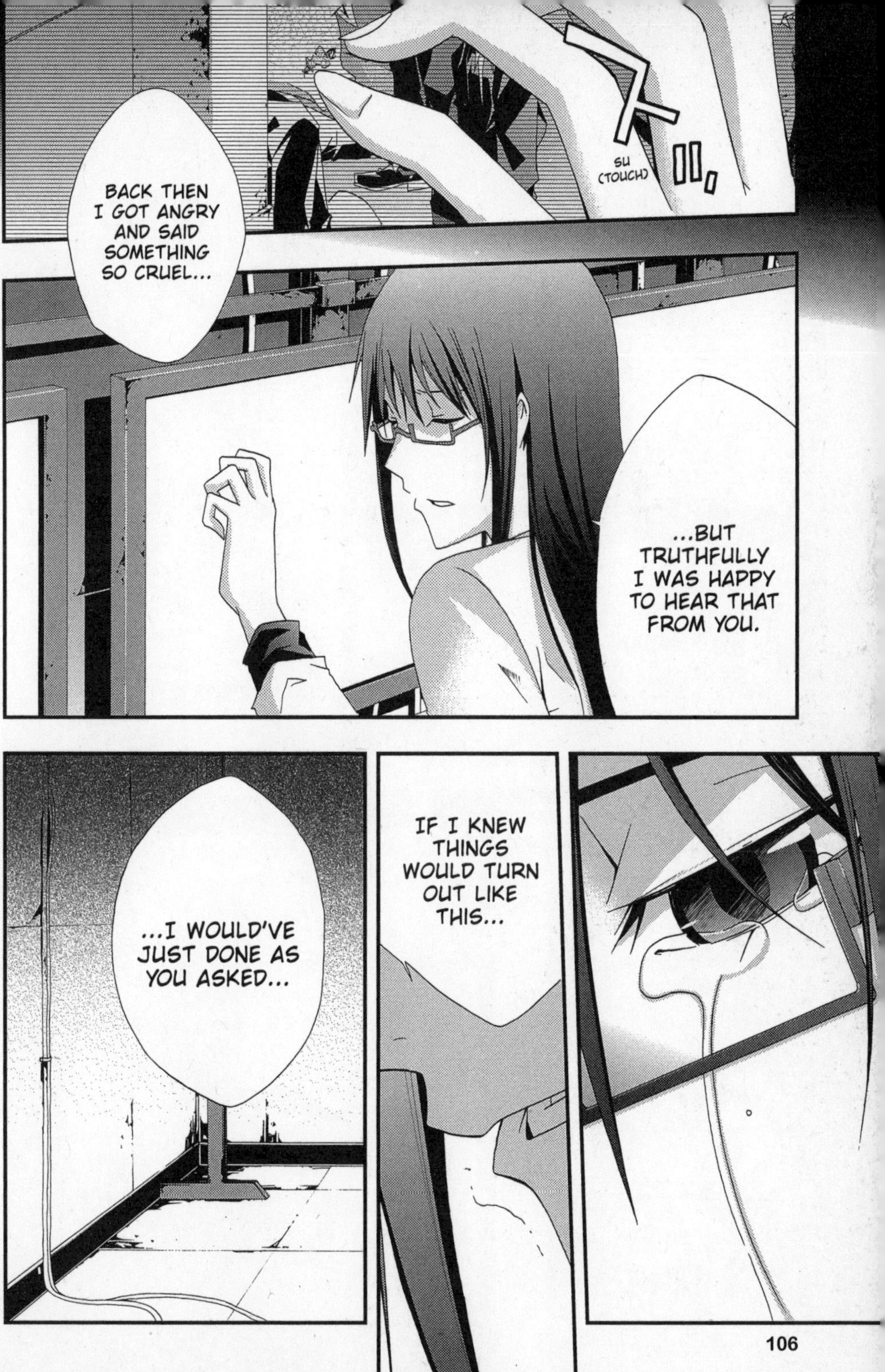
SU (TOUCH)
BACK THEN I GOT ANGRY AND SAID SOMETHING SO CRUEL...
...BUT TRUTHFULLY I WAS HAPPY TO HEAR THAT FROM YOU.
IF I KNEW THINGS WOULD TURN OUT LIKE THIS...
...I WOULD'VE JUST DONE AS YOU ASKED...

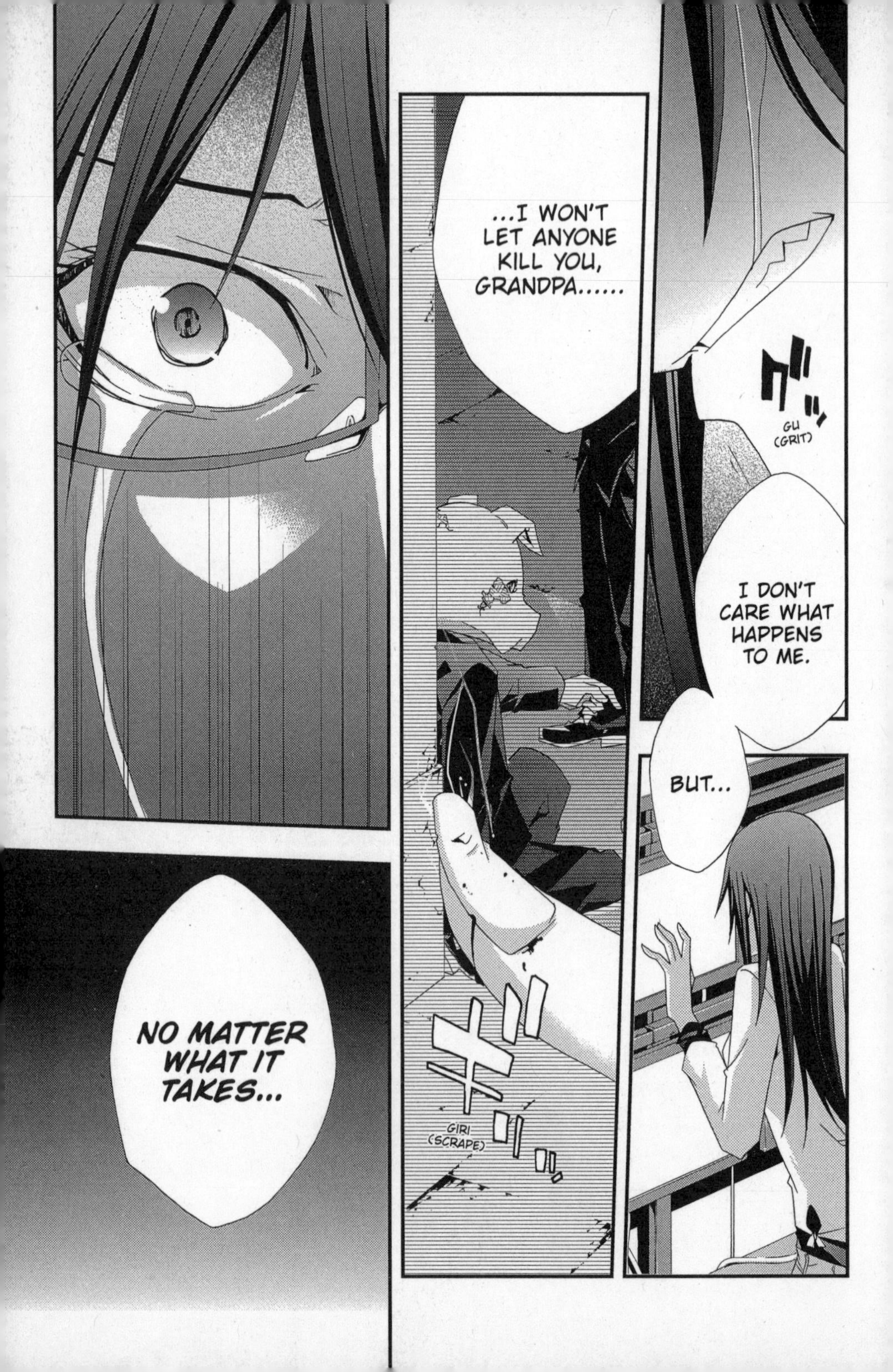

GU (GRIT)
I DON'T CARE WHAT HAPPENS TO ME.
BUT...
...I WON'T LET ANYONE KILL YOU, GRANDPA......
GIRI (SCRAPE)
NO MATTER WHAT IT TAKES...

JUDGE

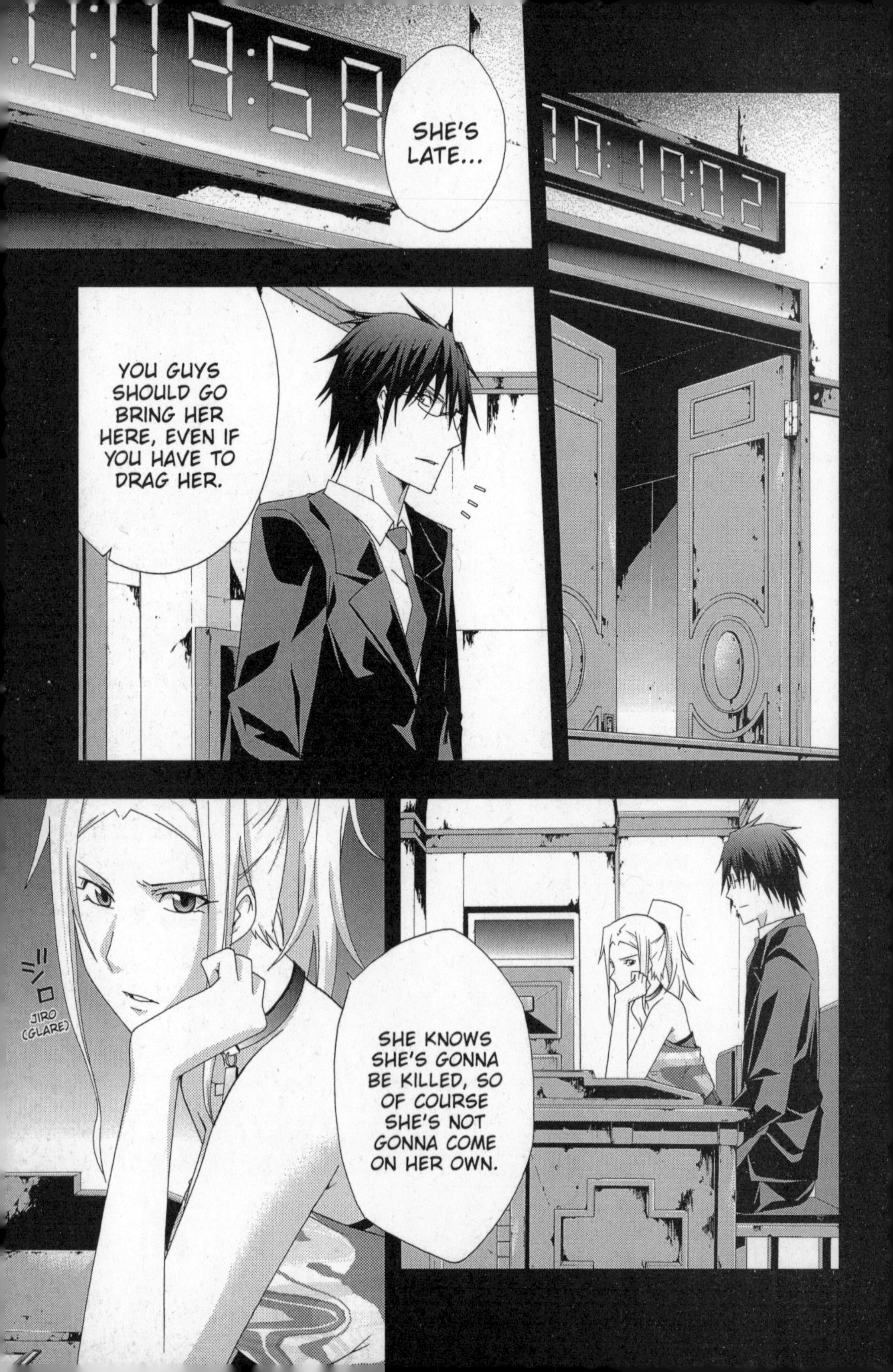
SHE'S LATE...
YOU GUYS SHOULD GO BRING HER HERE, EVEN IF YOU HAVE TO DRAG HER.
SHE KNOWS SHE'S GONNA BE KILLED, SO OF COURSE SHE'S NOT GONNA COME ON HER OWN.
JIRO (GLARE)

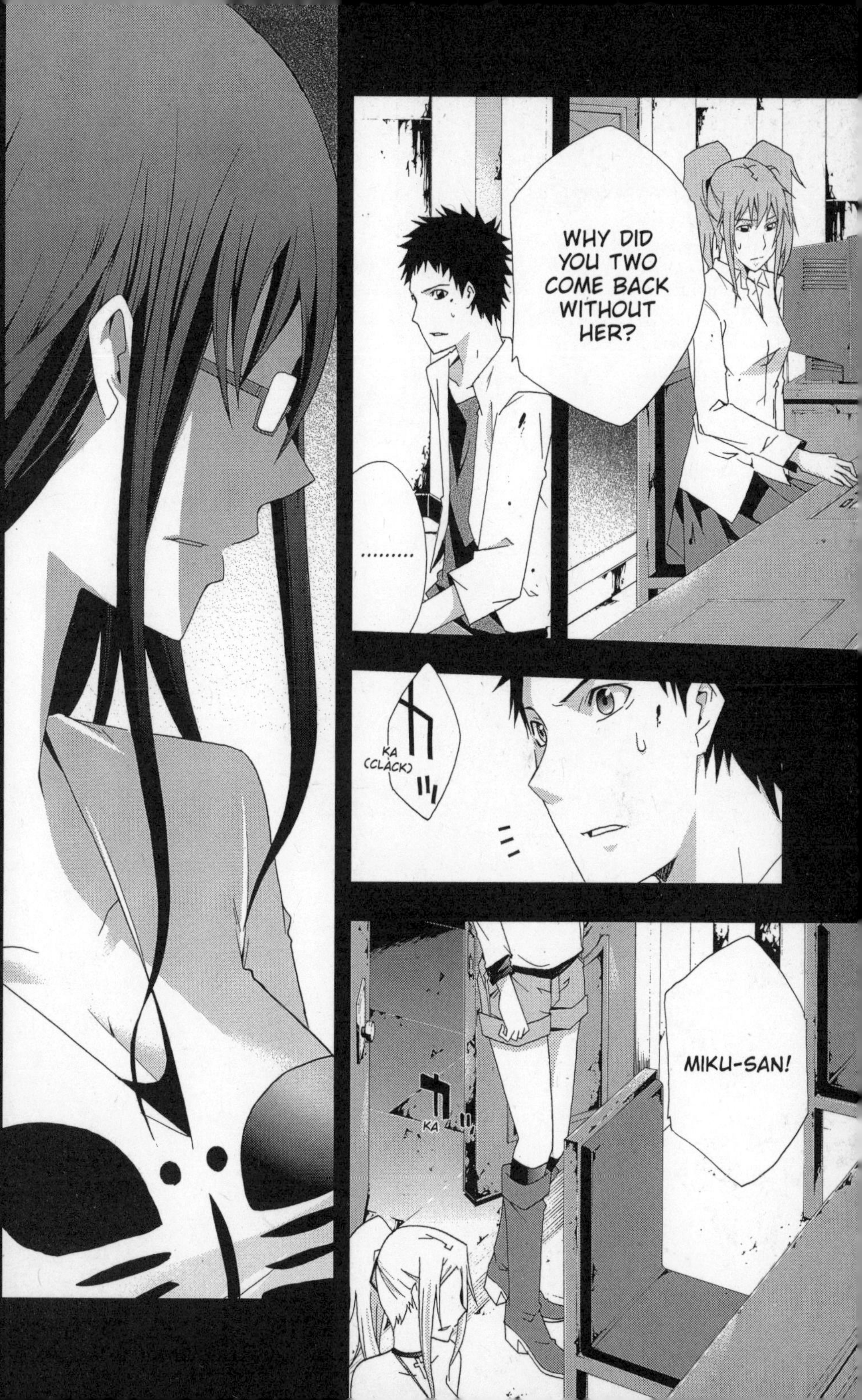
WHY DID YOU TWO COME BACK WITHOUT HER?
....
KA (CLACK)
MIKU-SAN!
KA

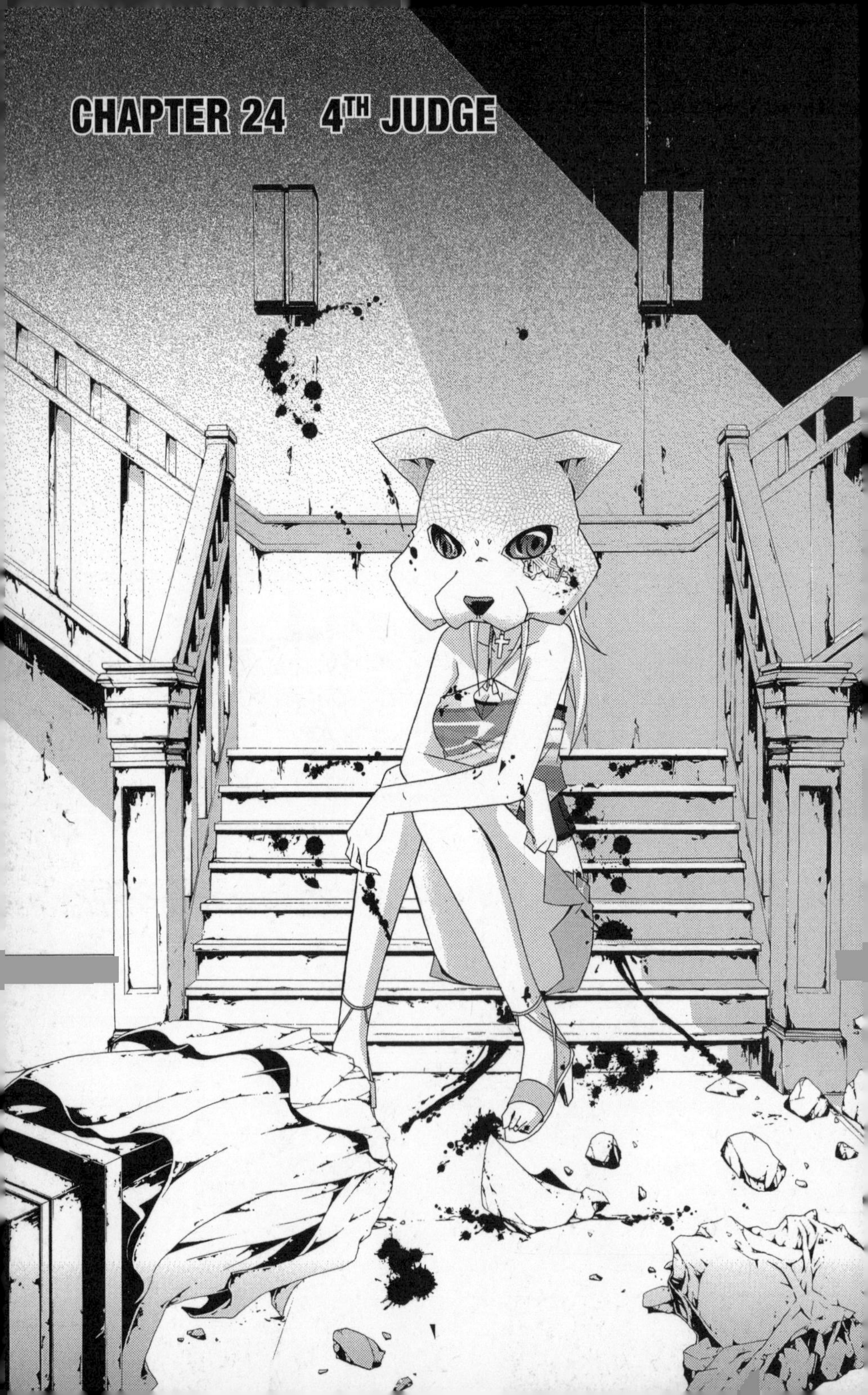
CHAPTER 24 4TH JUDGE

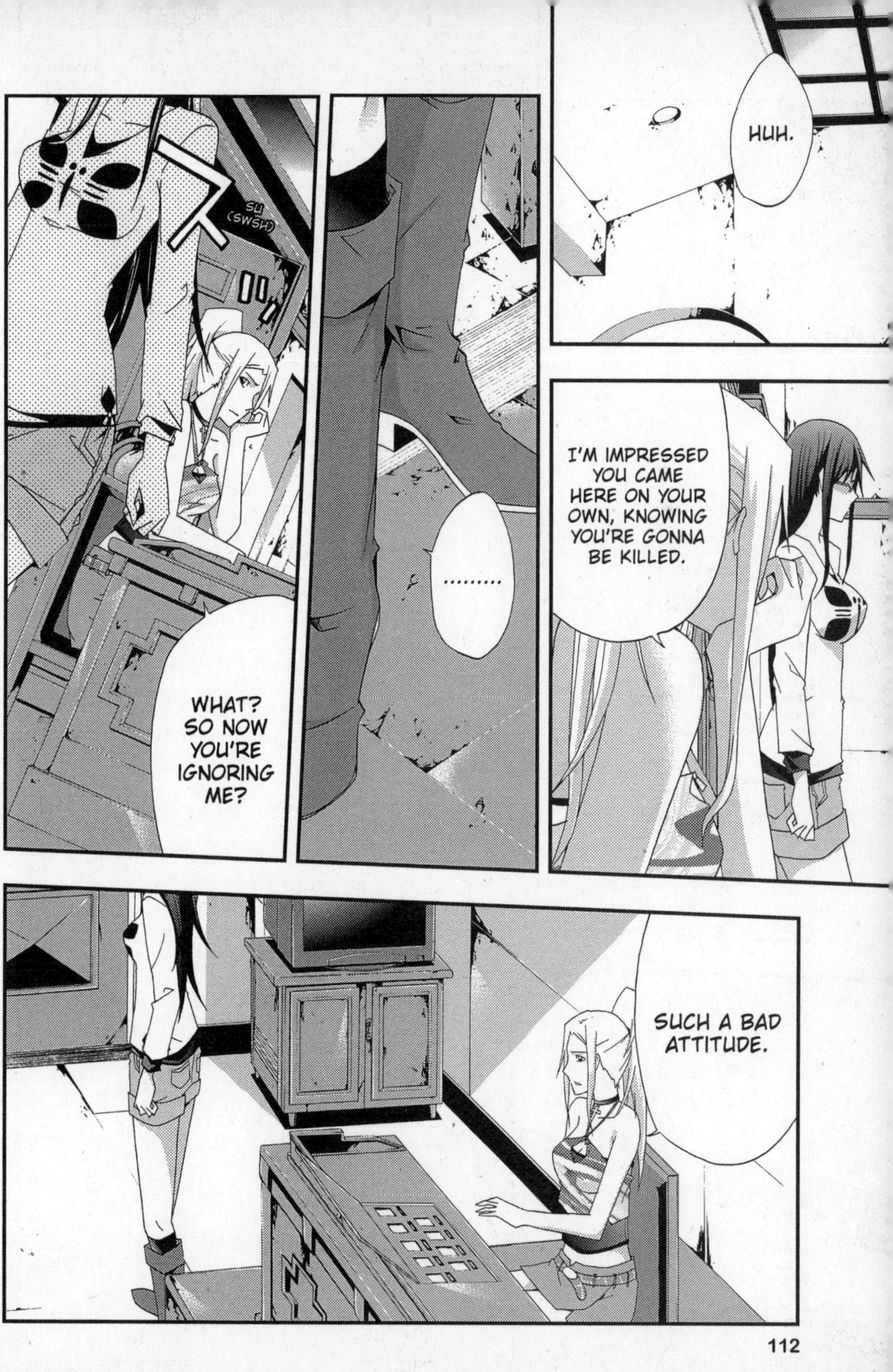
HUH.
I'M IMPRESSED YOU CAME HERE ON YOUR OWN, KNOWING YOU'RE GONNA BE KILLED.
....
SU (SWSH)
WHAT? SO NOW YOU'RE IGNORING ME?
SUCH A BAD ATTITUDE.

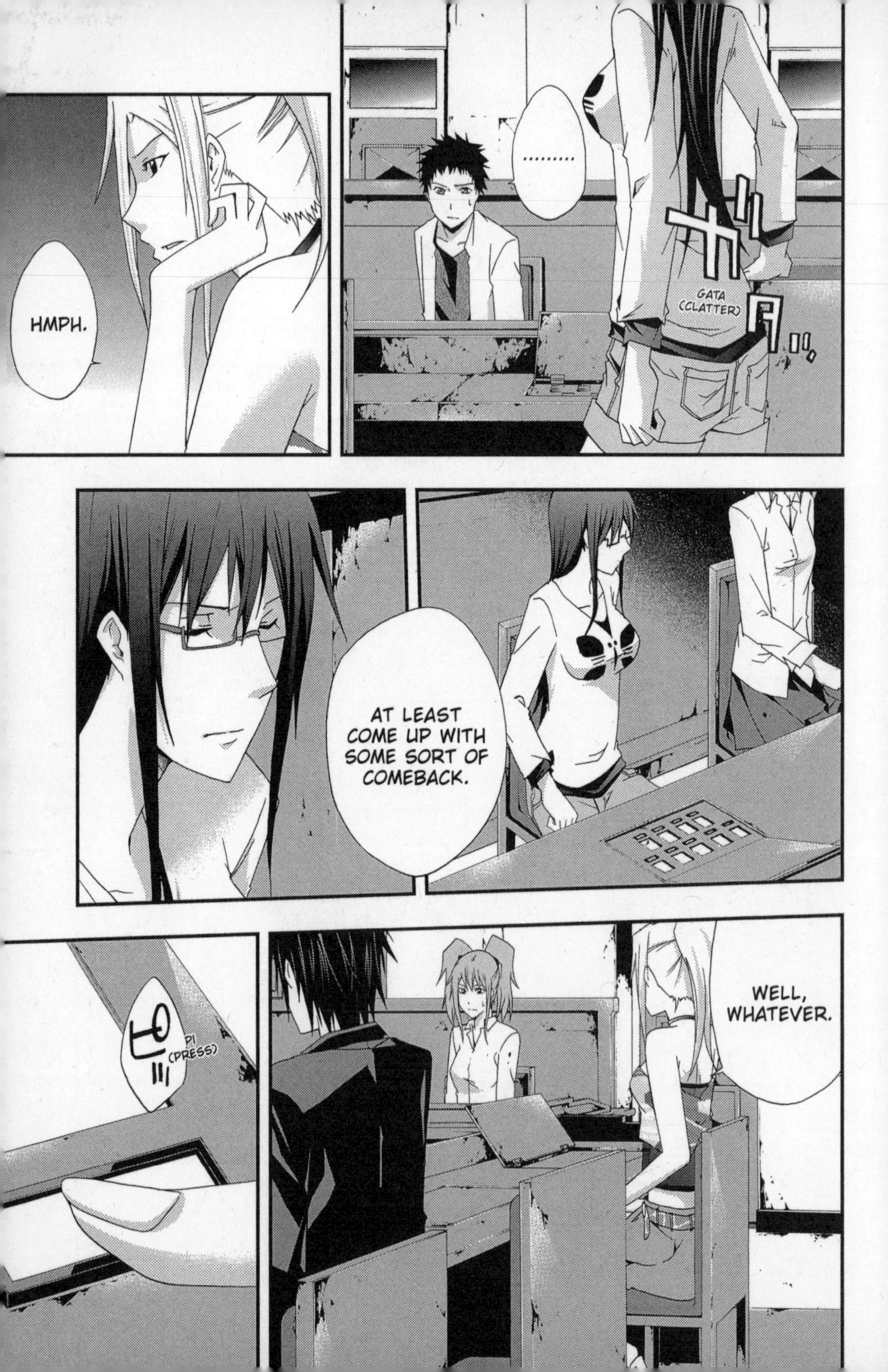
....
GATA (CLATTER)
HMPH.
AT LEAST COME UP WITH SOME SORT OF COMEBACK.
WELL, WHATEVER.
PI (PRESS)

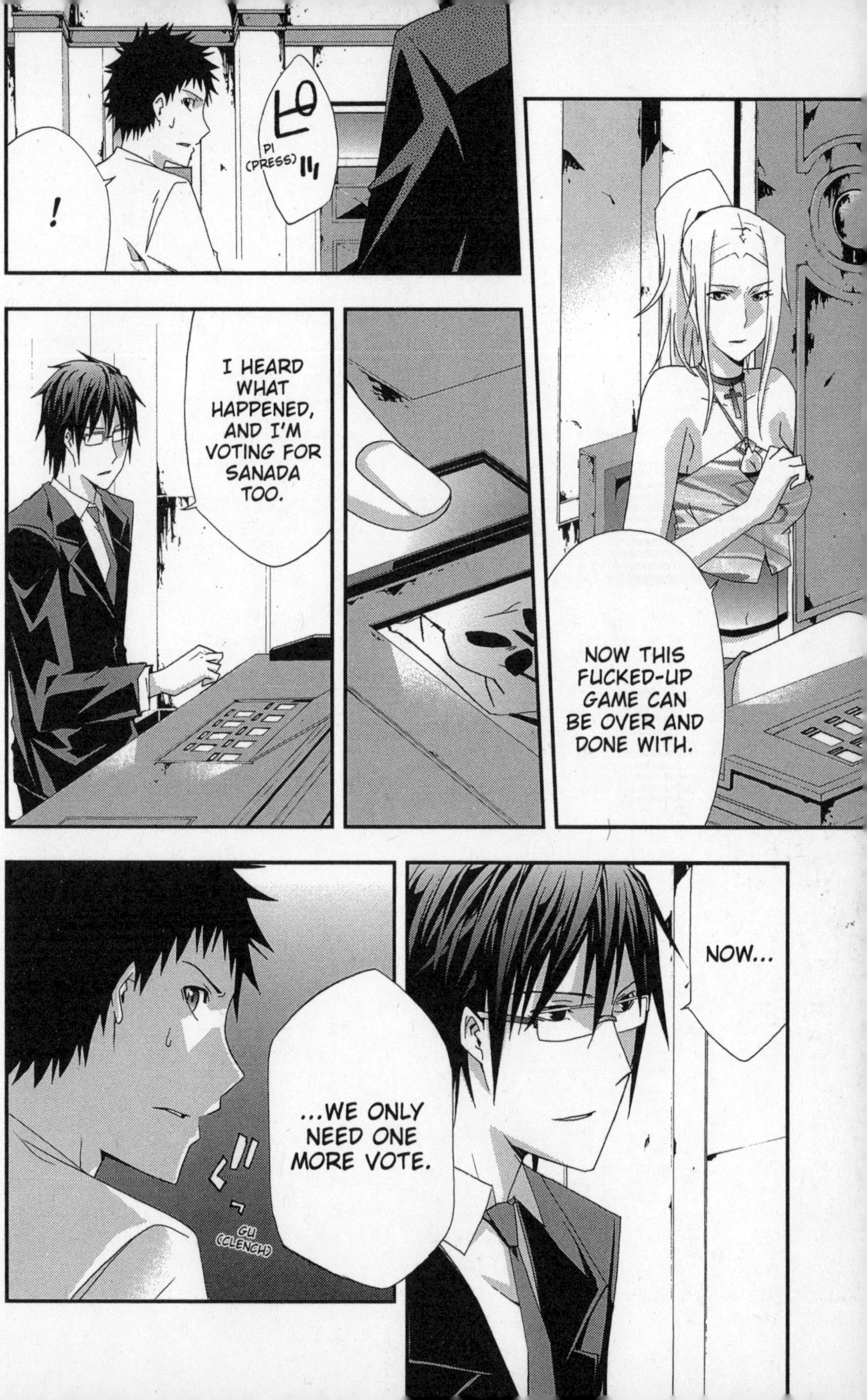
NOW THIS FUCKED-UP GAME CAN BE OVER AND DONE WITH.
PI (PRESS)
!
I HEARD WHAT HAPPENED, AND I'M VOTING FOR SANADA TOO.
NOW...
...WE ONLY NEED ONE MORE VOTE.
GU (CLENCH)

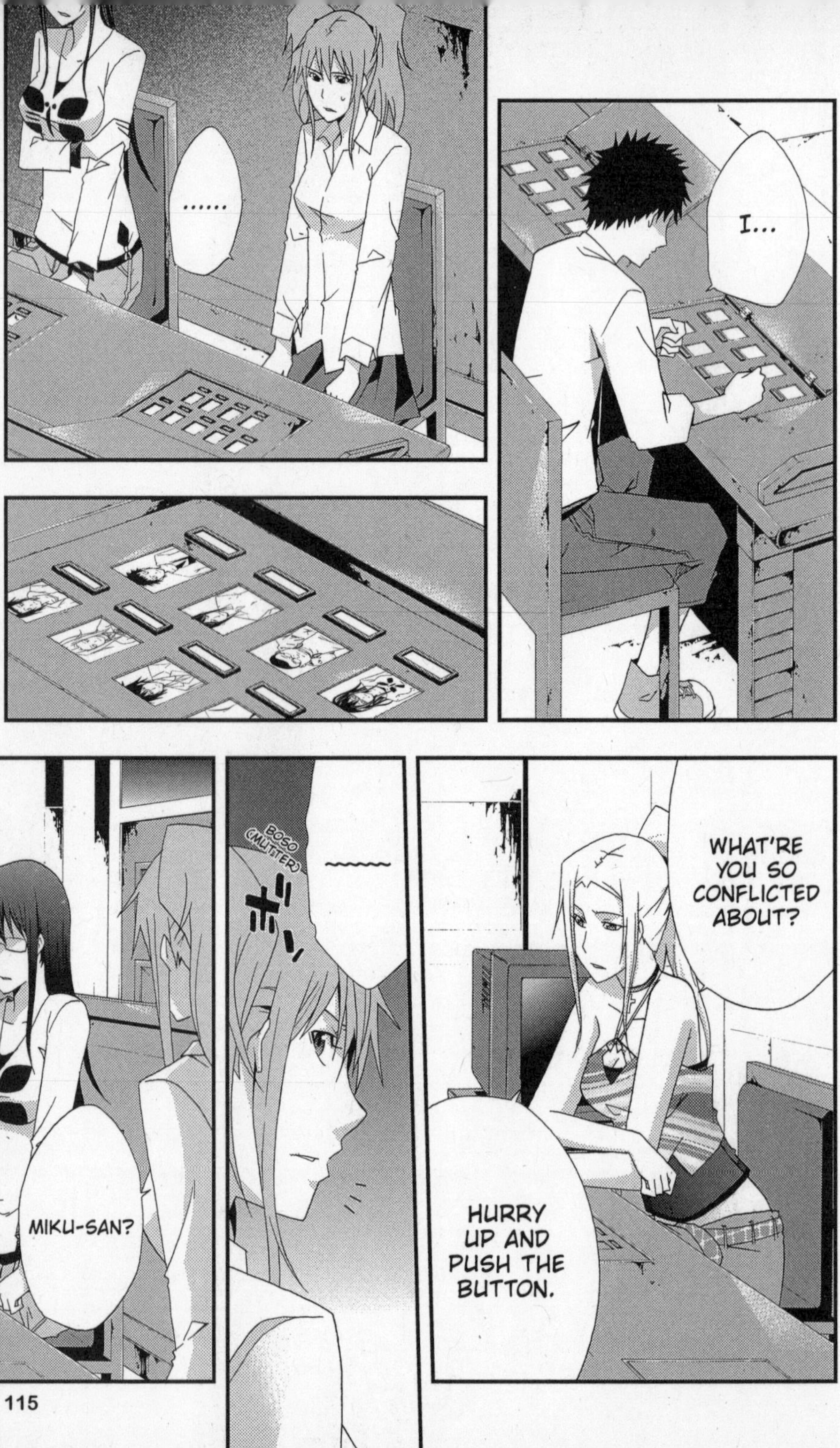
I...
......
WHAT'RE YOU SO CONFLICTED ABOUT?
HURRY UP AND PUSH THE BUTTON.
BOSO (MUTTER)
~~~~~
MIKU-SAN?
~~~~~

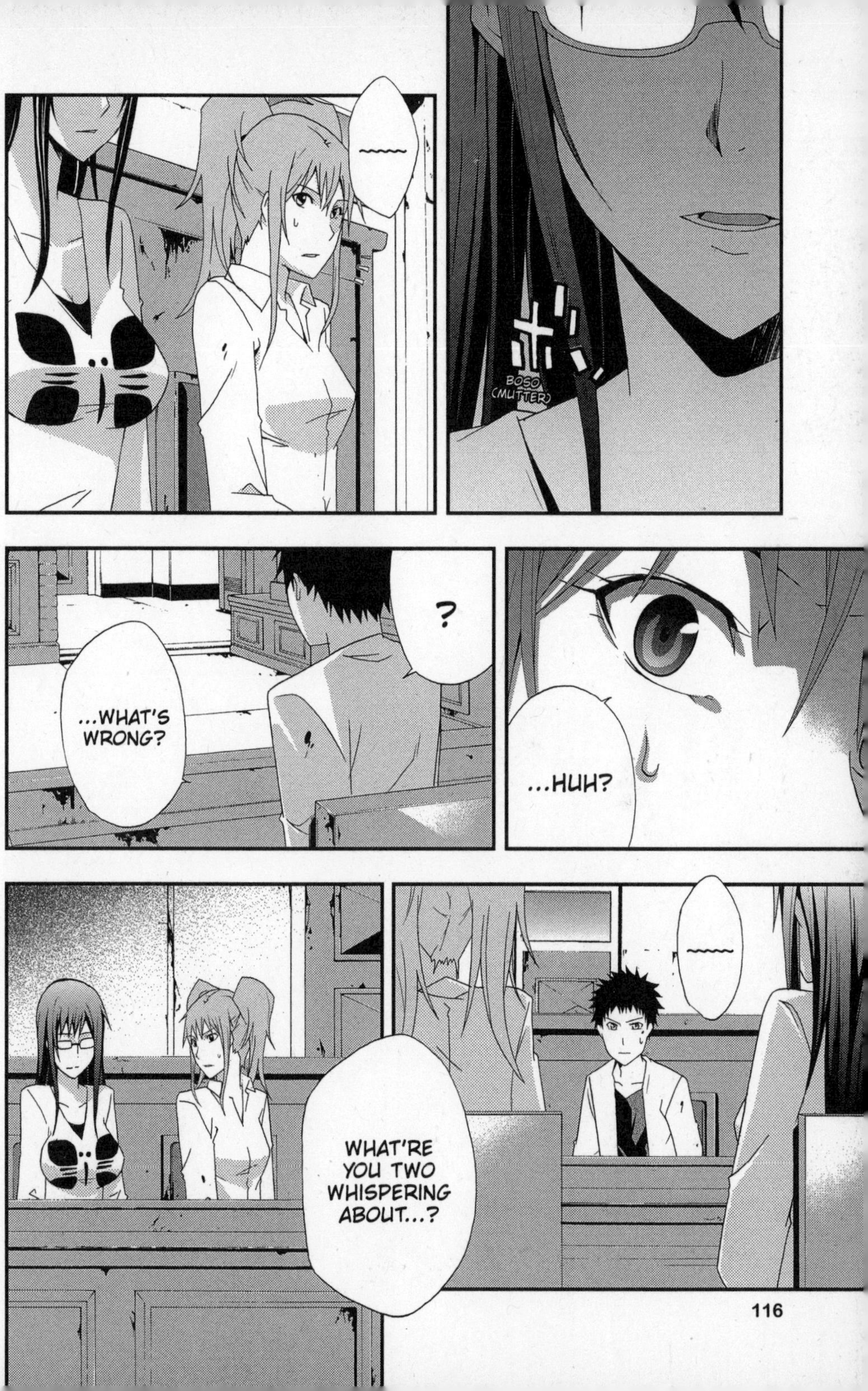

BOSO (MUTTER)
~~~~
...HUH?
?
...WHAT'S WRONG?
~~~~
WHAT'RE YOU TWO WHISPERING ABOUT...?

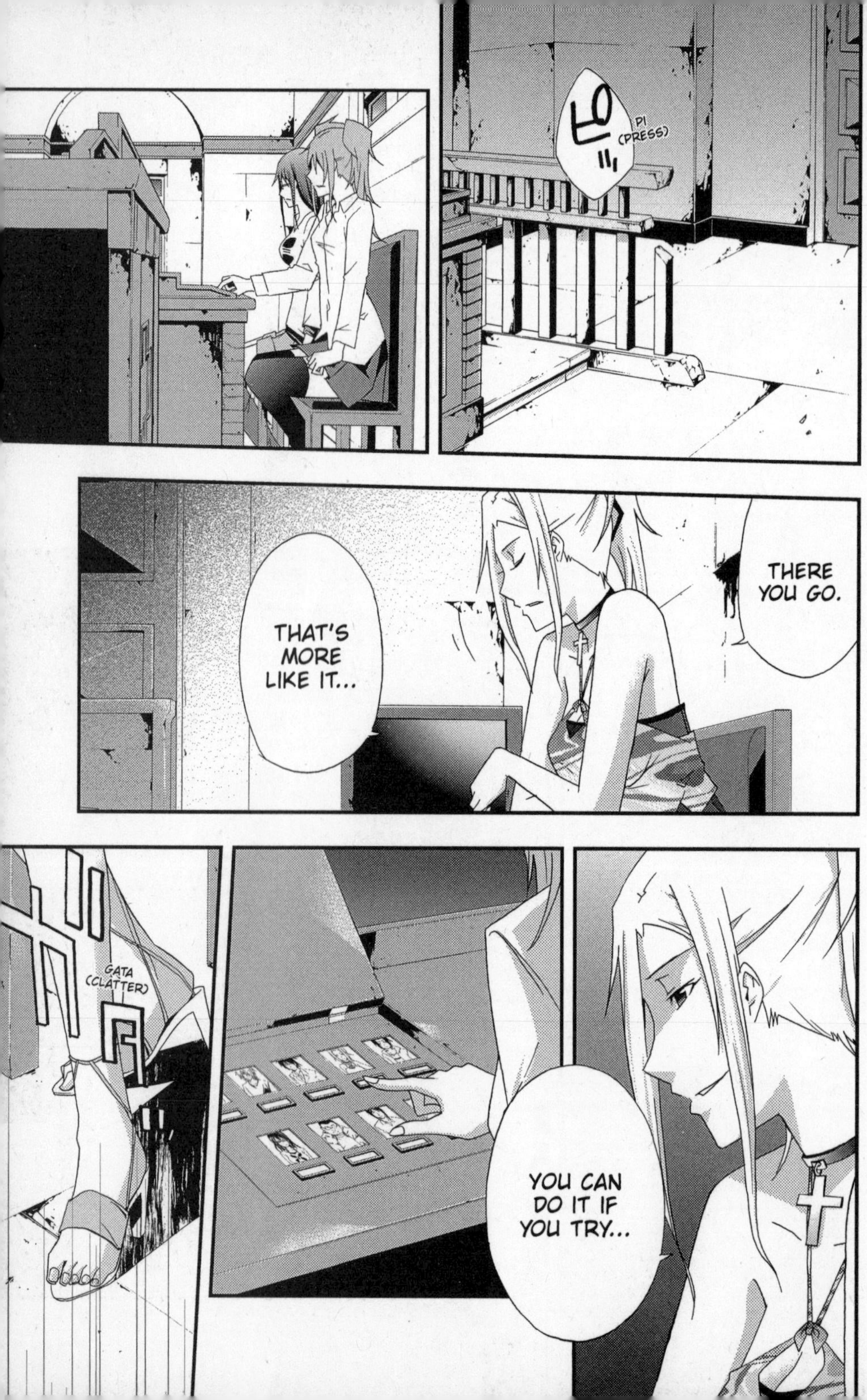

PI (PRESS)
THERE YOU GO.
THAT'S MORE LIKE IT...
YOU CAN DO IT IF YOU TRY...
GATA (CLATTER)

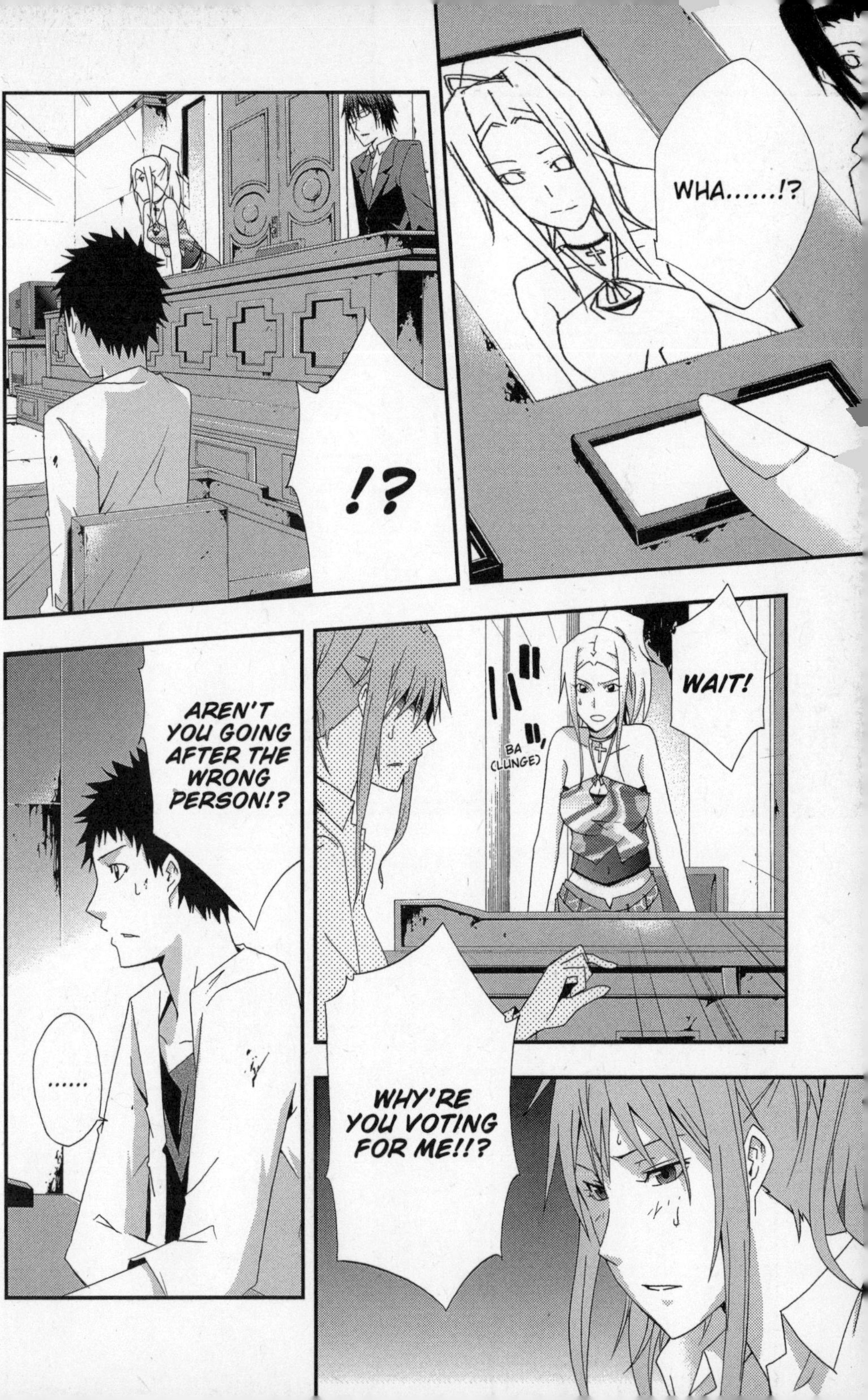
WHA......!?
!?
WAIT!
BA (LUNGE)
WHY'RE YOU VOTING FOR ME!!?
AREN'T YOU GOING AFTER THE WRONG PERSON!?
......

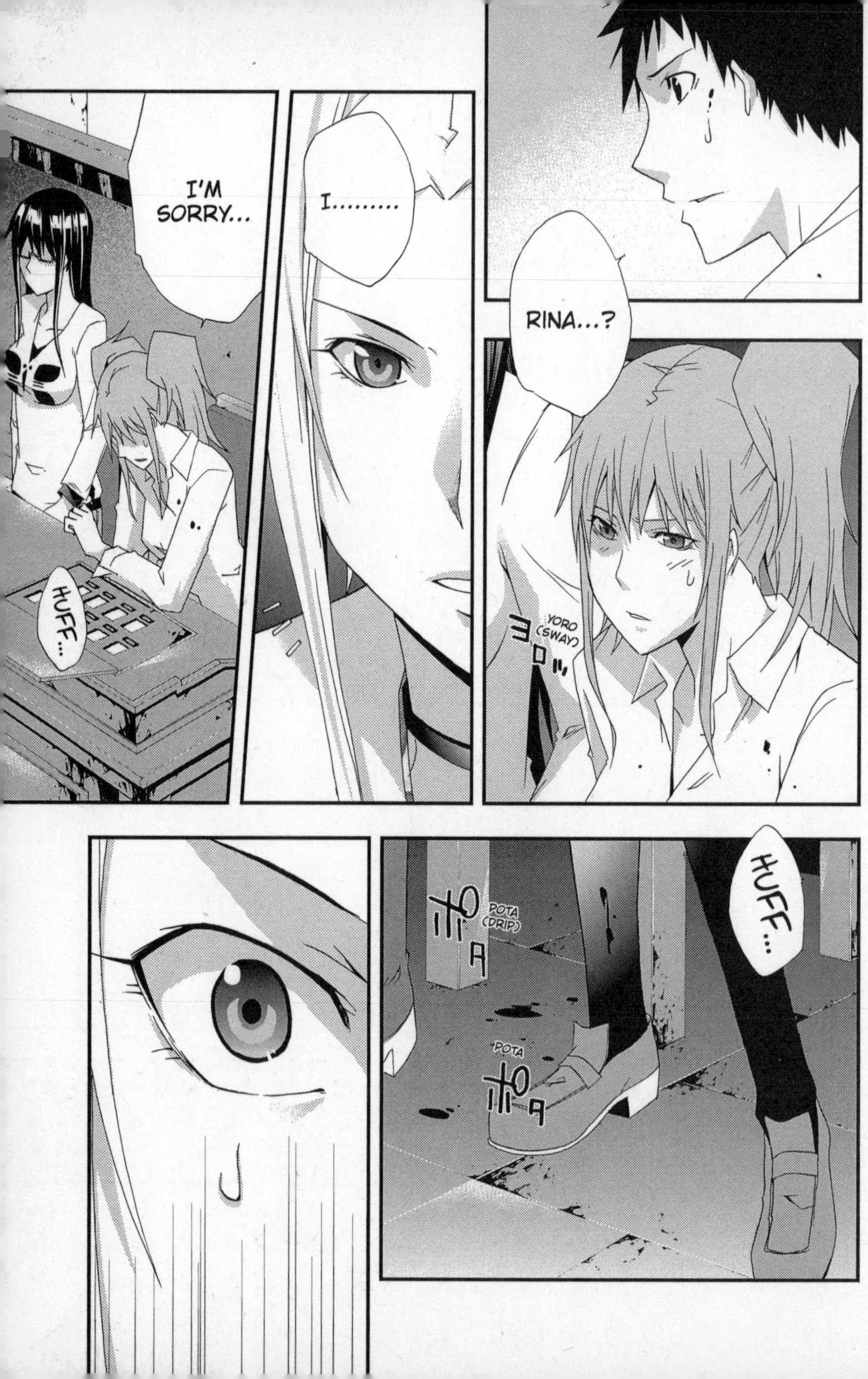
RINA...?
YORO (SWAY)
I........
I'M SORRY...
HUFF...
HUFF...
POTA (DRIP)
POTA

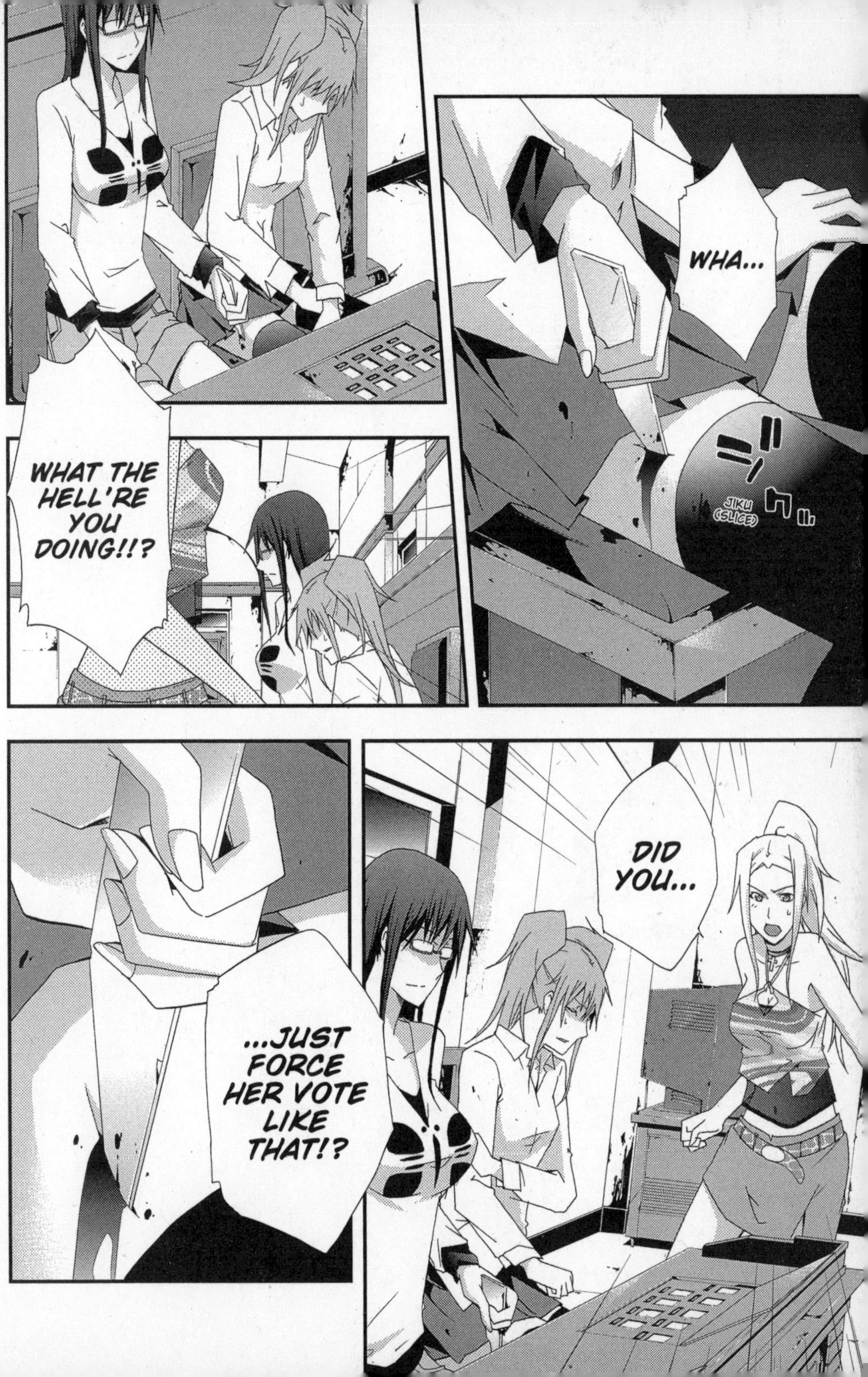
WHA...
JIKU (SLICE)
WHAT THE HELL'RE YOU DOING!!?
DID YOU...
...JUST FORCE HER VOTE LIKE THAT!?

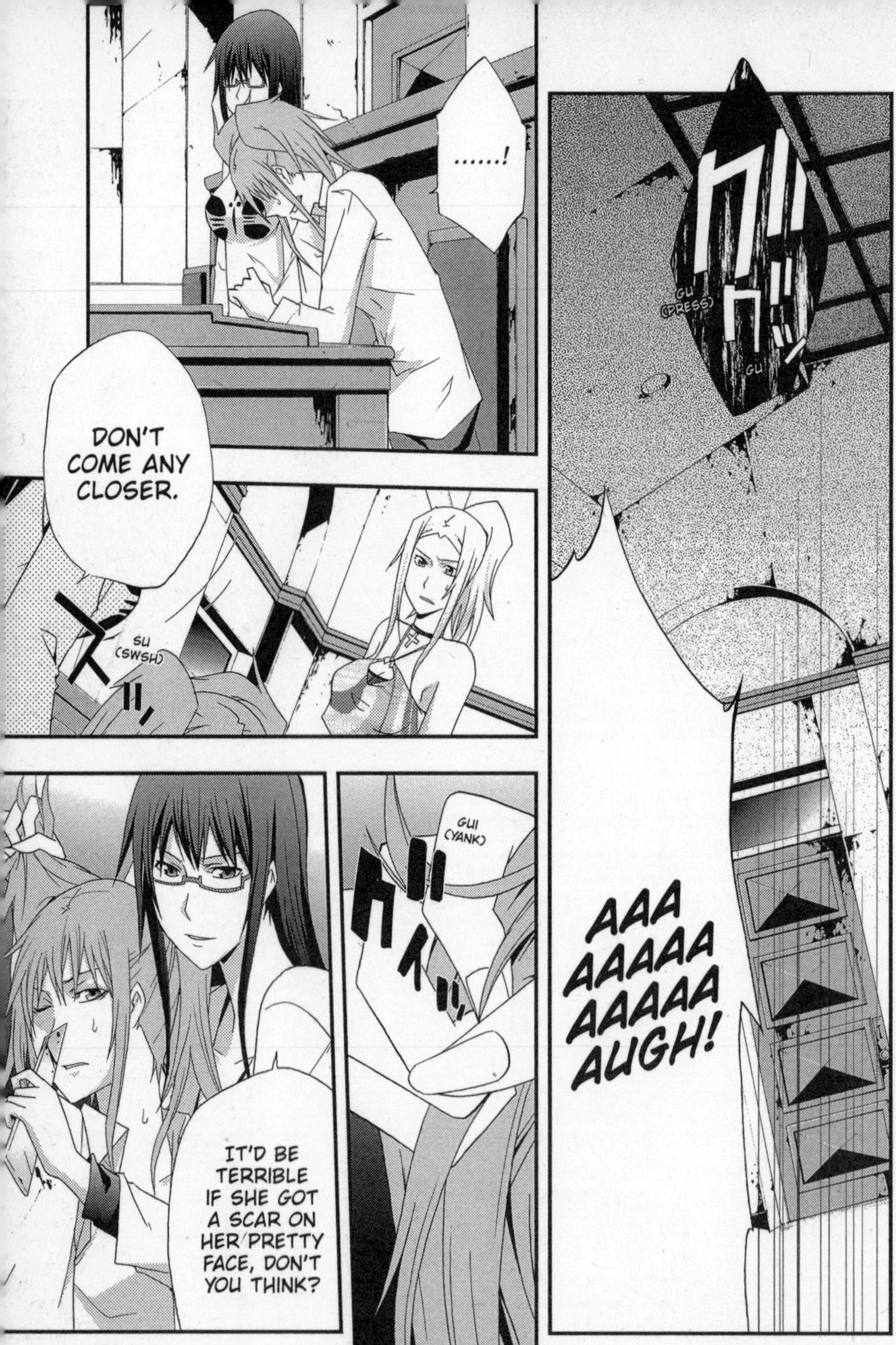
GU (PRESS)
GU
AAAAAAAAAAAAAAUGH!
......!
DON'T COME ANY CLOSER.
SU (SWSH)
GUI (YANK)
IT'D BE TERRIBLE IF SHE GOT A SCAR ON HER PRETTY FACE, DON'T YOU THINK?

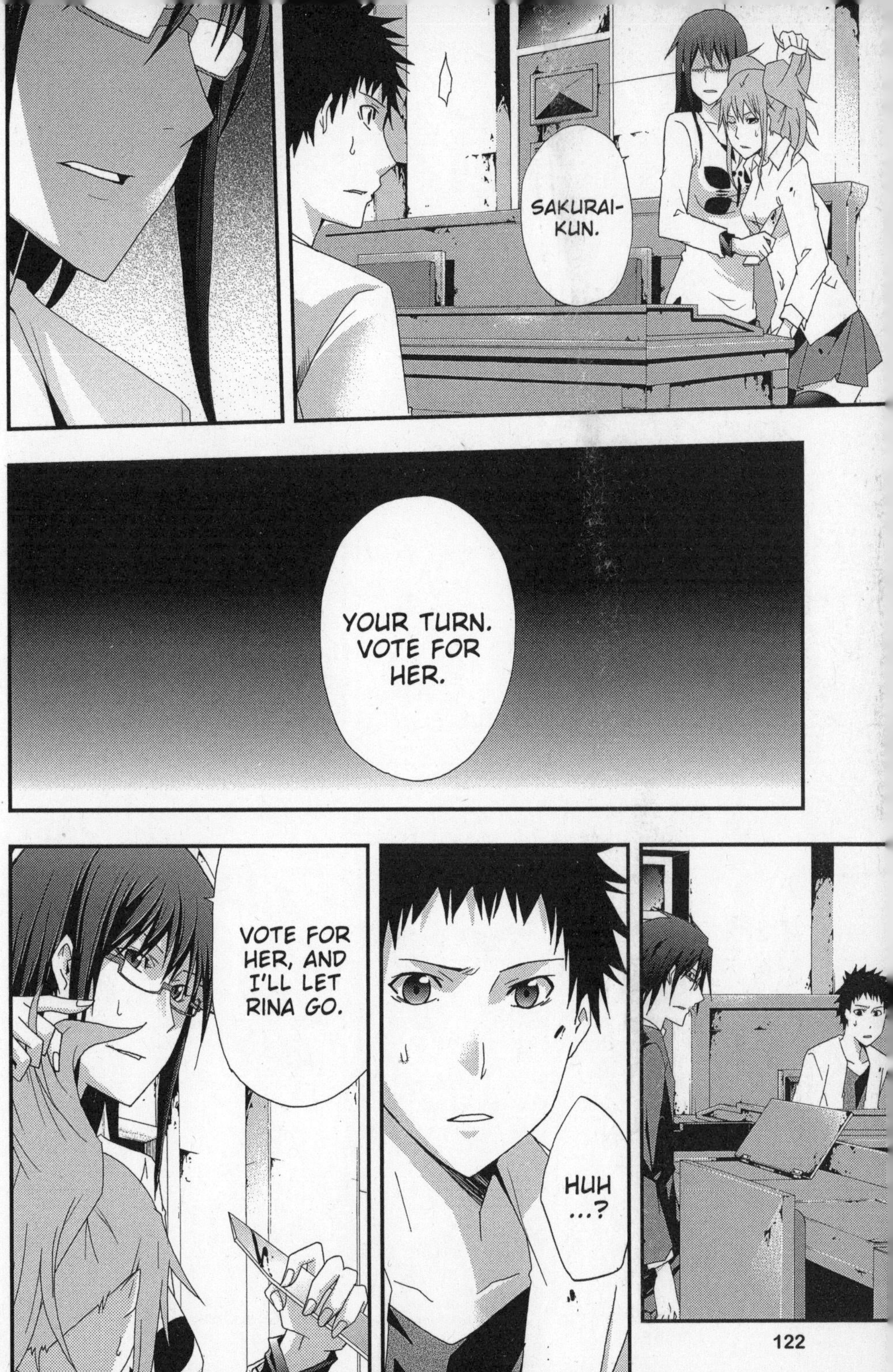
SAKURAI-KUN.
YOUR TURN. VOTE FOR HER.
VOTE FOR HER, AND I'LL LET RINA GO.
HUH ...?

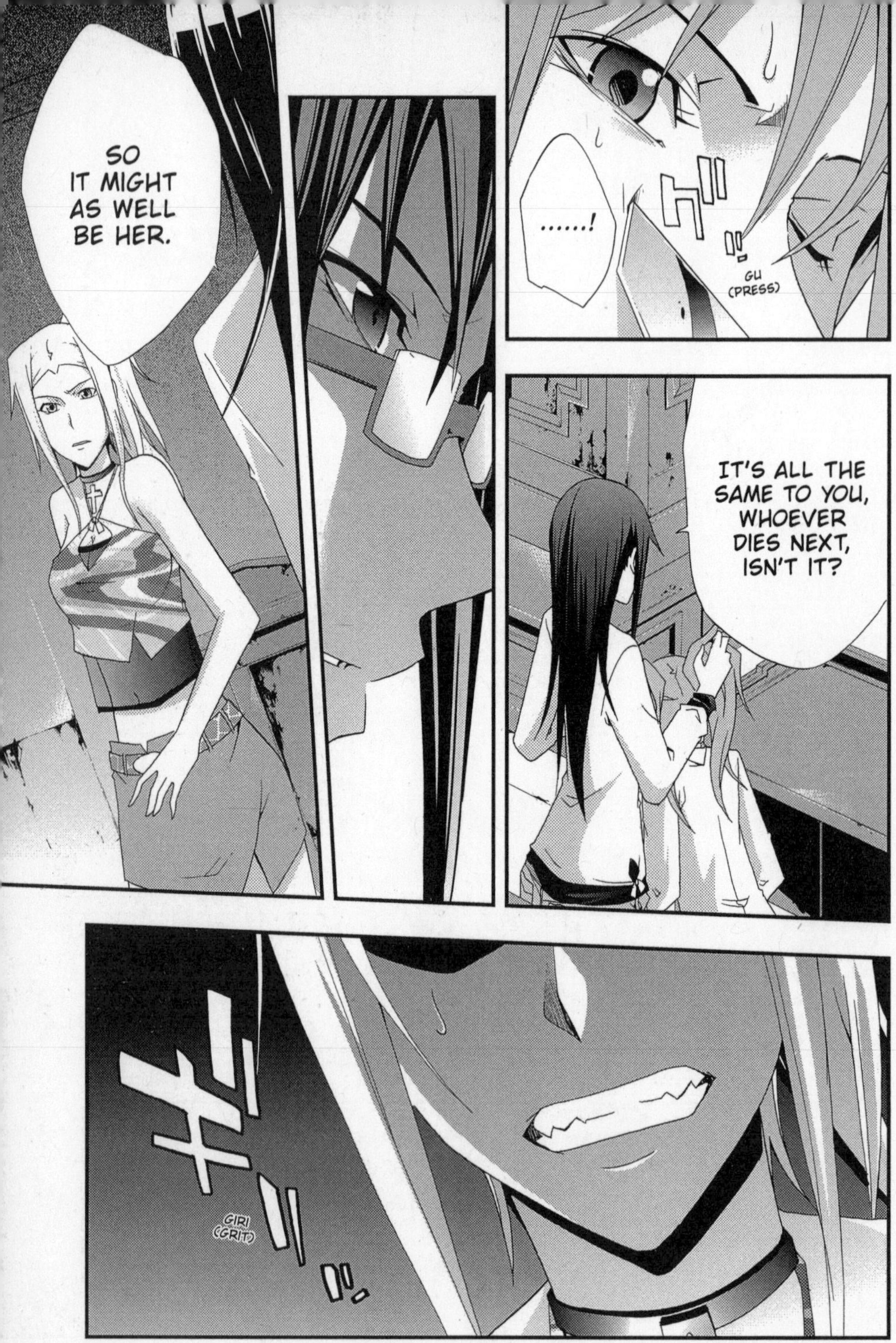
......!
GU (PRESS)
IT'S ALL THE SAME TO YOU, WHOEVER DIES NEXT, ISN'T IT?
SO IT MIGHT AS WELL BE HER.
GIRI (GRIT)

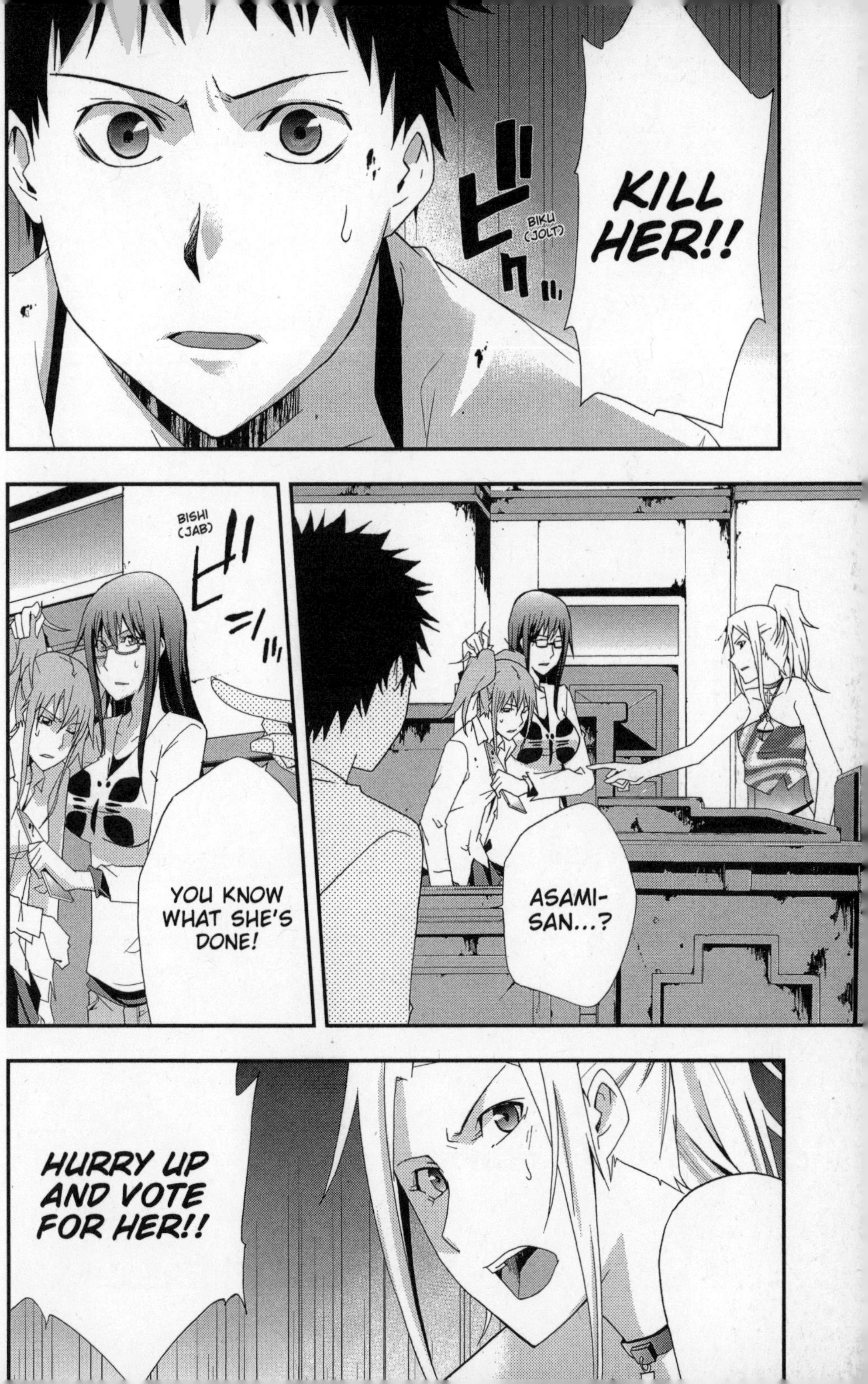

KILL HER!!
BIKU (JOLT)
ASAMI-SAN...?
BISHI (JAB)
YOU KNOW WHAT SHE'S DONE!
HURRY UP AND VOTE FOR HER!!

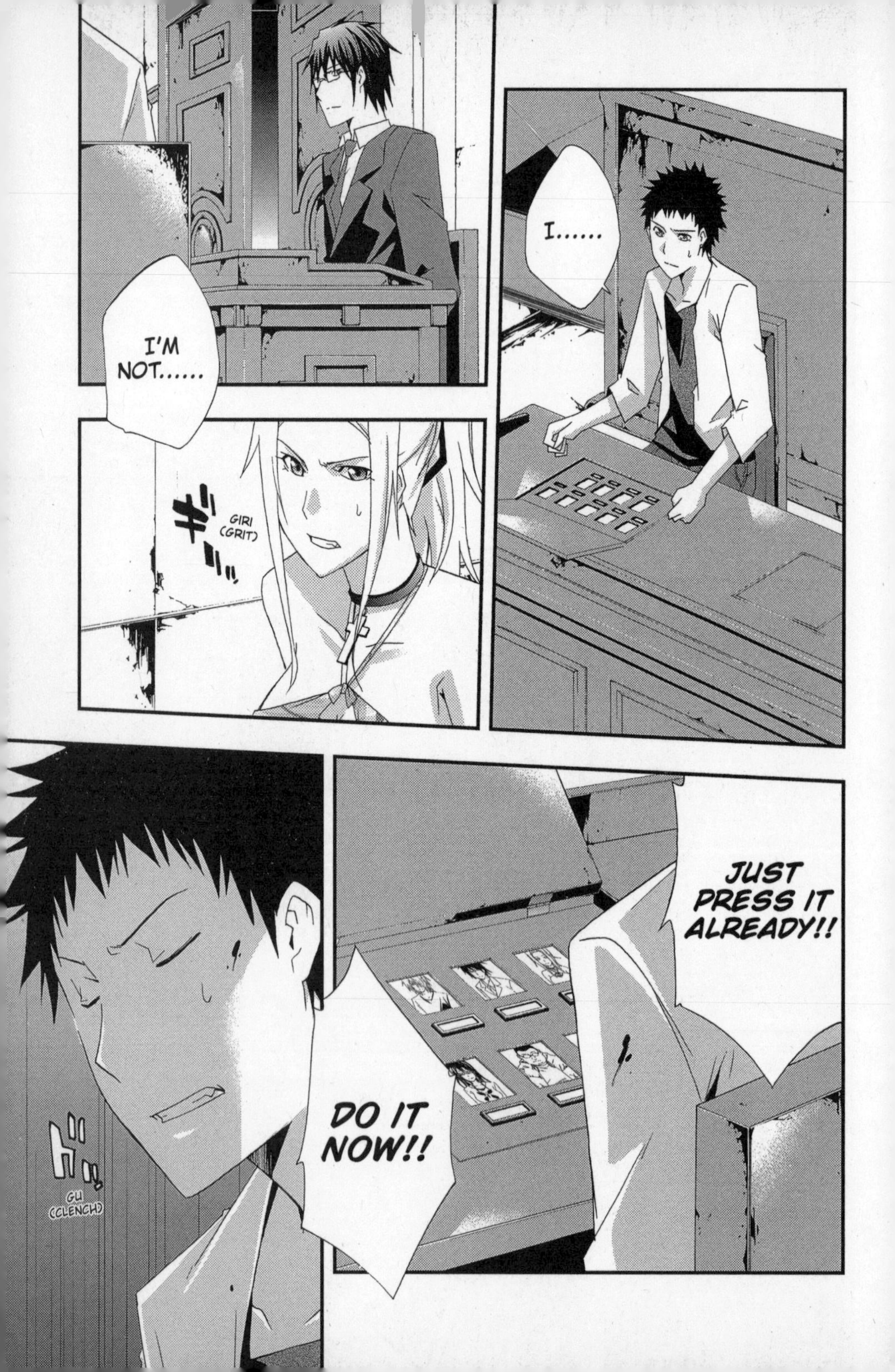
I......
I'M NOT......
GIRI (GRIT)
JUST PRESS IT ALREADY!!
DO IT NOW!!
GU (CLENCH)

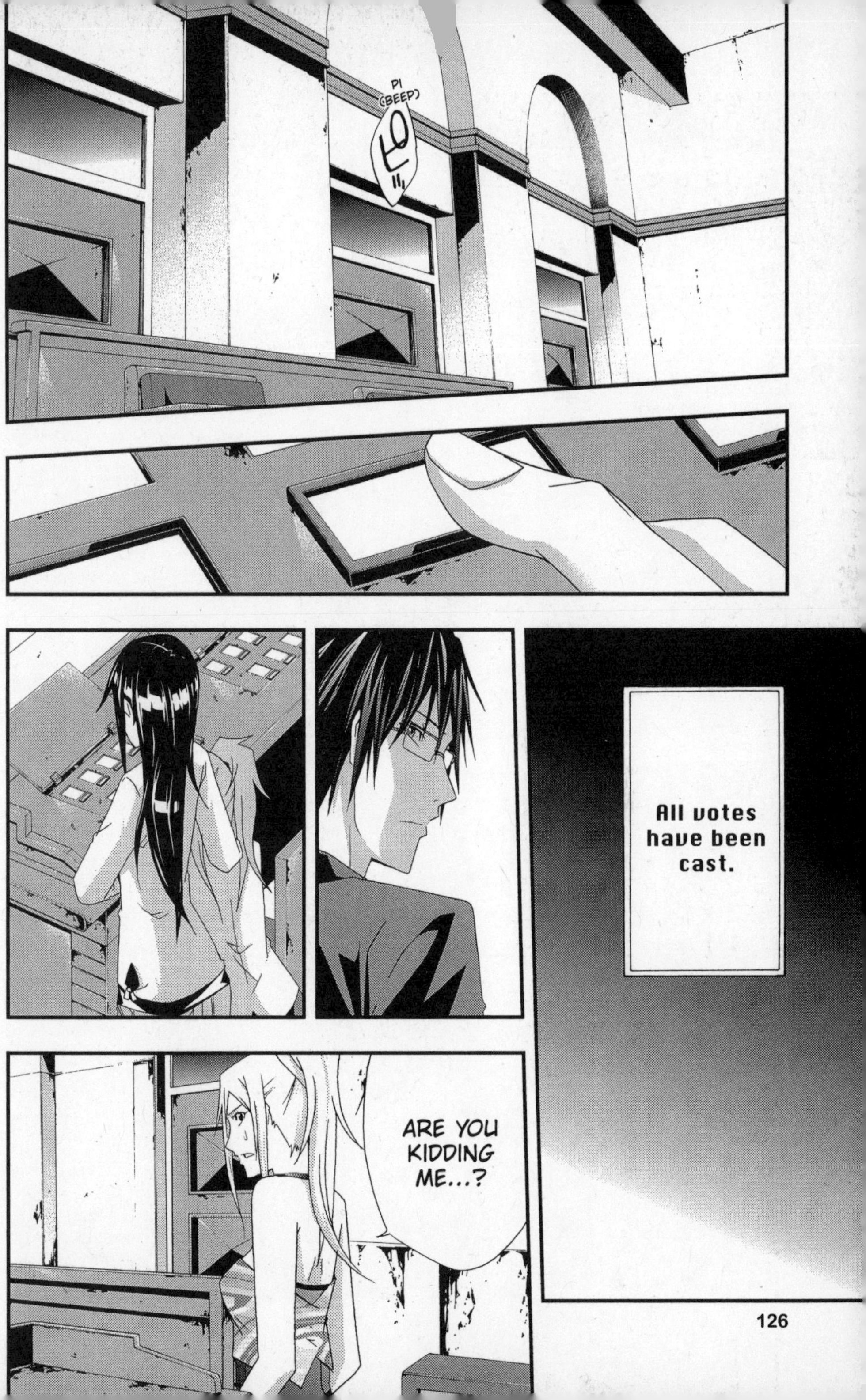
PI (BEEP)
ピ…
All votes have been cast.
ARE YOU KIDDING ME...?

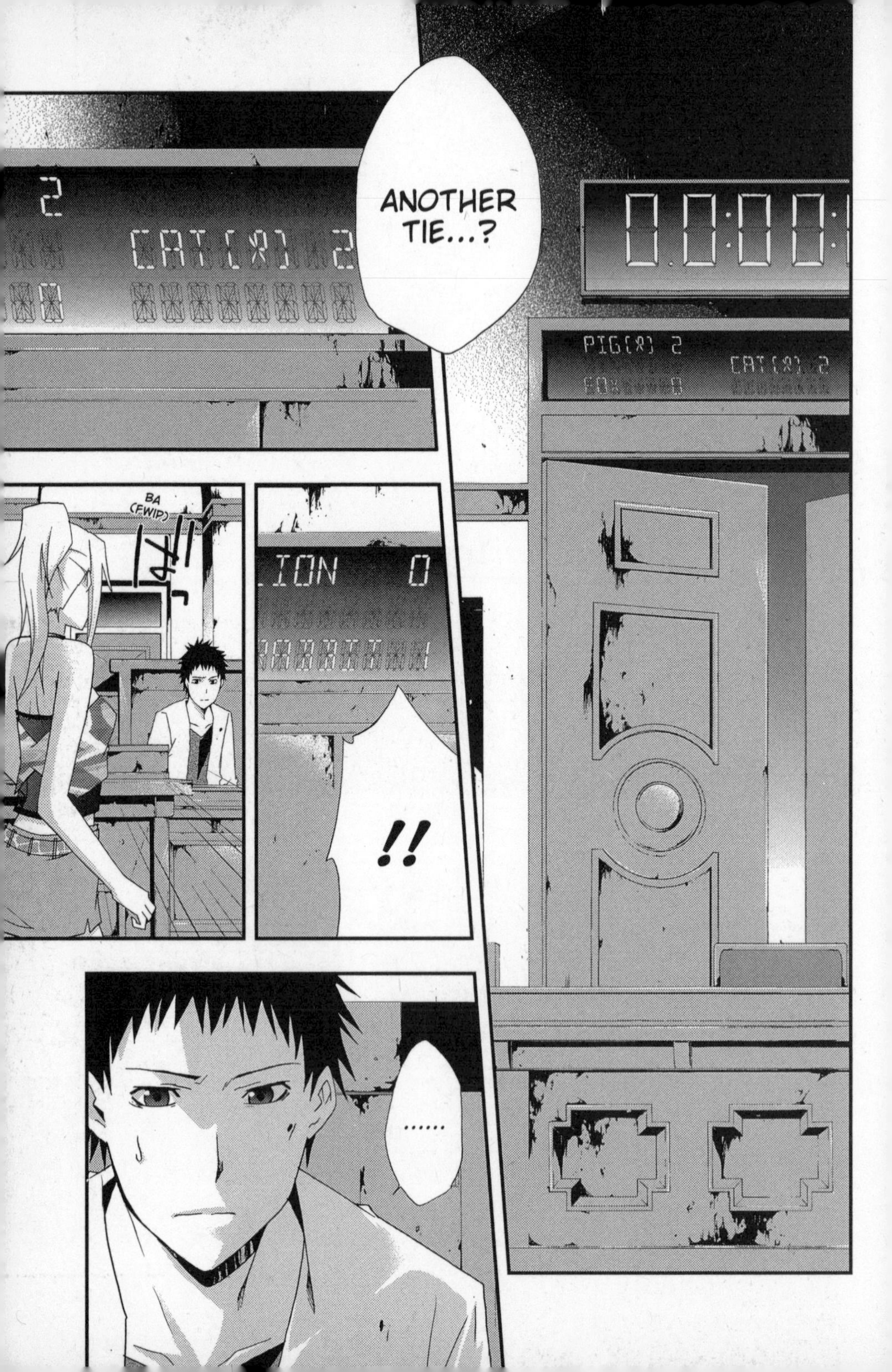
ANOTHER TIE...?
PIG(※) 2
CAT(※) 2
BA (FWIP)
!!
......

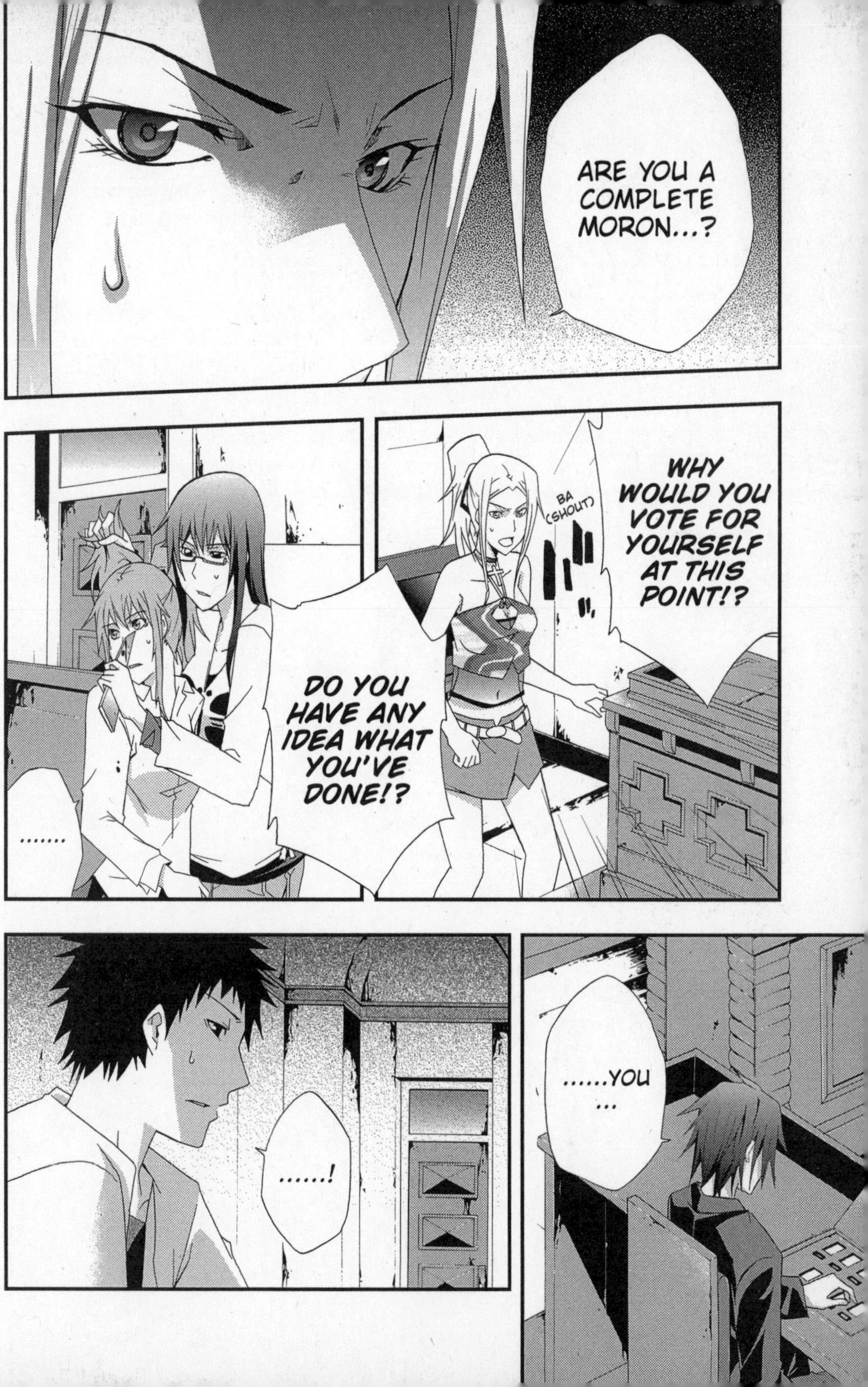
ARE YOU A COMPLETE MORON...?
WHY WOULD YOU VOTE FOR YOURSELF AT THIS POINT!?
BA (SHOUT)
DO YOU HAVE ANY IDEA WHAT YOU'VE DONE!?
....
......YOU ...
......!

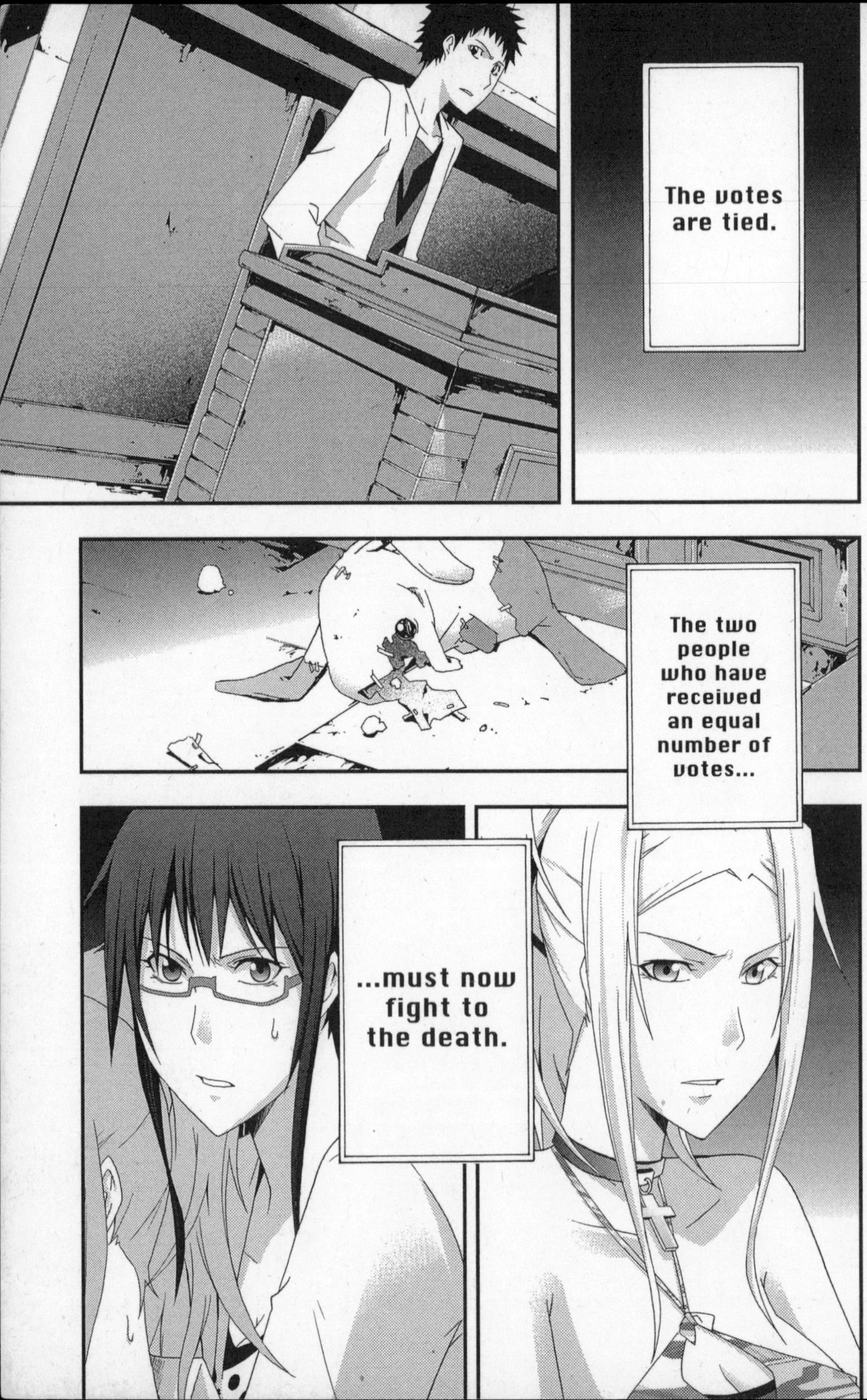

The votes are tied.
The two people who have received an equal number of votes...
...must now fight to the death.

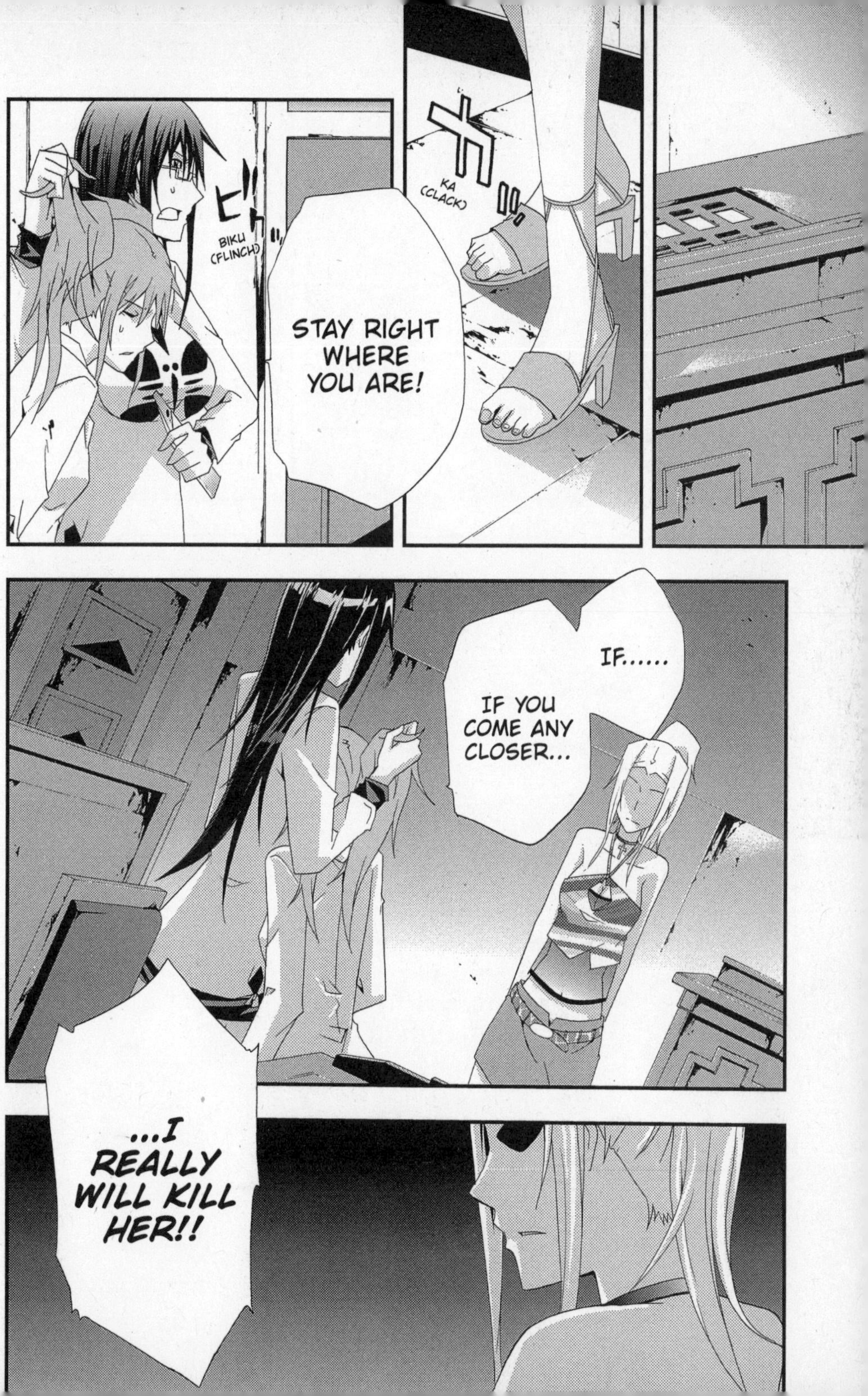
KA (CLACK)
STAY RIGHT WHERE YOU ARE!
BIKU (FLINCH)
IF......
IF YOU COME ANY CLOSER...
...I REALLY WILL KILL HER!!

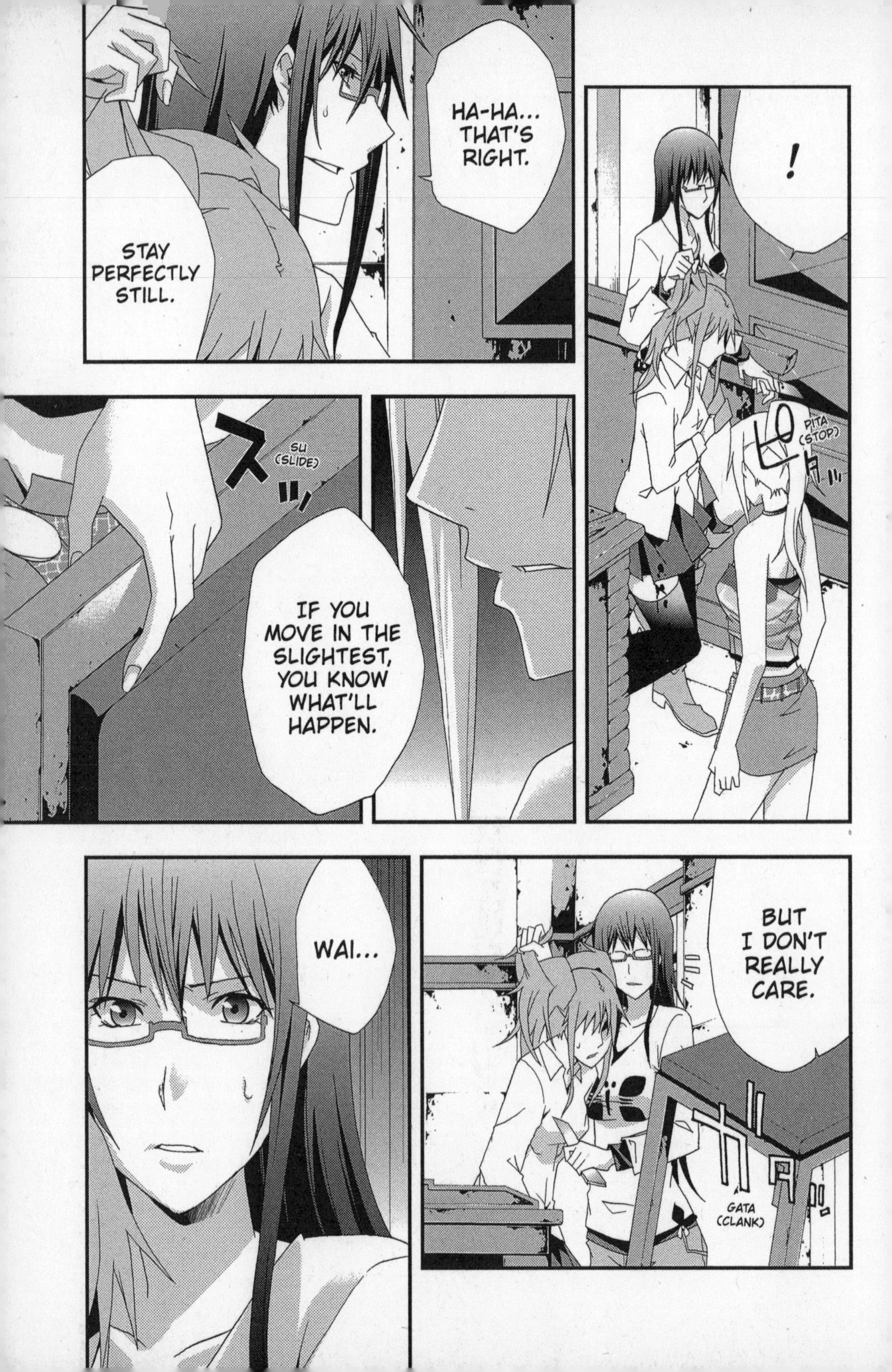
!
PITA (STOP)
HA-HA... THAT'S RIGHT.
STAY PERFECTLY STILL.
SU (SLIDE)
IF YOU MOVE IN THE SLIGHTEST, YOU KNOW WHAT'LL HAPPEN.
BUT I DON'T REALLY CARE.
GATA (CLANK)
WAI...

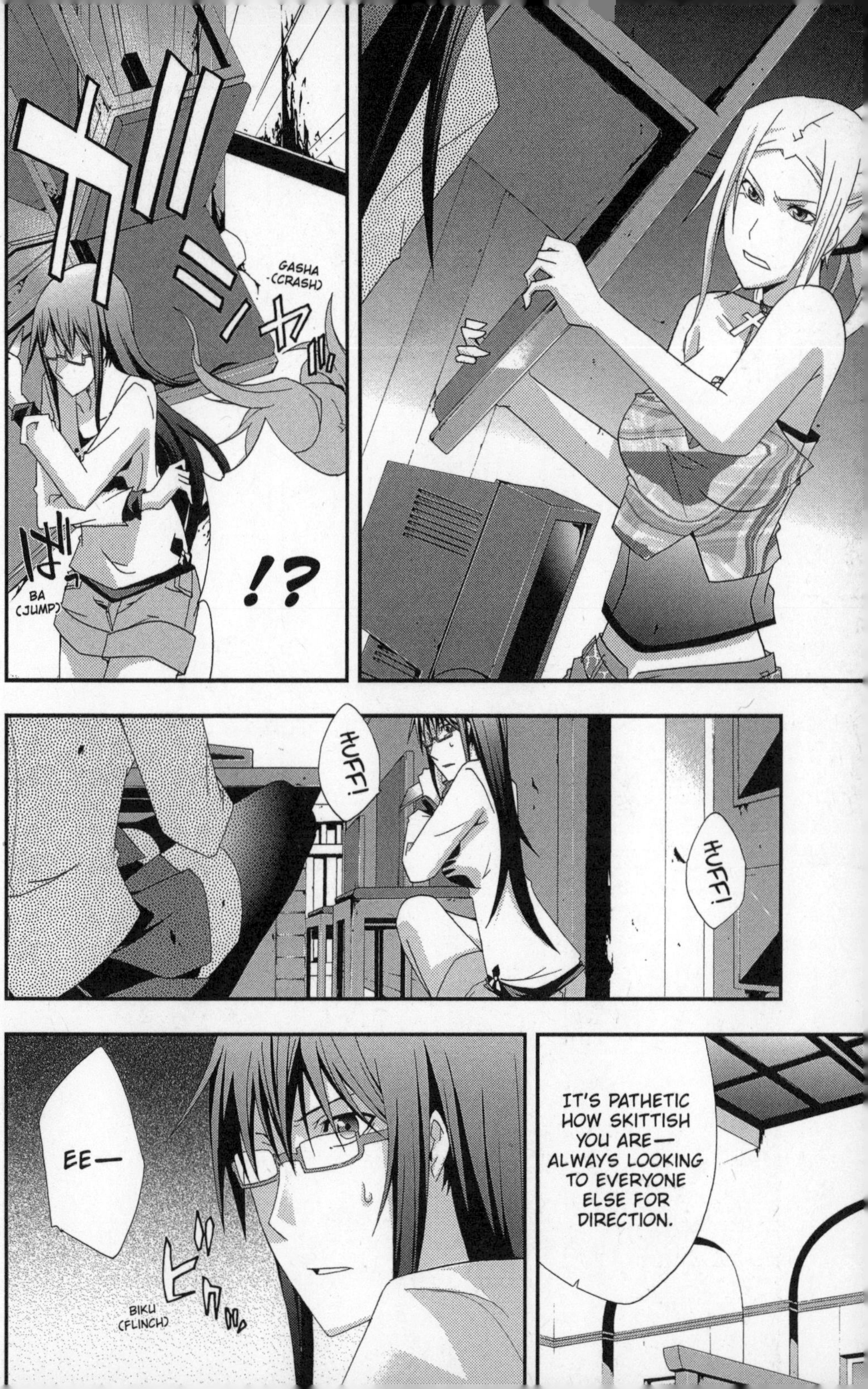
GASHA
-(CRASH)
!?
BA
(JUMP)
HUFF!
HUFF!
IT'S PATHETIC HOW SKITTISH YOU ARE— ALWAYS LOOKING TO EVERYONE ELSE FOR DIRECTION.
EE—
BIKU
(FLINCH)

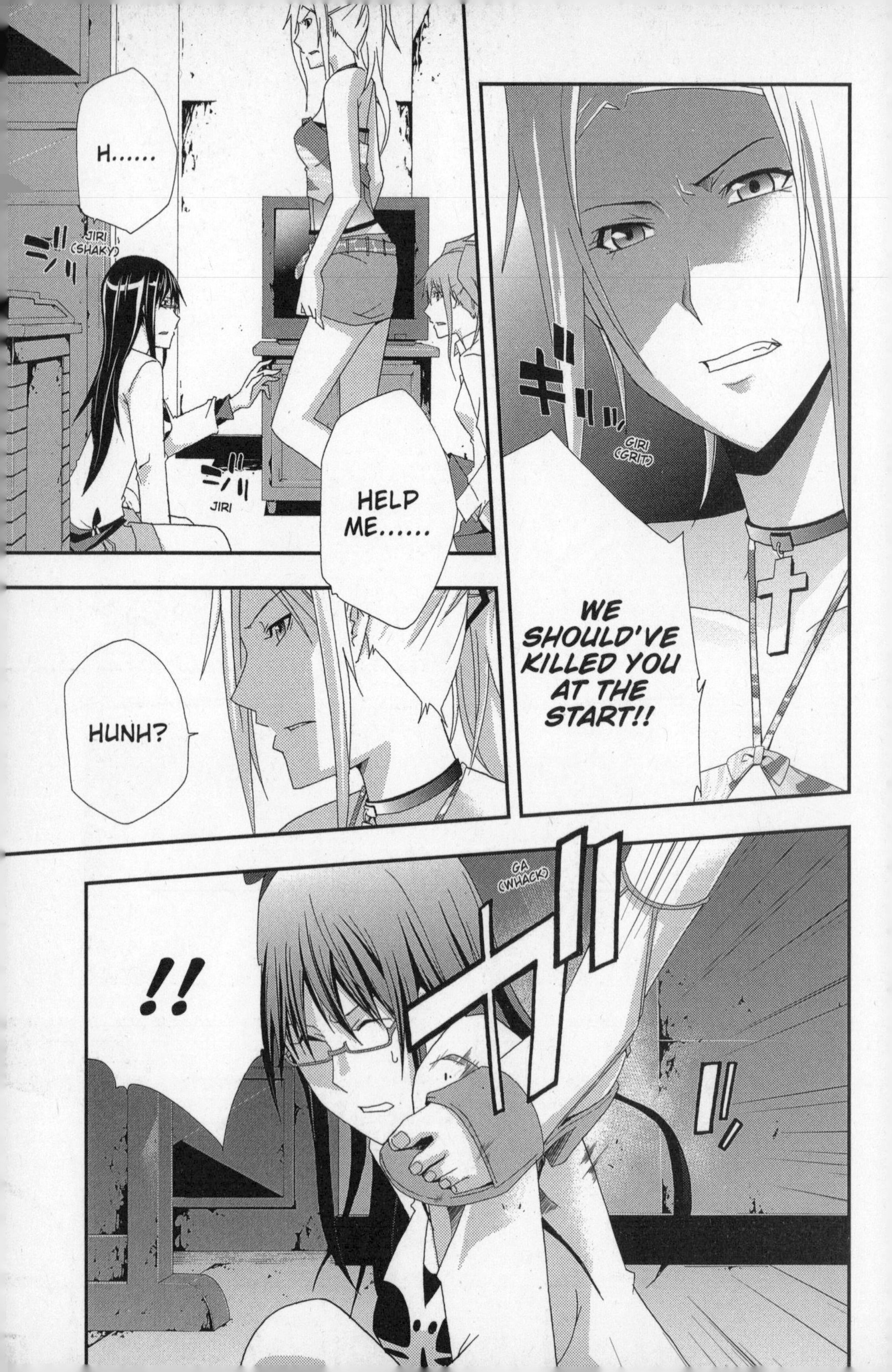
H......
JIRI (SHAKY)
JIRI
HELP ME......
HUNH?
GIRI (GRIT)
WE SHOULD'VE KILLED YOU AT THE START!!
GA (WHACK)
!!

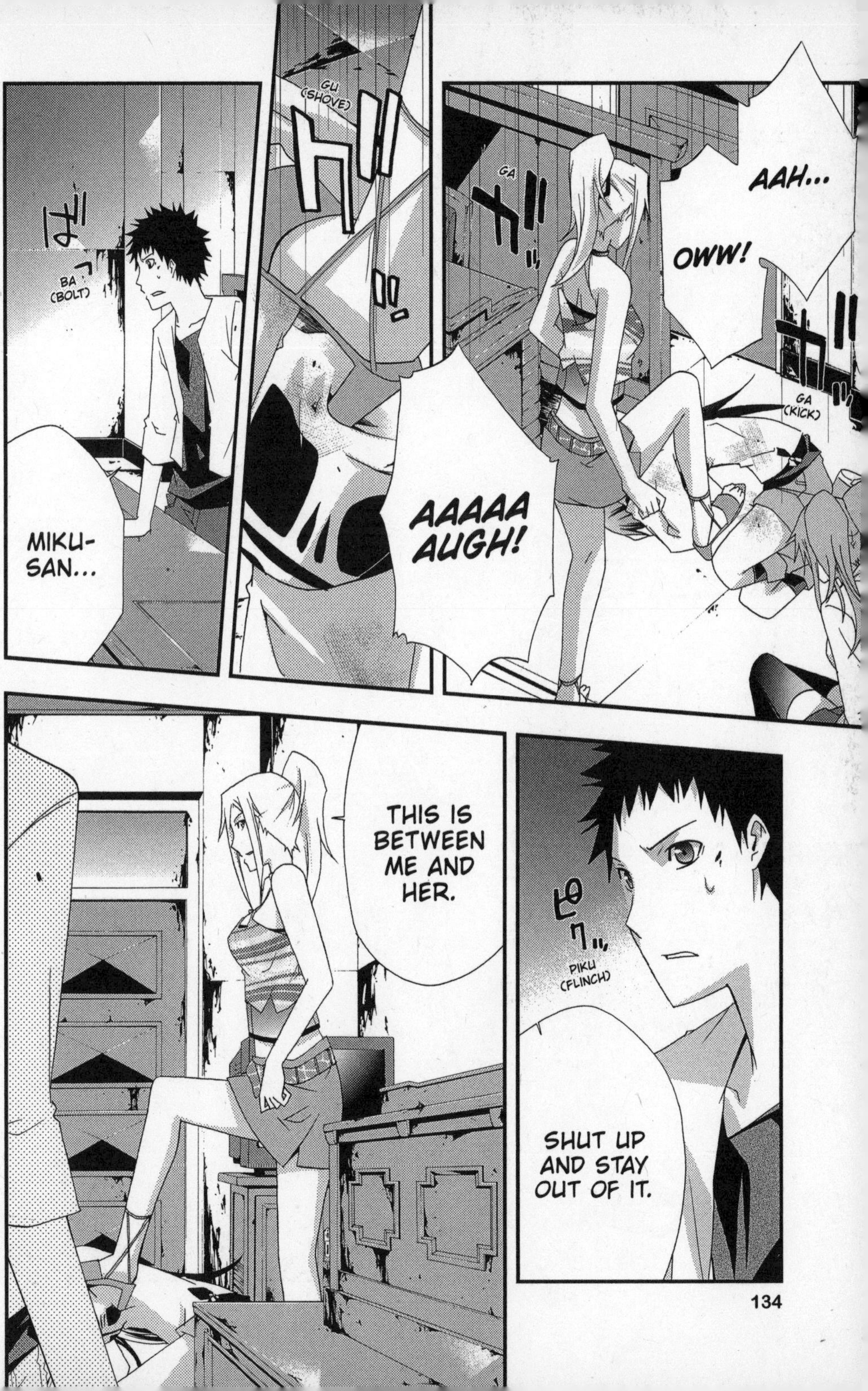

AAH...
OWW!
GA
GA (KICK)
GU (SHOVE)
AAAAA AUGH!
BA (BOLT)
MIKU-SAN...
PIKU (FLINCH)
SHUT UP AND STAY OUT OF IT.
THIS IS BETWEEN ME AND HER.

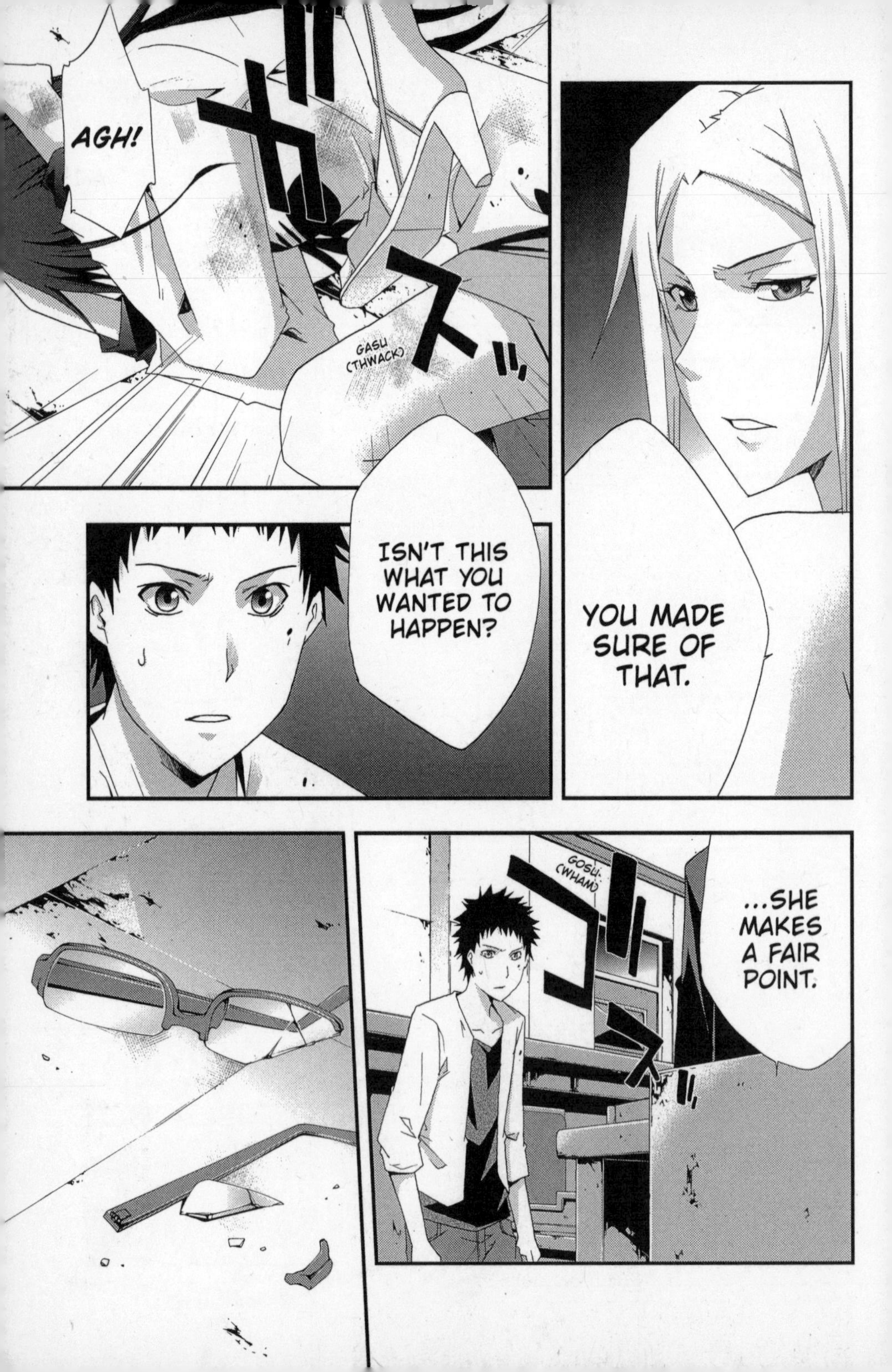
ISN'T THIS WHAT YOU WANTED TO HAPPEN?
AGH!
GASU (THWACK)
YOU MADE SURE OF THAT.
GOSU (WHAM)
...SHE MAKES A FAIR POINT.

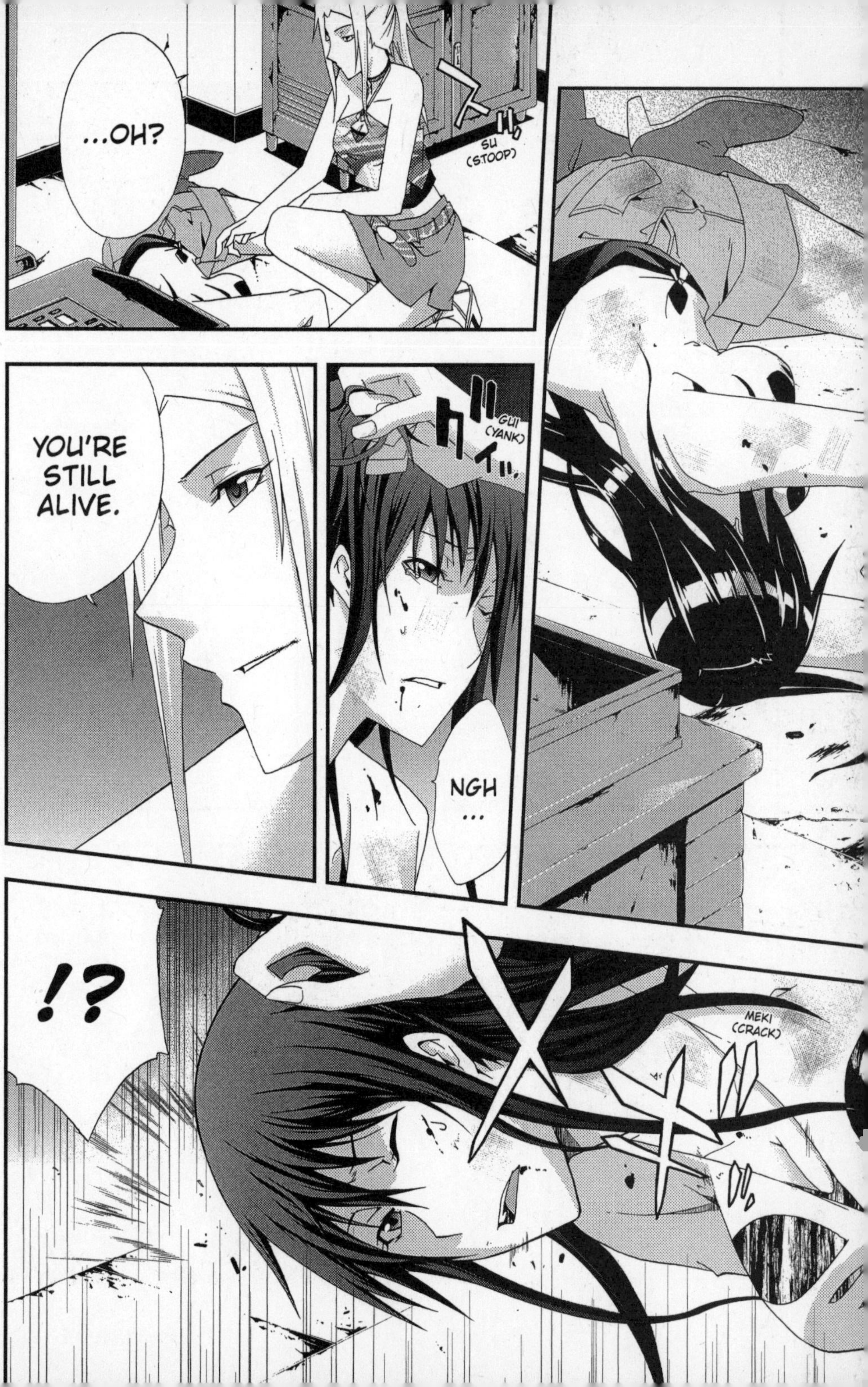

...OH?
SU (STOOP)
GUI (YANK)
NGH ...
YOU'RE STILL ALIVE.
MEKI (CRACK)
!?

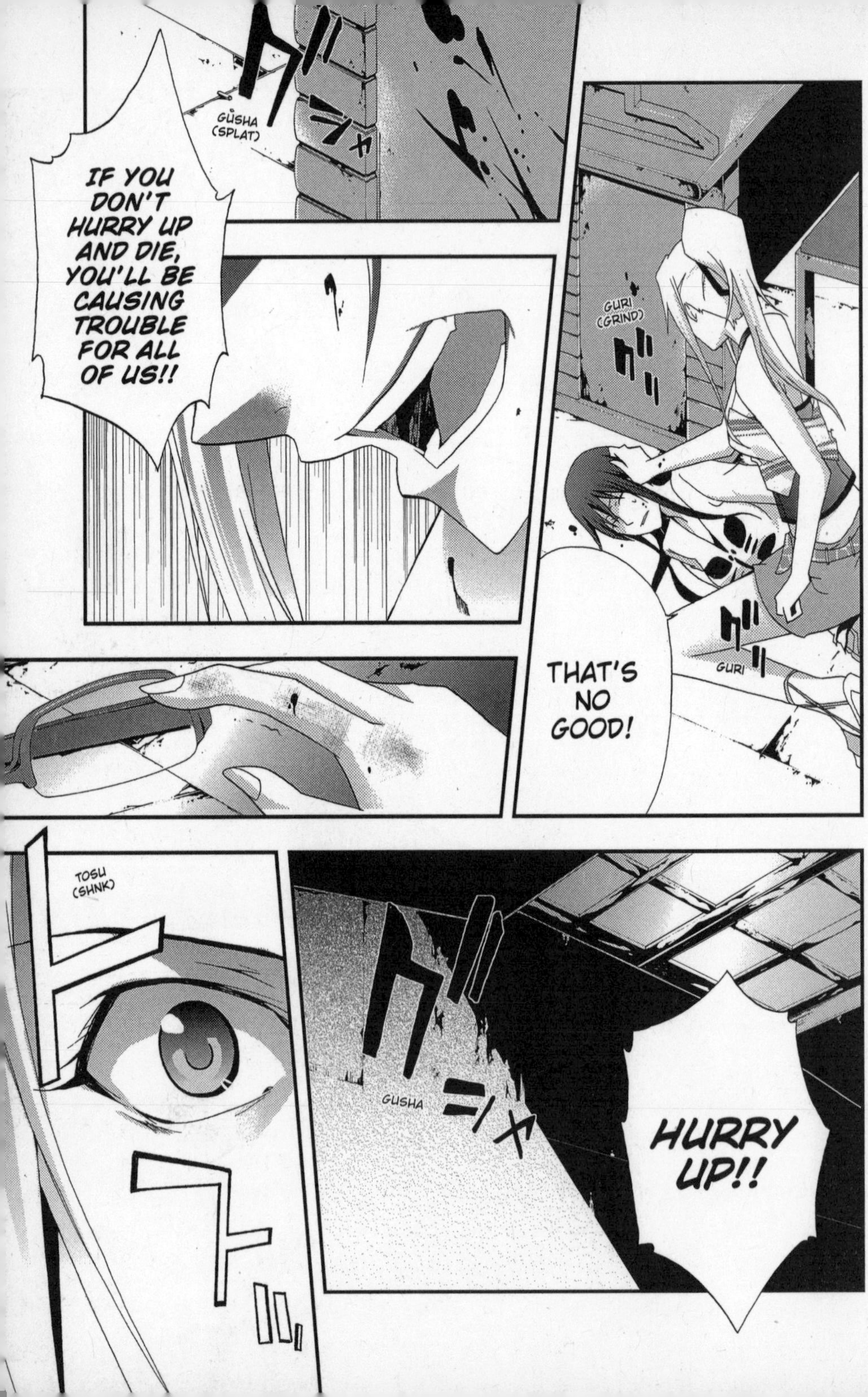
GURI (GRIND)
THAT'S NO GOOD!
GURI
GÜSHA (SPLAT)
IF YOU DON'T HURRY UP AND DIE, YOU'LL BE CAUSING TROUBLE FOR ALL OF US!!
HURRY UP!!
GUSHA
TOSU (SHNK)

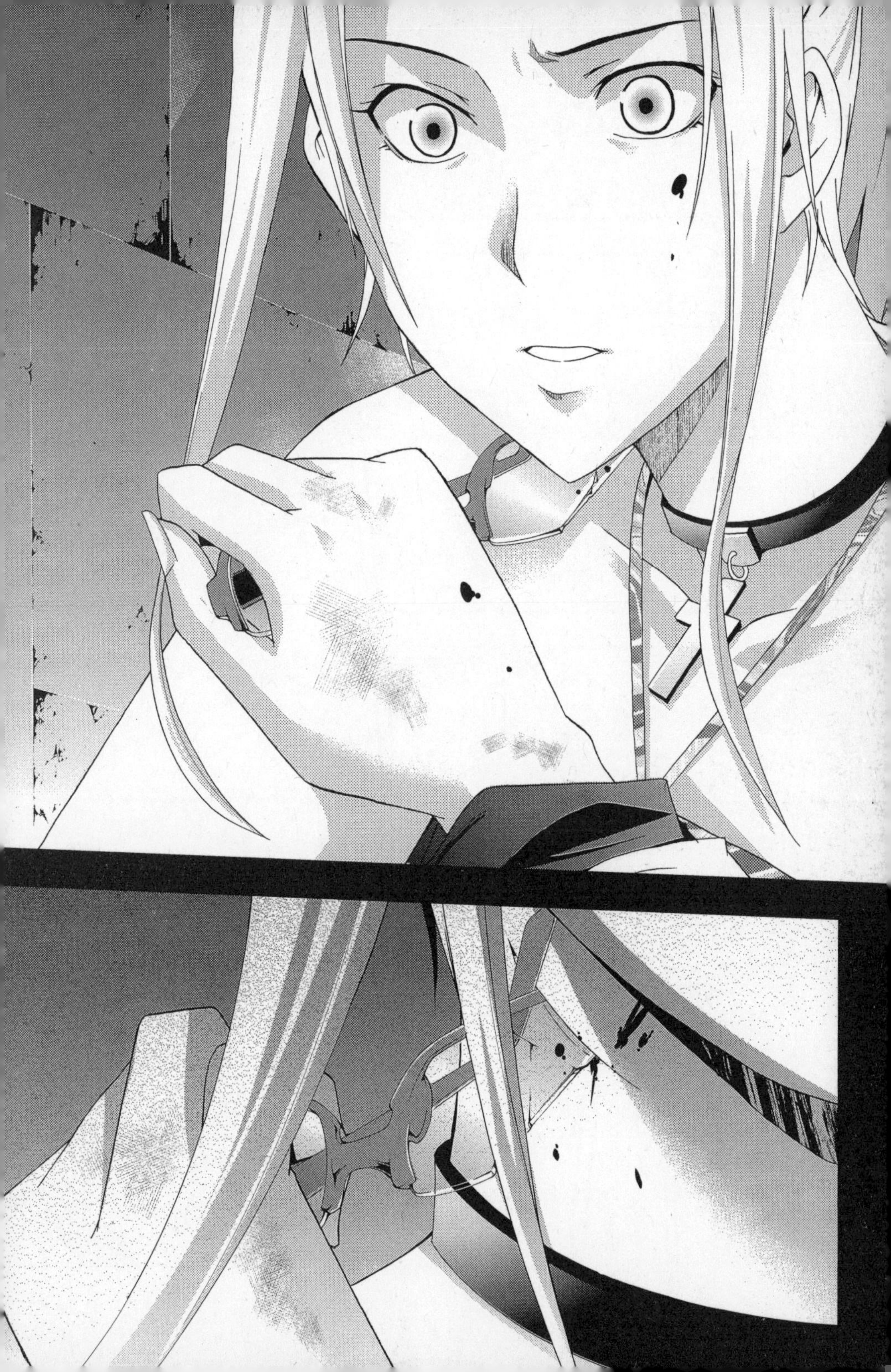

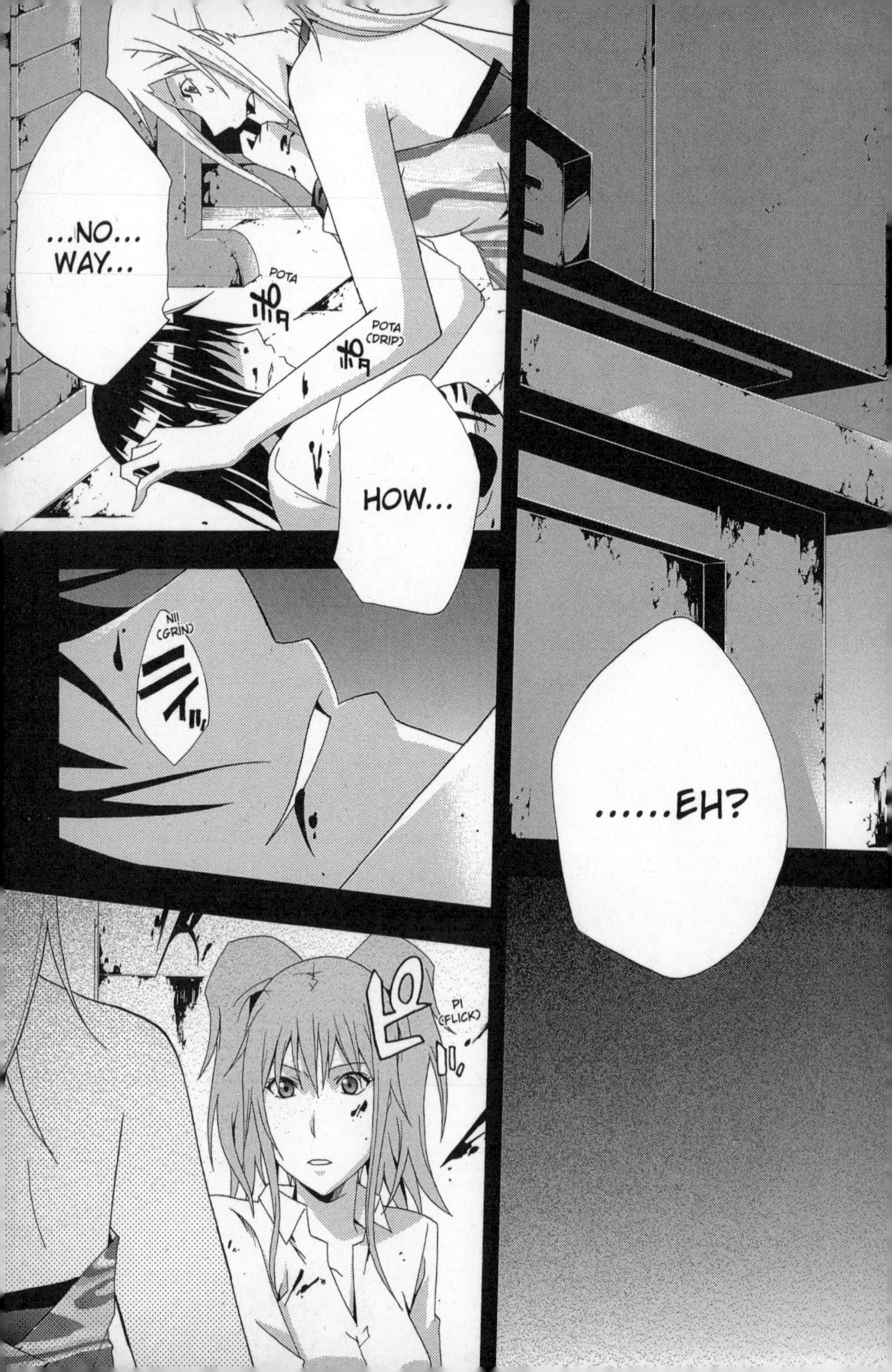

...NO...
WAY...
POTA
POTA (DRIP)
HOW...
NII (GRIN)
......EH?
PI (FLICK)

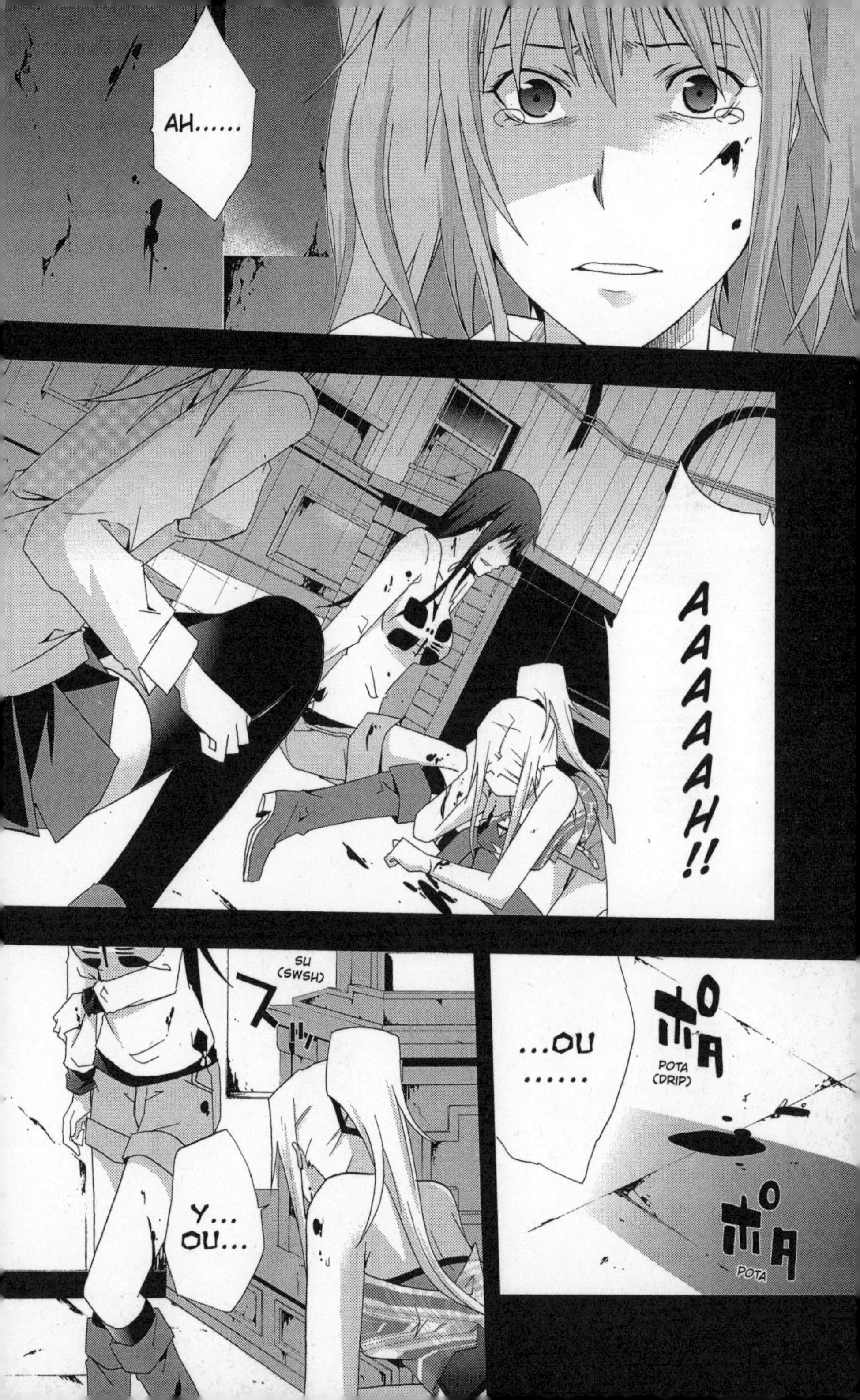
AH......
AAAAAAH!!
ポタ
POTA
(DRIP)
...OU
......
ポタ
POTA
スッ
SU
(SWSH)
Y...
OU...

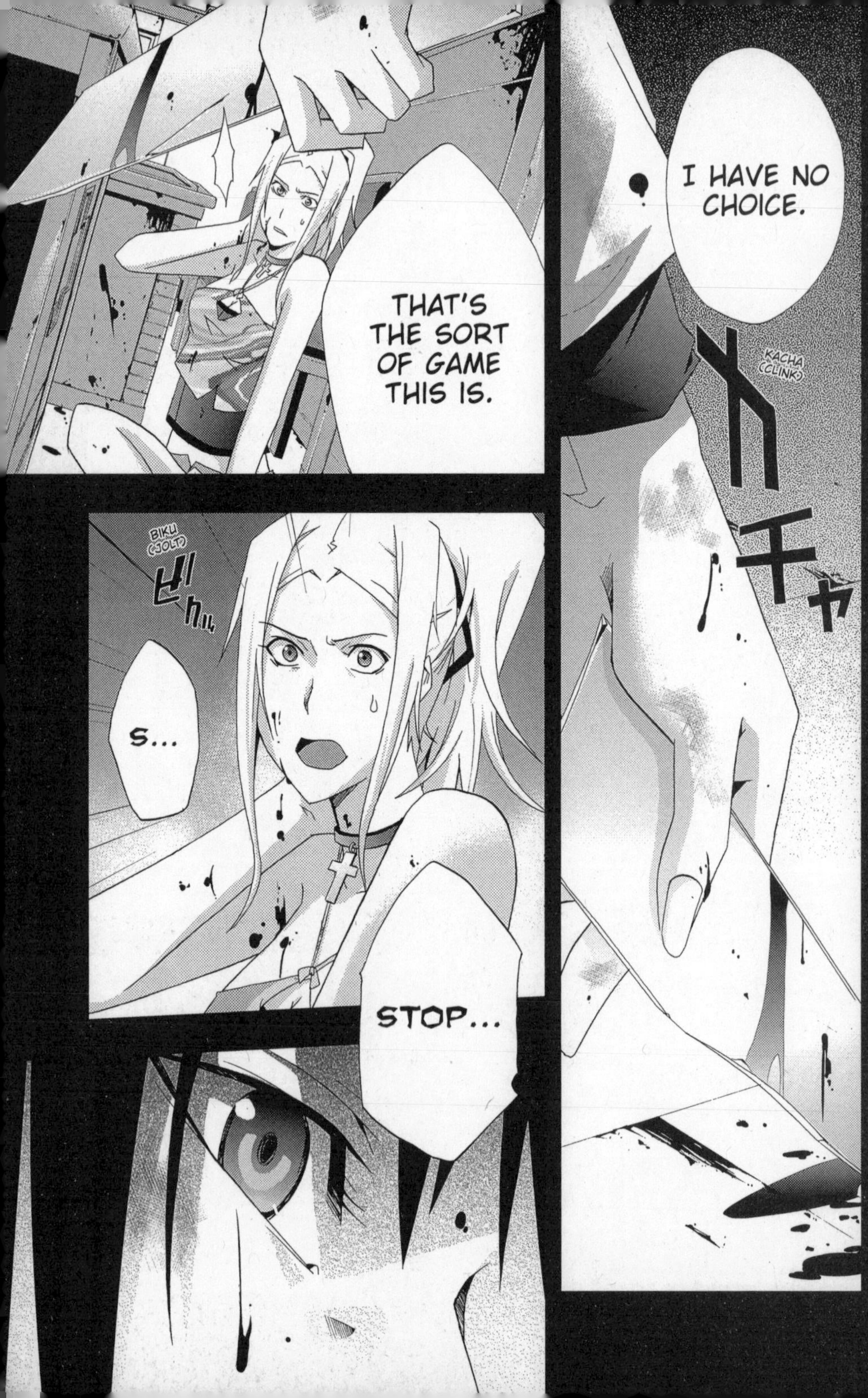
I HAVE NO CHOICE.
KACHA (CLINK)
THAT'S THE SORT OF GAME THIS IS.
BIKU (JOLT)
S...
STOP...

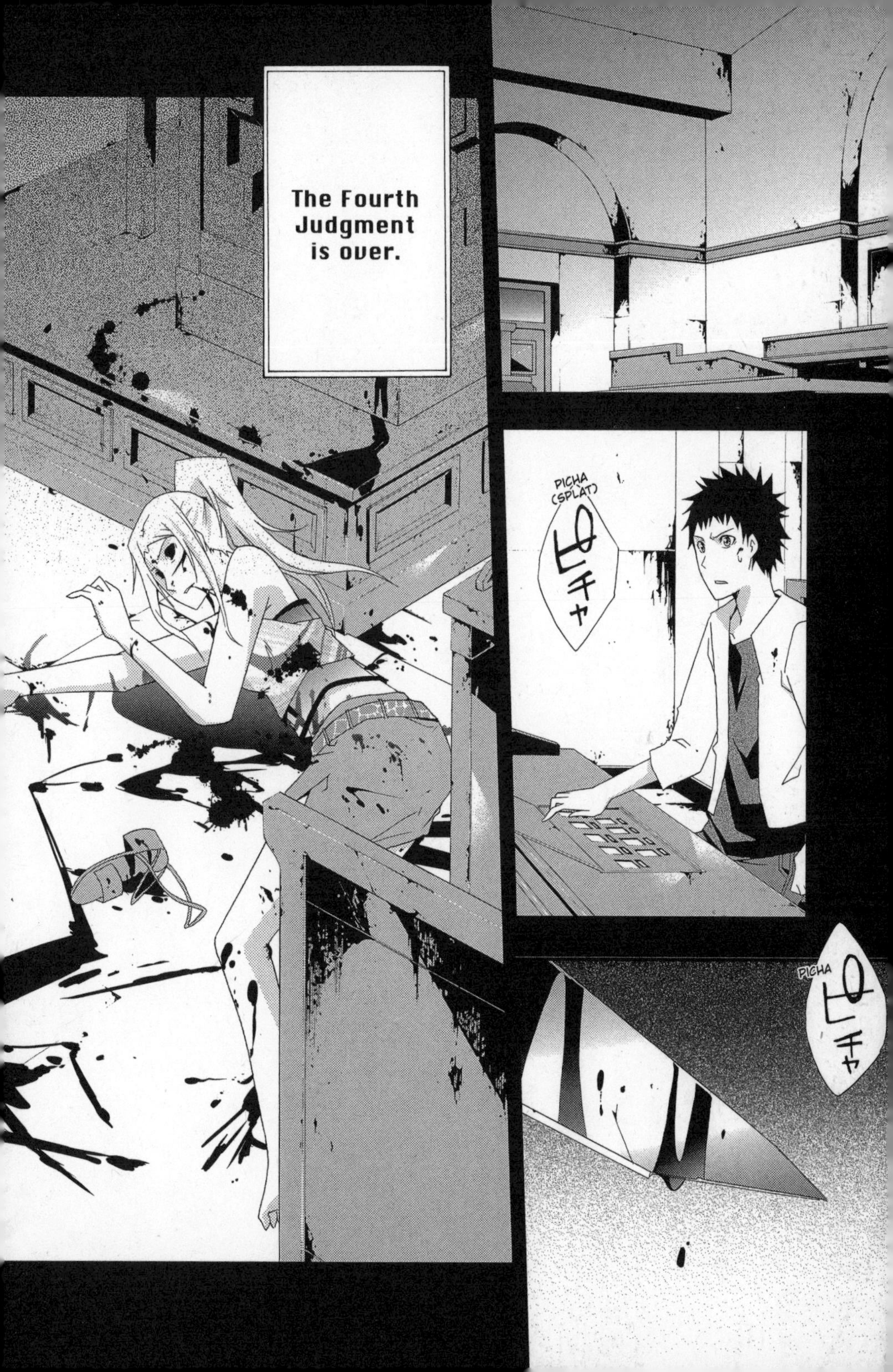
PICHA (SPLAT)
ピチャ
PICHA
ピチャ
The Fourth Judgment is over.

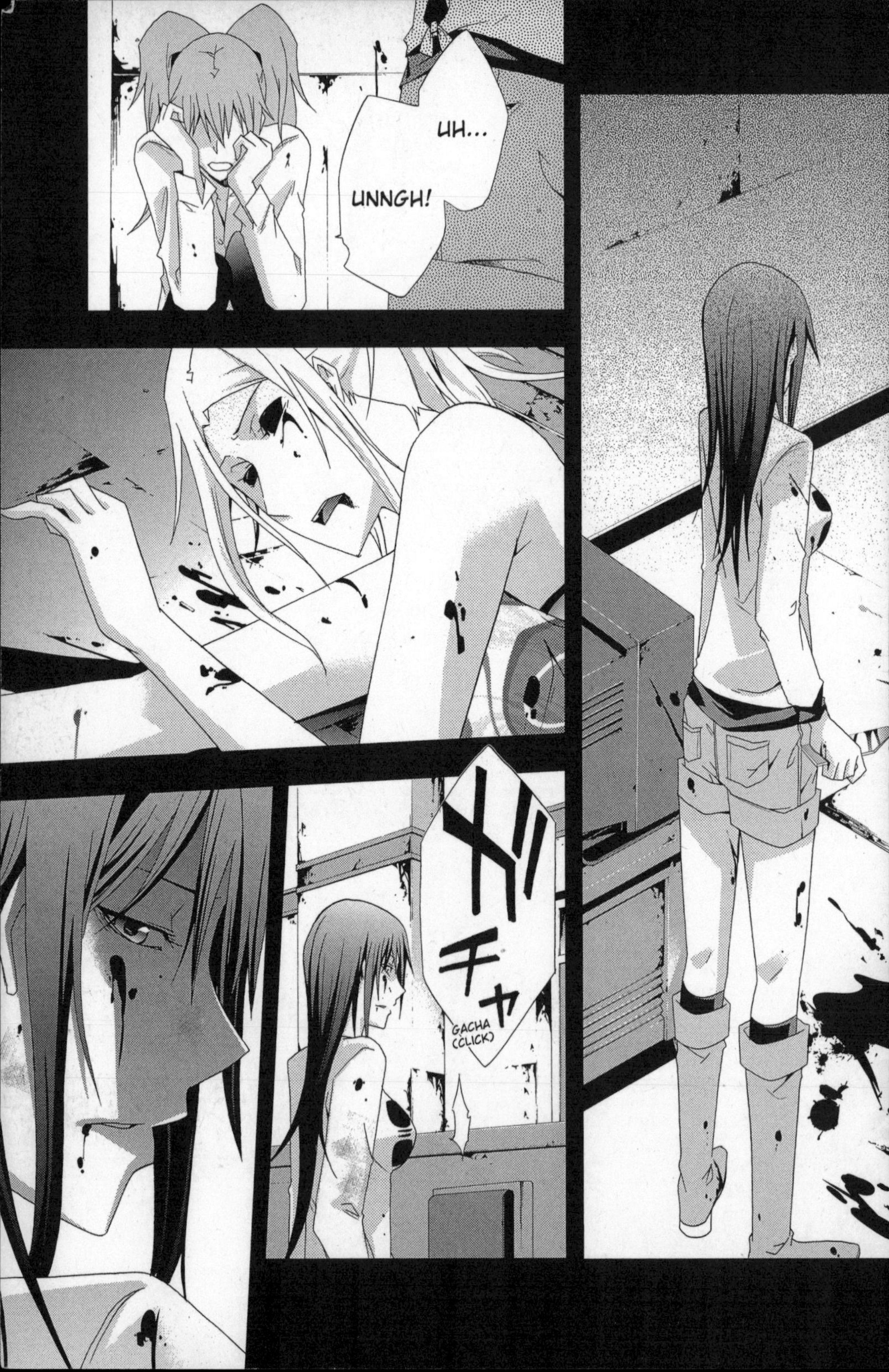
UH...
UNNGH!
ガチャ
GACHA (CLICK)

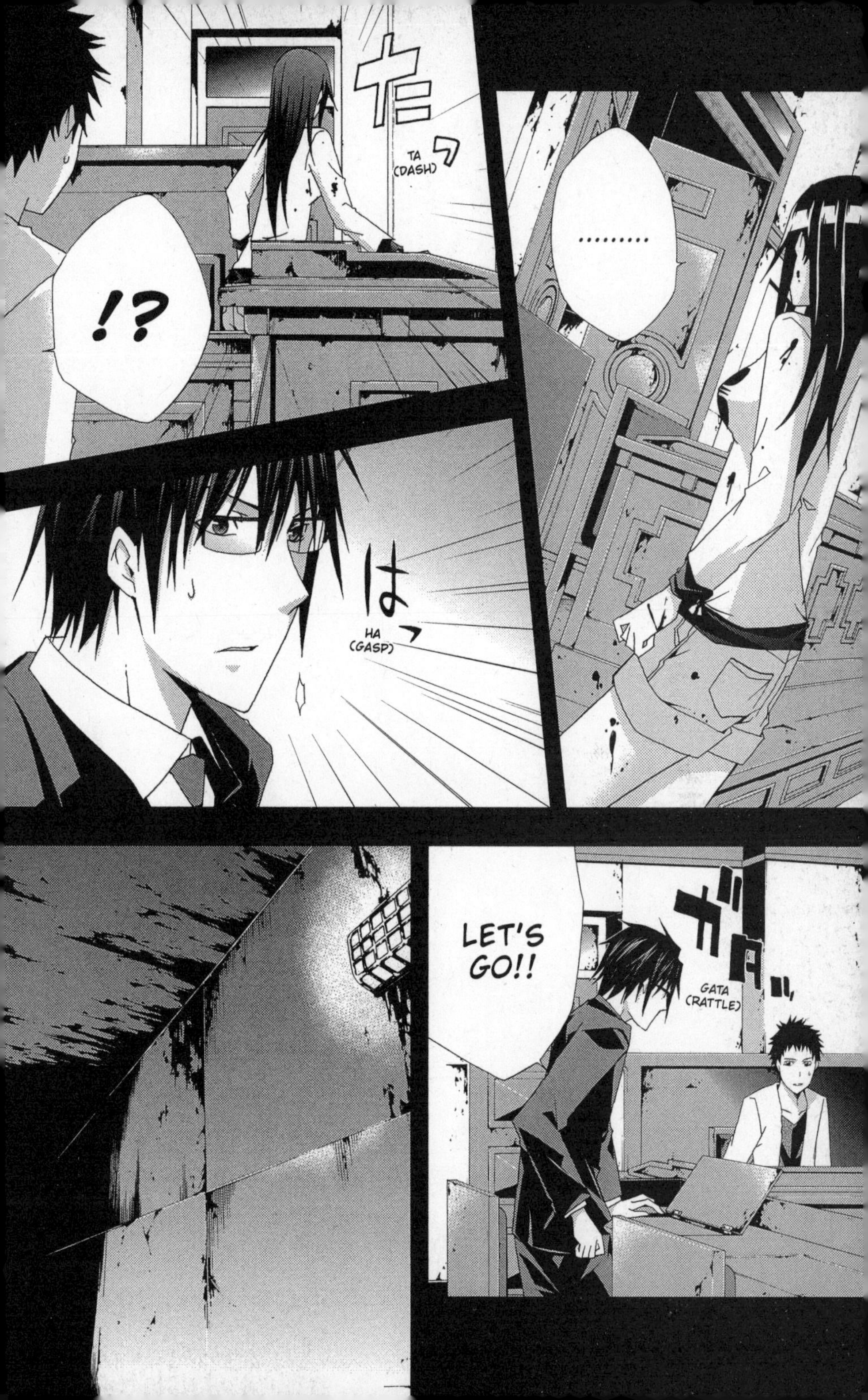
....
タッ
TA (DASH)
!?
はっ
HA (GASP)
LET'S GO!!
ガタッ
GATA (RATTLE)

GARAN
(CLANG)

!?

GII
(CREAK)

SU
(SLIDE)

MIKU-SAN...

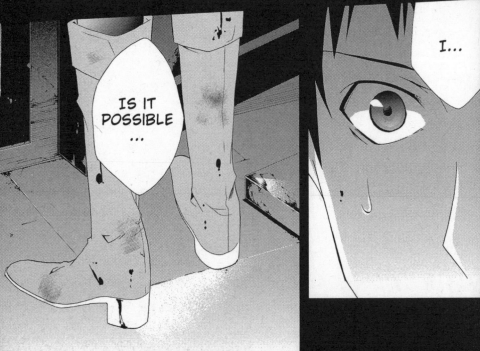

IS IT
POSSIBLE
...

I...

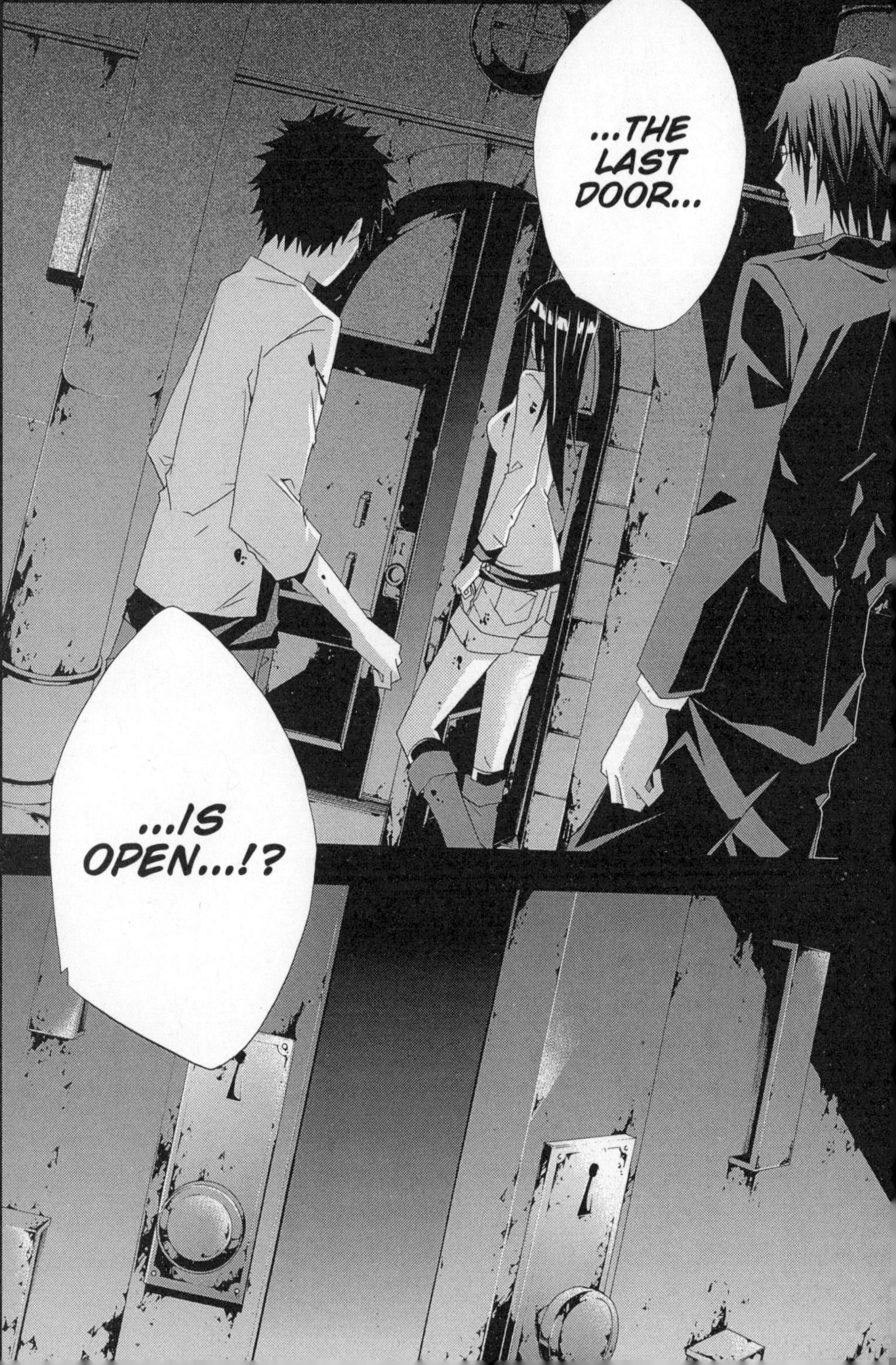
...THE LAST DOOR...
...IS OPEN...!?

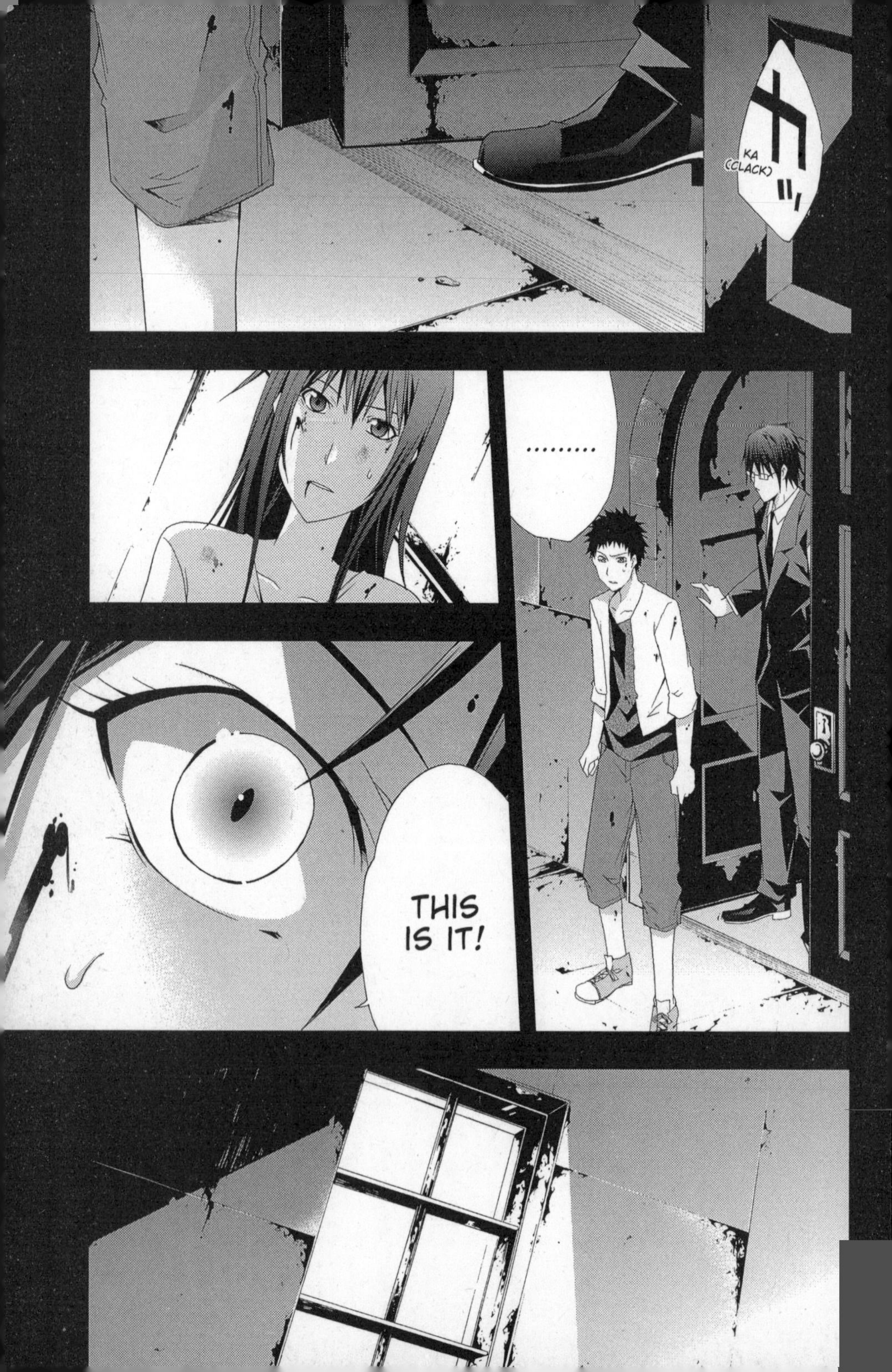

カッ
KA (CLACK)
………
THIS IS IT!

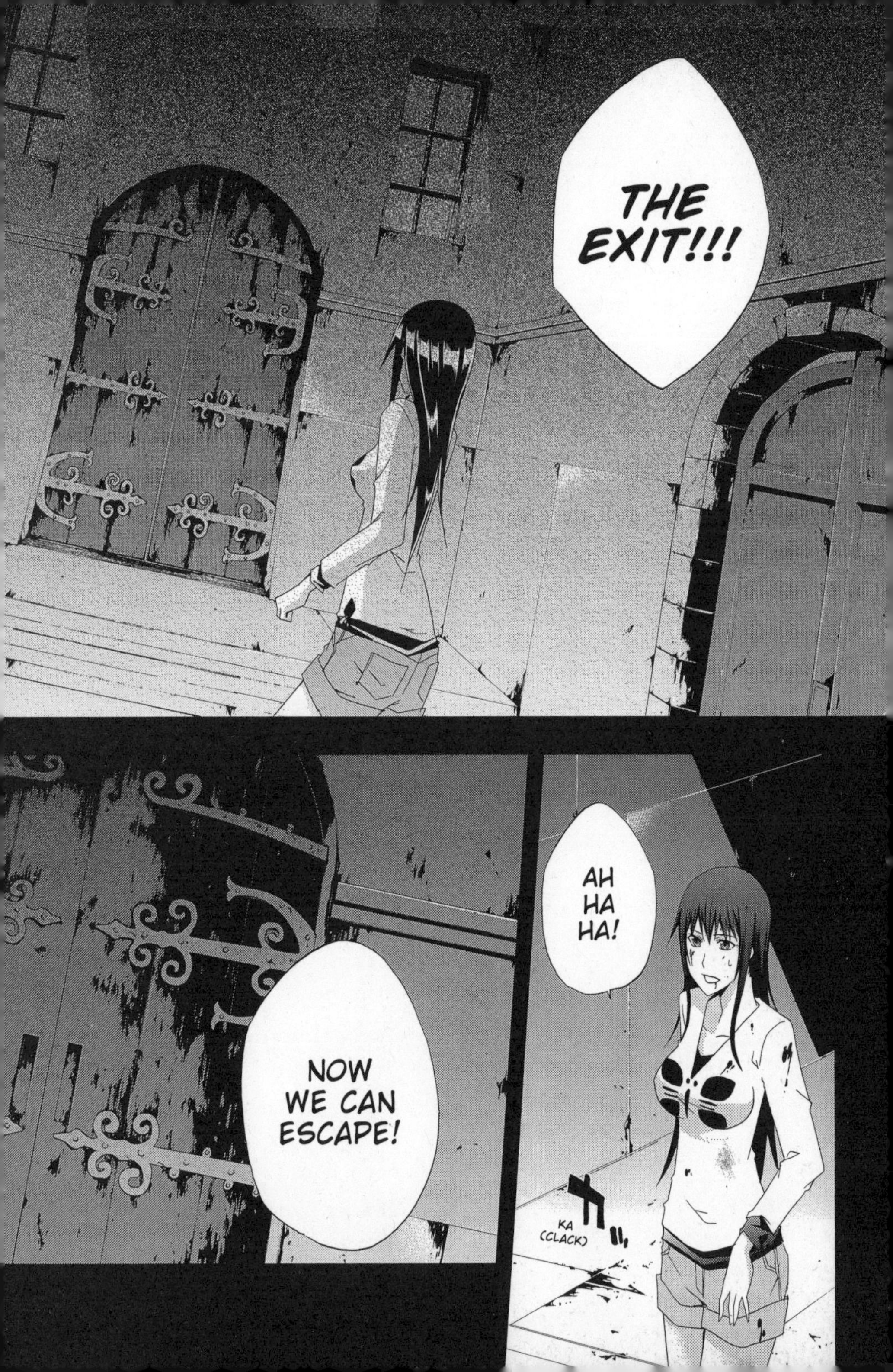
THE EXIT!!!
AH HA HA!
KA (CLACK)
NOW WE CAN ESCAPE!

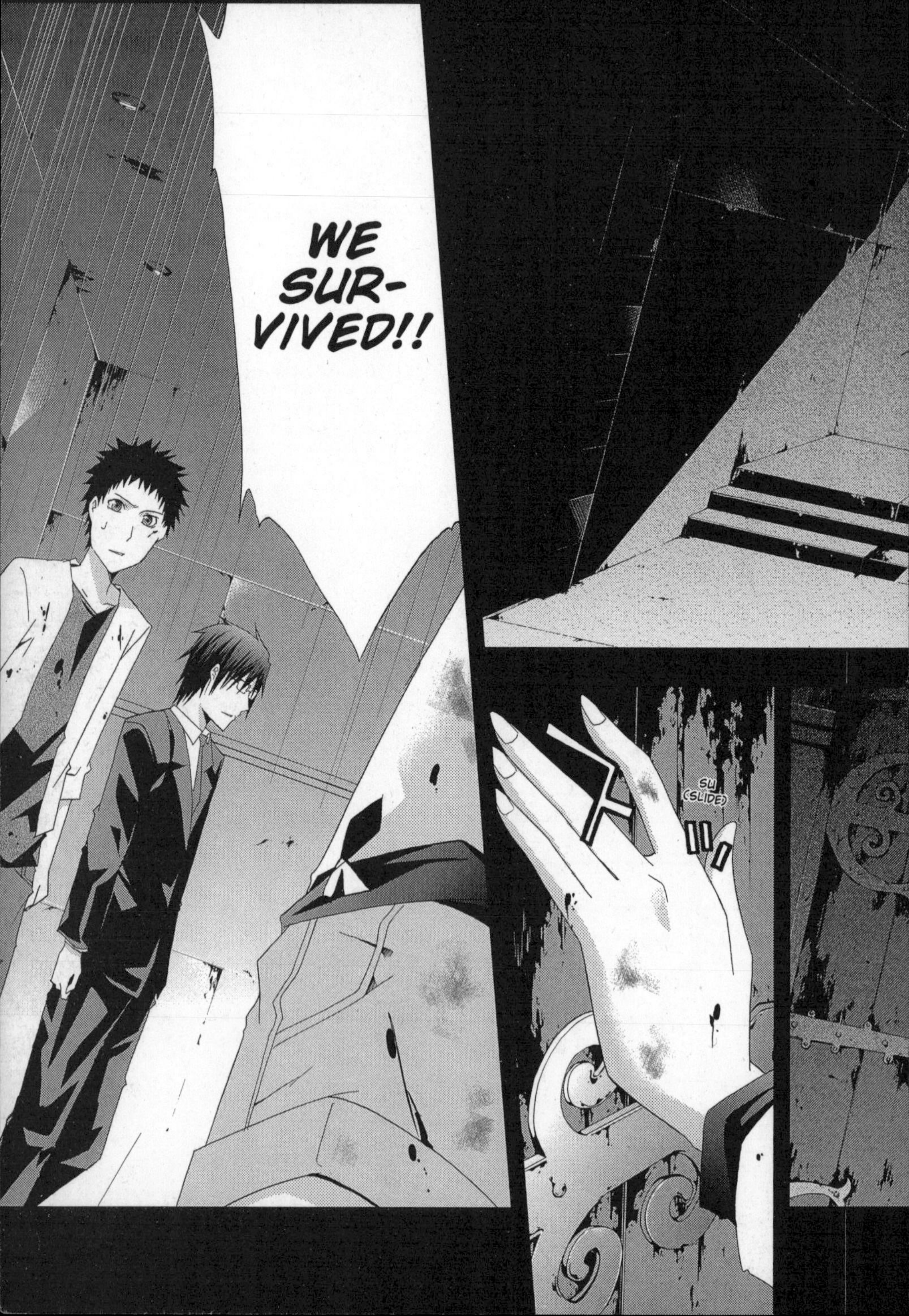
WE SUR-VIVED!!
SU (SLIDE)

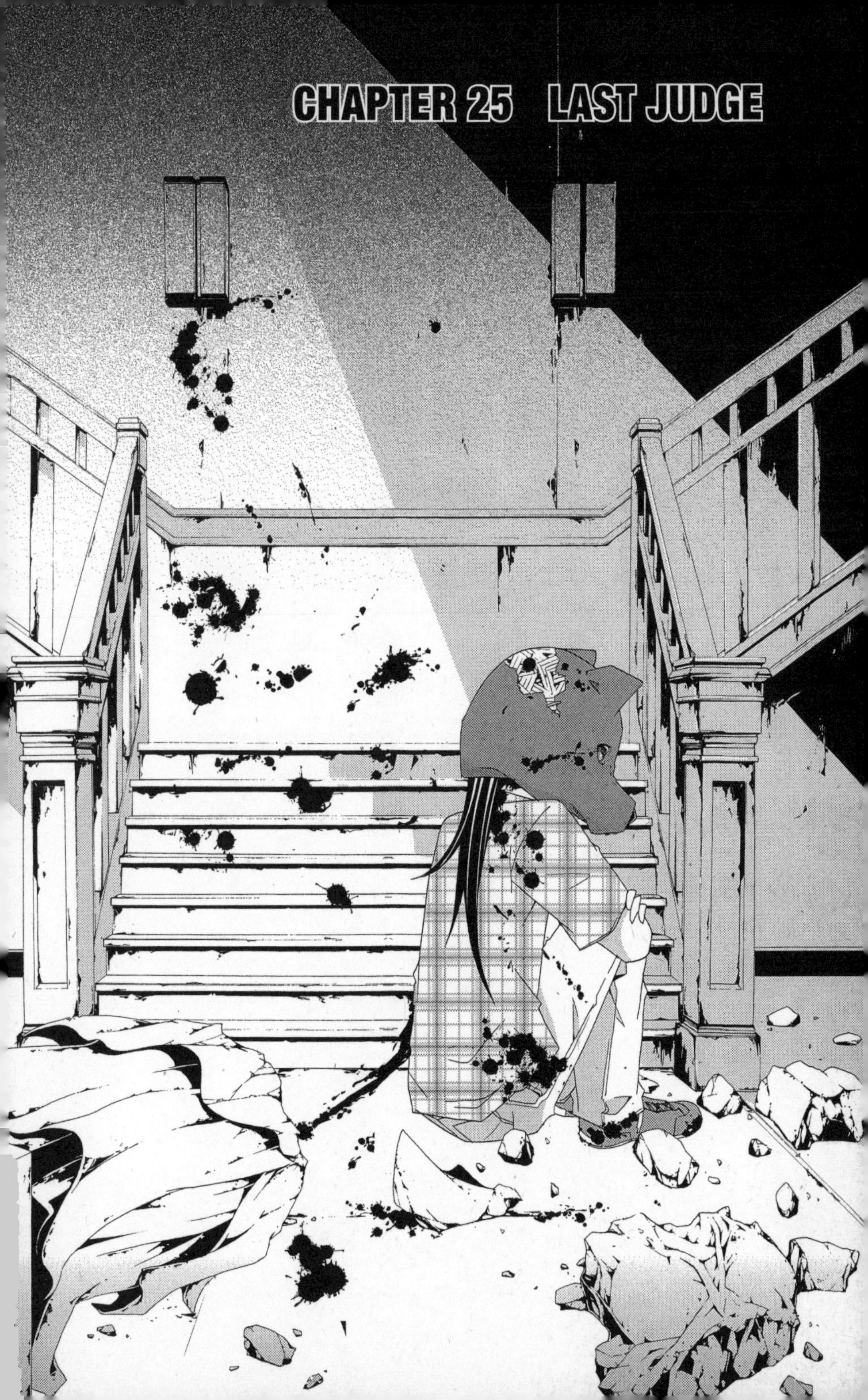
CHAPTER 25 LAST JUDGE

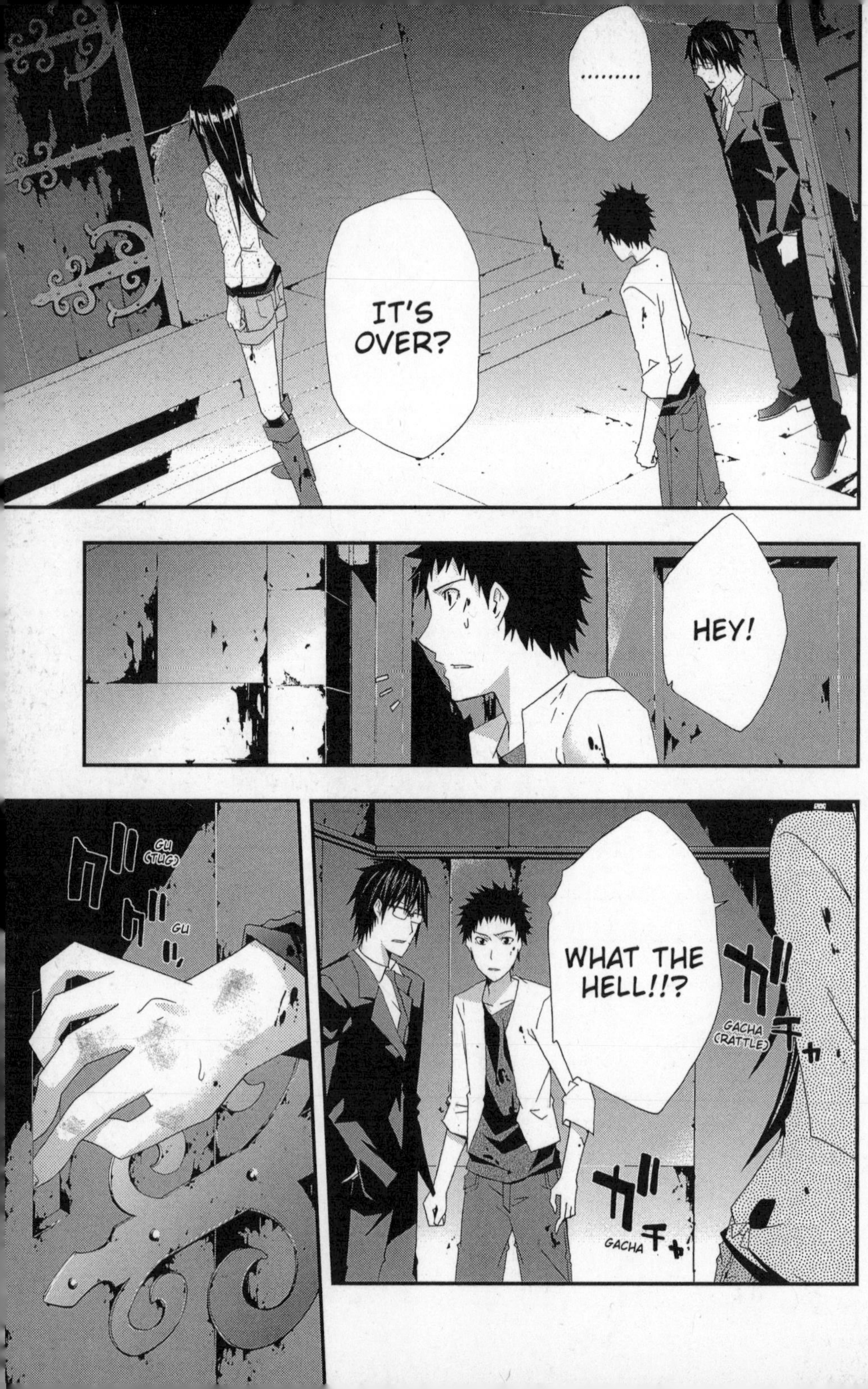

....
IT'S OVER?
HEY!
WHAT THE HELL!!?
GACHA (RATTLE)
GACHA
GU (TUG)
GU

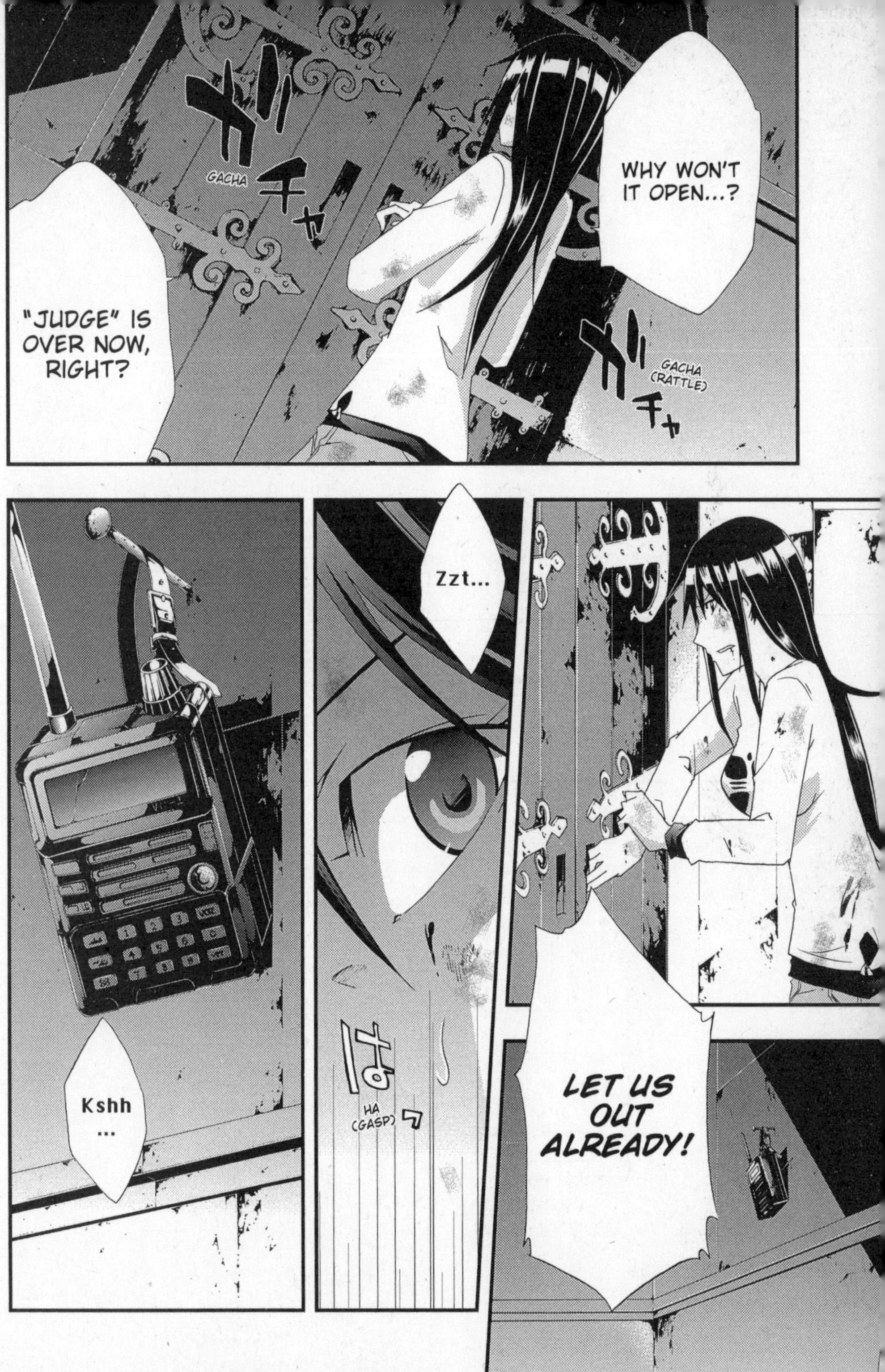
WHY WON'T IT OPEN...?
ガチャ
GACHA
"JUDGE" IS OVER NOW, RIGHT?
ガチャ
GACHA (RATTLE)
LET US OUT ALREADY!
Zzt...
はっ
HA (GASP)
Kshh ...

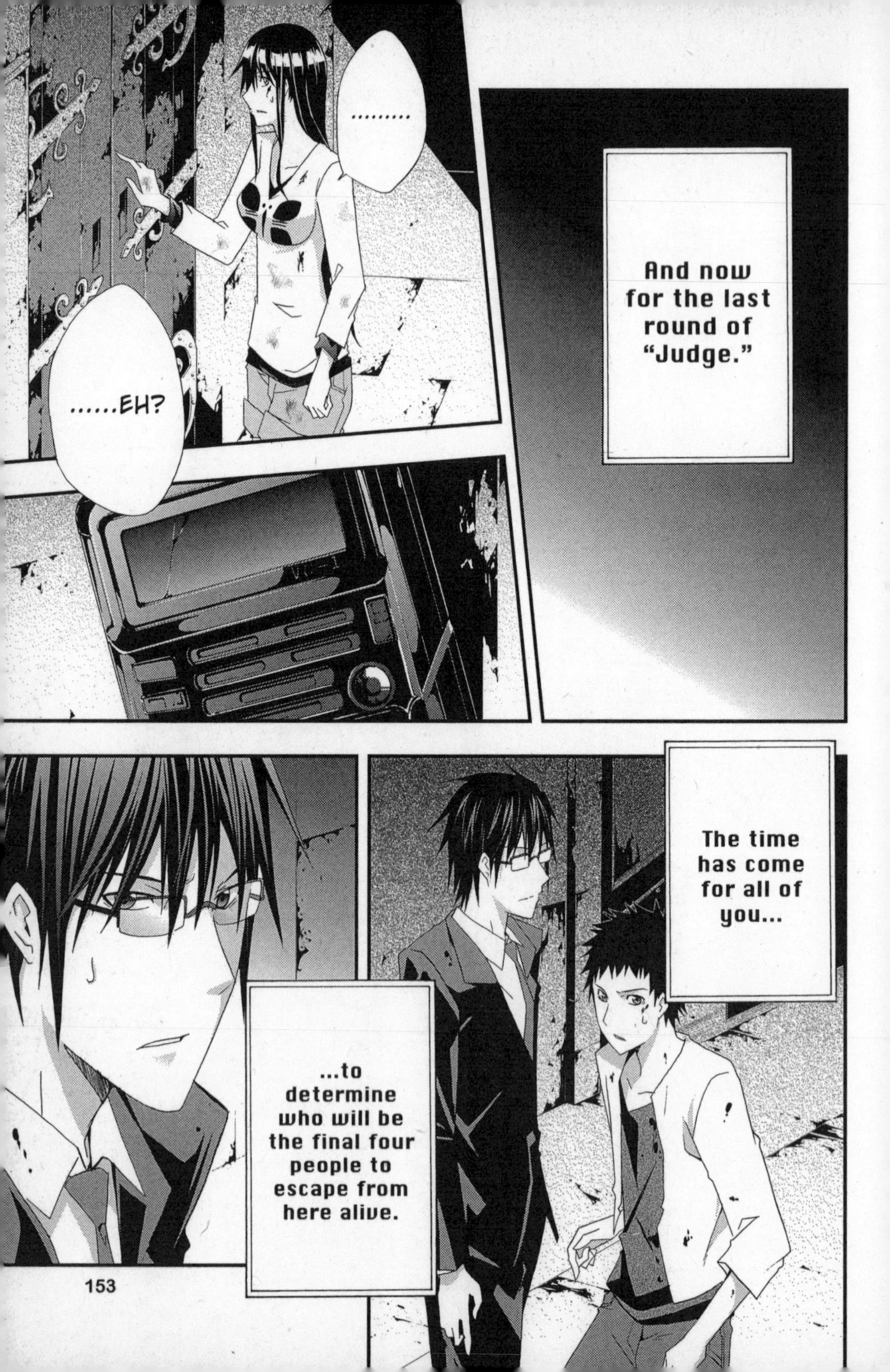
And now for the last round of "Judge."
....
......EH?
The time has come for all of you...
...to determine who will be the final four people to escape from here alive.

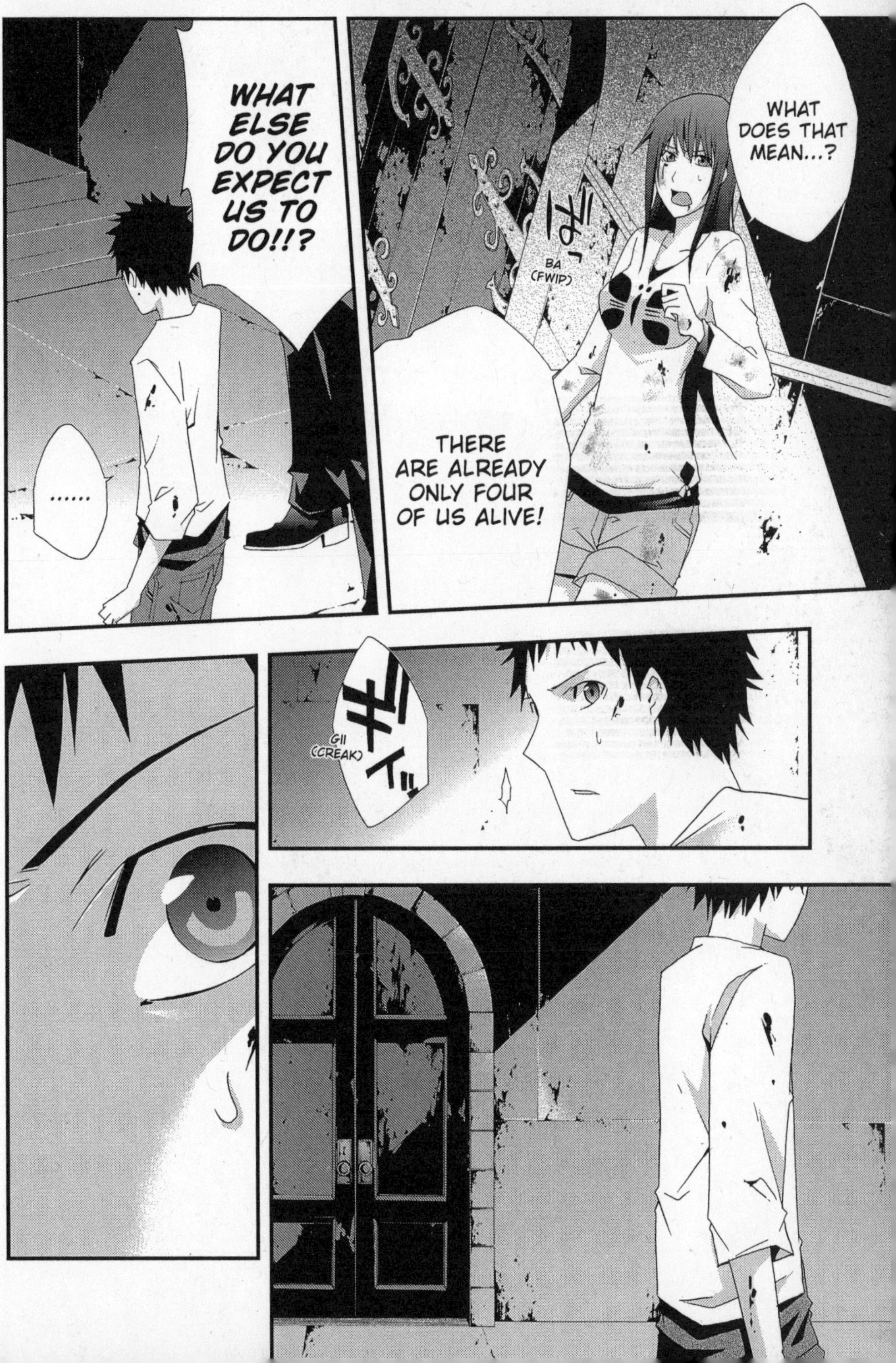
WHAT DOES THAT MEAN...?
ばっ
BA (FWIP)
THERE ARE ALREADY ONLY FOUR OF US ALIVE!
WHAT ELSE DO YOU EXPECT US TO DO!!?
......
ギイッ
GII (CREAK)

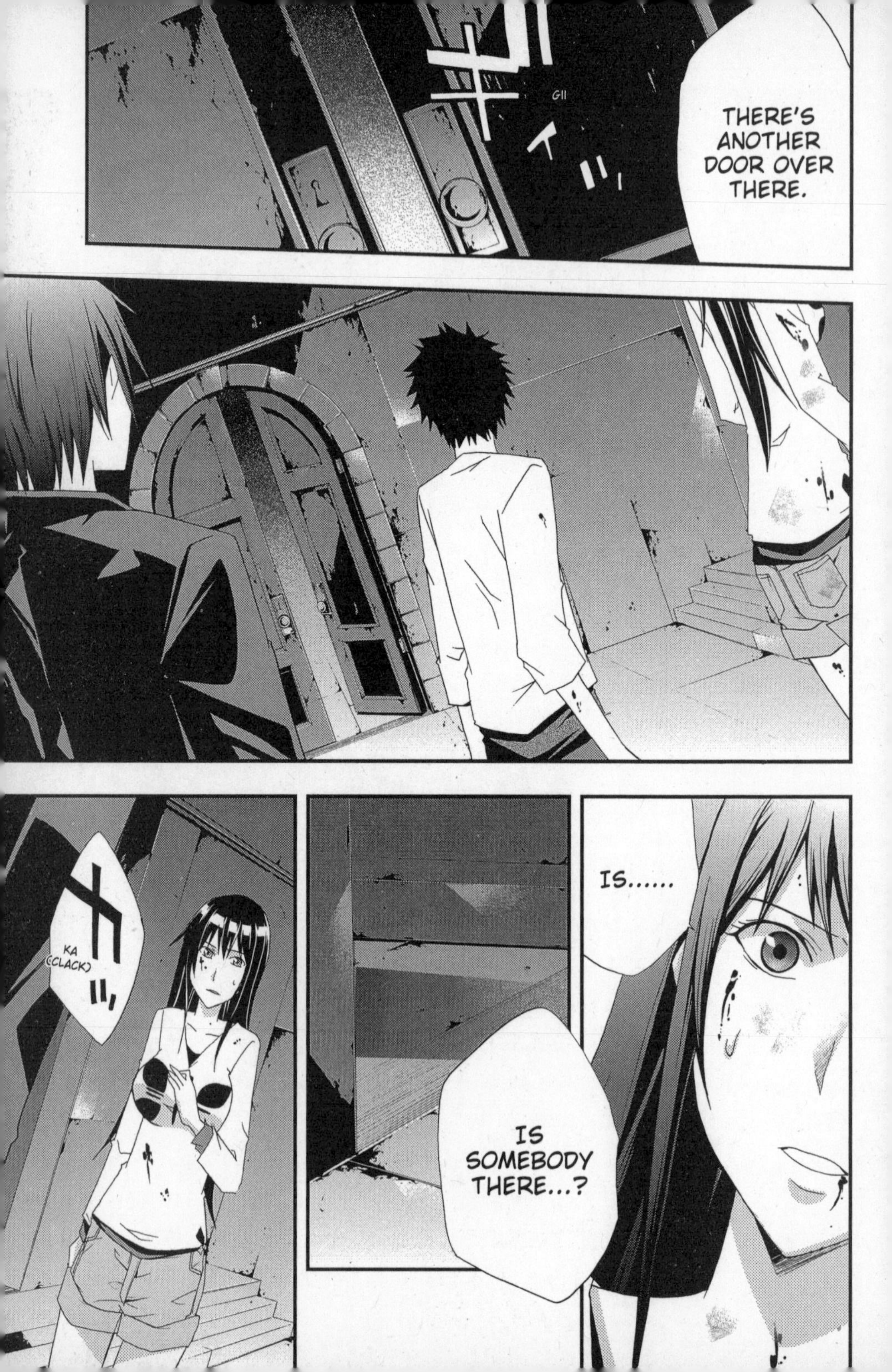
THERE'S ANOTHER DOOR OVER THERE.
GII
IS......
IS SOMEBODY THERE...?
KA (CLACK)

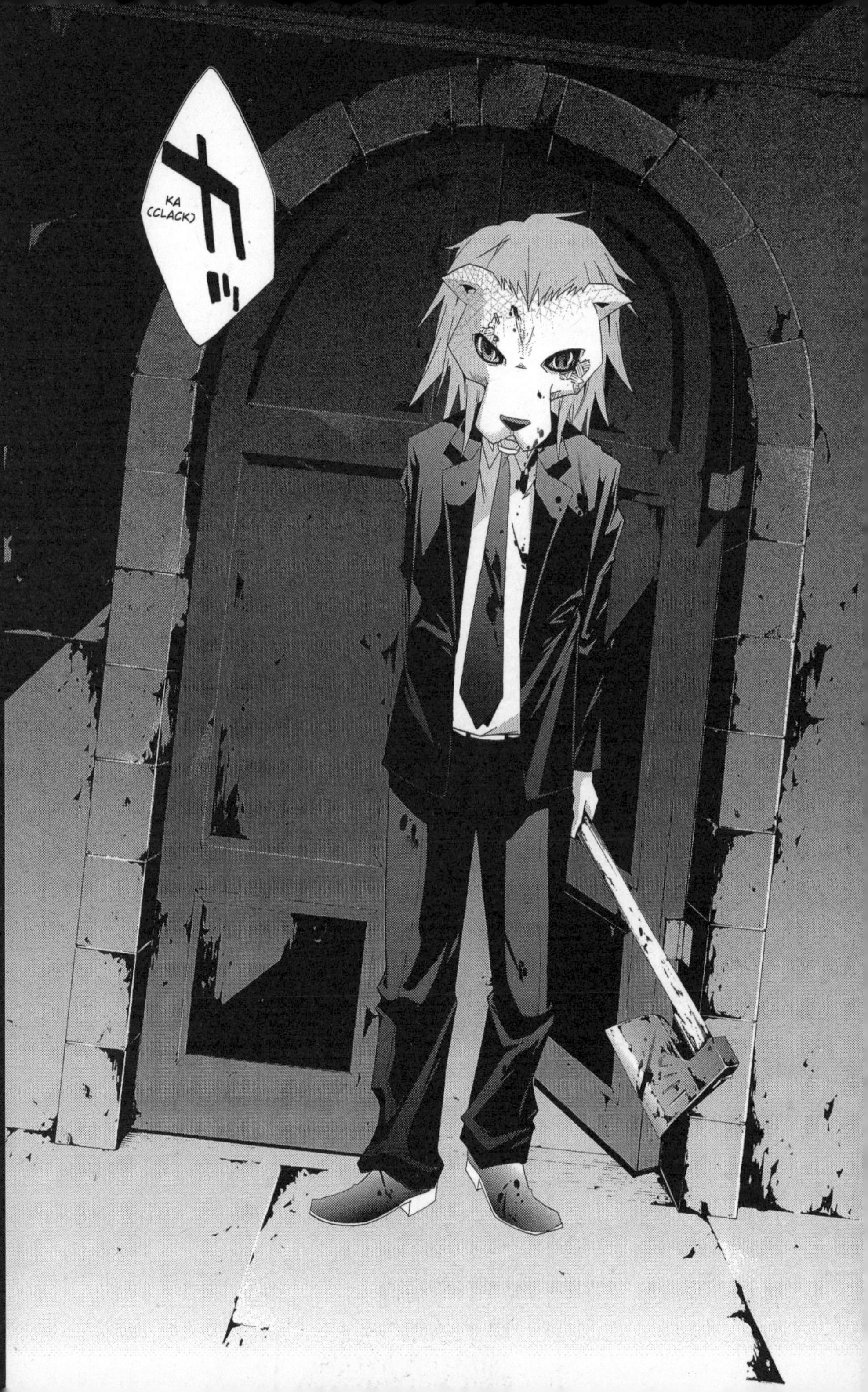

カッ
KA (CLACK)

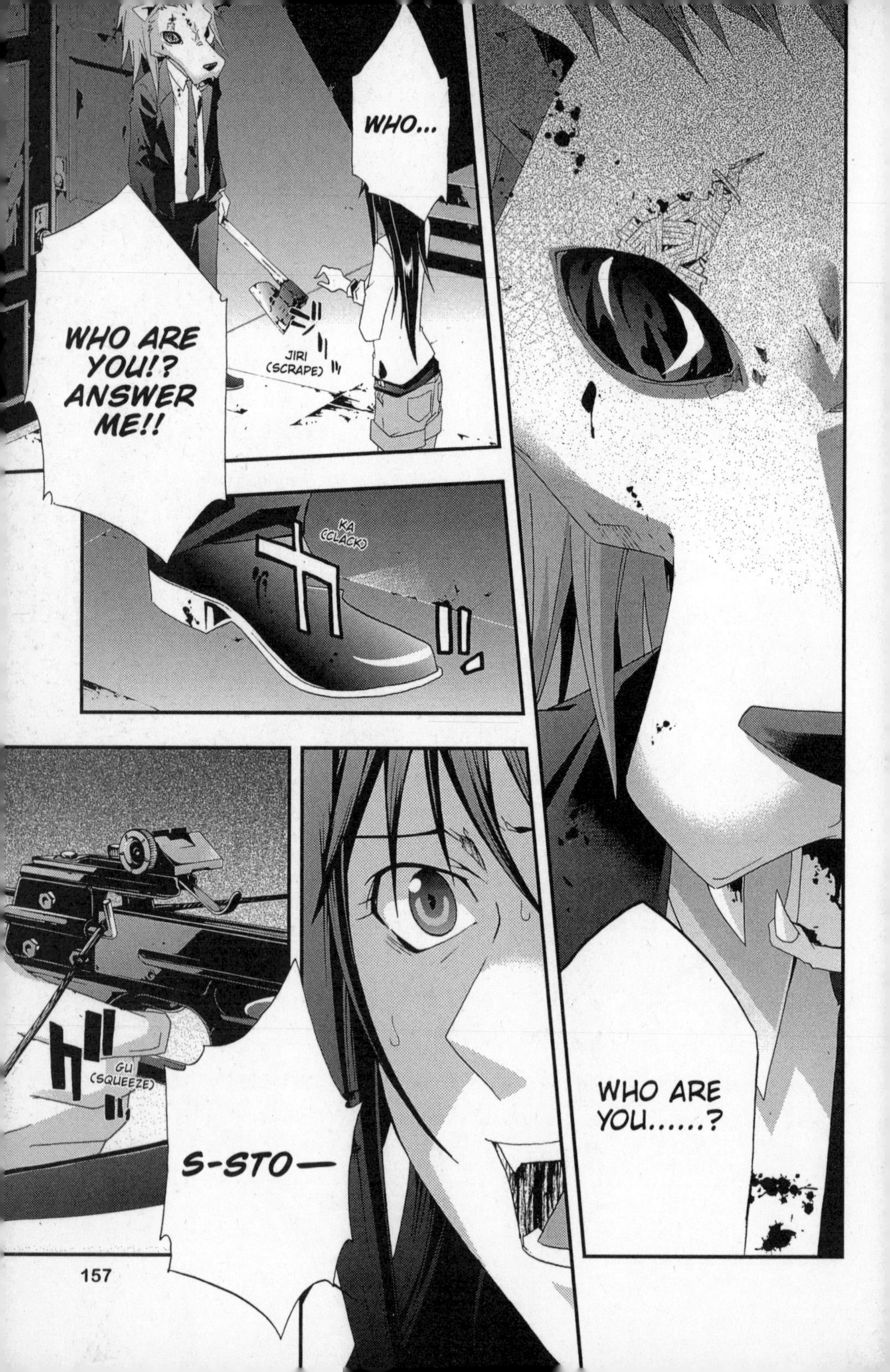
WHO ARE YOU......?
WHO...
WHO ARE YOU!? ANSWER ME!!
JIRI (SCRAPE)
KA (CLACK)
S-STO—
GU (SQUEEZE)

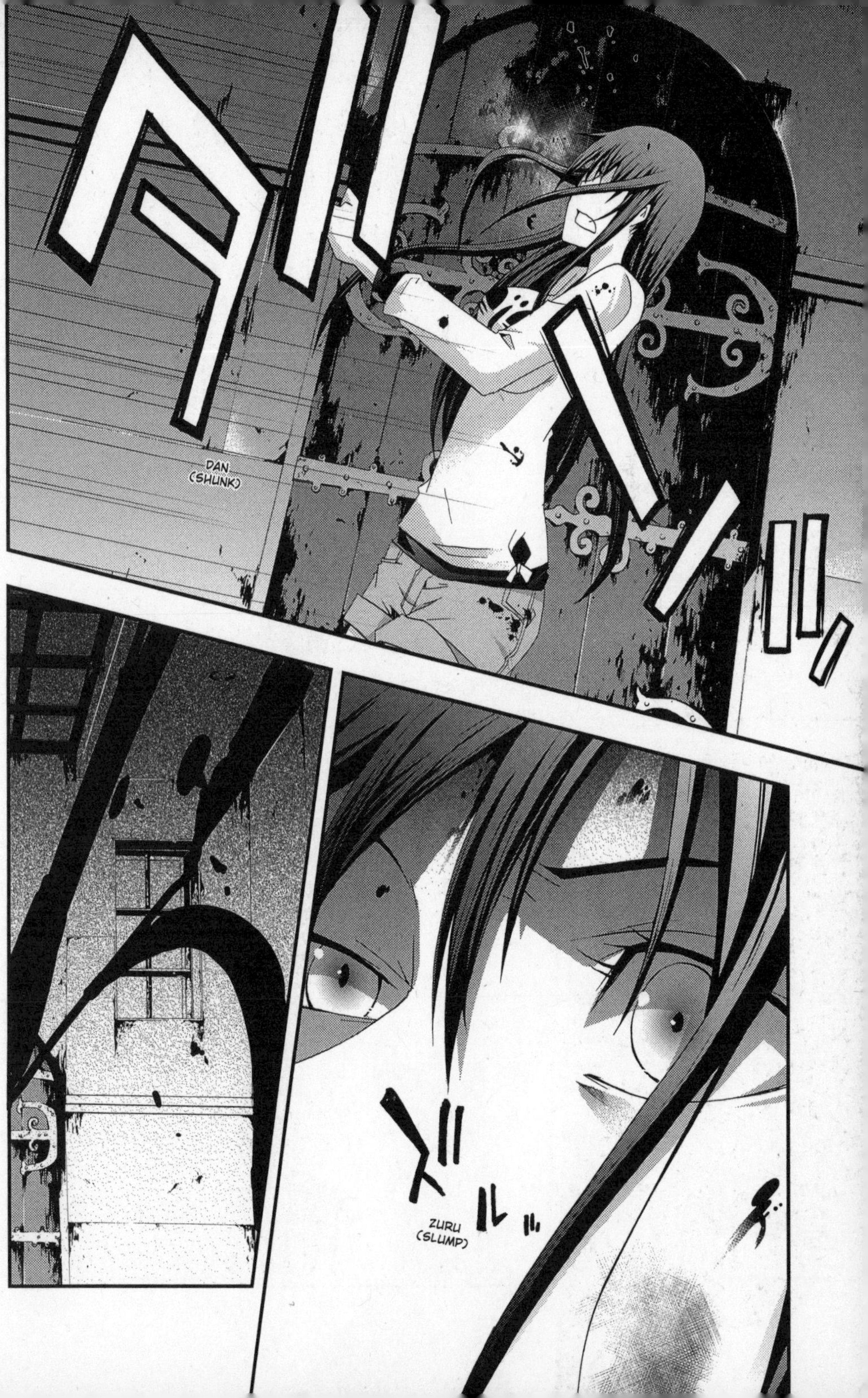
DAN
(SHUNK)
ZURU
(SLUMP)

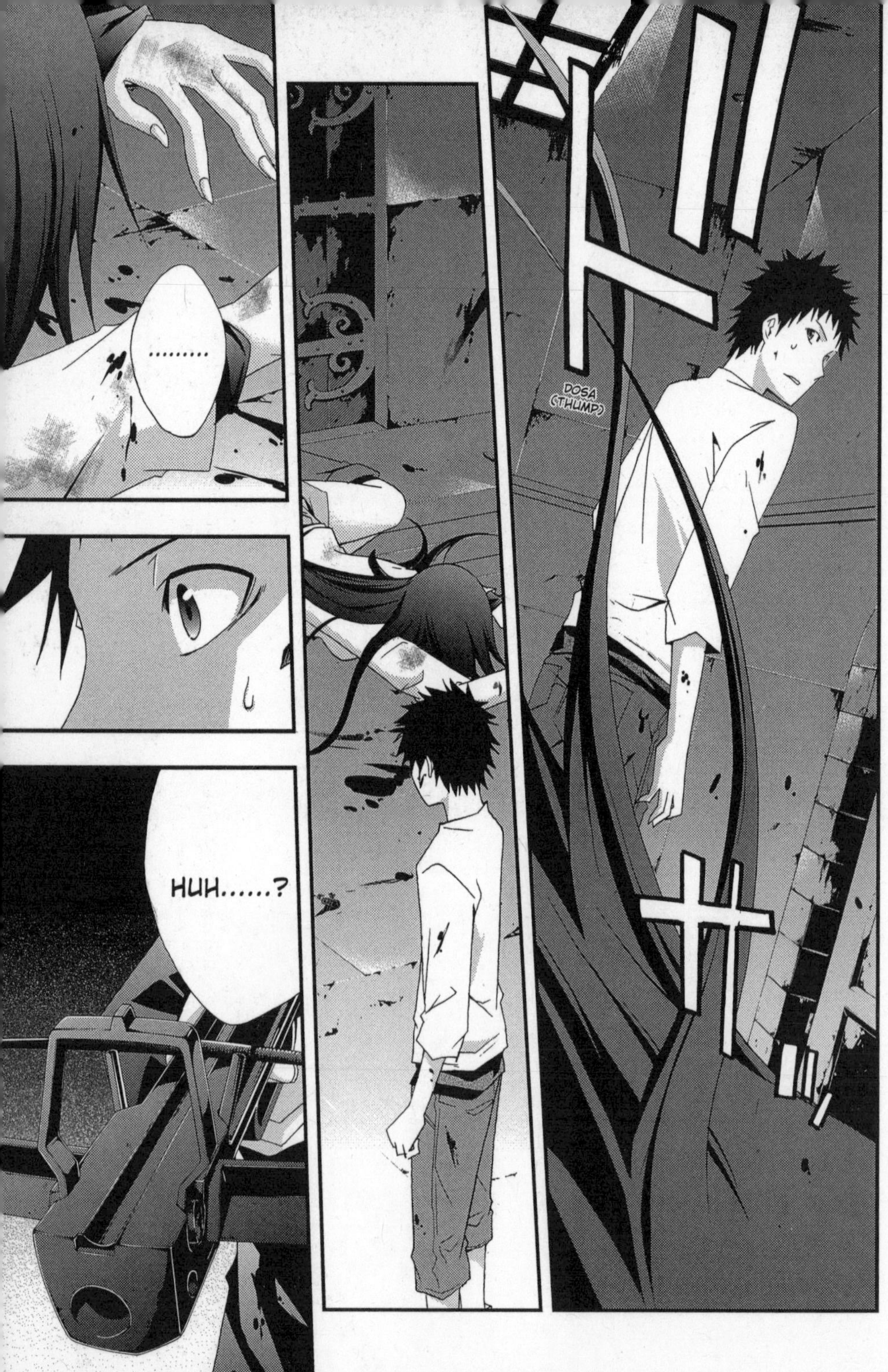
DOSA
(THUMP)
....
HUH......?

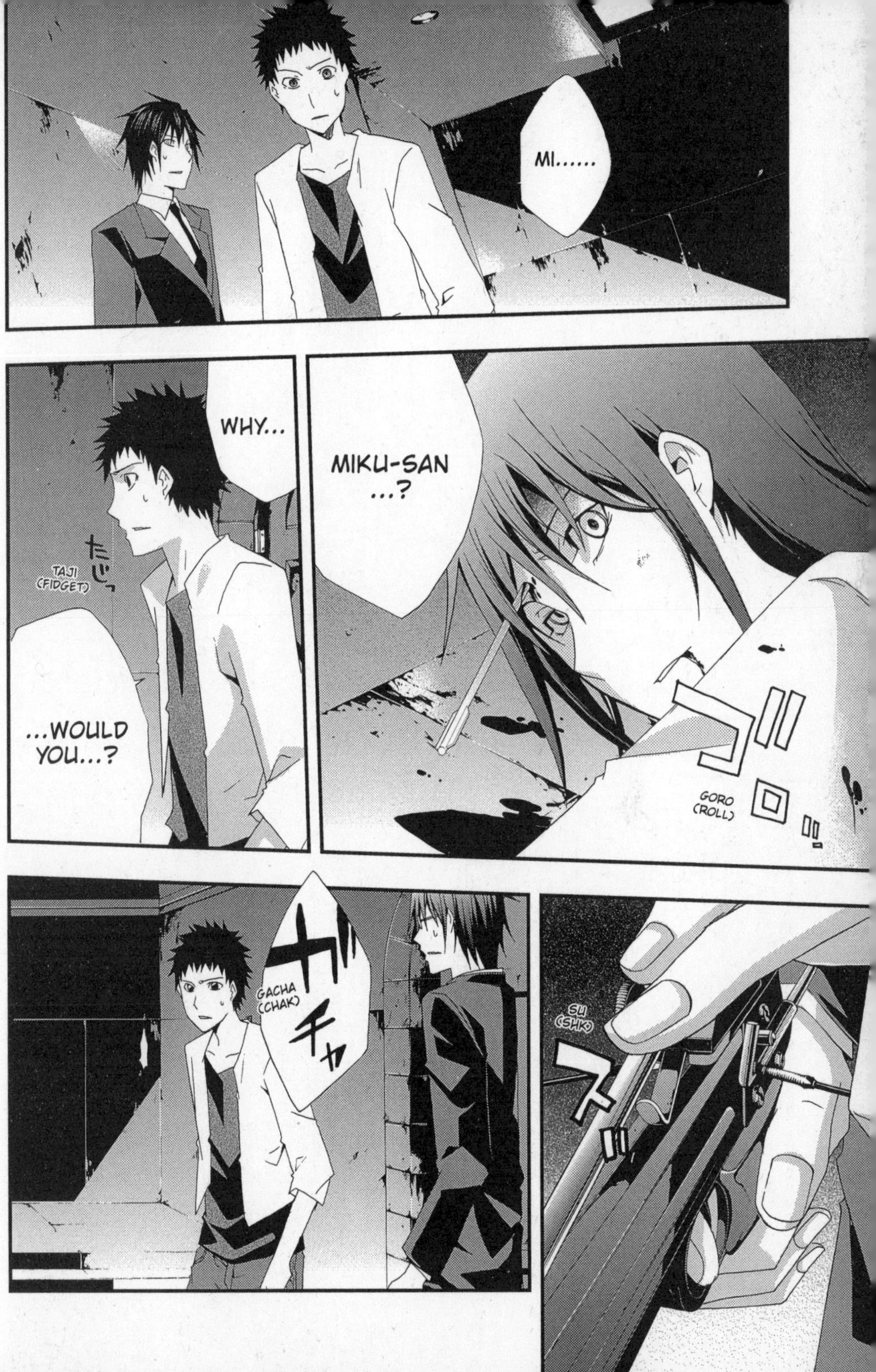

MI......
MIKU-SAN ...?
ゴロ
GORO (ROLL)
WHY...
たじっ
TAJI (FIDGET)
...WOULD YOU...?
スッ
SU (SHK)
ガチャ
GACHA (CHAK)

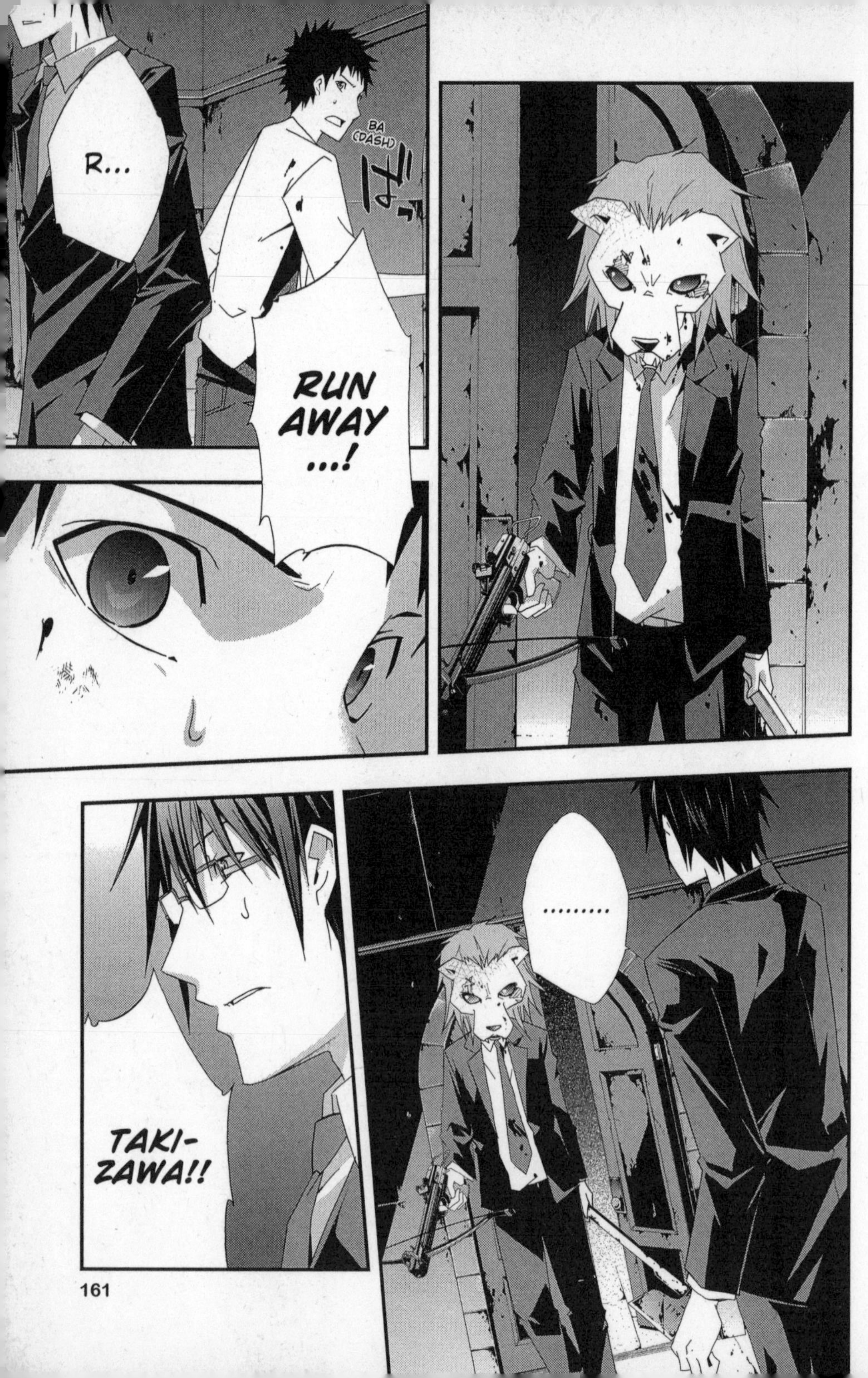
BA (DASH)
ばっ
R...
RUN AWAY ...!
....
TAKI-ZAWA!!

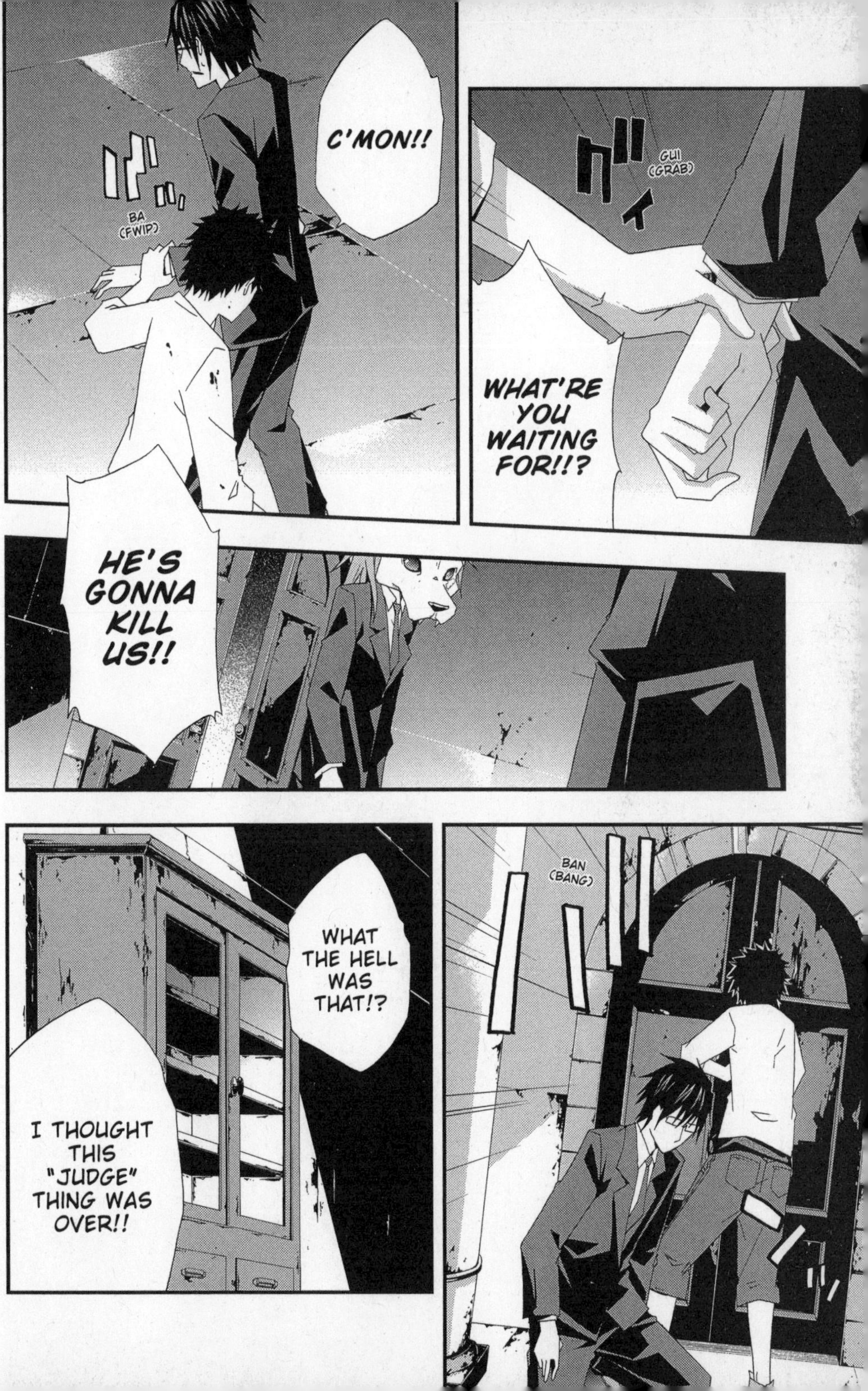
GUI
(GRAB)
WHAT'RE YOU WAITING FOR!!?
C'MON!!
BA
(FWIP)
HE'S GONNA KILL US!!
BAN
(BANG)
WHAT THE HELL WAS THAT!?
I THOUGHT THIS "JUDGE" THING WAS OVER!!

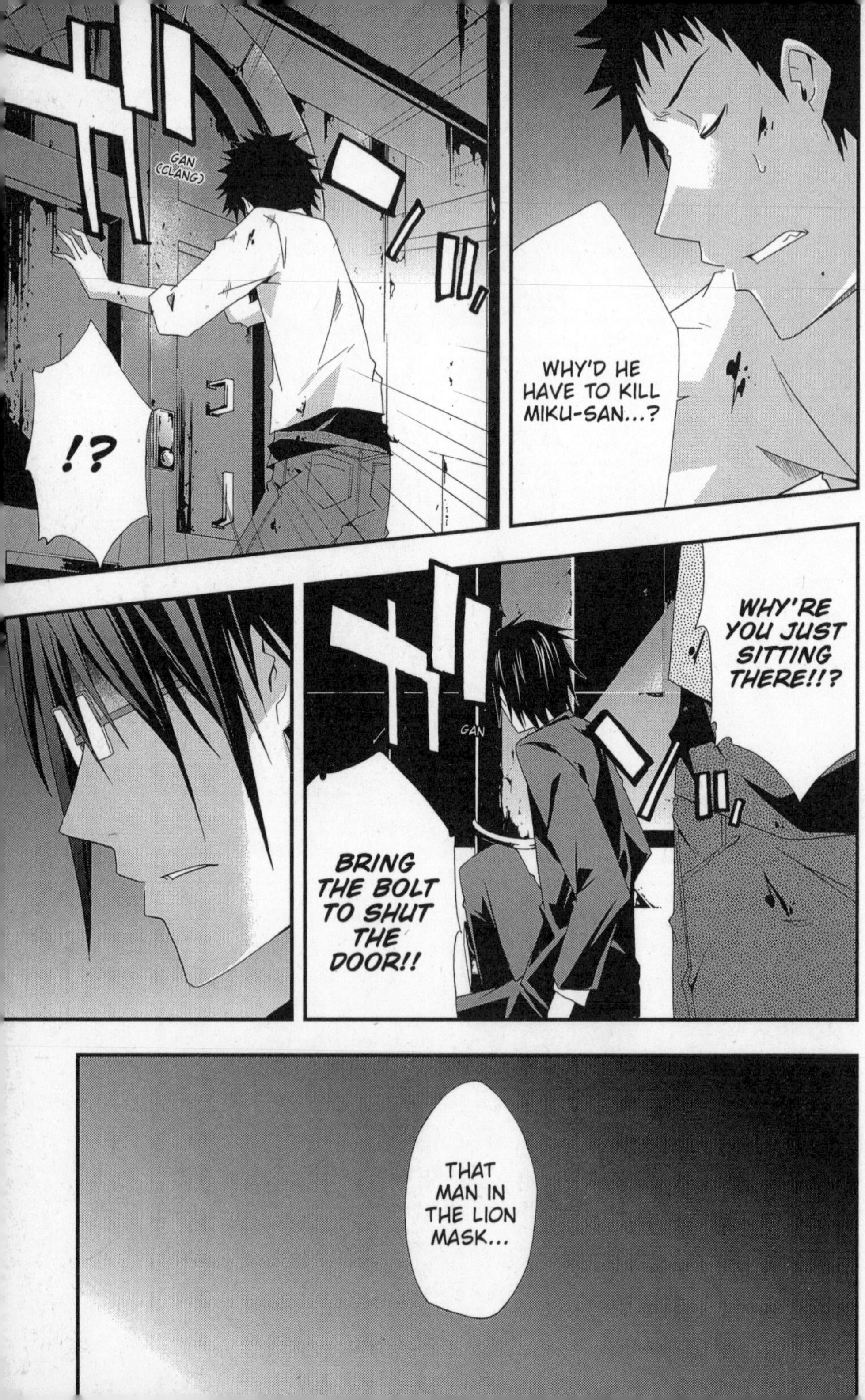
WHY'D HE HAVE TO KILL MIKU-SAN...?
GAN (CLANG)
!?
WHY'RE YOU JUST SITTING THERE!!?
GAN
BRING THE BOLT TO SHUT THE DOOR!!
THAT MAN IN THE LION MASK...

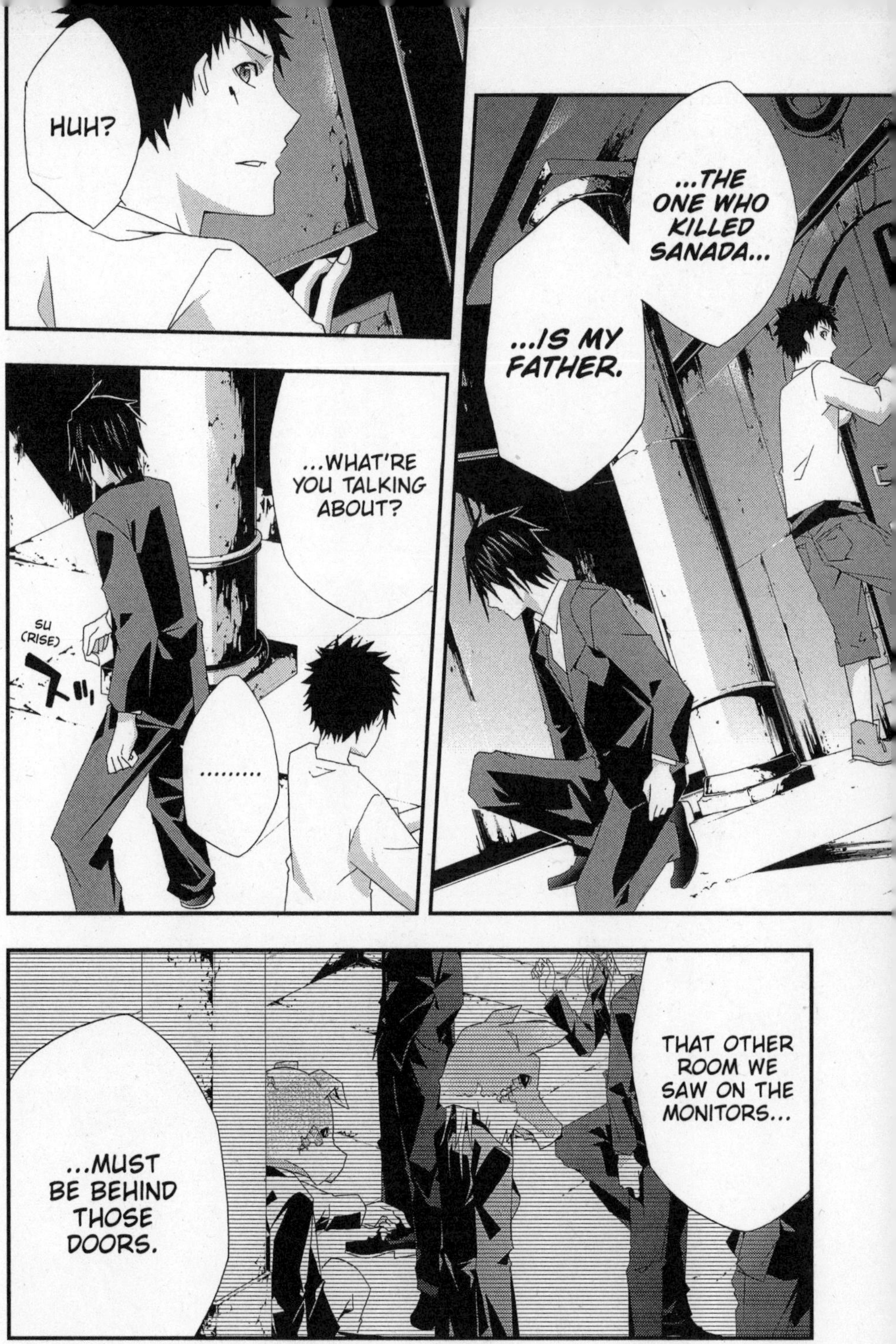
...THE ONE WHO KILLED SANADA...
...IS MY FATHER.
HUH?
...WHAT'RE YOU TALKING ABOUT?
SU (RISE)
....
THAT OTHER ROOM WE SAW ON THE MONITORS...
...MUST BE BEHIND THOSE DOORS.

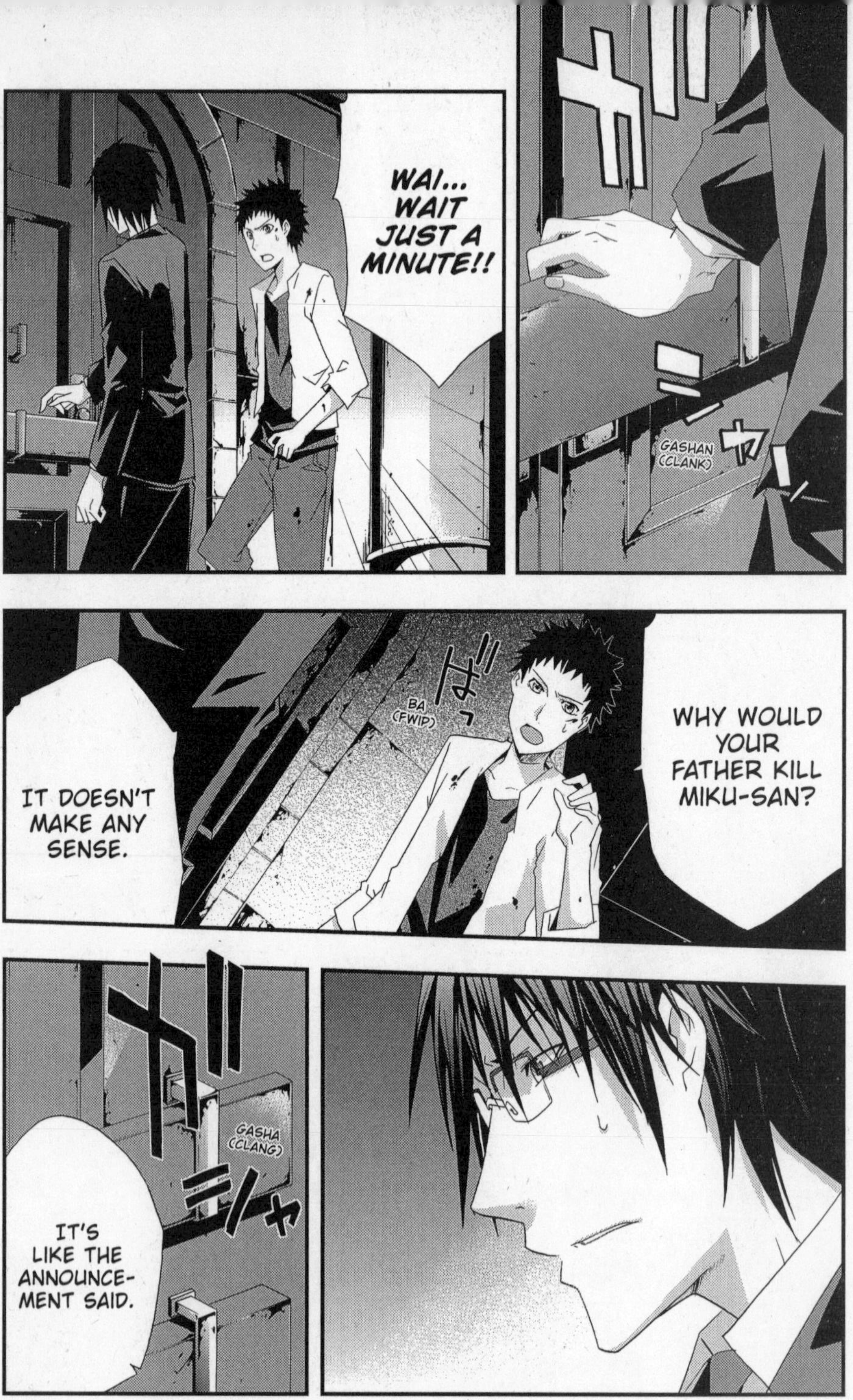
GASHAN (CLANK)
WAI... WAIT JUST A MINUTE!!
WHY WOULD YOUR FATHER KILL MIKU-SAN?
BA (FWIP)
IT DOESN'T MAKE ANY SENSE.
GASHA (CLANG)
IT'S LIKE THE ANNOUNCEMENT SAID.

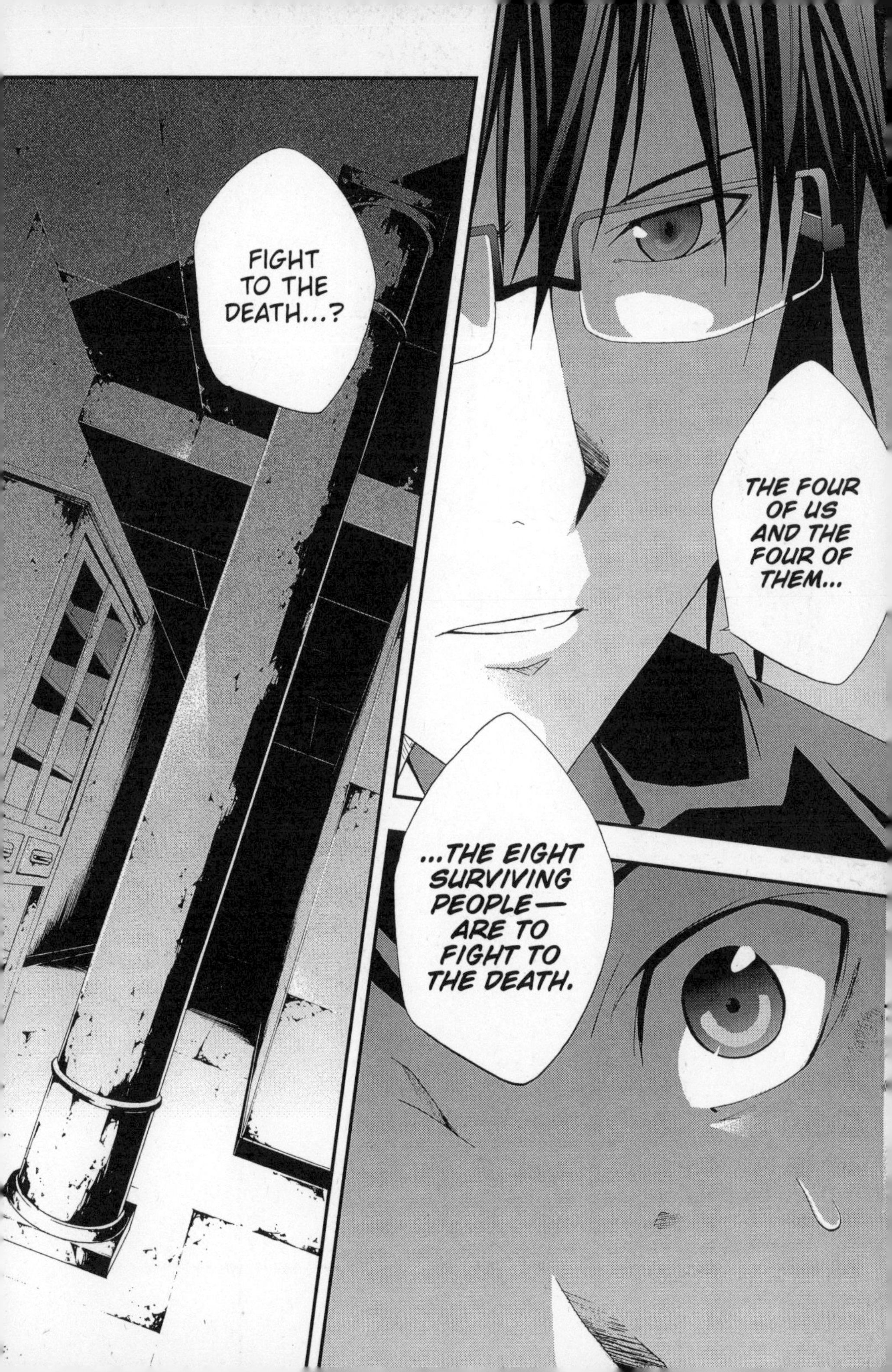
THE FOUR OF US AND THE FOUR OF THEM...
...THE EIGHT SURVIVING PEOPLE—ARE TO FIGHT TO THE DEATH.
FIGHT TO THE DEATH...?

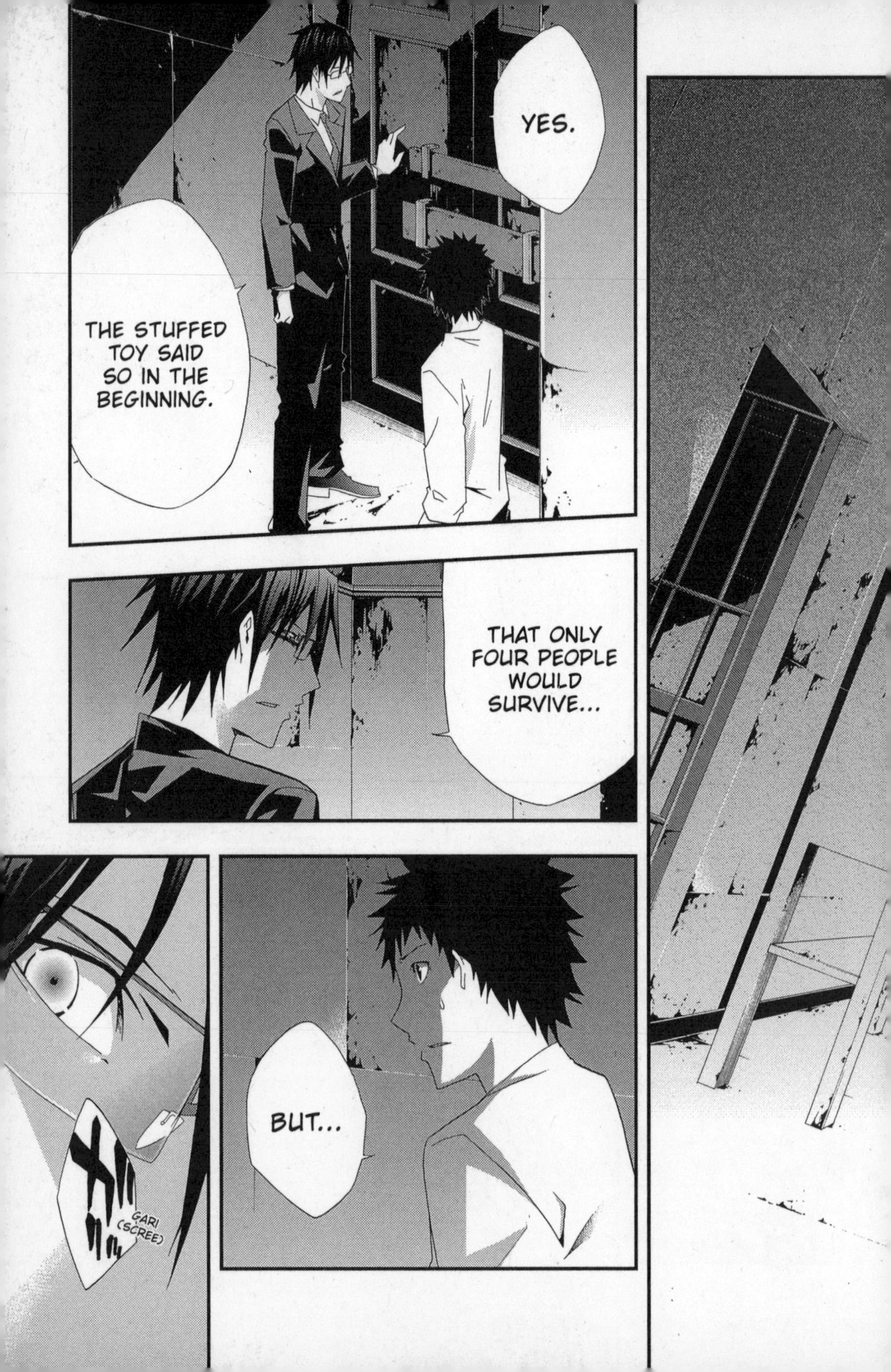
YES.
THE STUFFED TOY SAID SO IN THE BEGINNING.
THAT ONLY FOUR PEOPLE WOULD SURVIVE...
BUT...
GARI (SCREE)

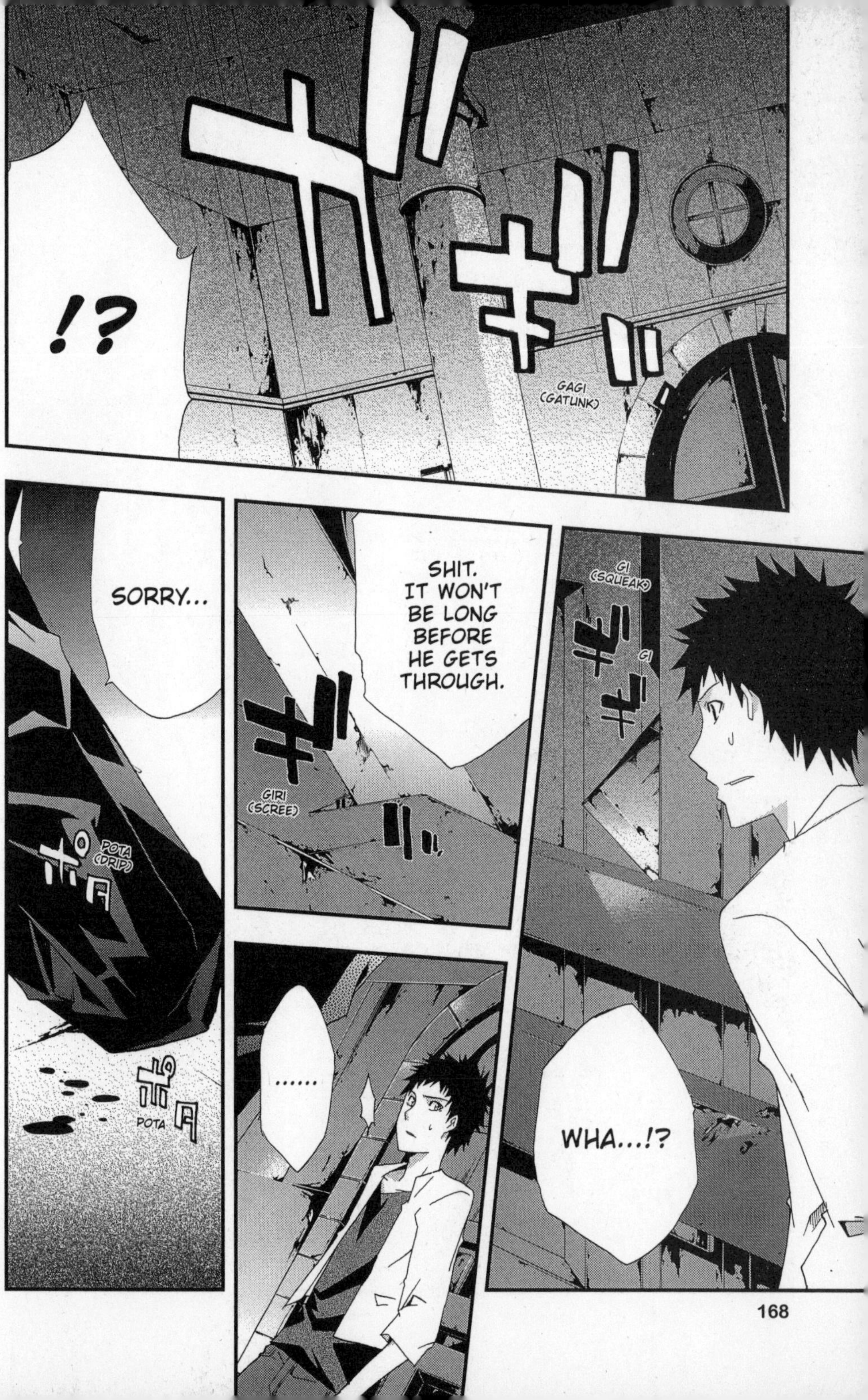
!?
GAGI (GATUNK)
GI (SQUEAK)
GI
WHA...!?
SHIT. IT WON'T BE LONG BEFORE HE GETS THROUGH.
GIRI (SCREE)
......
SORRY...
POTA (DRIP)
POTA

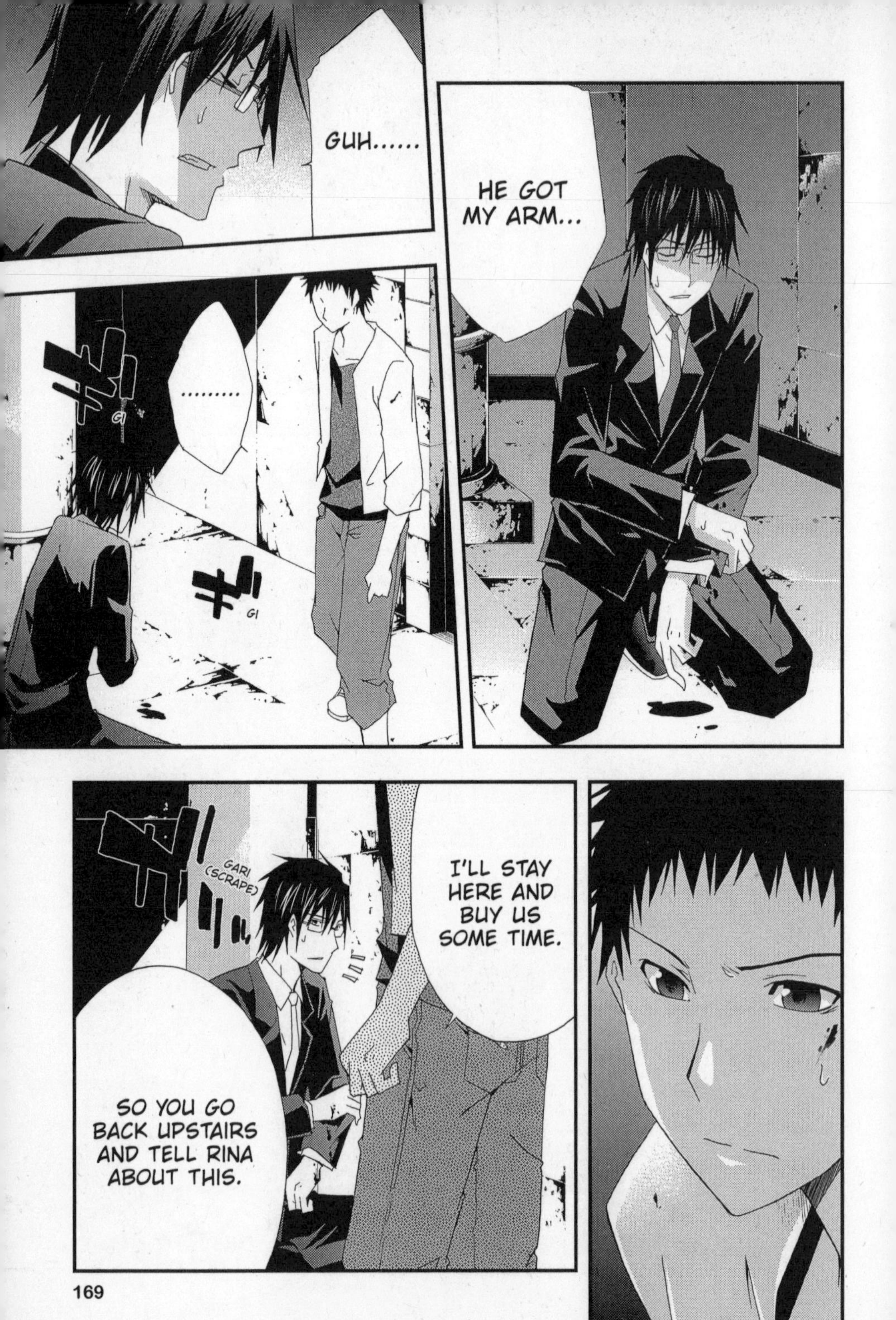
GUH......
HE GOT MY ARM...
....
GI
GI
I'LL STAY HERE AND BUY US SOME TIME.
GARI (SCRAPE)
SO YOU GO BACK UPSTAIRS AND TELL RINA ABOUT THIS.

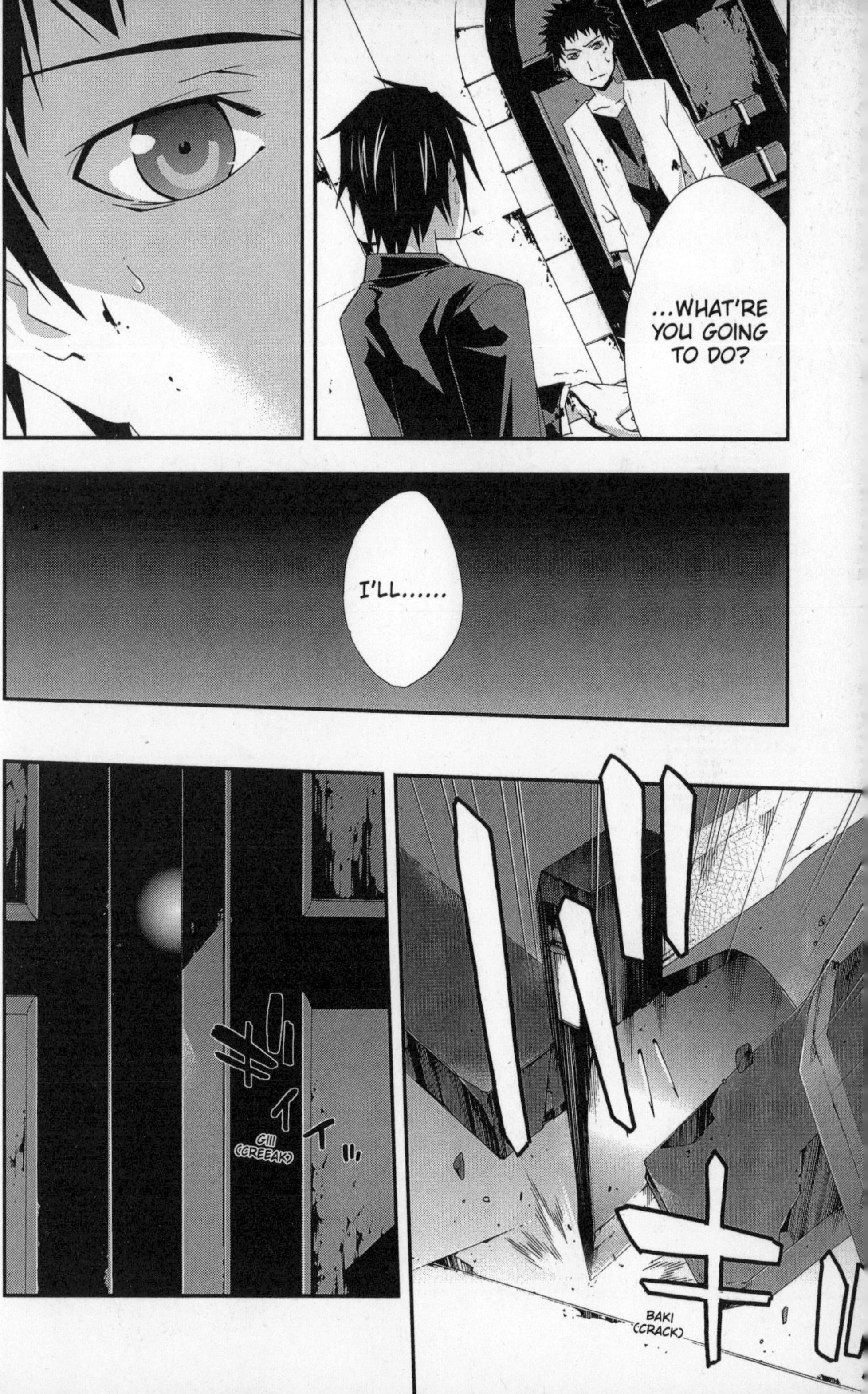
...WHAT'RE YOU GOING TO DO?
I'LL......
BAKI (CRACK)
GIII (CREEAK)

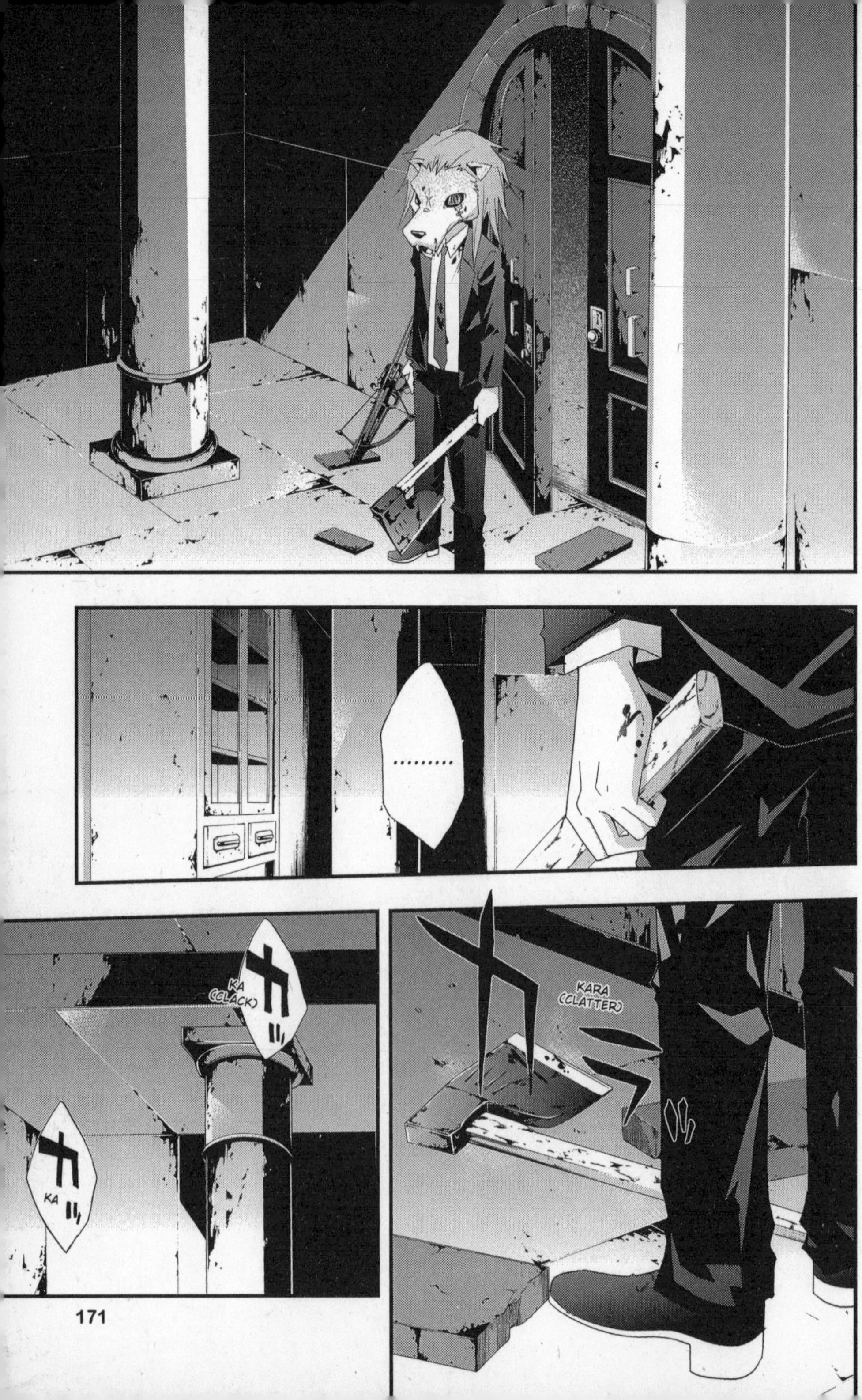
....
KARA (CLATTER)
KA (CLACK)
KA

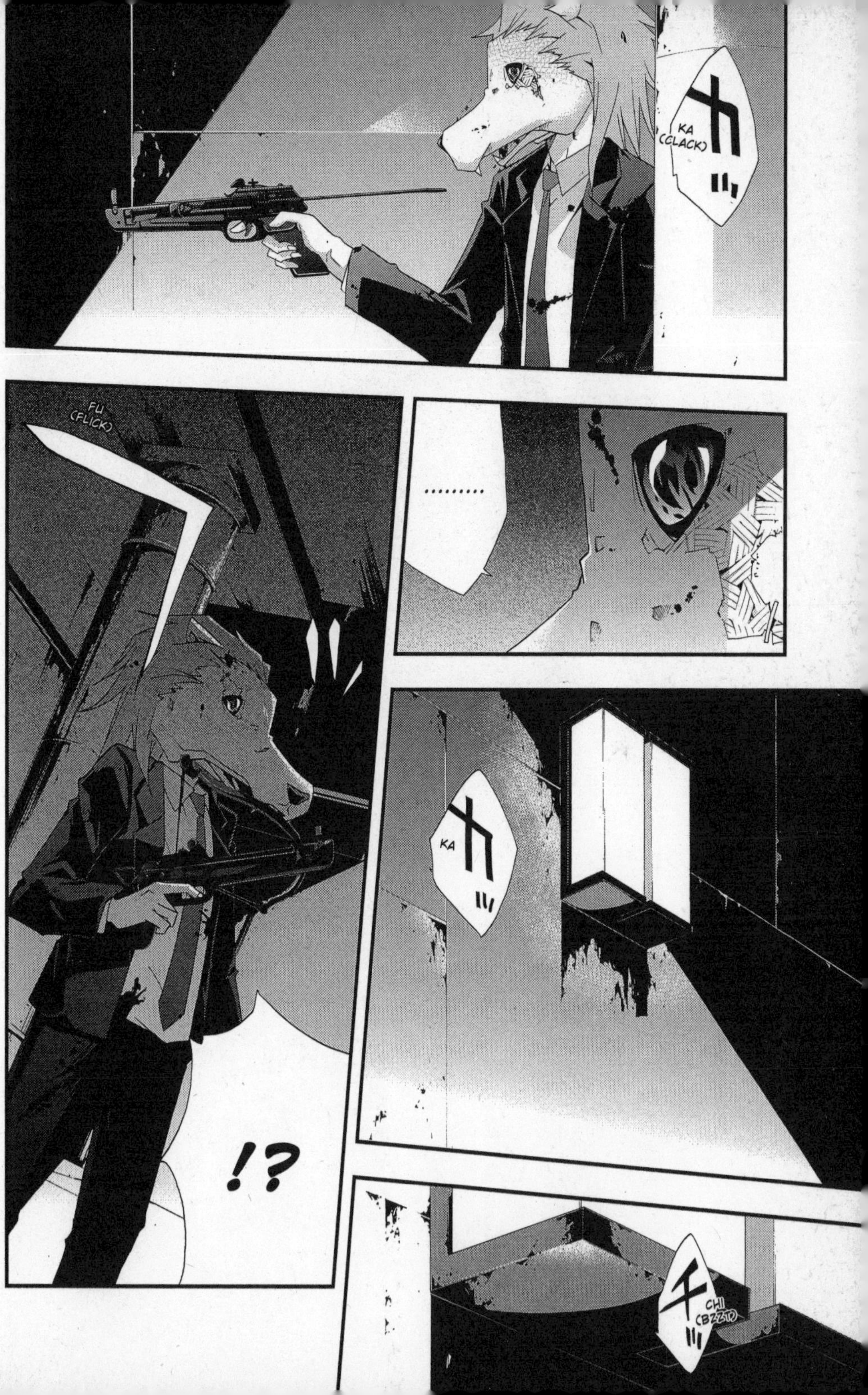
カッ
KA (CLACK)
....
カッ
KA
チッ
CHI (BZZT)
FU (FLICK)
!?

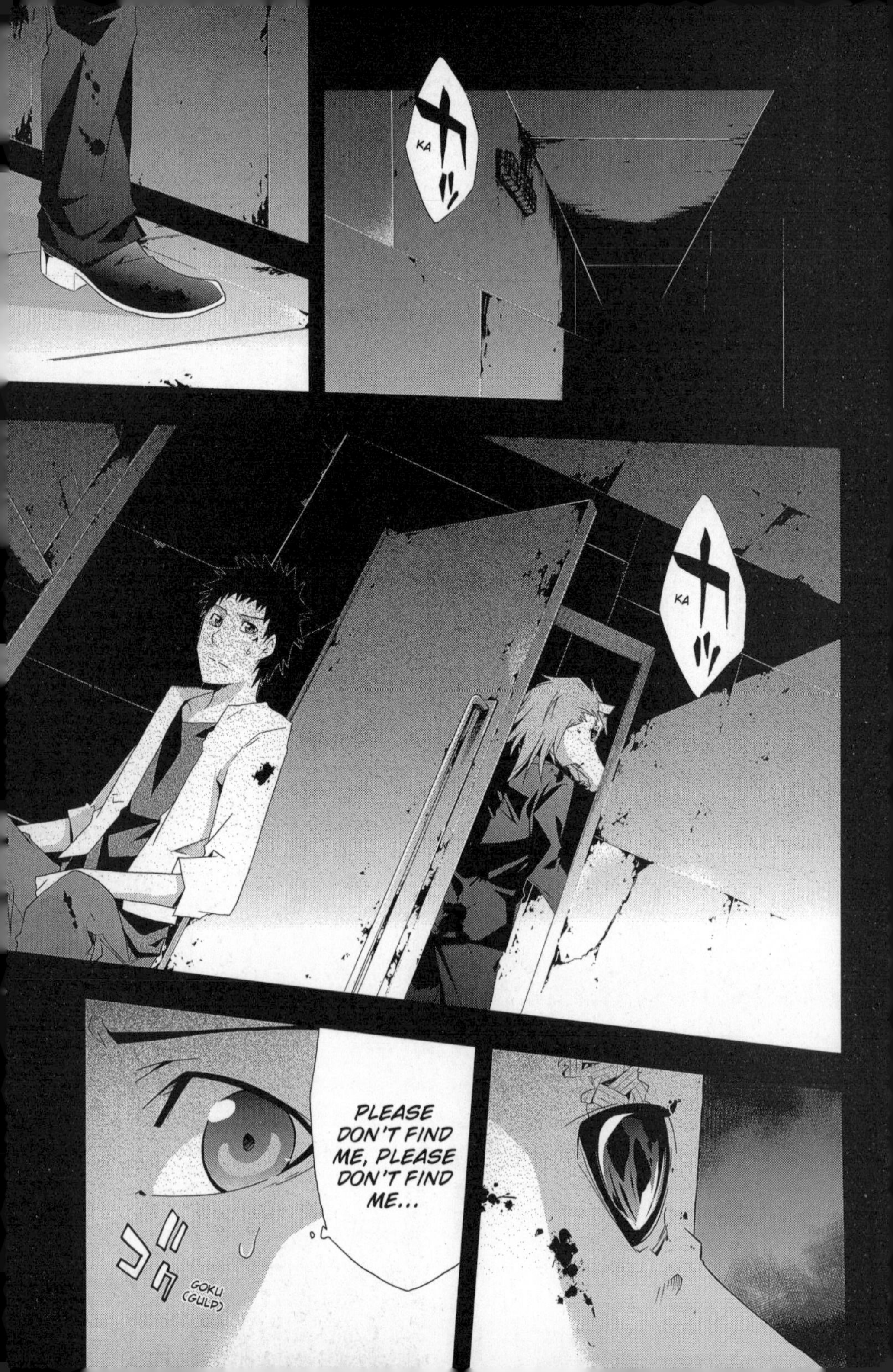
KA
KA
PLEASE DON'T FIND ME, PLEASE DON'T FIND ME...
GOKU (GULP)

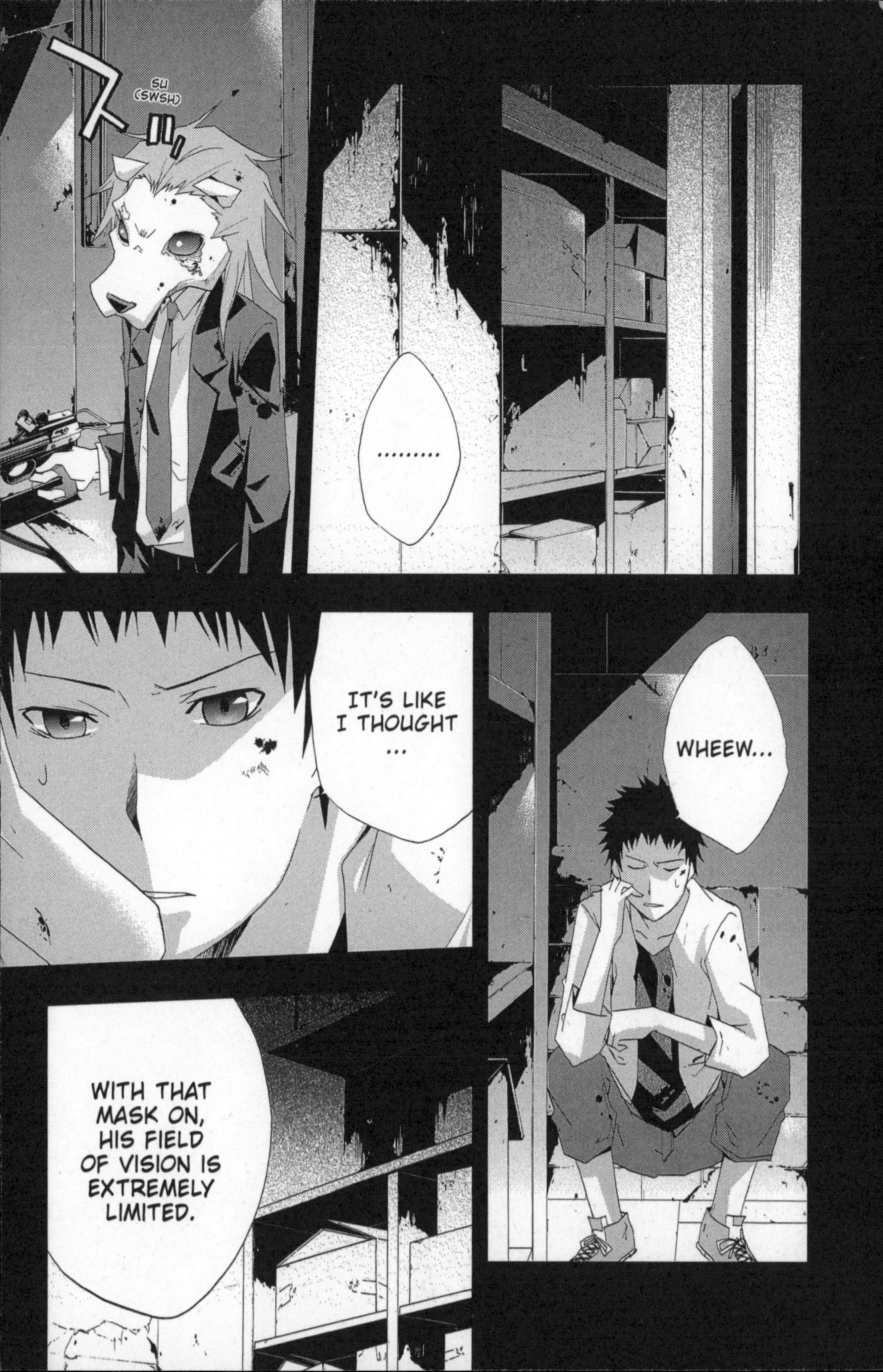
....
SU (SWSH)
WHEEW...
IT'S LIKE I THOUGHT ...
WITH THAT MASK ON, HIS FIELD OF VISION IS EXTREMELY LIMITED.

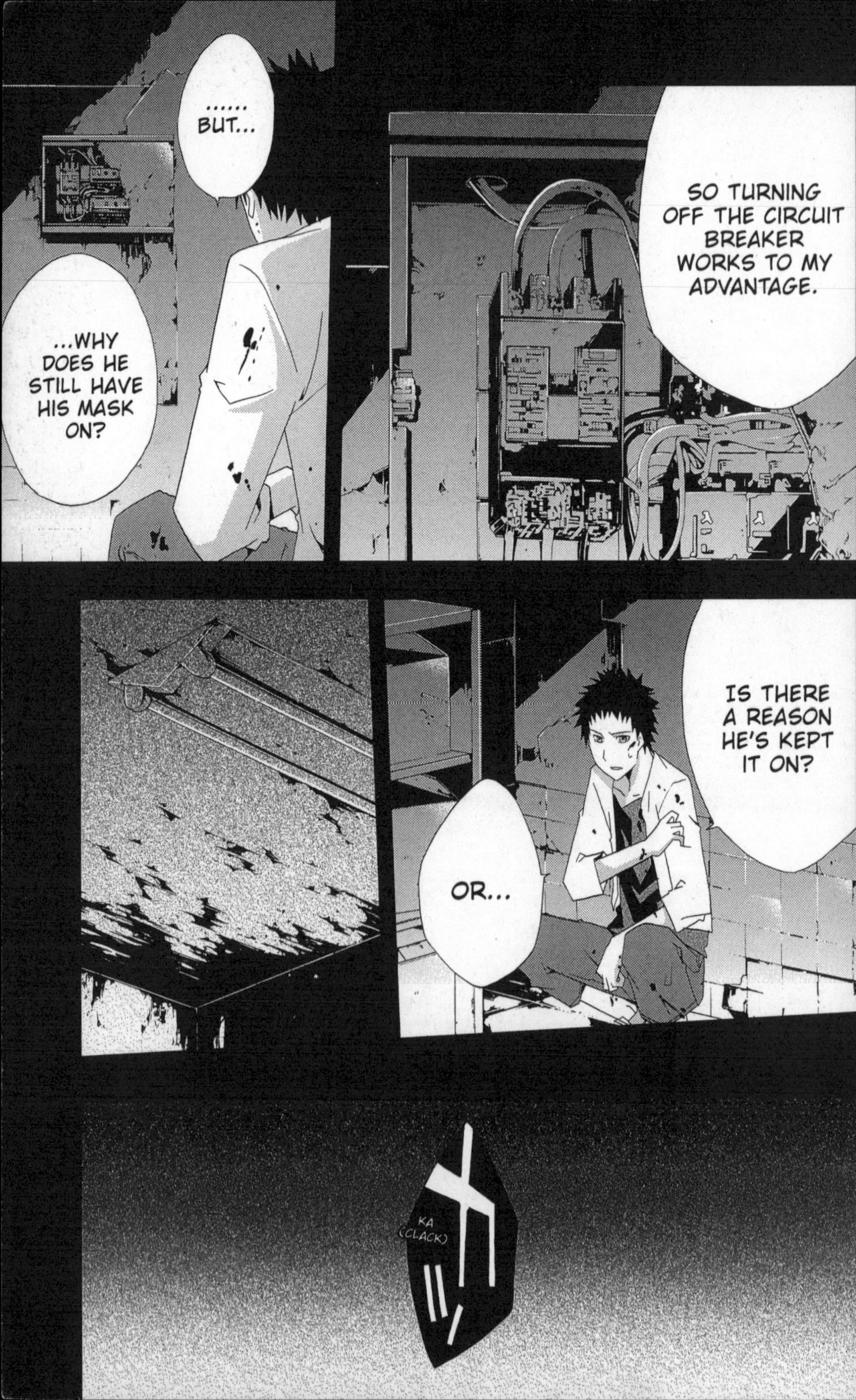
SO TURNING OFF THE CIRCUIT BREAKER WORKS TO MY ADVANTAGE.
...... BUT...
...WHY DOES HE STILL HAVE HIS MASK ON?
IS THERE A REASON HE'S KEPT IT ON?
OR...
KA (CLACK)

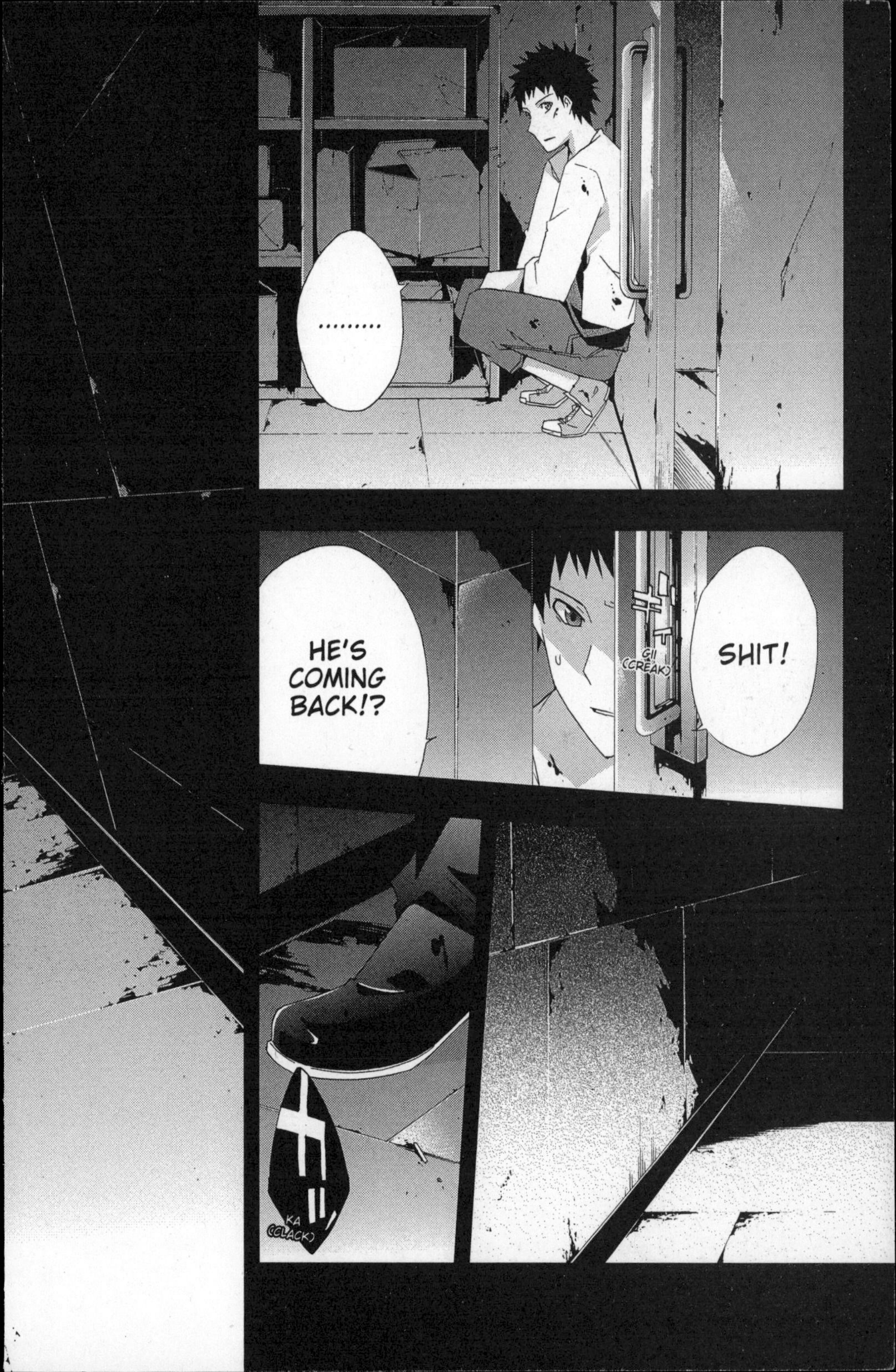
....
SHIT!
GII (CREAK)
HE'S COMING BACK!?
KA (CLACK)

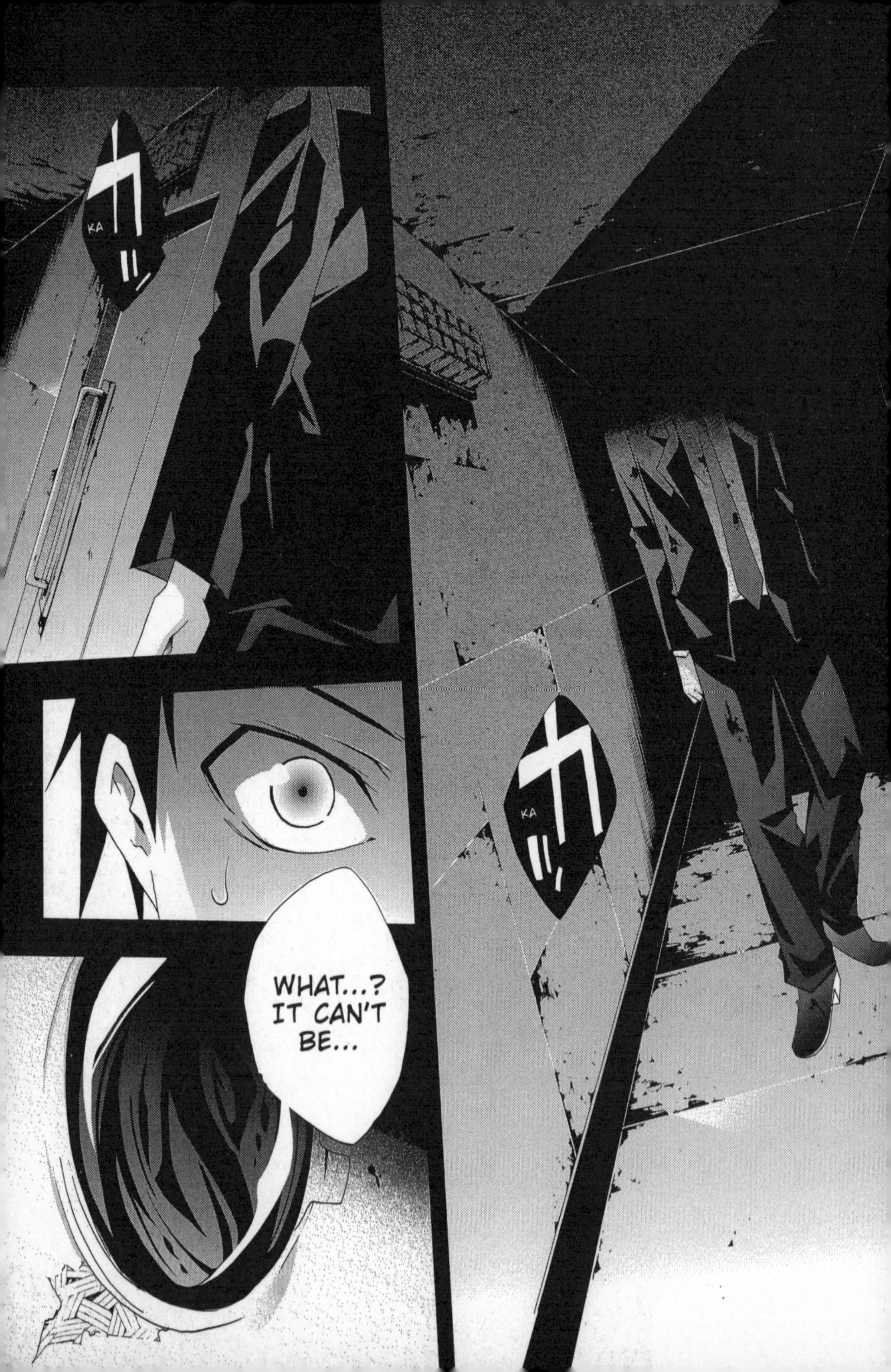
KA
KA
WHAT...? IT CAN'T BE...

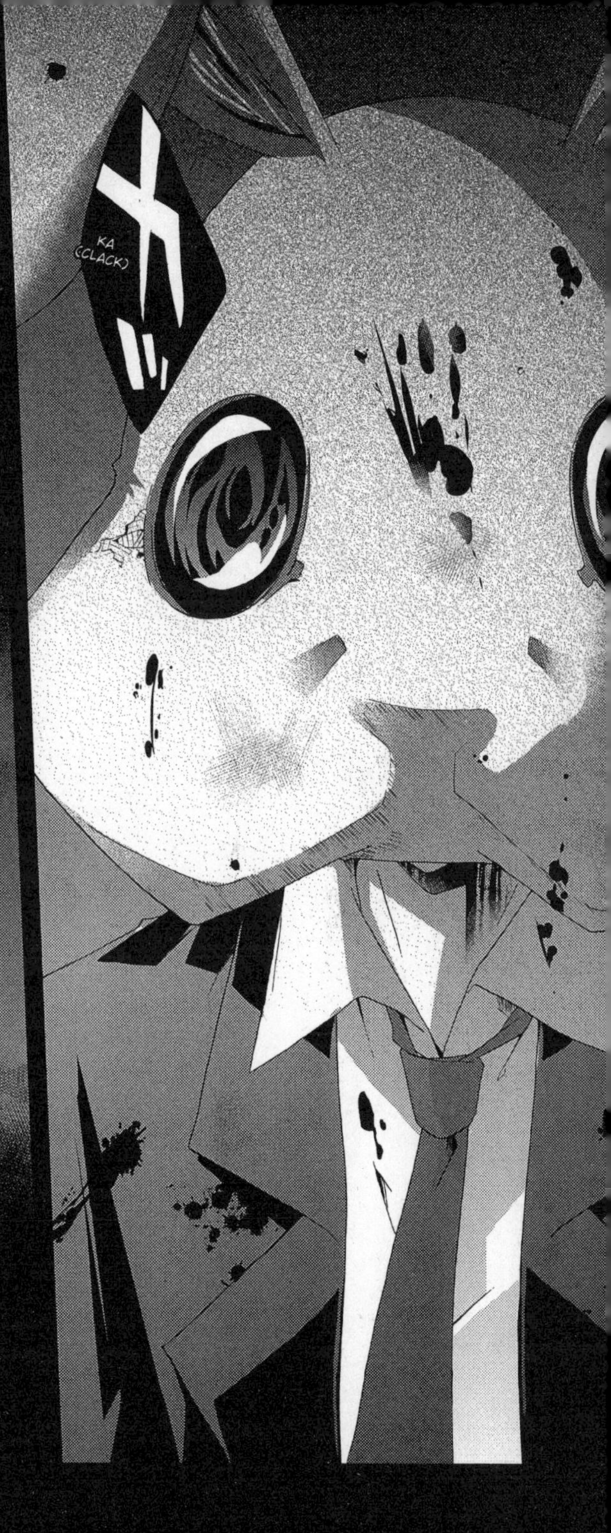
KA
(CLACK)
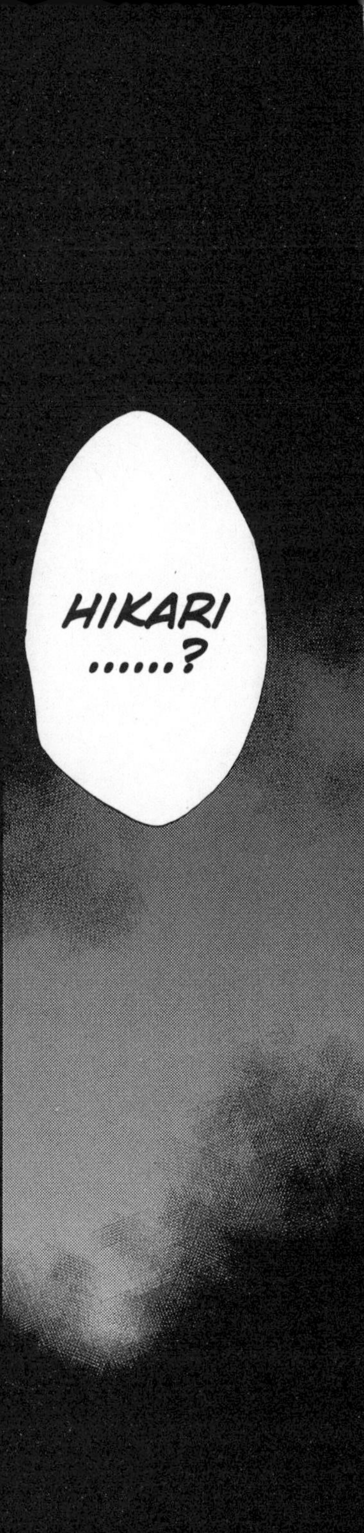
HIKARI
......?

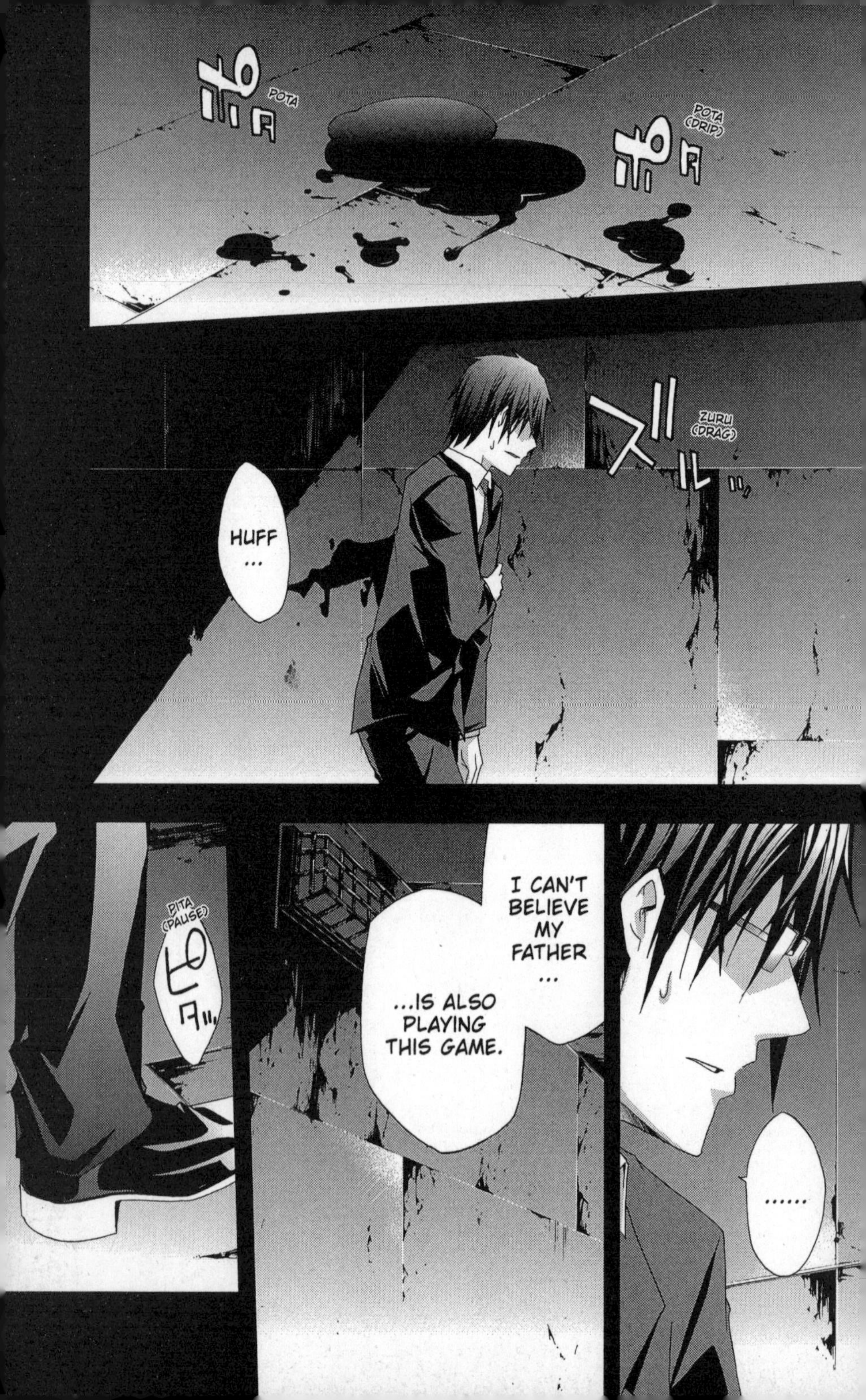

POTA (DRIP)
ポタ
POTA
ポタ
ZURU (DRAG)
ズル
HUFF...
......
I CAN'T BELIEVE MY FATHER...
...IS ALSO PLAYING THIS GAME.
PITA (PAUSE)
ピタ

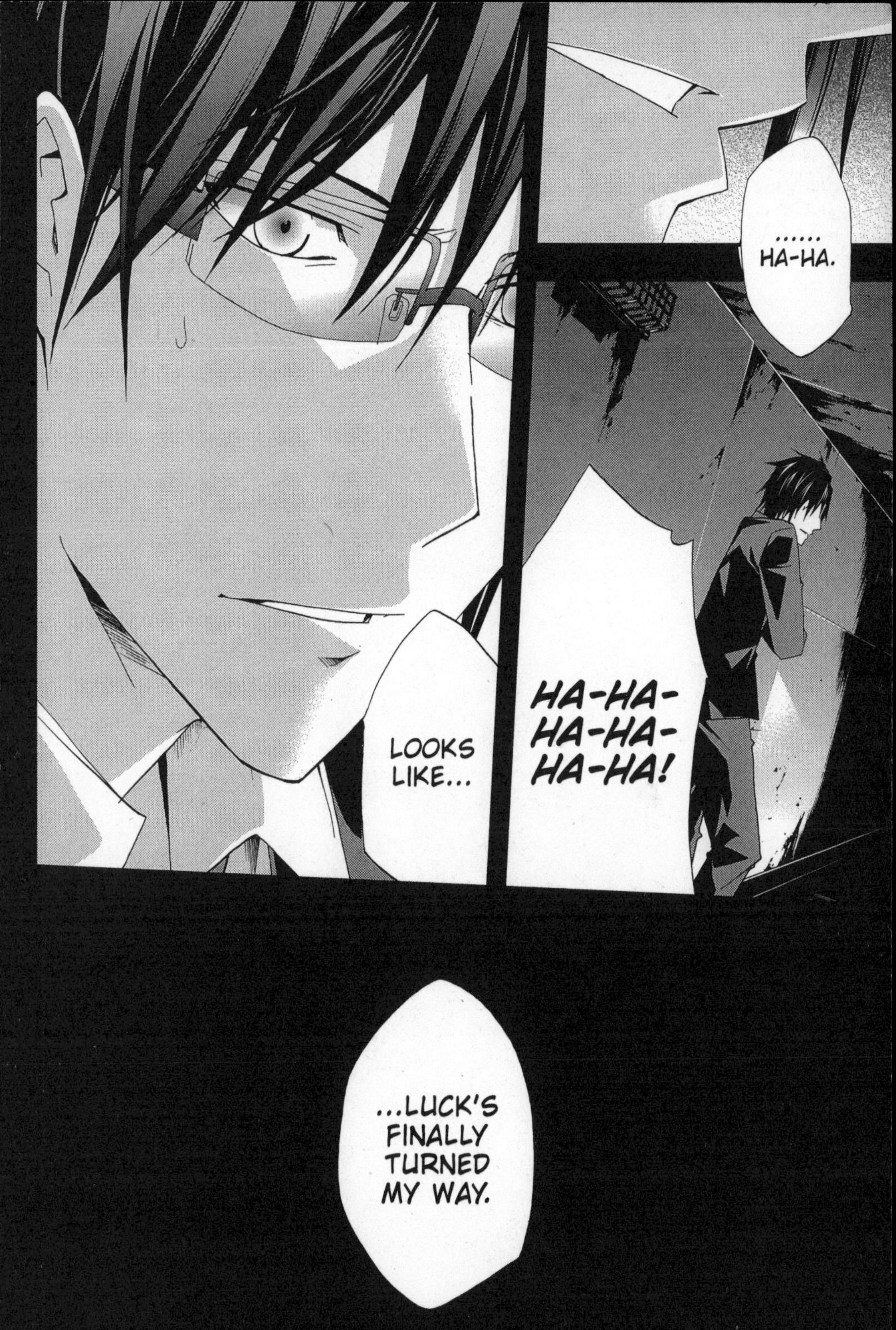
......HA-HA.
HA-HA-HA-HA-HA-HA!
LOOKS LIKE...
...LUCK'S FINALLY TURNED MY WAY.

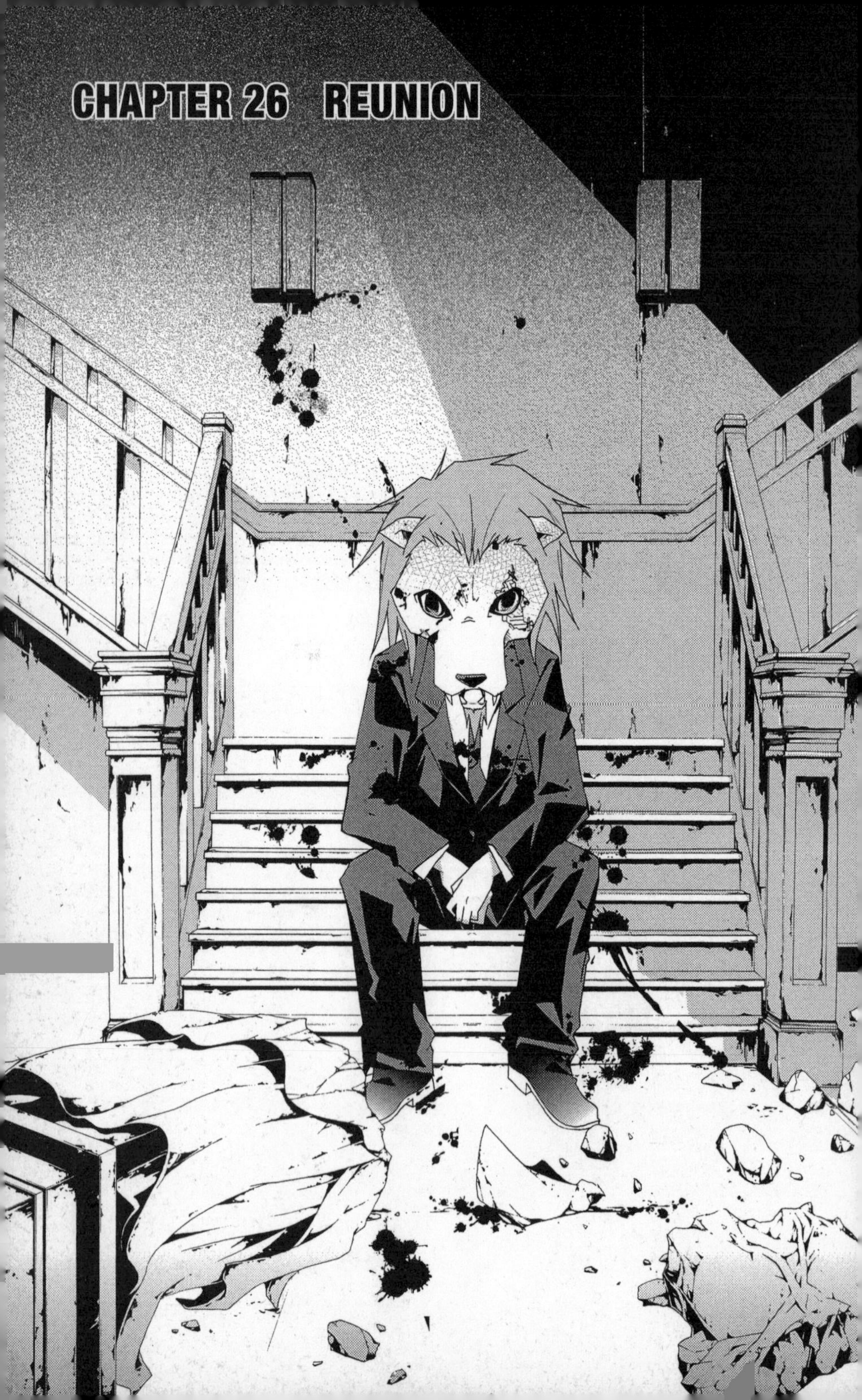
CHAPTER 26 REUNION

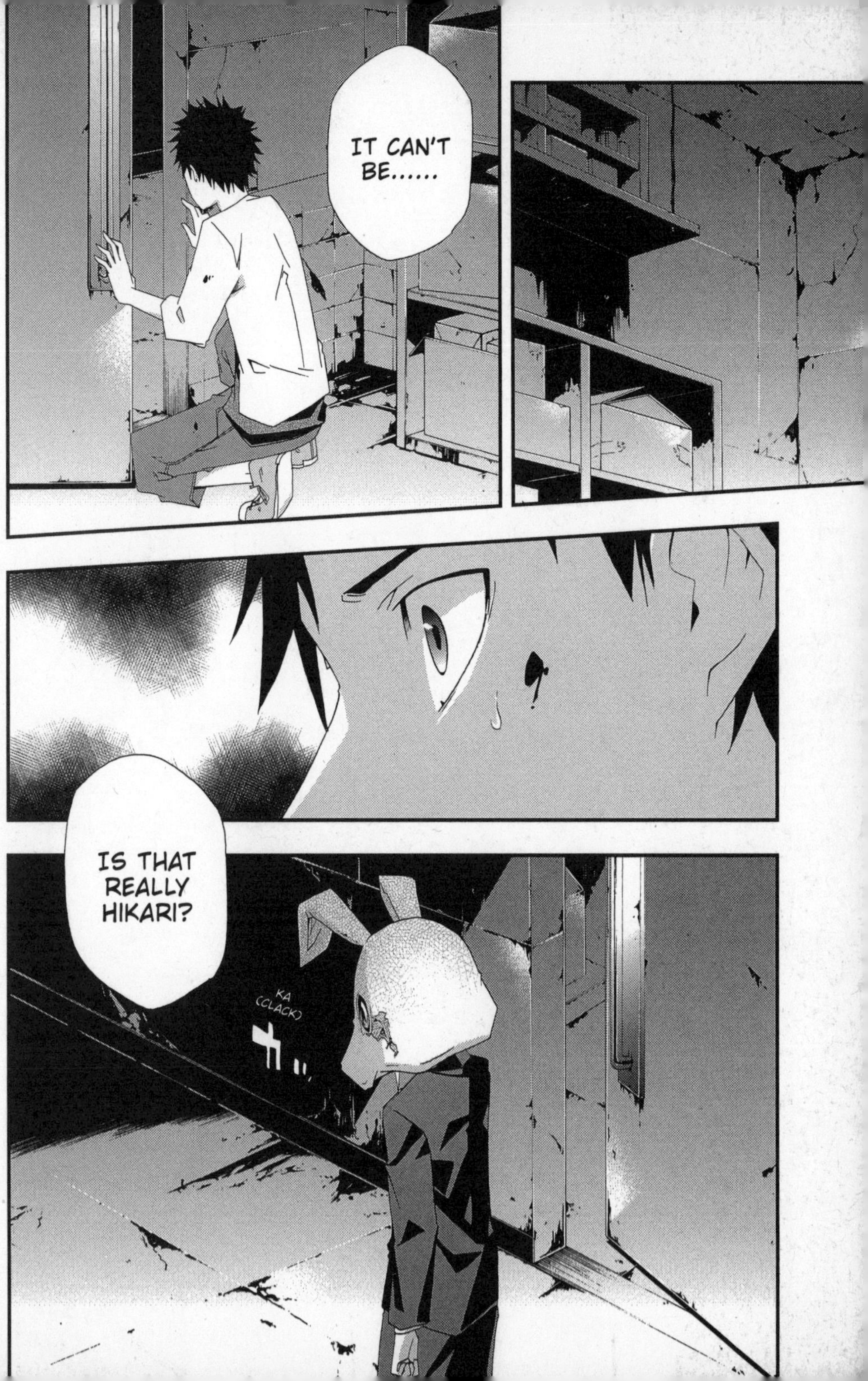
IT CAN'T BE......
IS THAT REALLY HIKARI?
KA (CLACK)

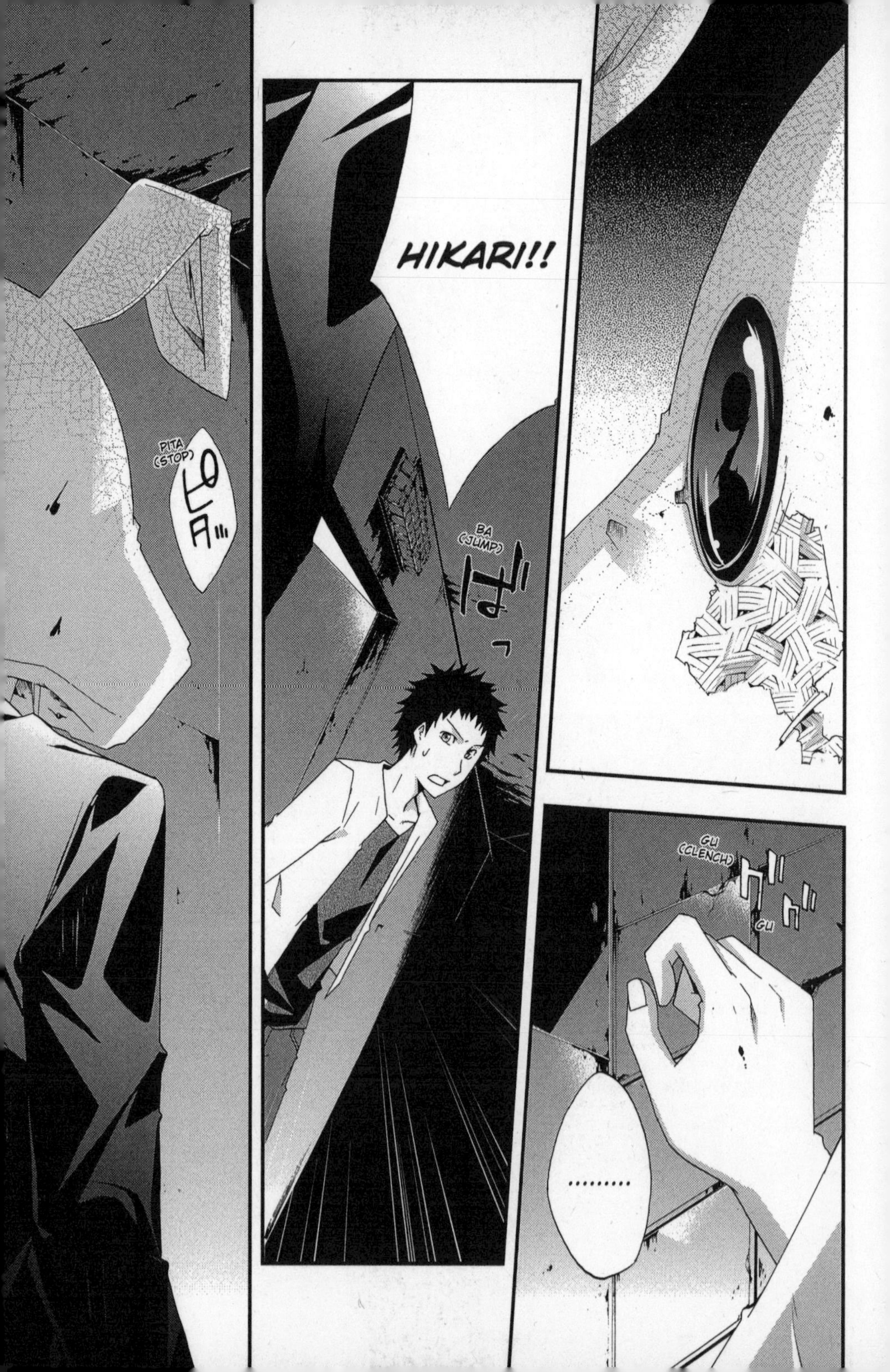
GU
(CLENCH)
GU
....
HIKARI!!
BA
(JUMP)
PITA
(STOP)

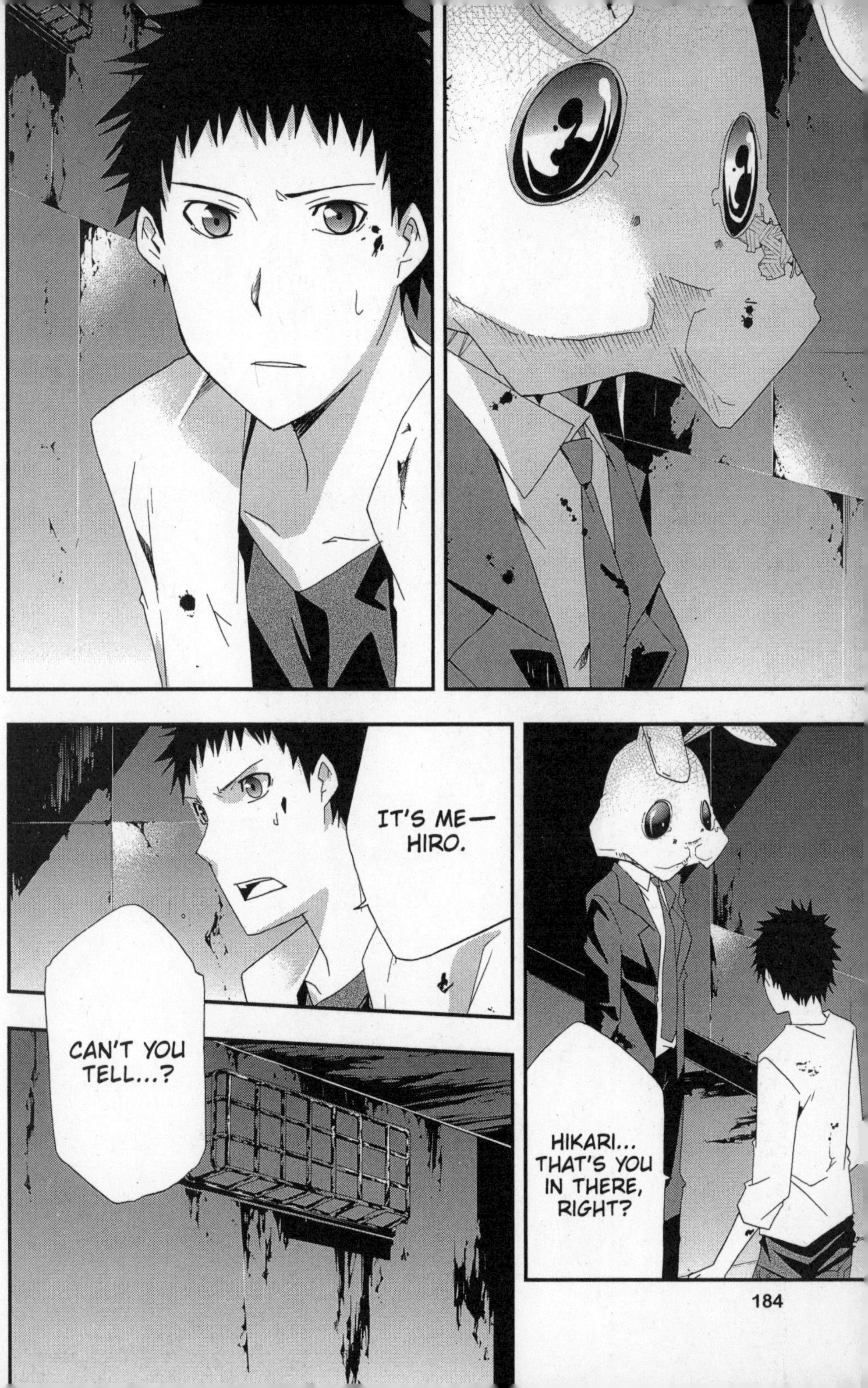
HIKARI... THAT'S YOU IN THERE, RIGHT?
IT'S ME—HIRO.
CAN'T YOU TELL...?

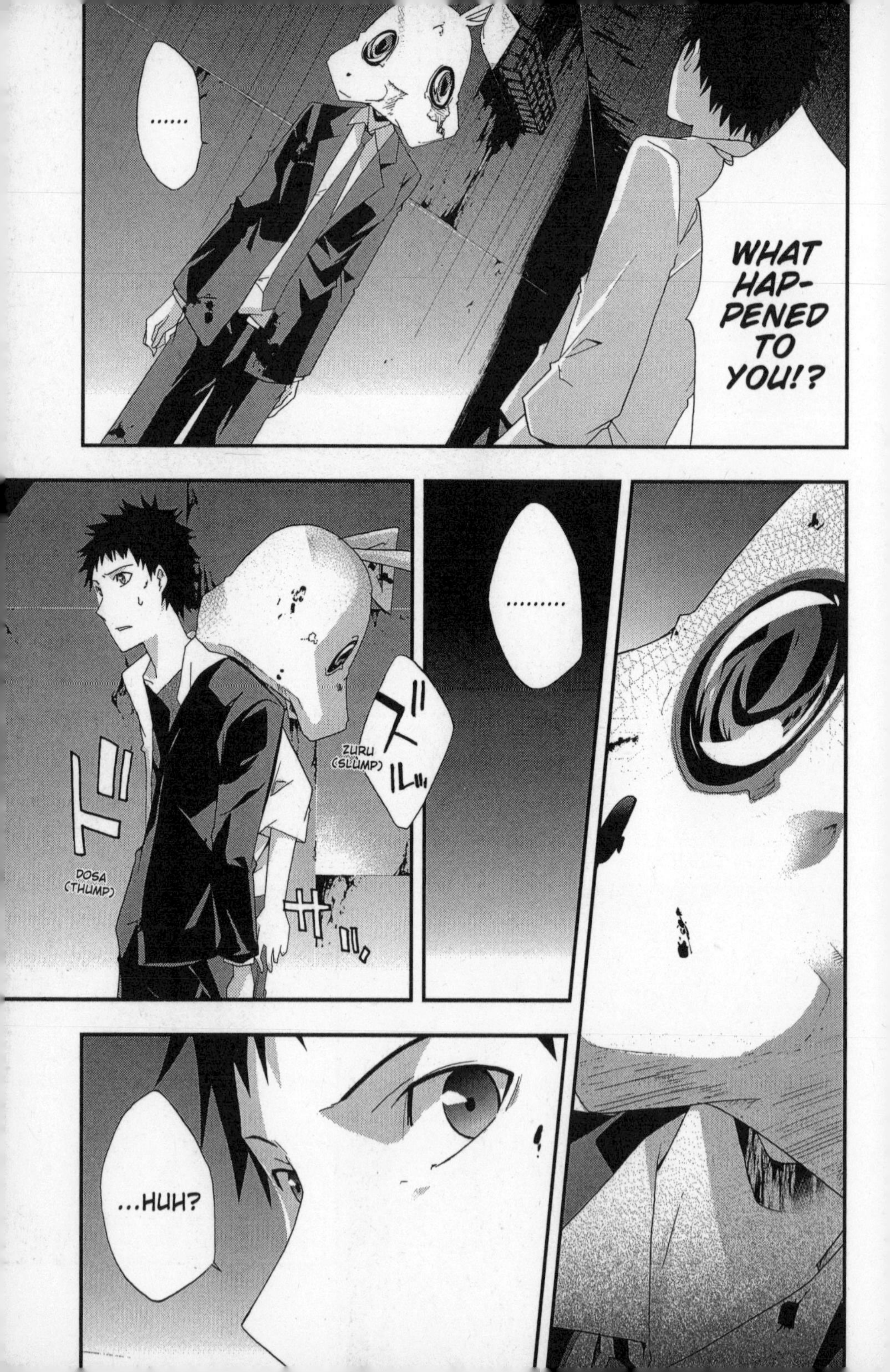
WHAT HAP-PENED TO YOU!?
......
....
ズルッ
ZURU (SLUMP)
ドサッ
DOSA (THUMP)
...HUH?

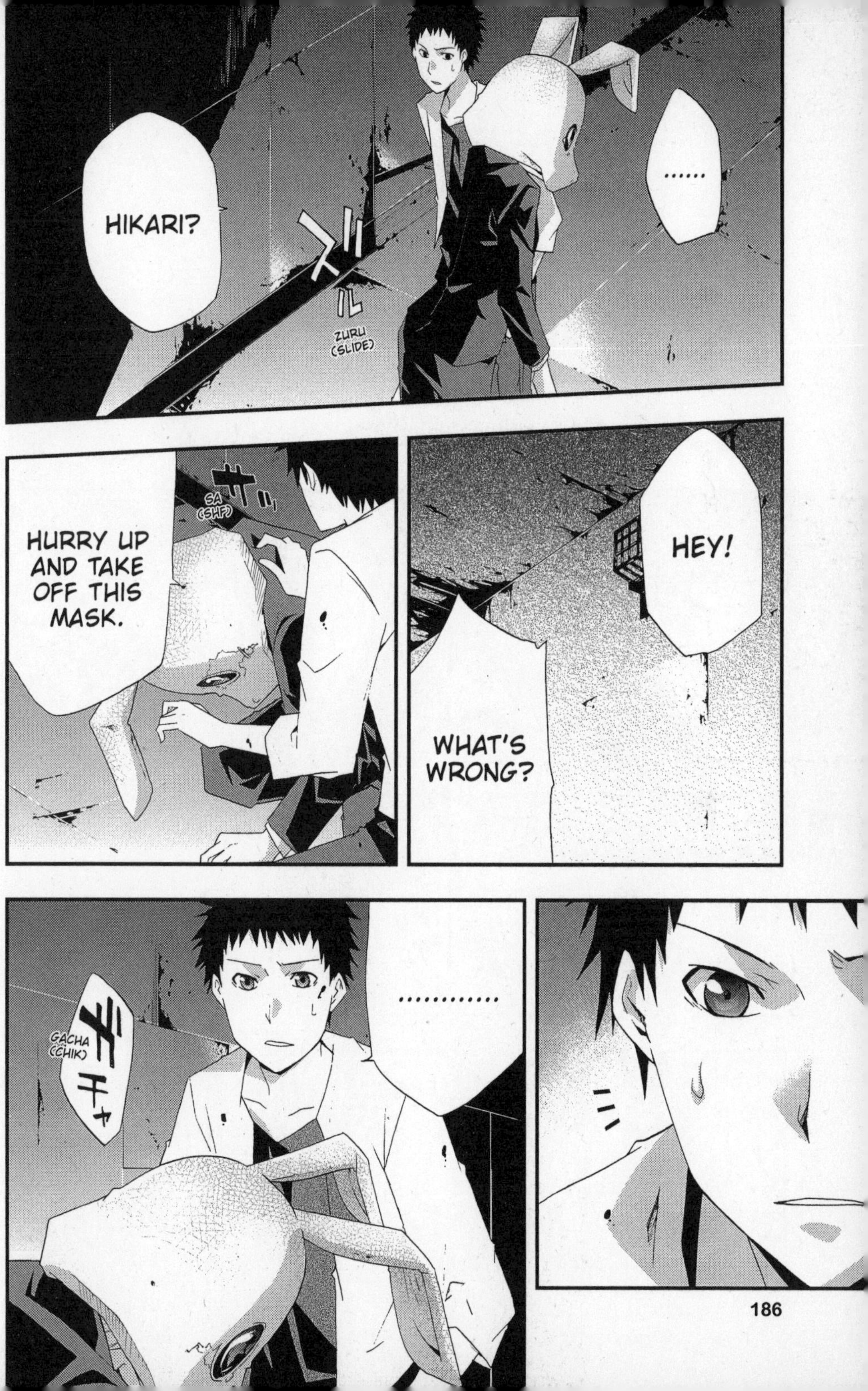
......
ZURU (SLIDE)
HIKARI?
HEY!
WHAT'S WRONG?
SA (SHF)
HURRY UP AND TAKE OFF THIS MASK.
....
GACHA (CHIK)

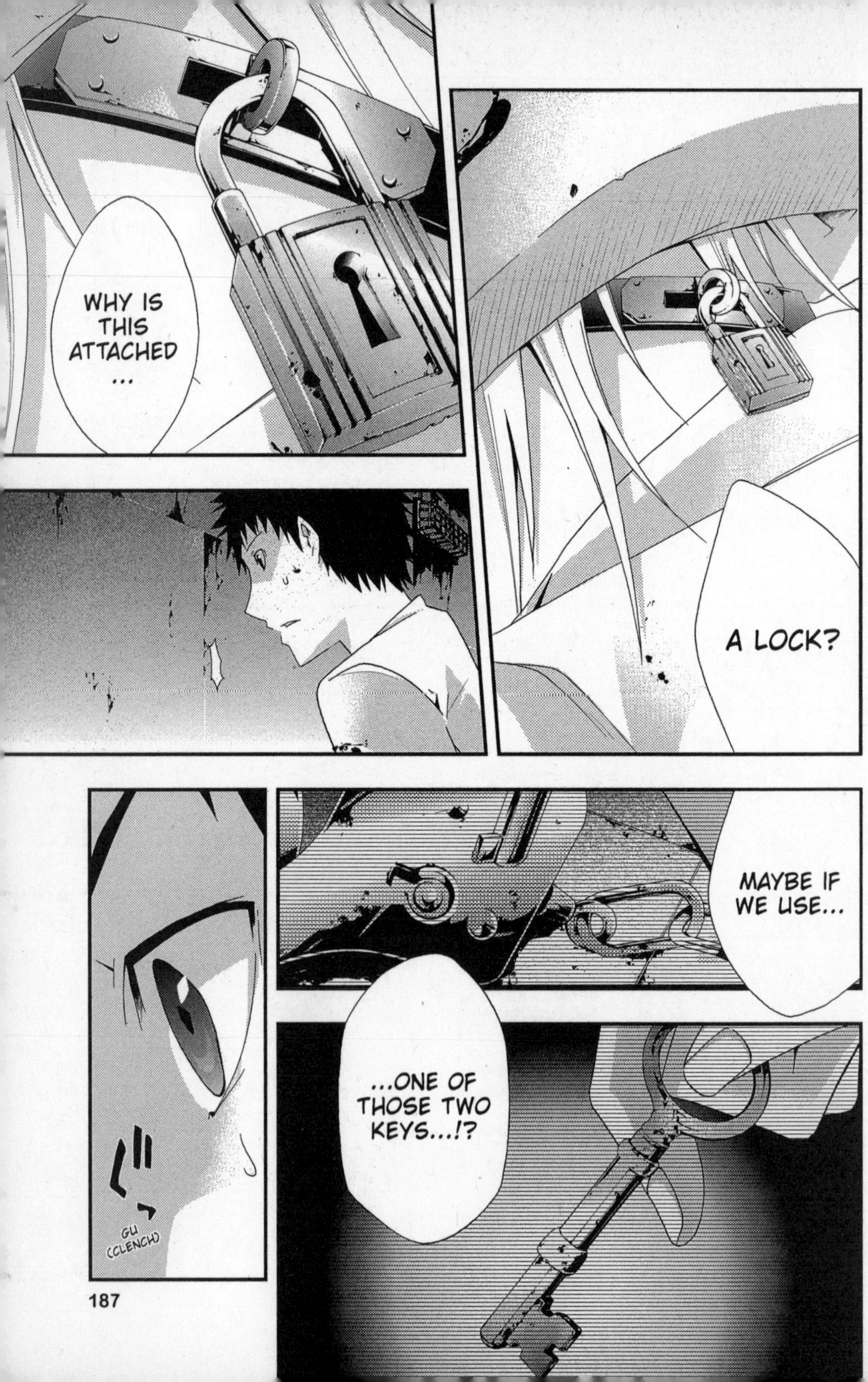
A LOCK?
WHY IS THIS ATTACHED ...
MAYBE IF WE USE...
...ONE OF THOSE TWO KEYS...!?
GU (CLENCH)

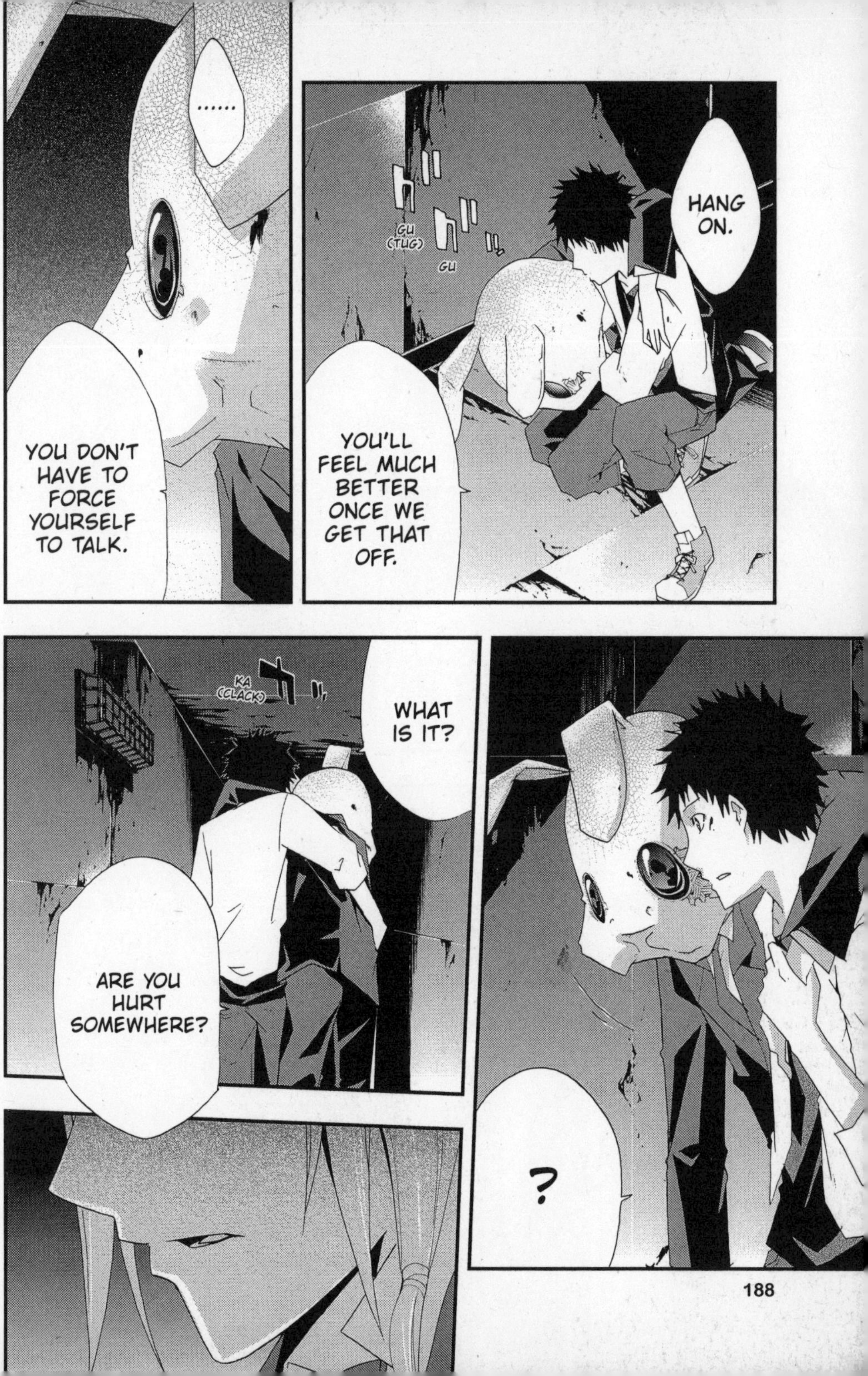
HANG ON.
GU (TUG)
GU
YOU'LL FEEL MUCH BETTER ONCE WE GET THAT OFF.
......
YOU DON'T HAVE TO FORCE YOURSELF TO TALK.
?
KA (CLACK)
WHAT IS IT?
ARE YOU HURT SOMEWHERE?

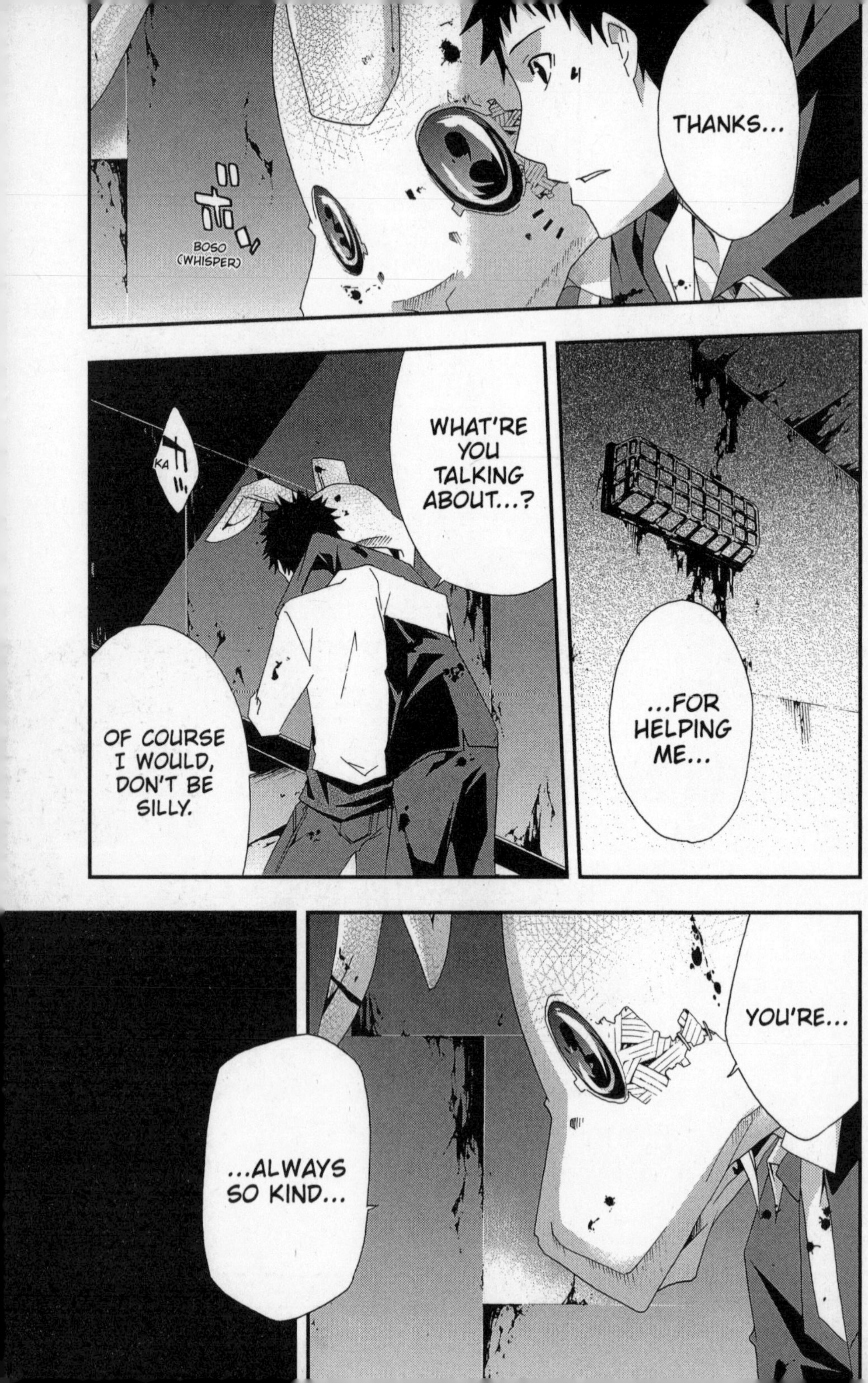
THANKS...
BOSO (WHISPER)
...FOR HELPING ME...
WHAT'RE YOU TALKING ABOUT...?
KA
OF COURSE I WOULD, DON'T BE SILLY.
YOU'RE...
...ALWAYS SO KIND...

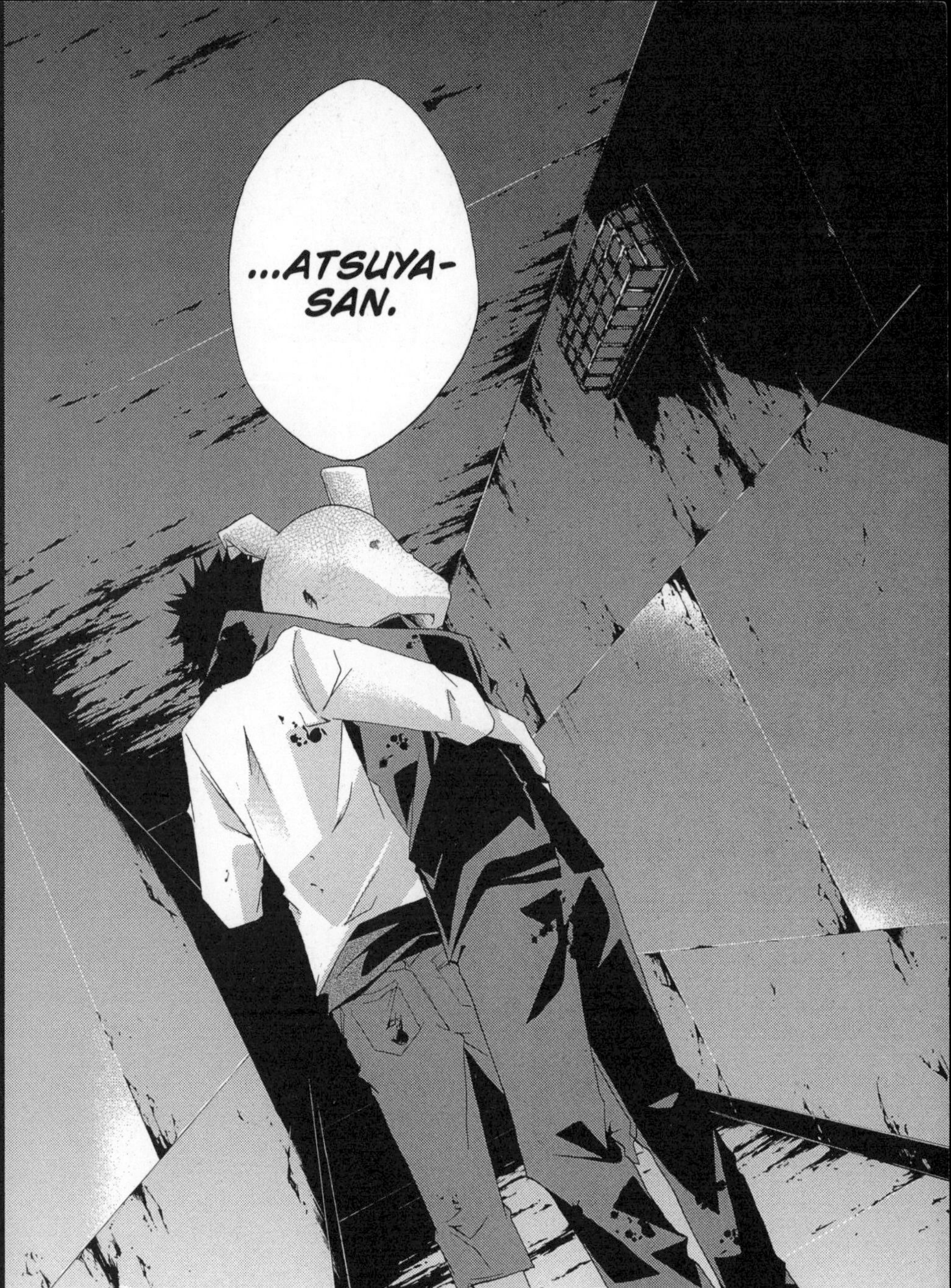
...ATSUYA-SAN.

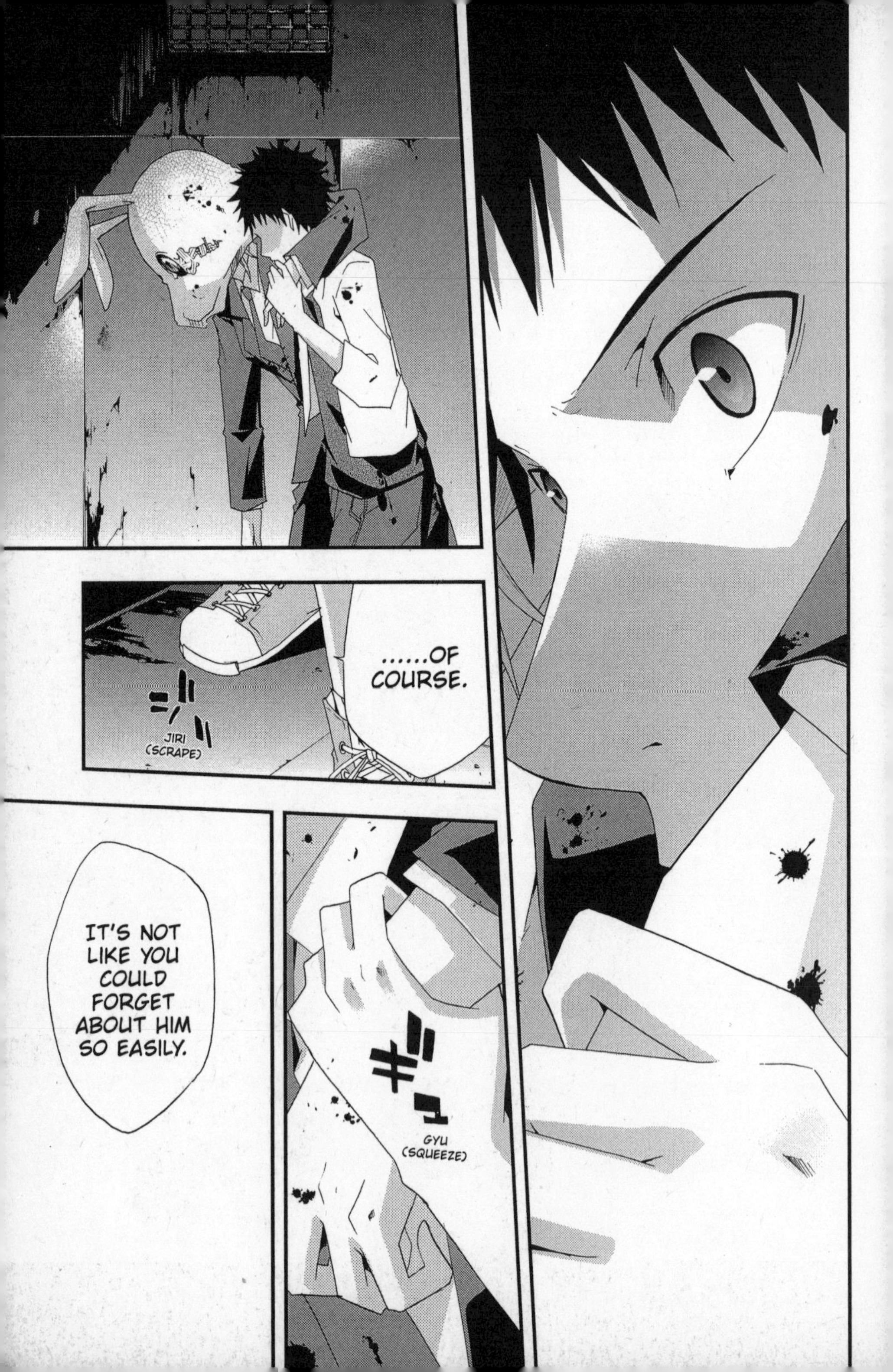

......OF COURSE.
JIRI (SCRAPE)
GYU (SQUEEZE)
IT'S NOT LIKE YOU COULD FORGET ABOUT HIM SO EASILY.

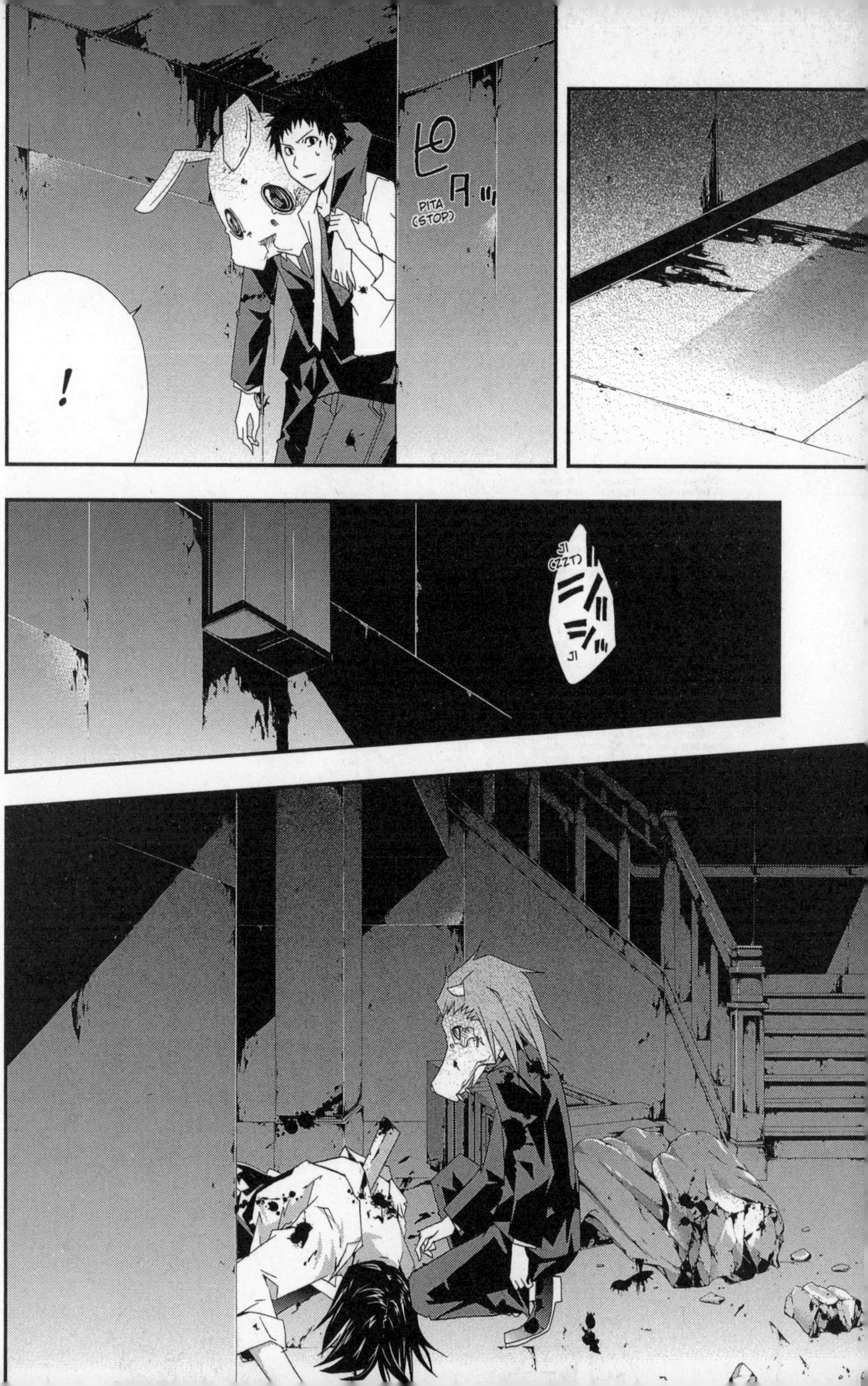
PITA (STOP)
!
JI (ZZZT)
JI

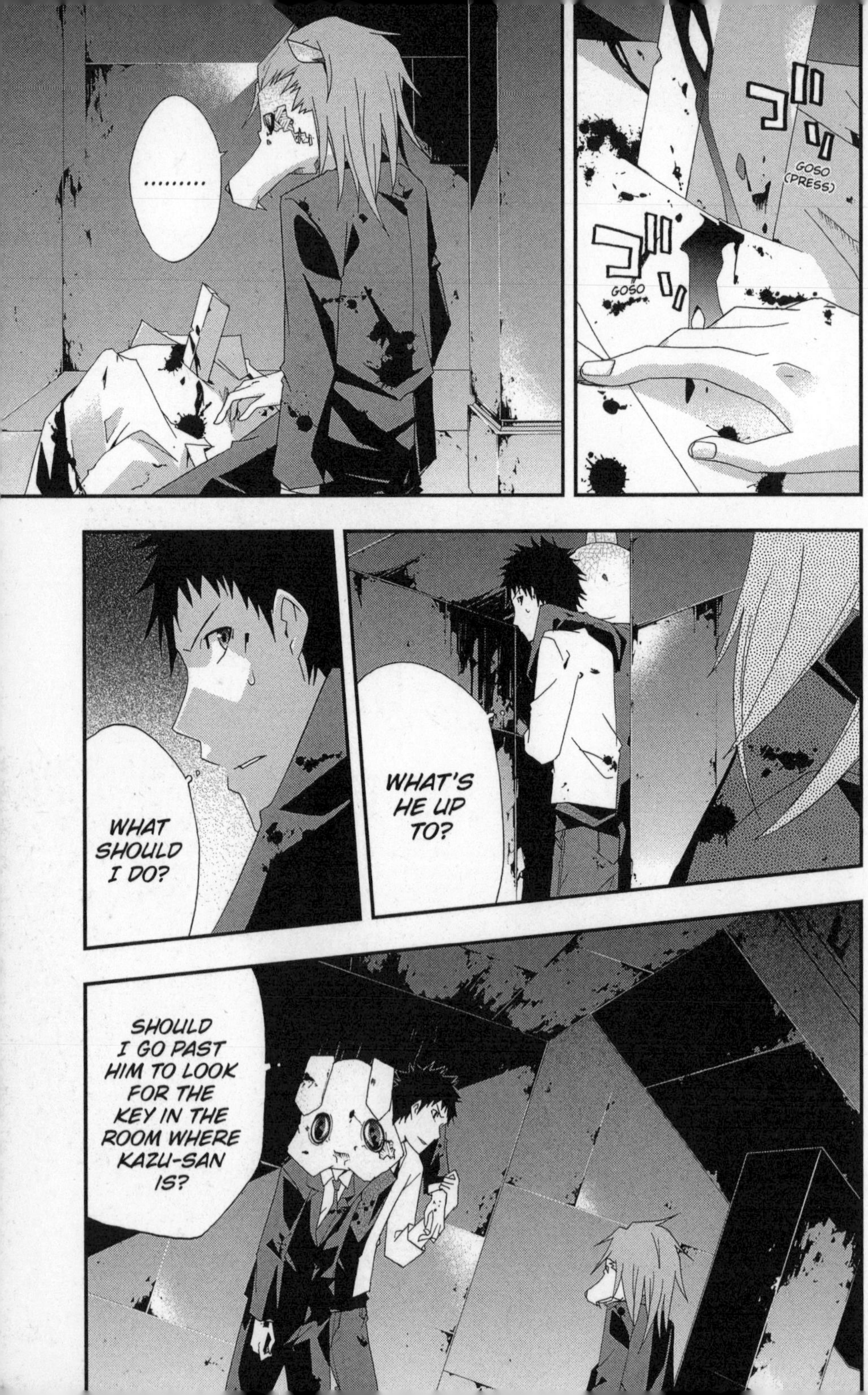
GOSO (PRESS)
GOSO
....
WHAT'S HE UP TO?
WHAT SHOULD I DO?
SHOULD I GO PAST HIM TO LOOK FOR THE KEY IN THE ROOM WHERE KAZU-SAN IS?

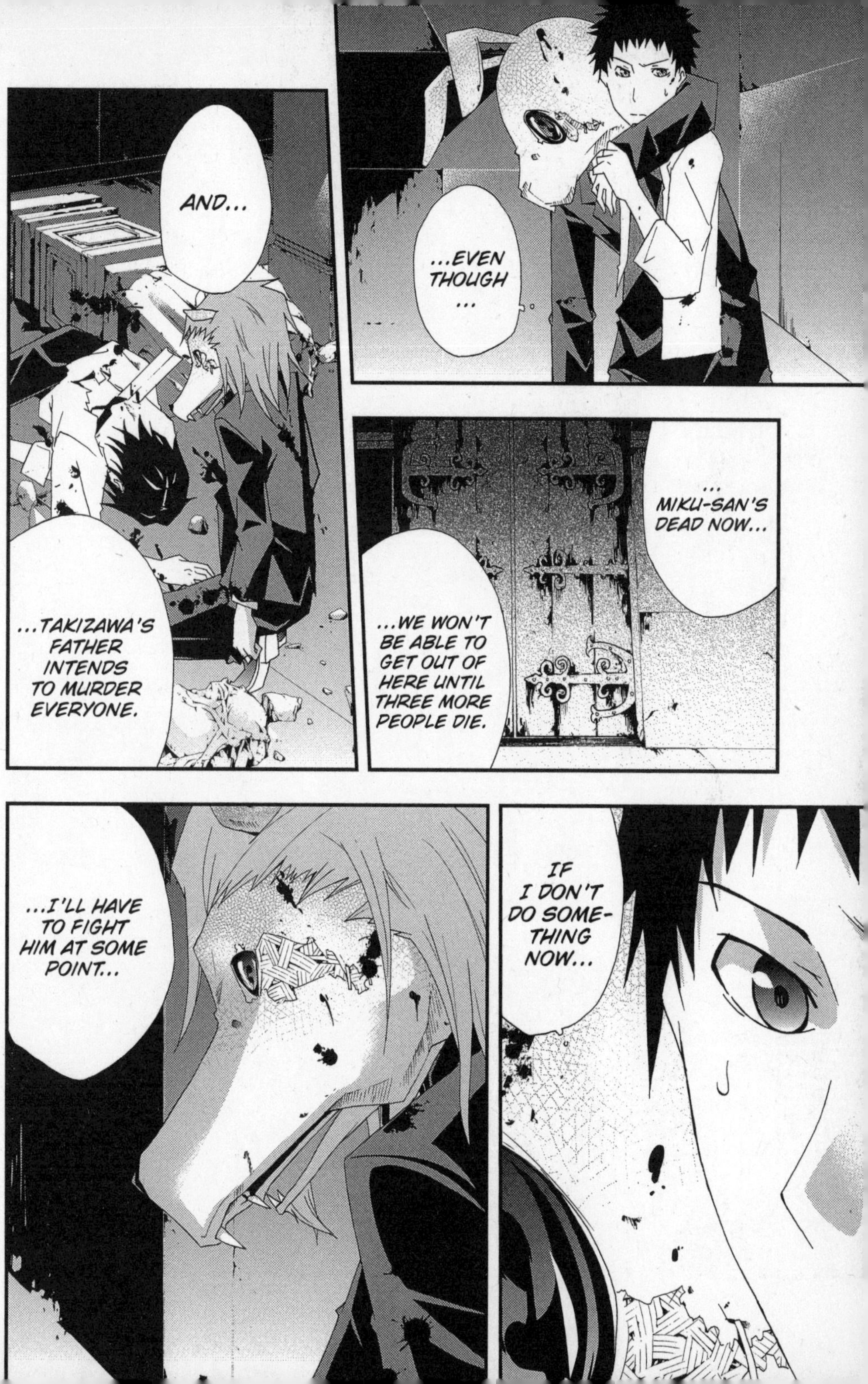
...EVEN THOUGH ...
... MIKU-SAN'S DEAD NOW...
...WE WON'T BE ABLE TO GET OUT OF HERE UNTIL THREE MORE PEOPLE DIE.
AND...
...TAKIZAWA'S FATHER INTENDS TO MURDER EVERYONE.
IF I DON'T DO SOME-THING NOW...
...I'LL HAVE TO FIGHT HIM AT SOME POINT...

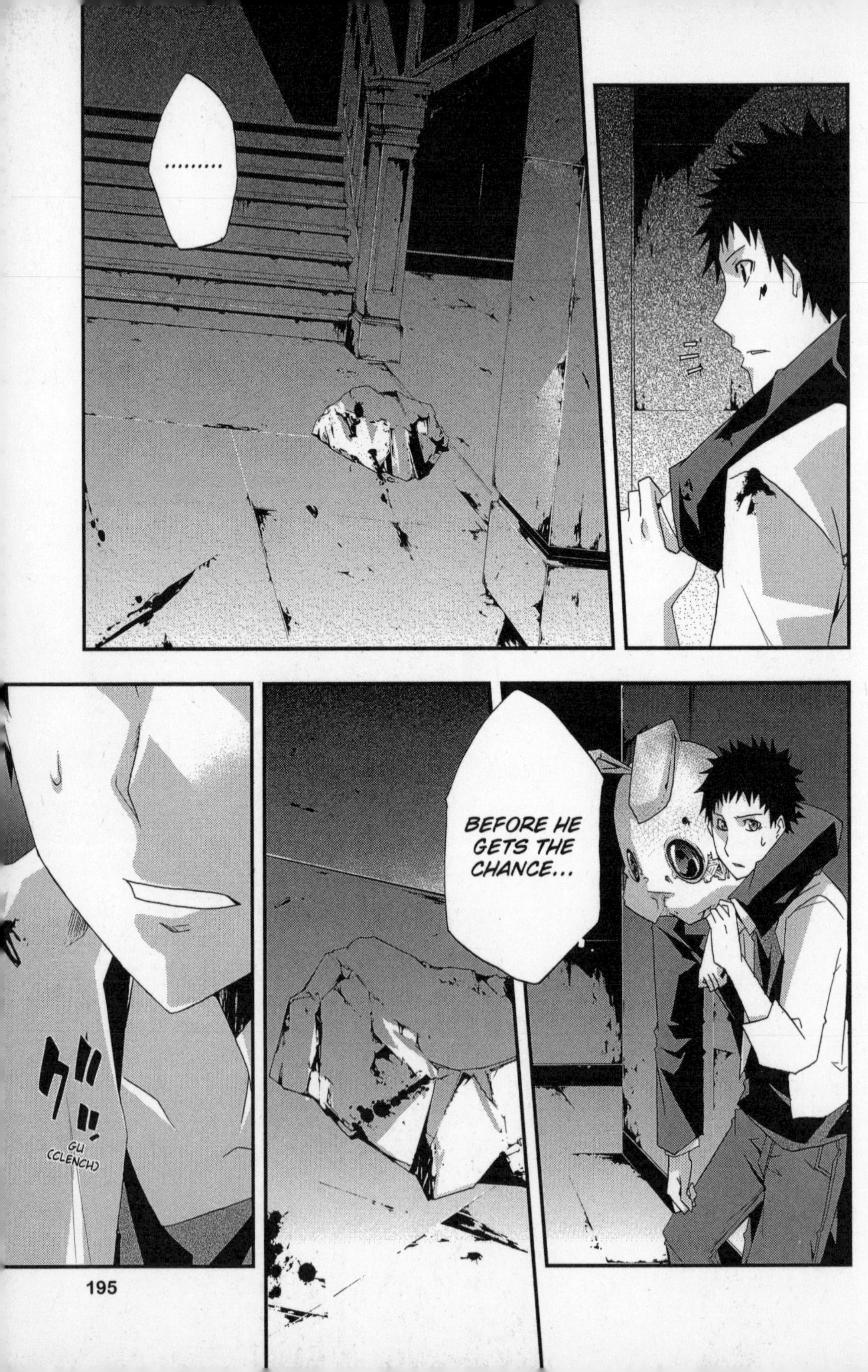
....
BEFORE HE GETS THE CHANCE...
GU (CLENCH)

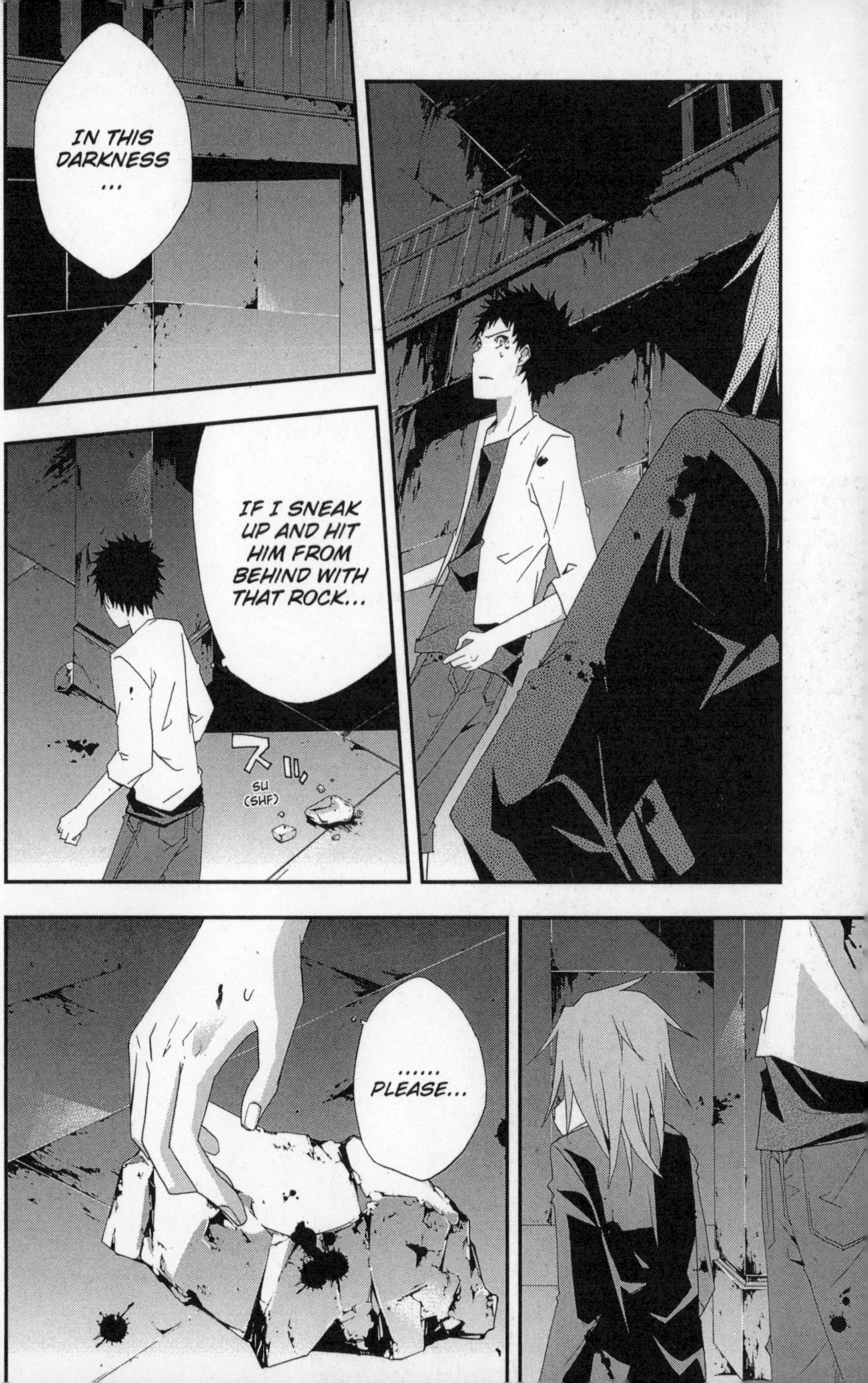
IN THIS DARKNESS ...
IF I SNEAK UP AND HIT HIM FROM BEHIND WITH THAT ROCK...
スッ
SU (SHF)
...... PLEASE...

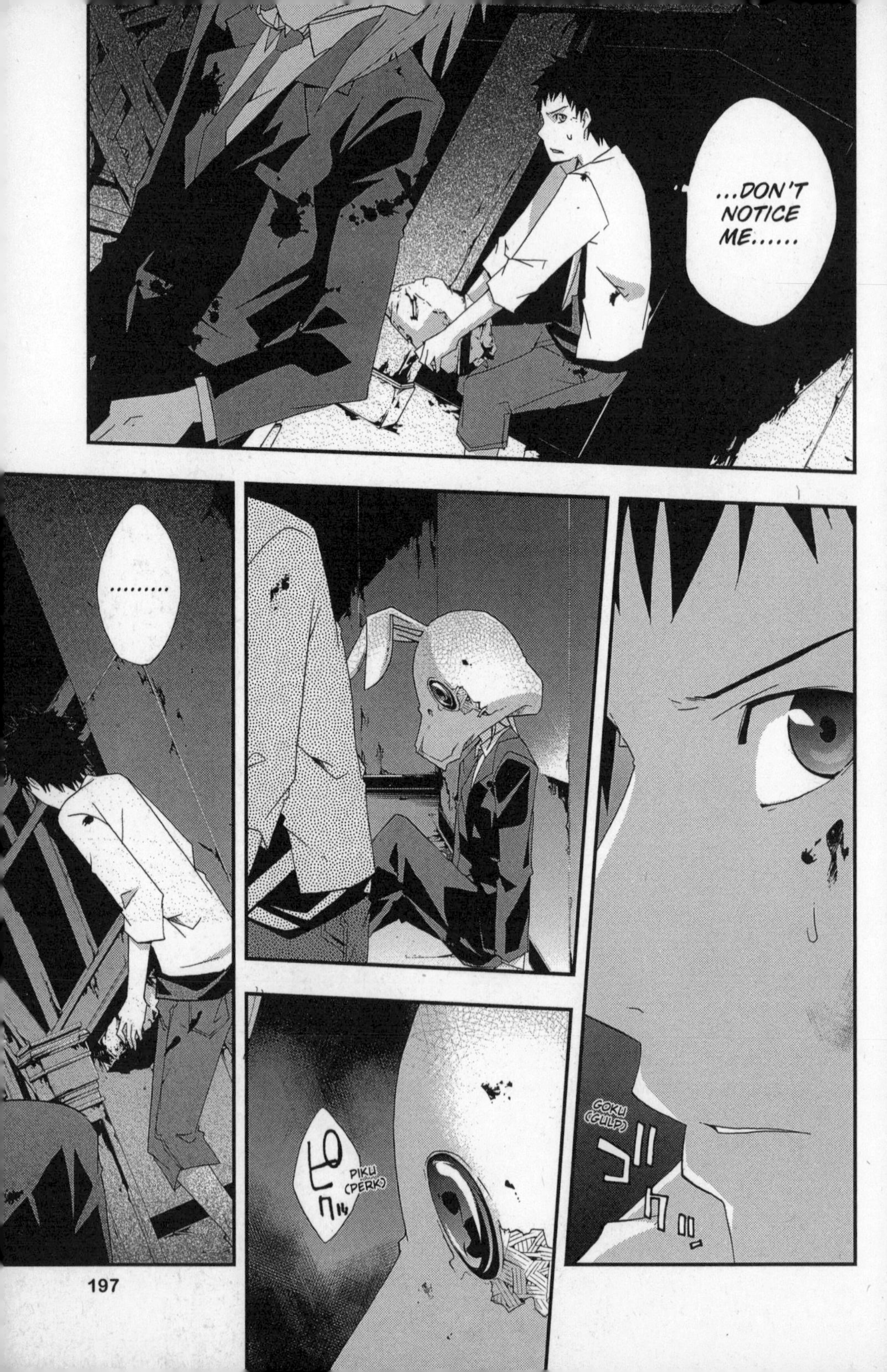
...DON'T NOTICE ME......
GOKU (GULP)
PIKU (PERK)
....

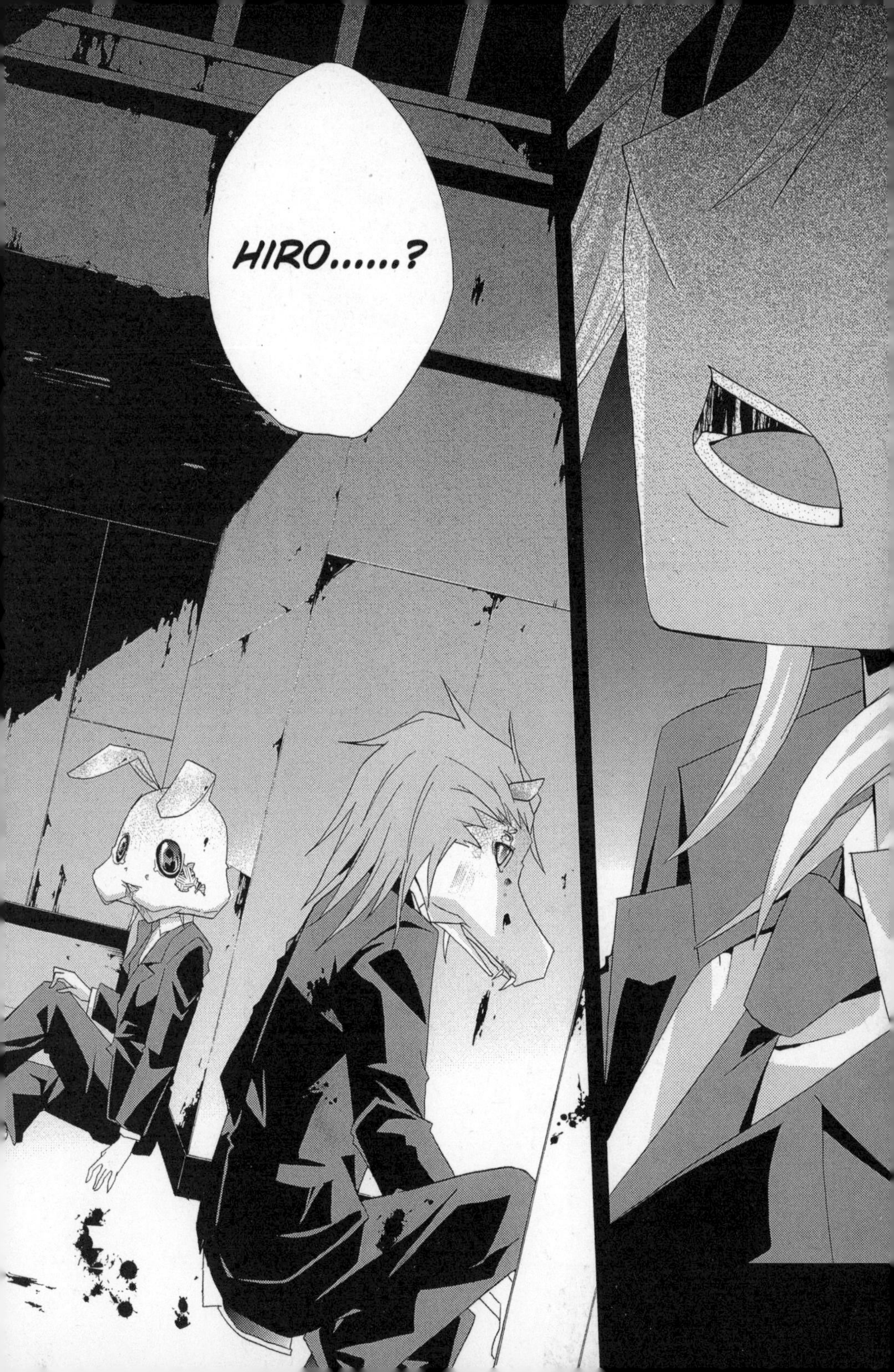
HIRO......?

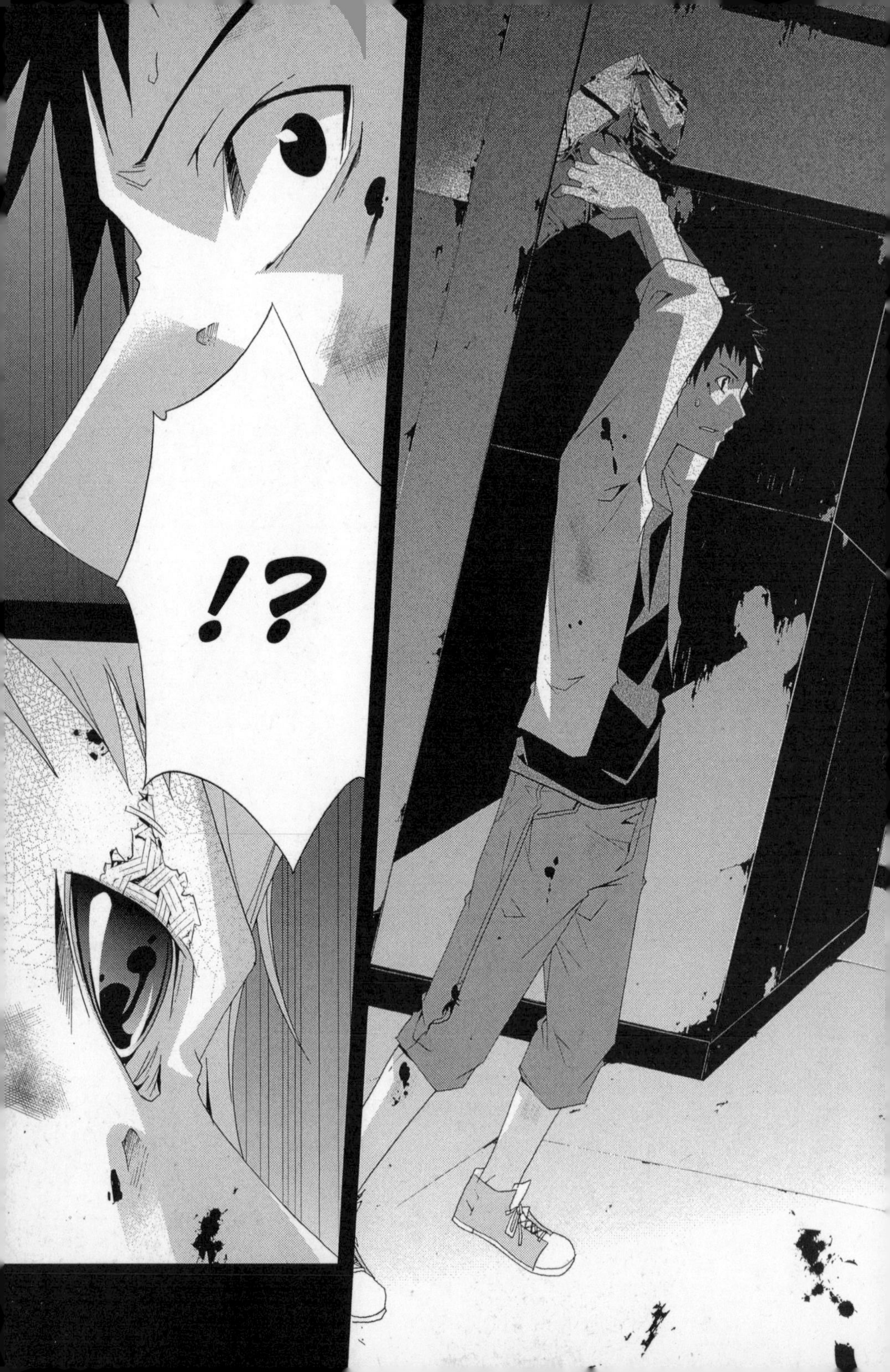
!?

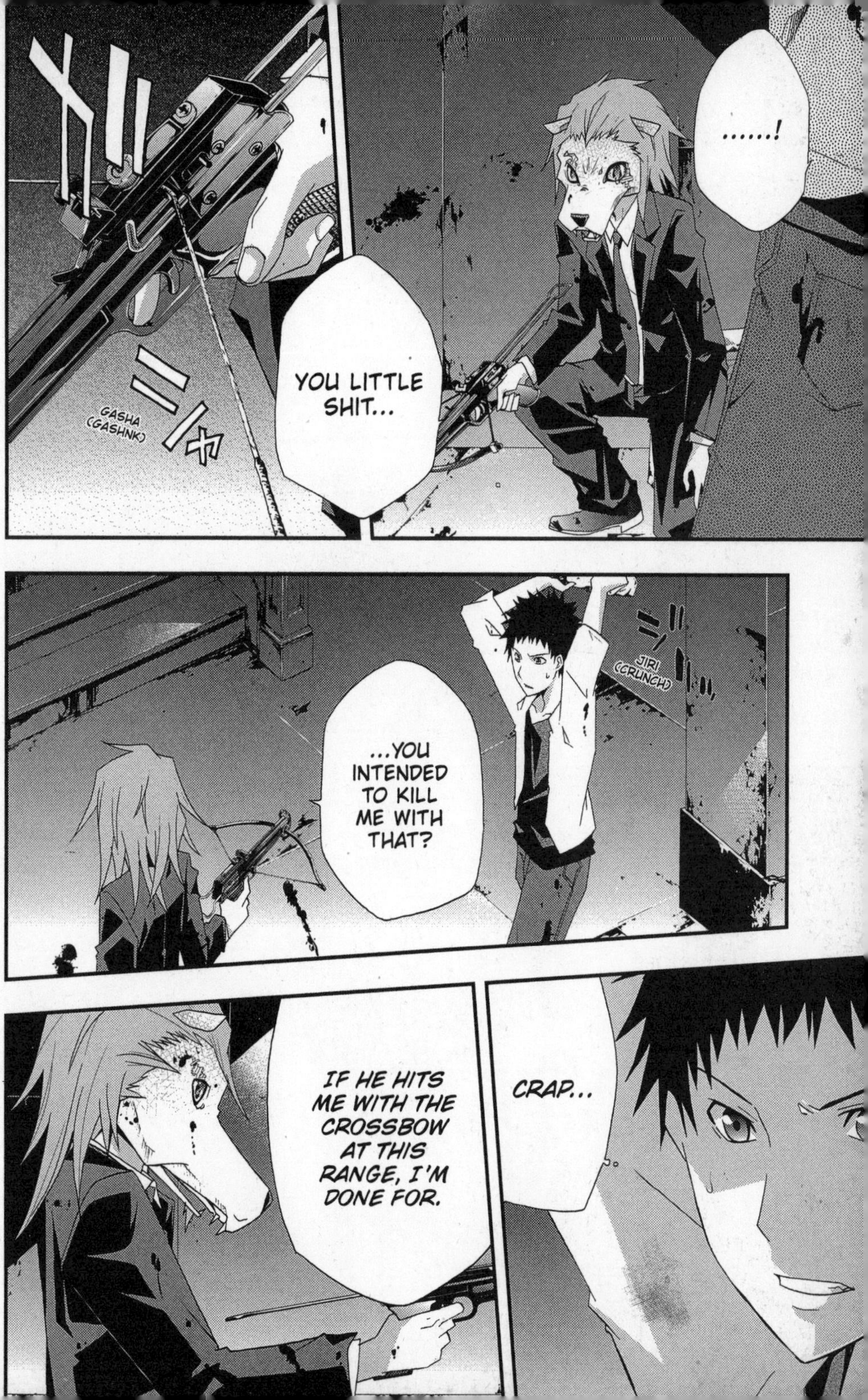
......!
YOU LITTLE SHIT...
GASHA (GASHNK)
JIRI (CRUNCH)
...YOU INTENDED TO KILL ME WITH THAT?
CRAP...
IF HE HITS ME WITH THE CROSSBOW AT THIS RANGE, I'M DONE FOR.

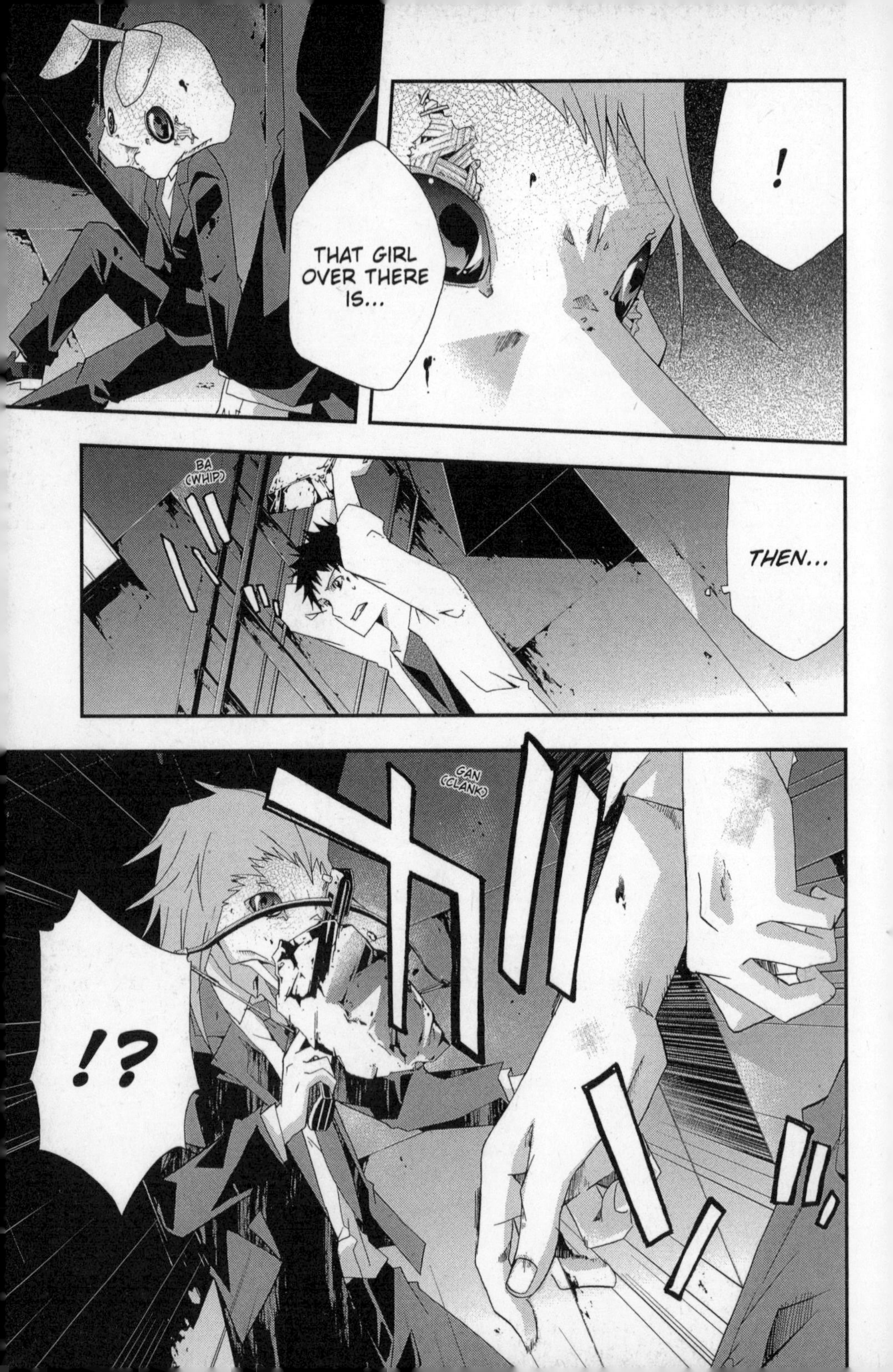
!
THAT GIRL OVER THERE IS...
THEN...
BA (WHIP)
GAN (CLANK)
!?

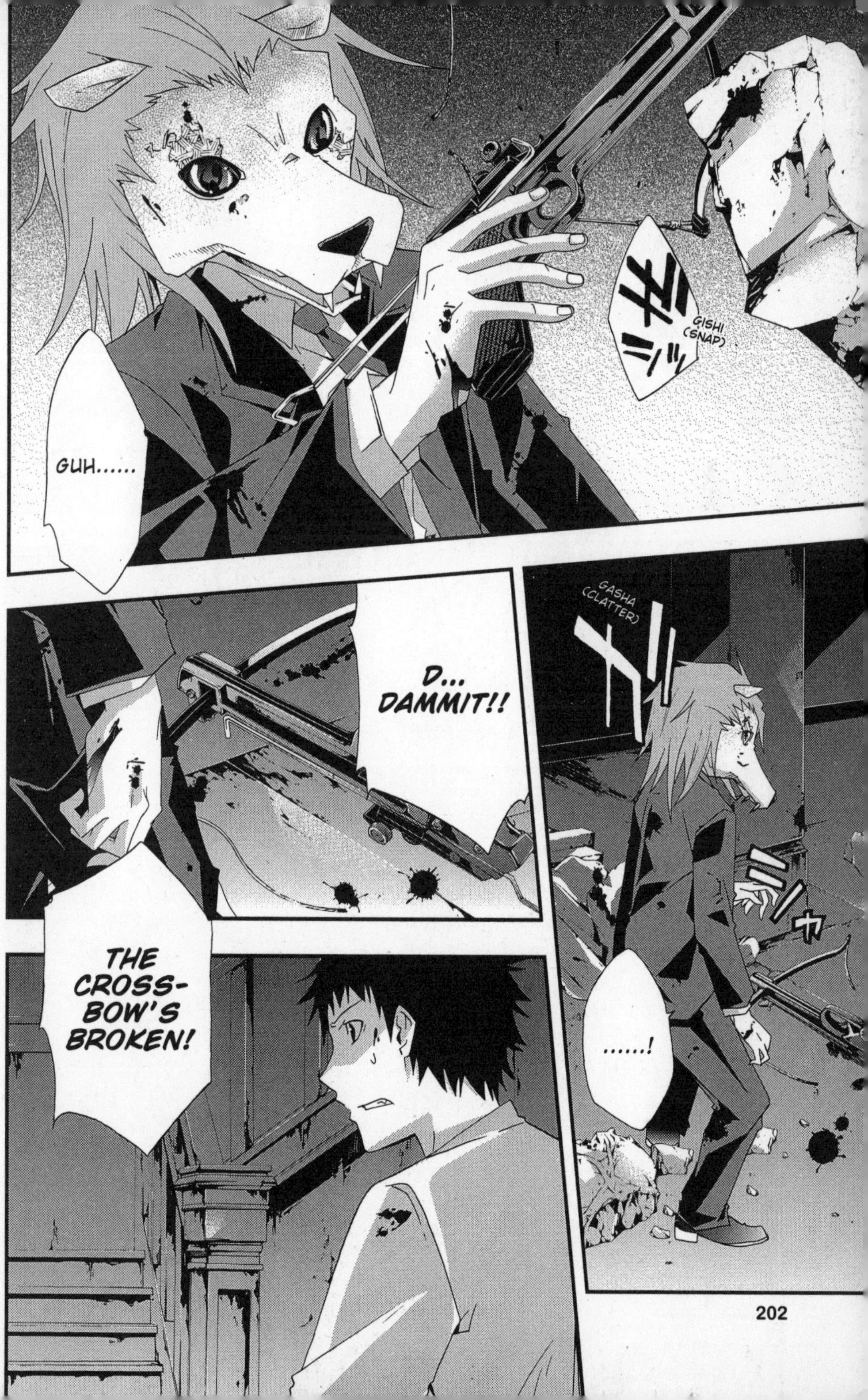
GISHI (SNAP)
GUH......
GASHA (CLATTER)
......!
D... DAMMIT!!
THE CROSS-BOW'S BROKEN!

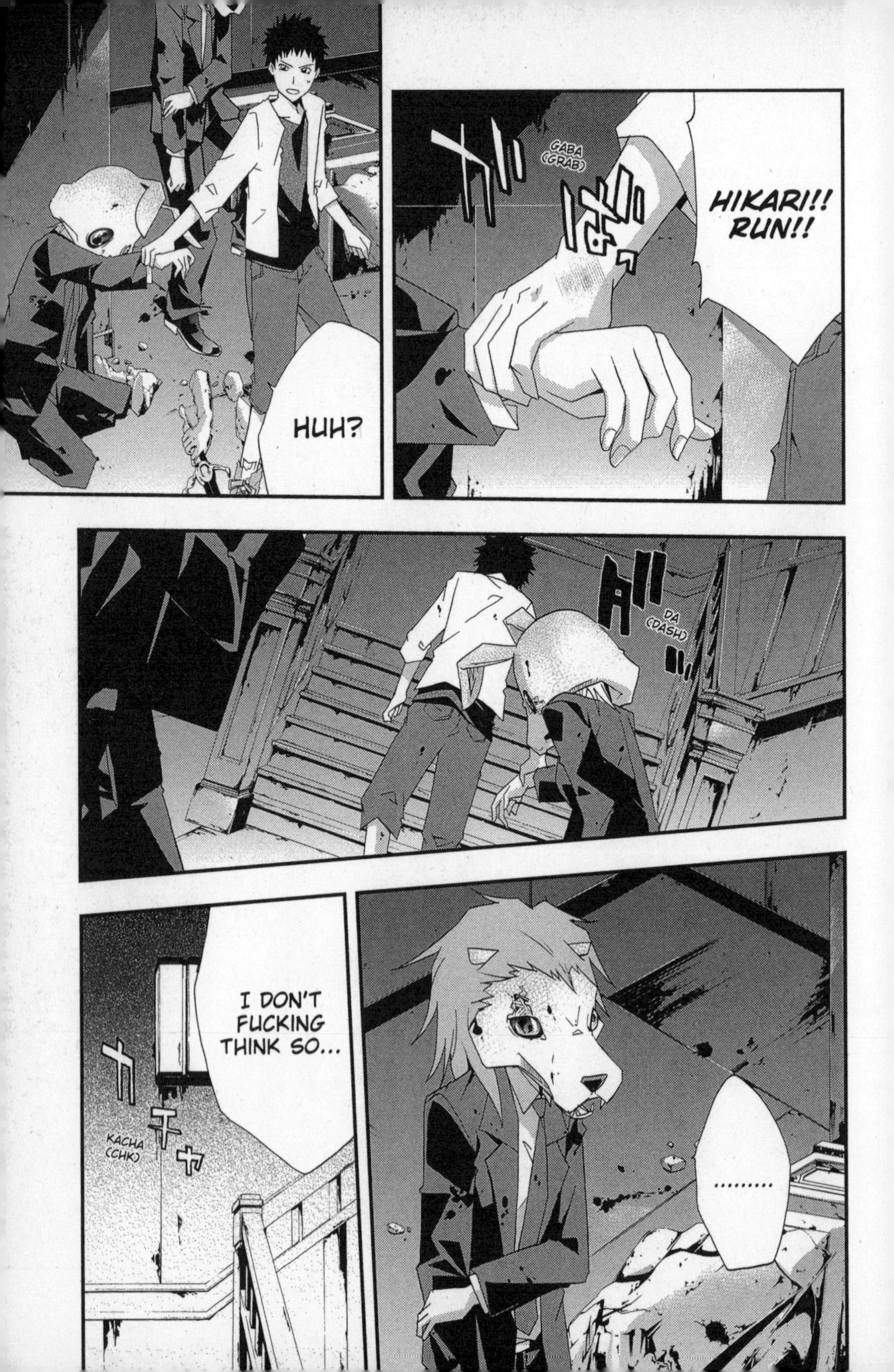
HIKARI!!! RUN!!
GABA (GRAB)
HUH?
DA (DASH)
....
I DON'T FUCKING THINK SO...
KACHA (CHK)

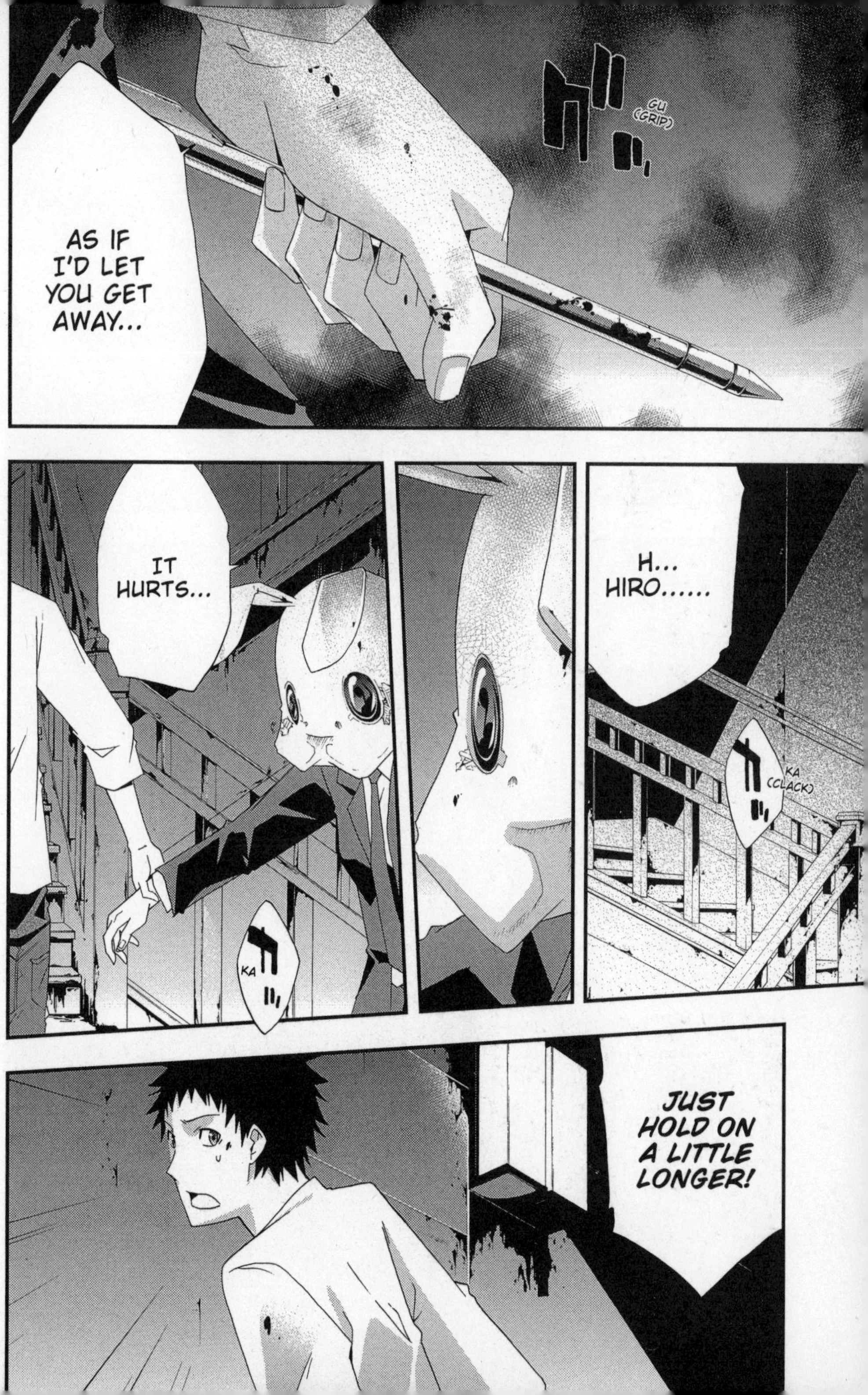
GU (GRIP)
AS IF I'D LET YOU GET AWAY...
H... HIRO......
KA (CLACK)
IT HURTS...
KA
JUST HOLD ON A LITTLE LONGER!

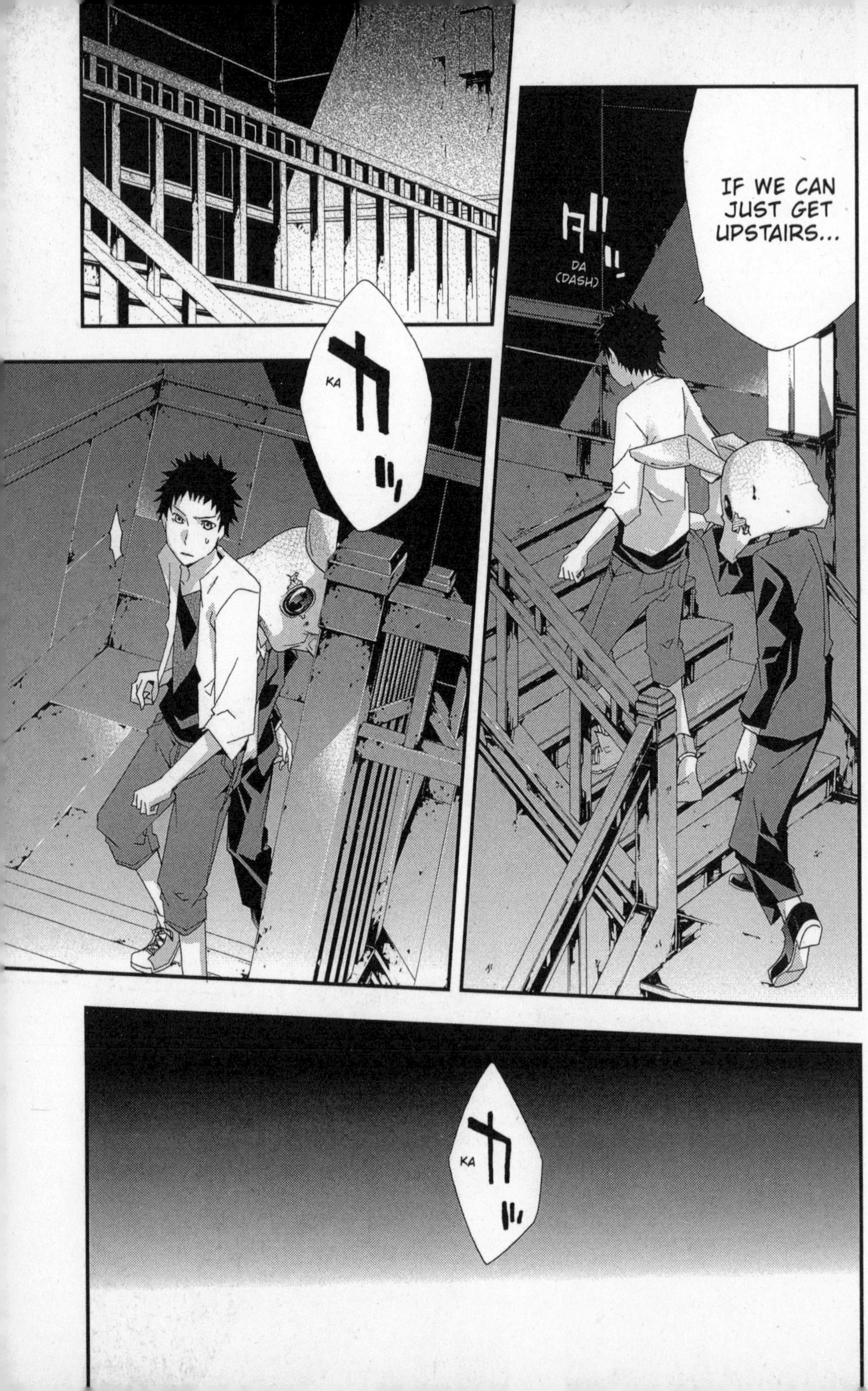
IF WE CAN JUST GET UPSTAIRS...
ダッ
DA (DASH)
カッ
KA
カッ
KA

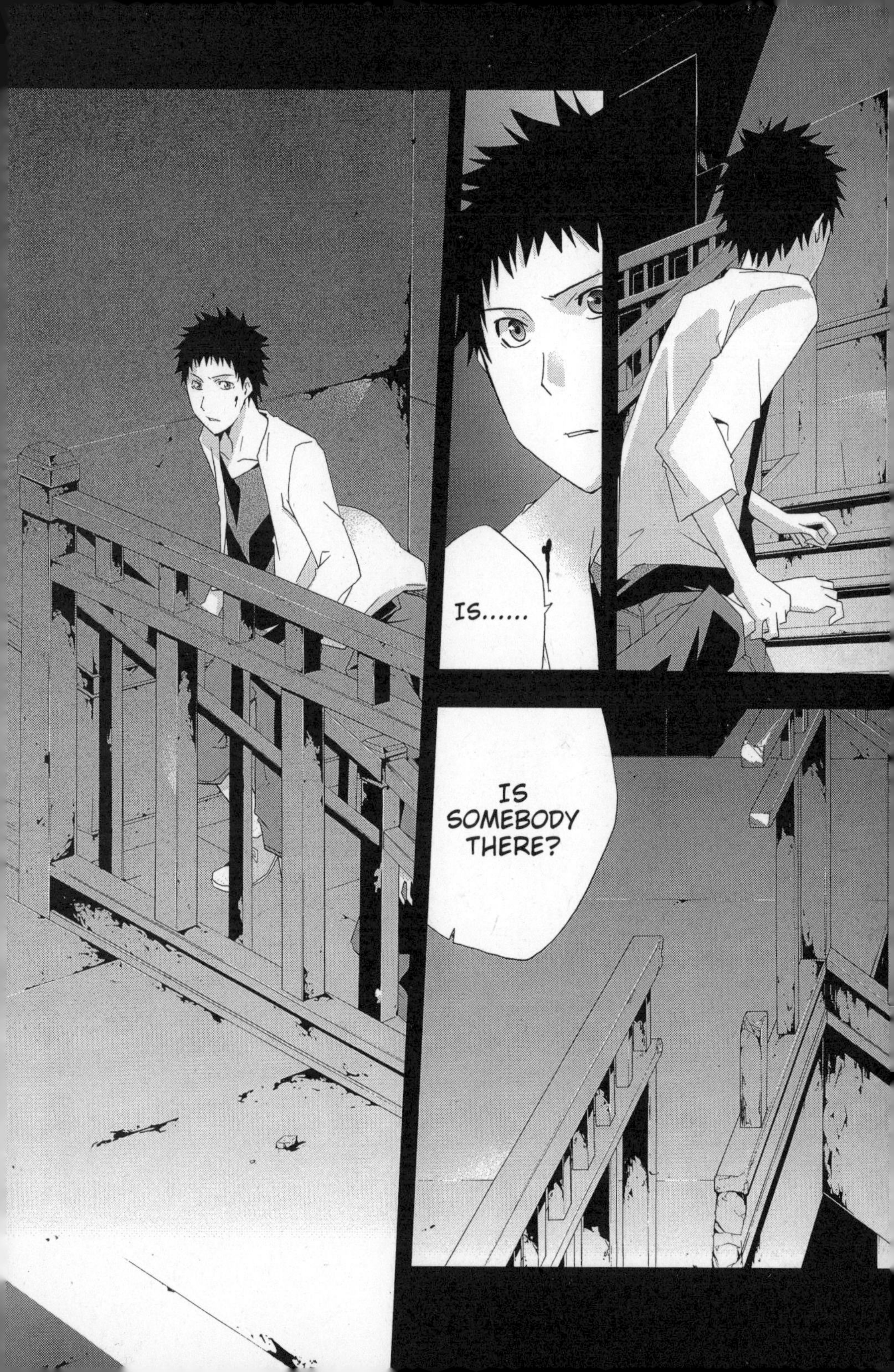
IS......
IS SOMEBODY THERE?

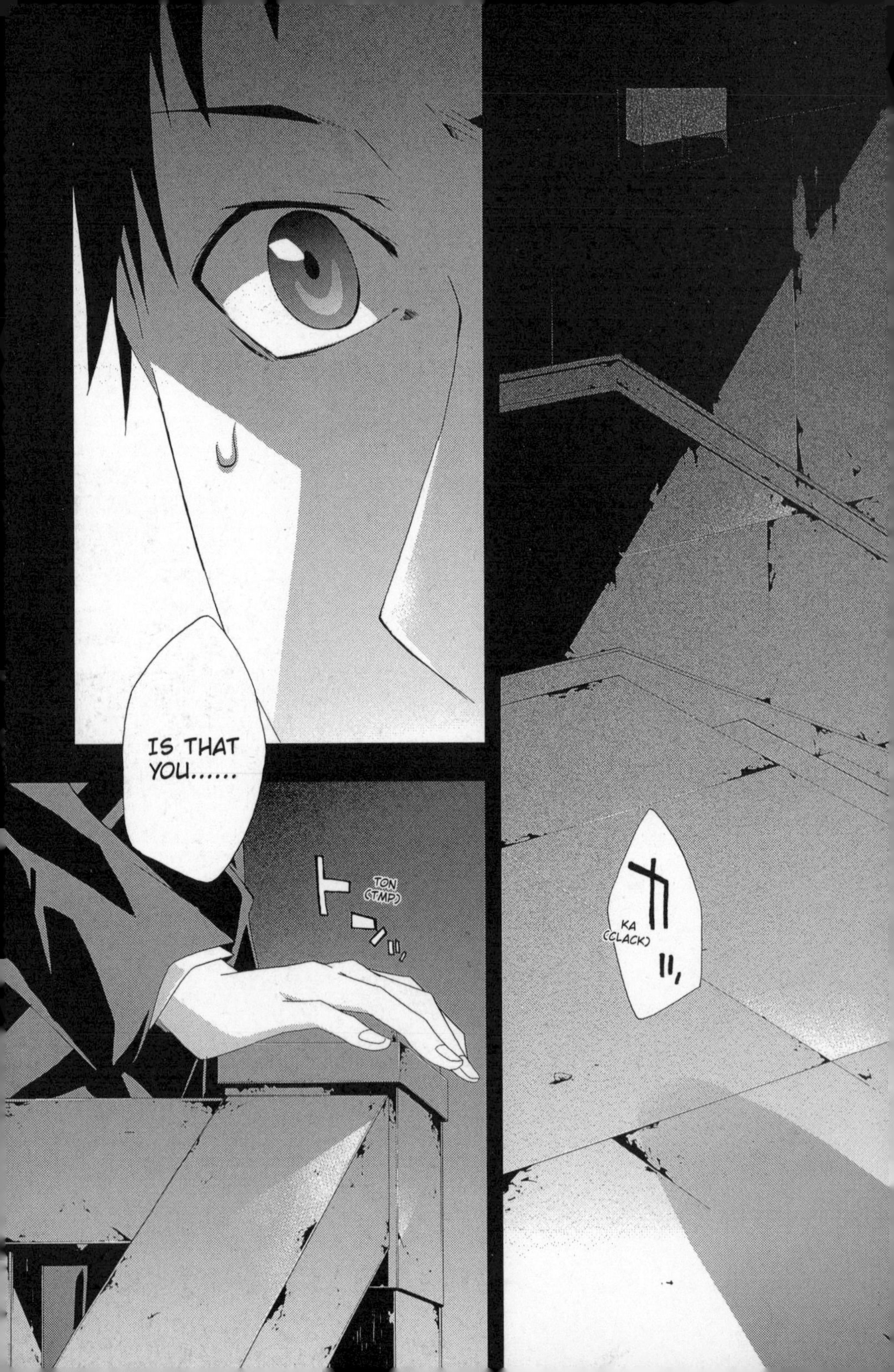
KA (CLACK)
IS THAT YOU......
TON (TMP)

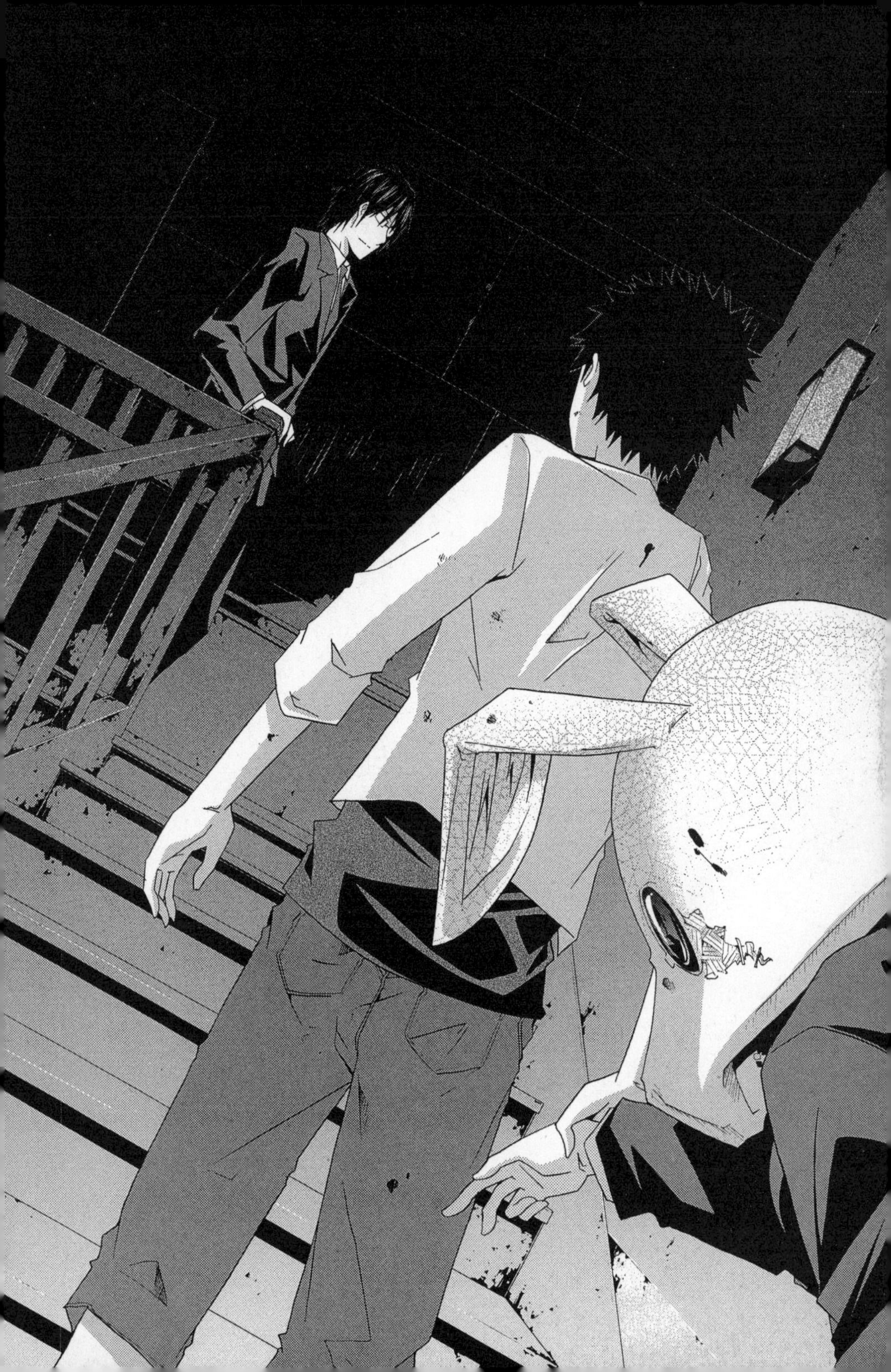

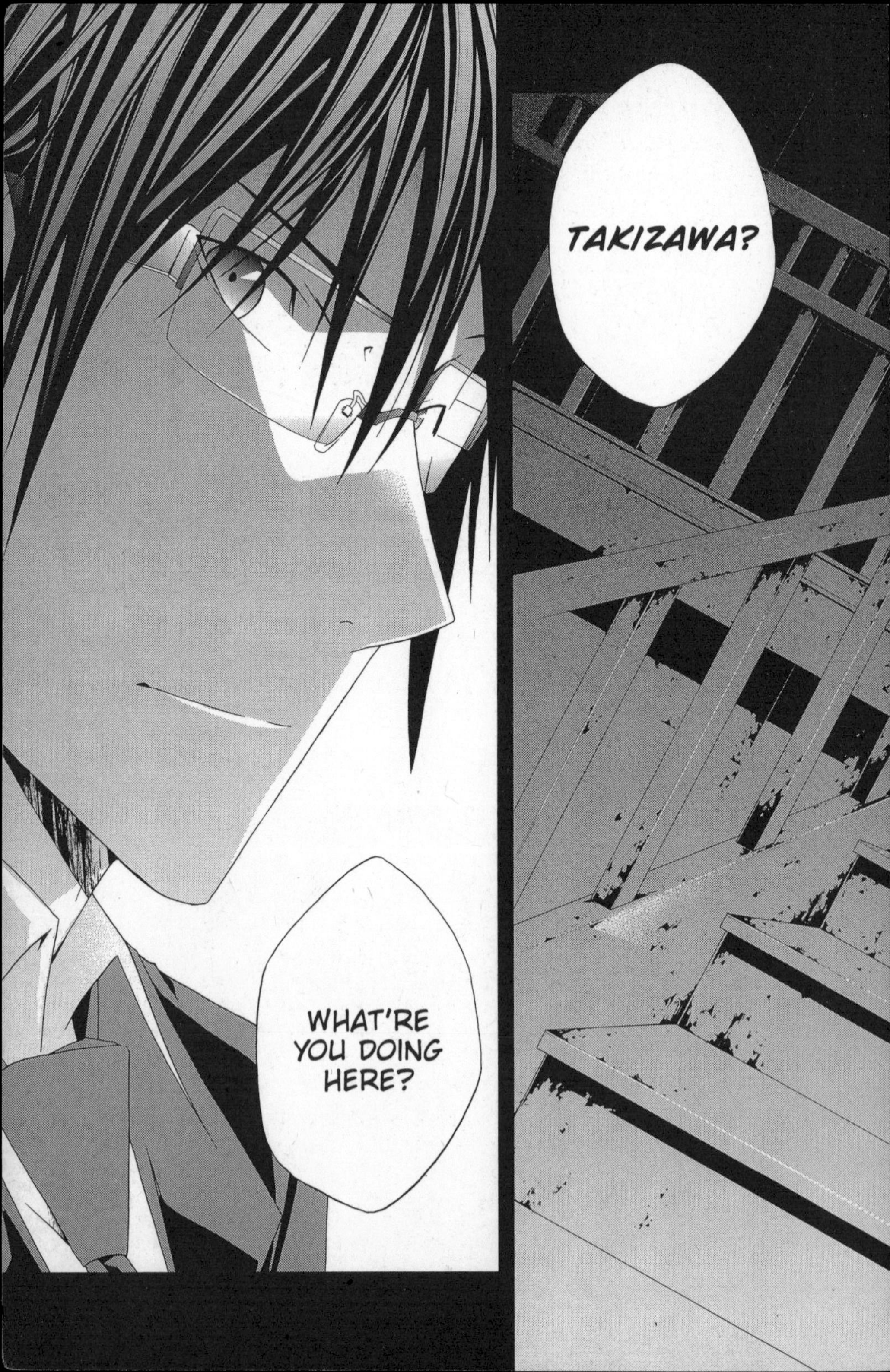
TAKIZAWA?
WHAT'RE YOU DOING HERE?

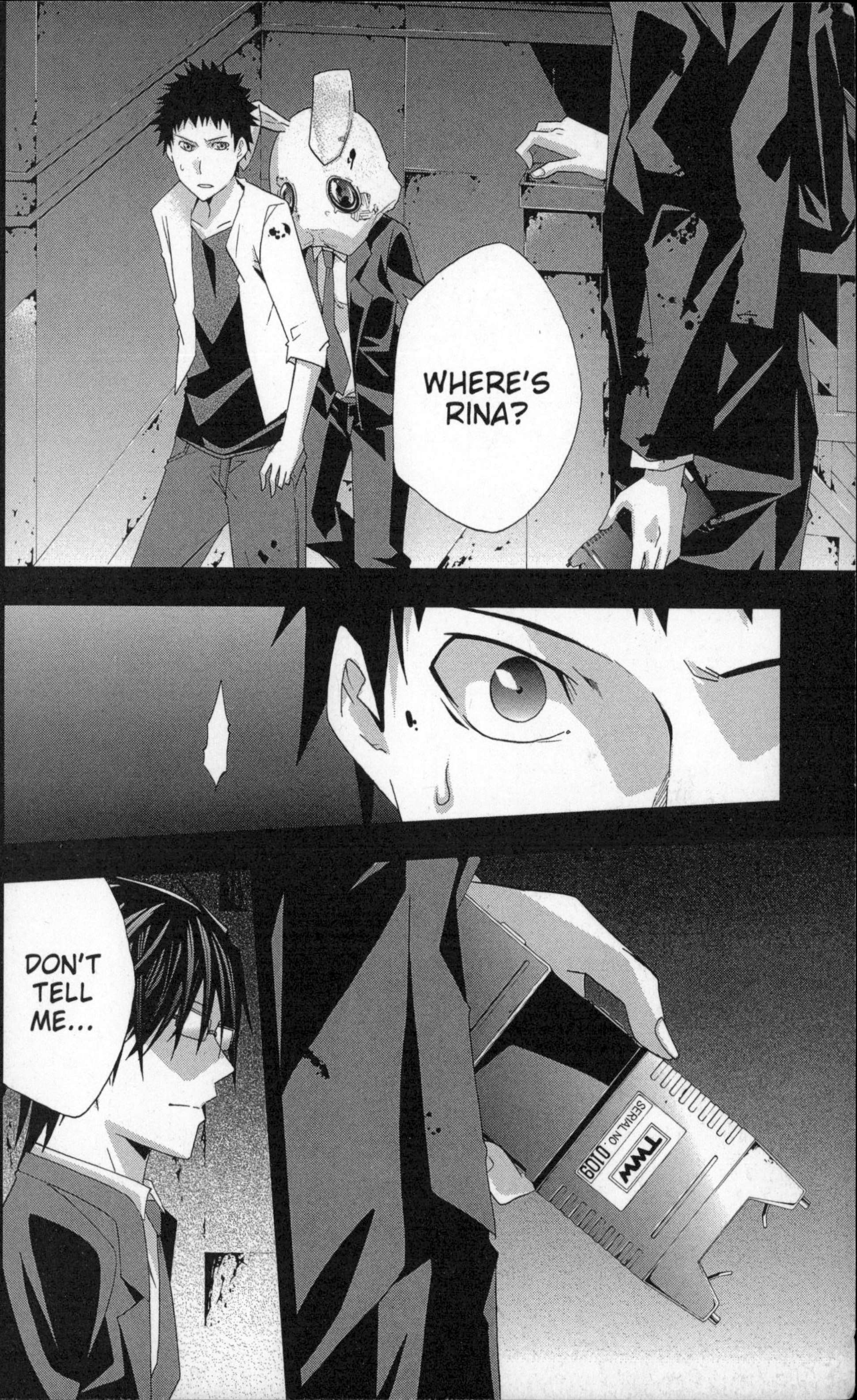
WHERE'S RINA?
DON'T TELL ME...
TWW
SERIAL NO. 0109

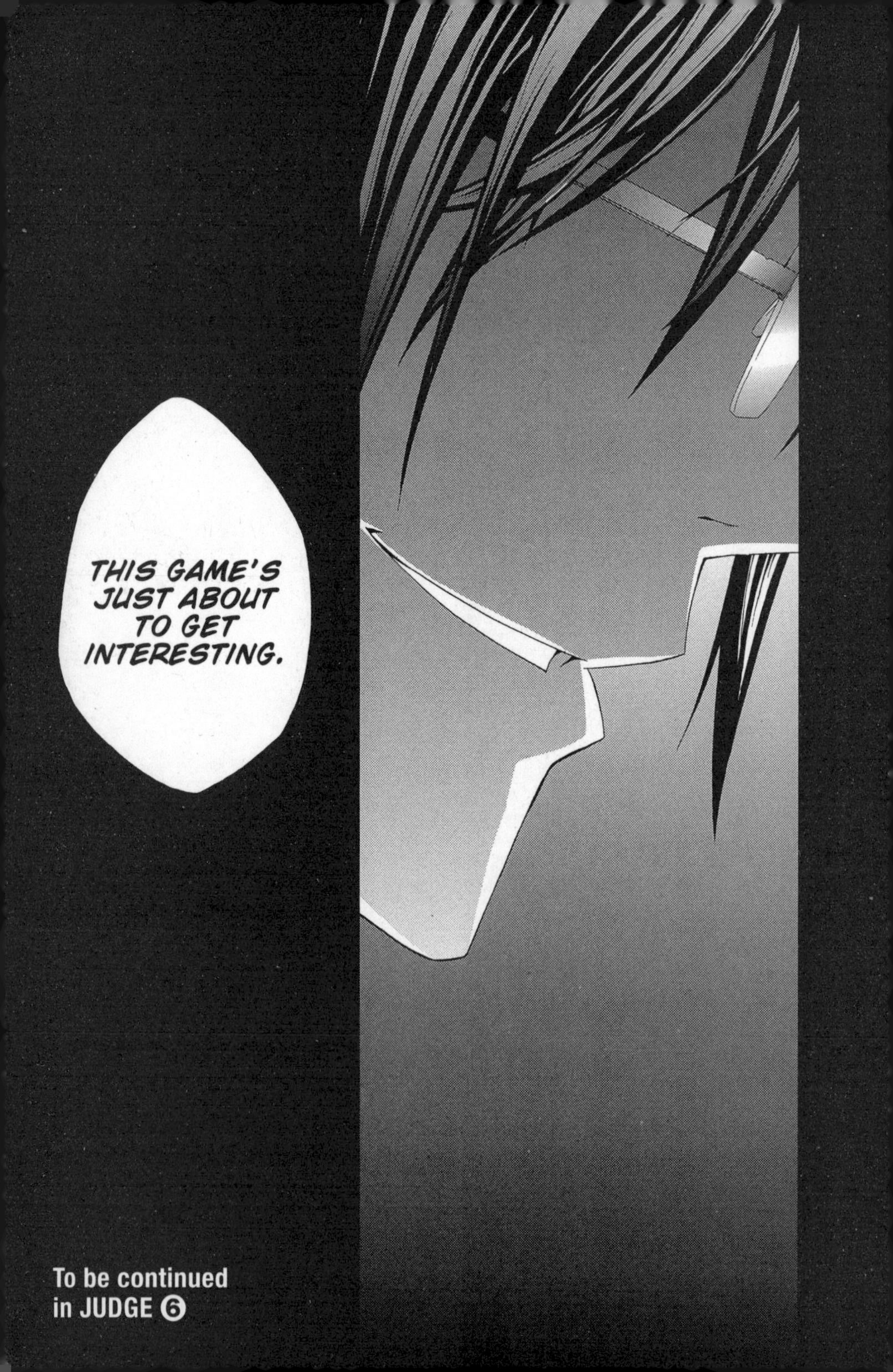
THIS GAME'S JUST ABOUT TO GET INTERESTING.
To be continued in JUDGE 6

JUDGE

STAFF

[MANGA]

TONOGAI

NOMURA

OIKAWA

TAKAHASHI

NAGASAWA

SASAI

YOSHIMURA

[EDITOR]

NOZAKI

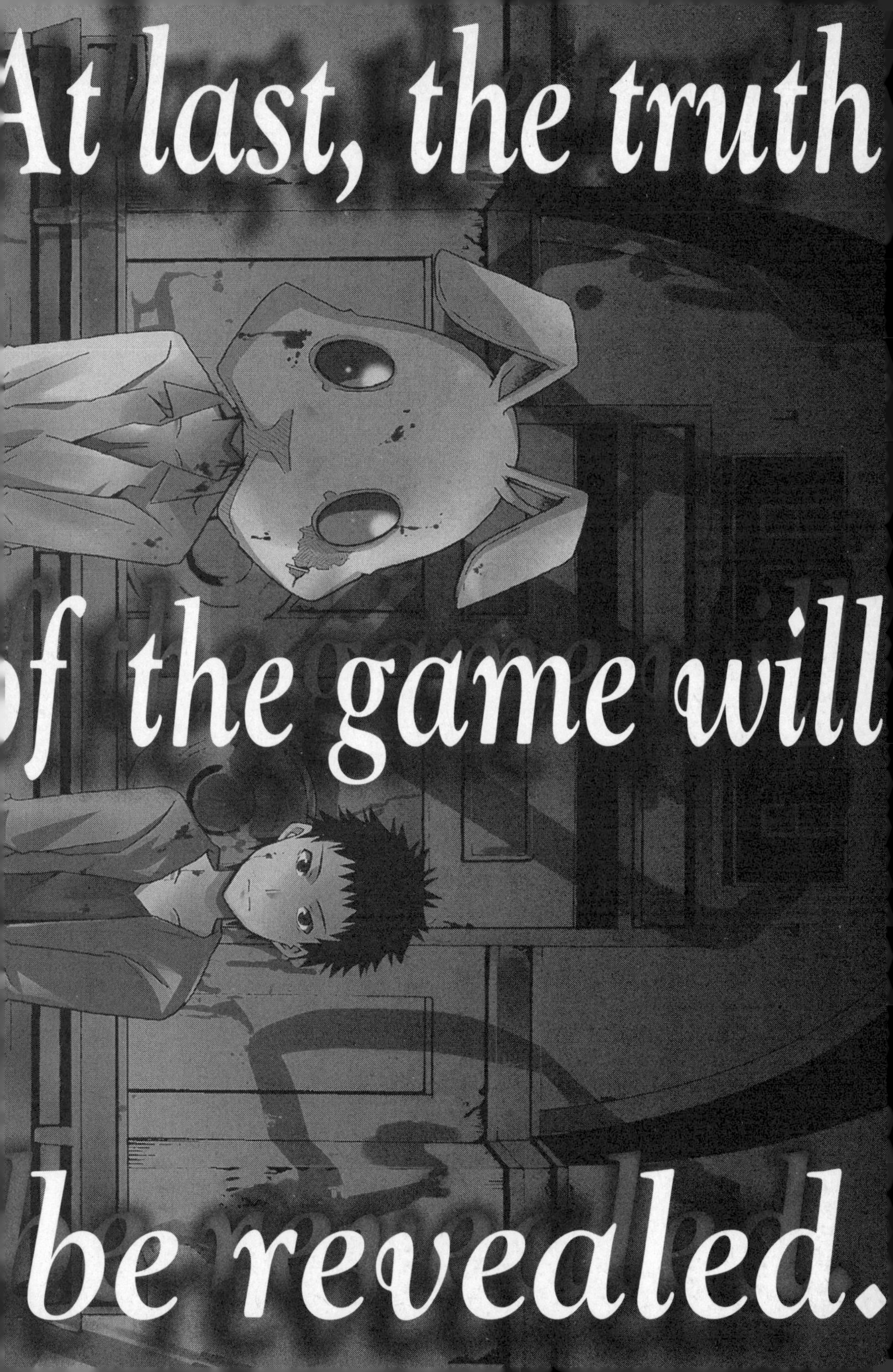
At last, the truth
of the game will
be revealed.

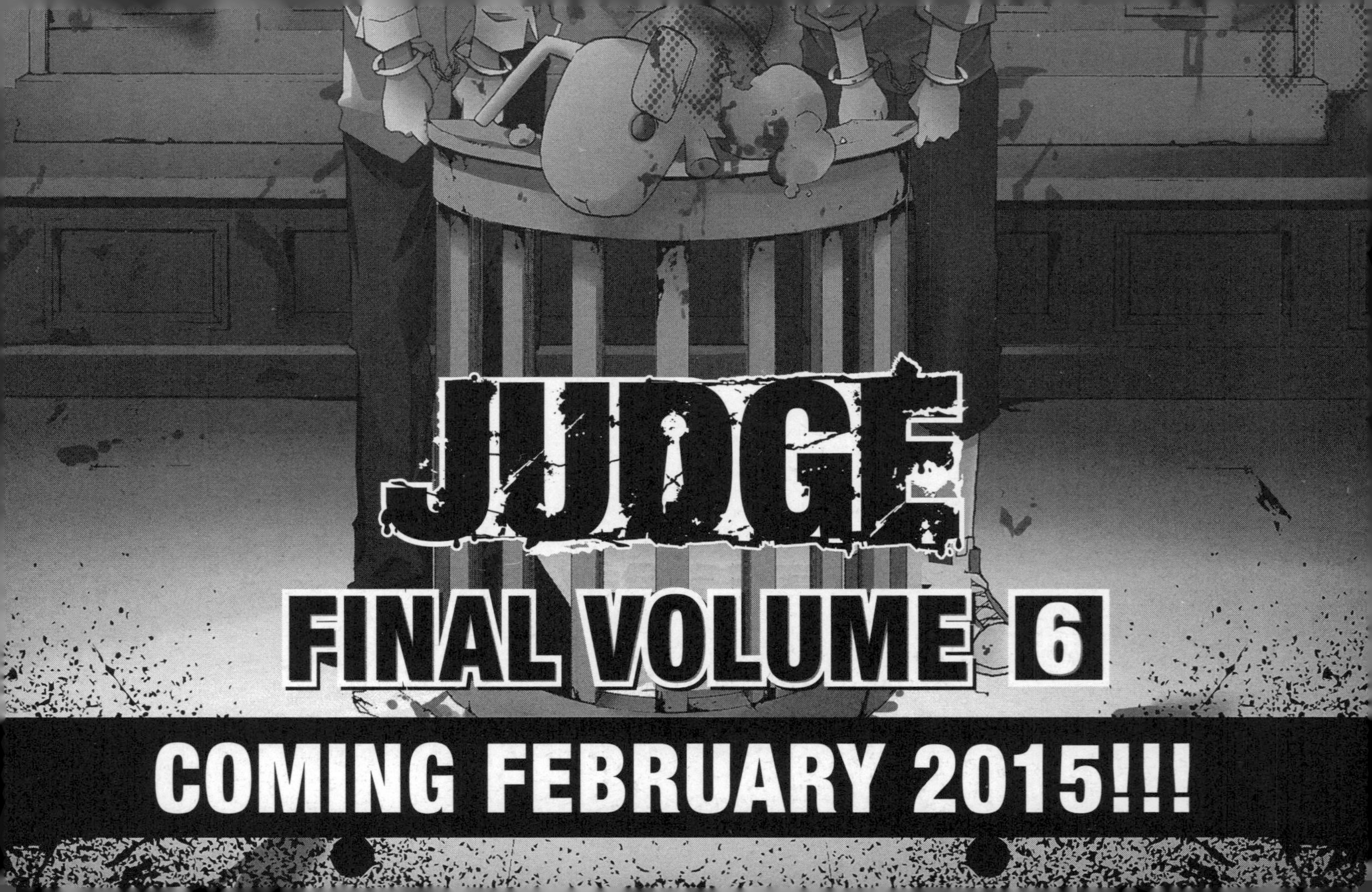
JUDGE
FINAL VOLUME 6
COMING FEBRUARY 2015!!!

DING-DONG! DEAD-DONG!

DON'T BE LATE FOR THE "NOT" CLASS AT DEATH WEAPON MEISTER ACADEMY!

Yen Press

SOUL EATER NOT!

ATSUSHI OHKUBO